The Causes of Suicide

Maurice Halbwachs

The Causes of Suicide

translated by
Harold Goldblatt

Routledge & Kegan Paul
London and Henley

*First published in French
as* Les Causes du suicide
*by Librairie Félix Alcan, Paris, 1930.
This English translation
first published in 1978
by Routledge & Kegan Paul Ltd
39 Store Street,
London WC1E 7DD and
Broadway House,
Newtown Road,
Henley-on-Thames,
Oxon RG9 1EN
Set in 10 on 11 pt Baskerville by
Computacomp (UK) Ltd, Fort William
and printed in Great Britain by
Redwood Burn Ltd,
Trowbridge and Esher
This translation © Routledge & Kegan Paul Ltd 1978*

British Library Cataloguing in Publication Data

Halbwachs, Maurice
The causes of suicide.
1. Suicide — Europe
I. Title   II. Goldblatt, Harold
364.1′552′094   HV6548.E/

ISBN 0 7100 8708X

In memory of
Ida Hillman Goldblatt
and
Ida Goldblatt Banks

Contents

Maps

Tables

Foreword to the English translation

Maurice Halbwachs was among the foremost of Durkheim's early followers. Together with Marcel Mauss, he played a leading role in furthering the influence of Durkheimian sociology in France during the period between the two World Wars, following the death of Durkheim himself. Halbwachs's own life ended tragically; in 1944 he was arrested by the Gestapo in Paris, and committed to Buchenwald where he died a few months later.

Halbwachs was never a doctrinaire Durkheimian. He was trained in philosophy, and was considerably influenced by the teachings of Bergson, whose philosophical vitalism contrasted quite sharply with Durkheim's conception of sociological method. Halbwachs, however, sought to incorporate notions borrowed from Bergson within a Durkheimian framework; one of the consequences of this was that he stressed the importance of psychology in the explanation of social conduct much more than Durkheim tended to do. This emphasis emerges strongly in several of his major writings, including his study of 'collective memory' (*La Mémoire collective*) and his work on social classes (*La Psychologie des classes*) – and is evident in his investigation of suicide.

The Causes of Suicide is best understood against the backdrop of a long-standing controversy in the study of suicide. Well before Durkheim published his *Suicide: a Study in Sociology* (1897) the relative importance of social versus psychological factors in the explanation of suicide, and the connected issue of the validity of statistical methods of observation as opposed to individual case-studies, had been matters of considerable debate. Many authors had declared that the official statistics of suicide were so unreliable as to be of little or no use in the analysis of the phenomenon they purported to measure, and had then drawn the inference that sociological studies of suicide, which almost universally relied upon such statistics, were similarly without value. Suicide, they argued, is an 'individual' act, whose causes have therefore to be sought in individual psychology, via detailed case-study. Some of these writers, most notably the famous psychiatrist Esquirol, held that suicide is universally an outcome or an expression of mental disorder, and hence that suicide has to be explained in terms of the proneness of the individual to manic-depressive illnesses.

Durkheim's intervention in this debate constituted a bolder and more forceful defence of the 'sociological thesis' than anyone had attempted before; thus it served to rekindle the controversy, and it became the chief target of those who wished to defend the idea that the explanation of suicide most properly belongs to psychology or psychiatry, rather than to sociology. In *Suicide* Durkheim made extensive use of official statistics to attempt to demonstrate that the distribution of suicide could be precisely charted. The study of suicide rates, he asserted, is the legitimate province of sociological analysis, and is distinct from the psychological investigation of individual cases, even though he did admit that the latter can usefully complement sociological research. Durkheim's theory of suicide identifies three main types of suicide, each held to be dependent upon particular sorts of social conditions. Altruistic suicide, which is the characteristic form of self-destruction found in small-scale, traditional societies, derives from the existence of strong moral codes which lead individuals, when placed in certain social circumstances, to value death more than life. The person who dies by his own hand is able either to bring honour upon his name, or to avoid shame. Egoistic and anomic suicide are characteristic of large-scale, developed societies having a differentiated division of labour, in which the traditional moral codes and beliefs have been largely destroyed. The first type is associated with the growth of individualism, and derives from the loosening of social ties associated with it; the second is the outcome of 'normlessness', of the lack of moral regulation of conduct that prevails precisely because traditional moral norms have become dissolved without having been replaced by new ones. In common with numerous other authors before him, Durkheim saw the increasing rates of suicide found in all Western European countries in the nineteenth century as evidence of a social pathology. He seems to have believed that egoistic suicide is a price that we have to pay for the achievement of individualism in the modern world. Anomic suicide, on the other hand, he expected to diminish with the remoralization of those areas of social conduct which were in a state of moral transition (especially the economic order).

Durkheim's theory was strongly criticized, both during his lifetime and afterwards, by those who rejected the sociological standpoint. One work which created something of a stir, and which took a resolutely anti-Durkheimian view, was that by de Fleury, *L'Angoisse humaine* (1926). De Fleury reiterated what came to be called the 'psychiatric thesis': suicide, he affirmed, is almost universally found among individuals of a specific temperament, inclined to manic-depressive psychosis. The origins of suicide have to be traced to individual psychopathology.

One of the main objects of Halbwachs's work was to try to resolve the opposition between the 'sociological thesis' and the 'psychiatric thesis'. His initial intention, as Mauss tells us in his foreword to the original edition, was merely to update Durkheim's work in the light of more recent statistics. But he soon came to see that the 'sociological thesis' could not simply be defended as it stood, and he 'felt compelled to undertake new research, pose new problems, and present the facts from another perspective' (p. 1). *The Causes of Suicide* attacks several problems simultaneously. Halbwachs begins with a new attempt to justify the usefulness of official statistics as a medium for the study of suicide; he then proceeds to examine Durkheim's empirical claims in the light of more modern figures; and finally he undertakes a revision of Durkheim's theoretical arguments. Many of Durkheim's readers (although certainly not his psychological critics), Halbwachs says, on closing the pages of *Suicide*, must have felt that the last word had been said on the subject. Not so at all, even for those with a sociological bent: Durkheim's ideas actually need quite a thorough overhaul if their general perspectives are to be effectively vindicated.

The main themes of Halbwachs's study can be briefly stated. So far as official statistics are concerned, Halbwachs argues that we are justified in using them as an index of the phenomenon of suicide. Halbwachs does what Durkheim did not do: he gives some space to considering possible sources of error in the collection and registration of the suicide statistics. The most obvious potential source of unreliability in the statistics, Halbwachs indicates, is likely to derive from a pressure on the part of those closely connected with a suicide to attempt to conceal the true cause of death. But in fact, he concludes, suicide is normally difficult to conceal, because it usually comes as a shock to relatives and friends who hence do not have time effectively to carry through the necessary dissimulations. We cannot be wholly certain that there are not sources of variation in the statistics which result from concealment; however, such variation might well be systematic, affecting all societies equally, in which case it can be effectively ignored, since it will not compromise the significance of comparisons made between them.

Most of Durkheim's empirical generalizations are borne out by the materials which Halbwachs analyses. But Halbwachs finds reason to qualify Durkheim's interpretation of them in an important way. Thus it is generally true that rates of suicide are lower among Catholics than among Protestants. However, Durkheim erred in treating such a differential as an isolated fact. There is no satisfactory way of separating out the religious factor from other influences with which it is intertwined. Durkheim's concept of social integration or cohesion has to be linked rather to the properties of communities as a whole. It is particularly important, according to Halbwachs, to note that Catholic communities tend to be predominantly rural, whereas Protestantism is more strongly represented in urban communities. Durkheim did not give sufficient attention to the influence of urbanization upon suicide rates. Thus the increase in suicide rates in the nineteenth century might well be explained as a consequence of the strains involved in the supplanting of agrarian society by the spread of urbanism. Some support is lent to this hypothesis by the fact, documented by Halbwachs, that suicide rates have levelled off in most Western European countries since the early part of the twentieth century.

On a more theoretical level, Halbwachs rejects the radical differentiation which Durkheim drew between the social causes of suicide and suicidal motives. In Durkheim's view, the motives of suicide – for example, the desire to escape from a situation of financial ruin, or the consequences of an unhappy love affair – are merely the precipitating circumstances, not the true causes, of the act of self-destruction: as Halbwachs expresses it, 'when one leaves a house which has several exits, the door through which one passes is not the cause of one's leaving' (p. 9). But the analogy, Halbwachs says, is not an apt one. Durkheim's thesis would be justifiable if motives were formed by completely different influences than those he identifies as causing suicide. But this is not the case. On the contrary, the main type of social circumstance underlying suicide, isolation from involvement in the nexus of community relationships, is closely associated with the most characteristic psychological state of the suicide: 'an unbearable feeling of loneliness.'

This approach also guides Halbwachs's examination of the 'psychiatric thesis'. We must abandon the idea that suicide is either caused by mental disorder, on the one hand, or by social factors on the other. In the first place, it is by no means demonstrated that the origins of mental illness are determined by heredity. It seems likely that mental disorders are themselves in substantial part a product of social influences, which thus may overlap with those causing suicide. But even if this were not the case, it would still be mistaken to maintain a clear-cut separation between the social and psychological causes of suicide. For suicide never occurs as a result of factors purely 'internal' to the individual: there is always an interaction between the individual and his social milieu. There are obviously differences between the person who is chronically prone to depression, and someone whose mental turmoil results from financial ruin: but the outcome, the dislocation of the individual from his surrounding social environment, is the same. 'The term "motives" must be retained for these events: mental illness, loss of money, mourning, or love-pangs, since they are so many different particular forms hiding the same condition' (p.275).

In the light of this analysis it is easy to see why Halbwachs rejects both the definition of suicide which Durkheim offered, and the typology of suicide that he developed. In conformity with his attempt to distance the explanation of suicide from psychology, Durkheim defined suicide in such a way as to exclude the notion of intention or purpose. Suicide was regarded by Durkheim as an act of an individual against himself which he knows (rather than intends) will result in his death. For Halbwachs, however, suicide is an intentional or motivated act. It can thus be differentiated from self-sacrifice, where the individual gives up his life for the sake of the group, not because he actively wishes to die; most of Durkheim's category of altruistic suicides are in fact more appropriately regarded as acts of self-sacrifice, and as distinct from other forms of self-destruction. Moreover, since Halbwachs regards the basic social influence on suicide as the detachment of the individual from his social milieu, he merges Durkheim's types of egoistic and anomic suicide into one.

Halbwachs's work still retains much of its interest, even though it is nearly fifty years since it was first published, and the statistics upon which he relied are as out-of-date today as those which Durkheim employed were when Halbwachs wrote. The controversies which were current then, with regard to the reliability of official statistics as a measure of the distribution of suicide, and the relevance of sociological explanations to suicidal conduct, are still with us. Halbwachs's work is particularly important in respect of the latter. For however we might seek to deal with the issues involved, Halbwachs was undoubtedly right to suggest that the analysis of the social conditions implicated in the causation of suicide has to be closely bound up with an appreciation of the motivated, purposive character of human behaviour.

Anthony Giddens

Translator's preface

One's first impression of Halbwachs's follow-up to Durkheim's *Suicide* is the strong resemblance of *The Causes of Suicide* to the parent study. One finds in both the same insistence that sociological theory is indispensable to the understanding of suicide, the same dependence on the official statistics of the same European countries, the same comparative, statistical tabulation of the same variables: age, sex, nationality, religion, marital status, rural–urban differences, occupation, etc., the same sense of the importance to sociology of a historical perspective, and not least, the same high fervor for utilizing the scientific method of inquiry towards achieving an understanding and perhaps a solution of a critical and vexing social problem.

But the translator's experience of poring over Halbwachs's text, word by word and thought by thought, modifies this first impression. One comes to perceive in Halbwachs's sociology of suicide major differences from that of Durkheim in theory, in research methods and methodology, and in the evaluation of the social significance of the rising rate of suicide among the nations of Europe.

THEORY

Halbwachs has dismissed Durkheim's classification of suicides. He continued to recognize the egoistic suicide but redefined the altruistic suicide, whether obligatory or optional, prescribed or merely permitted, as, instead, a self-sacrifice or a ritual human sacrifice (pp. 291–309), and the anomic suicide as caused instead by 'social accidents' (pp. 317–22). (Fatalistic suicides receive no more attention from him than they did from Durkheim.) Accordingly, he proposed a sociological definition of suicide that is substantially different (pp. 308–9 especially). Halbwachs retains Durkheim's two basic criteria of, first, the individual's responsibility for his self-destruction by acts of omission as well as commission, and, second, his knowledge that death would be the consequence of his behavior. But to these he adds three criteria that greatly narrow the scope of Durkheim's definition: first, the self-destructive behavior must not be socially prescribed. Thus he excludes such altruistic deaths as those of the religious martyr, the soldier courting certain death on the field of battle, the captain of an ill-fated ship who goes down with his vessel, the bankrupt or alcoholic who takes his own life to spare his family from ill-fortune, disgrace, or dishonor, and the like. Second, the suicide must be his own, sole executioner; the perpetrator of the murder and the victim are one and the same, death occurring without other human intervention. The consequence of this limitation is to exclude ritual human sacrifice in which the community participates along with the victim. Third, the suicide must desire, and must intend to die, either to atone for his misdeeds or his personal inadequacies, or to revenge himself upon his milieu or upon society for its misdeeds to him or its social inadequacies, or to efface himself from society which had given him to understand, or misunderstand, that it no longer had a place for him.

The additional stipulations tend to bring Halbwachs's definition in line with the commonsense definition of suicide held by the public officials whose judgments are tabulated in the official statistics. They reduce the danger that the definitions implicit in the official statistics run counter to his own. They also partially justify his own estimate of the essential validity of the statistics, especially for analysts who focus on intra-national comparisons (Chapter 2, especially pp. 42–3).

Halbwachs has elaborated a theory of suicide rather different from Durkheim's, whose complexity is not readily perceived by the reader because its component details are scattered through his text rather than presented in one place. Figure 1 assembles the components in a conceptual framework, or model, which interrelates the psychological, biological, social, and cultural determinants of suicide and charts them as a series of proximate, intermediate, and more remote causes of suicide. (The discussion to follow annotates this schema.)

By 'the causes of suicide' Halbwachs means, first, the motives, circumstances, or commonsense reasons for individual cases of suicide of which the unfortunate, his kinsmen, neighbors, and family physician are well aware, and which, upon communication to officials, coroners, and police agents, are then tabulated in official lists or statistics of suicide. 'The causes of suicide' are, second, the reasons given by psychiatrists, psychologists, and

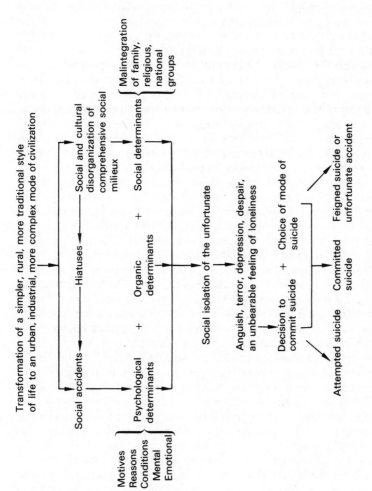

Figure 1 *The causes of suicide*

physicians (Chapter 14), mental, emotional, and organic illnesses such as manic-depressive psychosis, lypemania, hypochondria, and delirium tremens. Though not rare, all of these are uncommon complaints. Being uncommon, it must be these complaints that account for the uncommon though not rare act of suicide by people who surely must be unbalanced to engage in self-destruction. Finally, 'the causes of suicide' refers also to the reasons given by sociologists. These are characteristics of the unfortunate's social status, social milieu, or encompassing society of which the victim, the general public, and the professionals in other disciplines are not aware. The influence of these distal factors is discernible, writes Halbwachs, only through statistical analysis of the variations in rates of suicide among diverse social groups and social statuses, through time. Halbwachs's attempt to integrate the reasons given for suicide by common sense, by psychology, by medicine, and by sociology can therefore be properly called a psychosociological theory of suicide.

The most proximate cause of suicide as an individual event, the cause that triggers or precipitates the decision to take one's own life, is an emotional state or condition of anguish and terror so intense as to make life unbearable. 'The state of terror and anguish,' he writes, 'is alone what matters. There is nowhere beyond it to go when one wishes to explain suicide.'

But for Halbwachs, unlike Durkheim, the committed suicide is both decision and effective implementation. The first without the second is only an 'attempted suicide' which he has excluded from his definition (pp. 56–7), while the second without the first is no more than an unfortunate accident or else a 'feigned suicide' – the latter being particularly common among the very young.

Every commonsense reason for suicide assigned in the official statistics of suicide, writes Halbwachs, can be shown to have as its common element the isolation of the unfortunate from the social milieu which simultaneously sustains as well as constrains the lives of its members. The same is true of the reasons assigned by the physician, psychiatrist, and psychologist. Ill-health, whether due to mental, emotional, or organic factors, causes the suicide by isolating the sick from the community of the healthy. (Halbwachs dismisses the distinction between rational and irrational reasons for committing suicide. However calm and deliberate the decision may be, upon its implementation the causation of suicide is always psychosomatic, of the body and emotion as well as of the mind, external as well as internal.)

Society for Halbwachs is the great nurturant, but is neither omniscient nor omnipotent. Society cannot avoid failing a yearly quota of the unfortunates who suffer by reason of its imperfections. The events that unfortunates experience as the reasons for committing suicide and that are tabulated in the official statistics actually are 'social accidents.' But, writes Halbwachs, Durkheim was correct in his assessment of the lesser protectiveness of malintegrated families, religious communities, and political societies. Such social conditions reinforce individual reasons for suicide and both, acting jointly, isolate the unfortunate from his milieu, with suicidogenic consequences as we have seen. On the other hand, Durkheim was mistaken in abstracting for reasons of research procedure the institutions of the family, the religious community, and the political society from the complex of social facts that in ensemble form the suicide's total environment. It is the total environment, the comprehensive social milieux that must be investigated in the causation of suicide. Social and cultural disorganization produce social voids about the individual, social hiatuses in which persons psychologically disposed to suicide cannot sustain themselves. 'If there were no such hiatuses, there would be no suicides' (p. 290).

Nor are increases in the annual quota of unfortunates due to abrupt changes in the structure of society, sudden crises, as Durkheim mistakenly supposed. There is no reason to believe, writes Halbwachs, that modern society is more anomic, less well regulated today than heretofore. Rather it is the progressive transformation of modern society, the inevitable increase in social complexity required of the more advanced stage of civilization that accounts for the 'social accidents.' Ultimately, therefore, it is the style of life (pp. 322–7) characteristic of the modern urban industrial civilization which is the fundamental, if distal, cause of the rising tide of suicides during the nineteenth century.

RESEARCH

Halbwachs's work benefited not only from the improvements in the collection and mode of tabulation of data on suicide by the statistical bureaux of national governments (Chapter 1) and the longer duration of the time series available to him, but also from advances in demographic research procedures and methods of statistical analysis since Durkheim's time. Halbwachs knew he could not compare increases in absolute numbers of suicides (as Durkheim sometimes did) and that he must adjust rates of increase in suicide to the percentage of the population which is below fifteen years of age in order to exclude them from the population at risk. He also invented computations that go beyond simple percentage and proportions, such as measures of dispersion, of rank order correlation, and of cross tabulation, and index numbers for measuring fluctuations in rates of suicides, productivity, and foreign imports and exports, relative to carefully selected base years. Certainly Halbwachs's statistical methods by today's standards are crude. He did not have the analysis of variance to aid him in comparing within-group and between-group differences to study the convergence of suicide rates that are so important to his appraisal of the significance of suicide in modern European societies. Nor did he have Spearman's rank order correlation, which would have often been useful to him, Pearson's product-moment coefficient of correlation, or multivariate regression equations. Halbwachs believed that methods more refined than those he employed were not justified by the quality of the data at his disposal (p. 5).

Using these improved if crude statistical measures at his command, Halbwachs set out to confirm some and to challenge others of Durkheim's empirical findings. For example, he denied that suicide rates rise during crises of economic prosperity, as Durkheim had supposed. He showed that suicide rates diminished during World War I not only in belligerent but also in neutral countries, a finding which required an interpretation at odds with Durkheim's thesis that the egoistic disposition is submerged by wartime requirements for task-oriented, concerted activity in the face of the common enemy. He refined Durkheim's findings on the relationship between homicide and suicide. He showed the effects on the suicide rates of European Jews since 1870 of their social integration into Christendom.

Such achievements, however, are perhaps no more than the normal routine of an advancing discipline. The principal research accomplishment for which Halbwachs's book is notable may be the investigations he undertook to establish his law of convergence of suicide rates toward a common norm. He undertook to demonstrate the operation of this law among the nations of Europe, among provinces, counties, and geographical districts within given nations, and among rural–urban differences within provinces. Durkheim, too, had ventured into analysis of disaggregations of his data by region, but with him use of the method is occasional and not for the purpose of systematically demonstrating the convergence of the international, national, provincial and rural–urban rates of suicide.

The central empirical question to which Halbwachs addresses himself is the future of the rising rate of suicide in European nations. He presents eleven time series for the ninety years from 1836–45 to 1922–5 (Table 4.1, p. 59) which show during this period rapid increases in the incidence of self-destruction in nine of eleven European nations. Will these increases continue and

without limit? 'This is certainly one of the most important
problems that could be raised and that the most extended
observations in time and space at our disposal could permit us to
resolve' (p. 62). Halbwachs reports that they will not increase 'in a
continuous and unlimited manner.' Rather, 'everything seems to
indicate that, increasingly, the suicide rates in the different
countries are converging' toward a uniform level for Europe as a
whole (Table 4.5 and pp. 64 and 68). Halbwachs's initial
explanation is in demographic terms: suicide rates increase most
rapidly among nations whose initial rates are low and whose
populations are rapidly increasing; they increase least rapidly, or
even decline, among nations whose initial rates are high and
whose populations are increasing only slowly or are stable. But
since the population explosion and migrations are linked to the
industrialization and urbanization of Europe, this means that the
differences among European nations in mode of civilization and
style of life are diminishing. As this happens, differences in their
rates of suicide – since they reflect the stage of civilization – must
likewise diminish.

So important is the empirical result of Chapter 4 for
Halbwachs's evaluation of social and economic conditions of
European societies that he replicates the convergence of suicide
rates of geographical regions within those nations – their
seacoasts, mountainous areas, and great river valleys. He finds his
data to be adequate for such regional analyses in France (Chapter
5) and Germany, Italy, and England (Chapter 6). In each instance
he reports confirmation of his 'law of convergence.' (Halbwachs
provides a concise summary of his findings on pp. 122–4.)

Halbwachs had three things to gain from his emphasis on such
regional analysis. First, he sought to provide through intra-
national comparisons additional evidence for the 'law of
convergence' among national rates that he presents in Chapter 4.
Second, he hoped to avoid the difficulties attendant upon
international comparisons as a consequence of national
differences in the collection and tabulation of suicide data.

The third benefit stems from the problem of multicollinearity,
or intercorrelation among the analytically separate causes of
suicide. As noted, Halbwachs's fundamental explanation for the
variations and increases in rates of suicide among social groups is
the difference in their life styles. Styles of life or modes of
civilization are the macrosociological contexts within which are
intertwined national, economic, religious, political, and family
evolutionary changes. Halbwachs sought a territorial unit of
analysis smaller than the nation but coextensive with each variety
of style of life. This territorial unit may be the province, county,

department, or urban or rural area. Halbwachs employs this pattern of analysis repeatedly, especially in his chapter on Religion and Suicide.

SOCIAL SIGNIFICANCE

Now, what reason did Halbwachs have for so persistently inquiring into the convergence of these rates, first among the nations of Europe, then within individual nations, and then between rural and urban areas within provinces?

Halbwachs concurs with Durkheim that suicides are normal provided their numbers do not increase too much or too rapidly. But how much, he asks, is 'too much,' and how rapid is 'too rapid'? At what level do suicide rates become abnormal? The criterion Durkheim proposed is the universality of the phenomenon: how general is it among nations at a like level of social development? Durkheim saw in suicide rates, which are stable in the short run but rising in the long run, an indication of the socially disruptive influence of rapid social and economic change, whether the movement of the business cycle was toward hard times or toward prosperity. Halbwachs saw, or believed he saw, an asymptotic convergence of suicide rates toward a norm among and within the European nations. To him, this indicated not an indefinitely continuous increase in the anomization of societies but rather a temporarily painful transition toward a new, common form of industrial and urban civilization in which suicide rates higher than those of the past would be 'appropriate' to the new stage of civilization, normal to the new industrial and urban style of life. Halbwachs regards the higher suicide rates not as an abnormality but as merely an unfortunate cost of social progress. That is, Halbwachs accepts the methodological rule that Durkheim proposed for the evaluation of social pathology. But unlike Durkheim, he used it as evidence of the normality of the increases in suicide rates and, by implication, the normality of the industrial development and urbanization of Europe which are responsible for the changed mode of civilization or style of life causing the increases. Durkheim had written, 'All proofs combine to make us consider the enormous increase in the number of voluntary deaths within a century as a pathological phenomenon becoming daily a greater menace' (*Suicide*, p. 370). Halbwachs in reply asks, 'Are all European societies ill? Can a given society remain in a pathological state for three-quarters of a century?' (p. 311). He uses Durkheim's principle, 'When the same phenomenon is found not only in a great number of societies, but additionally, within each of them over so prolonged a period, we can say that it is general both in space and time.' Nevertheless, he answers differently: 'For our part' we have more than one reservation about [Durkheim's] pessimistic conclusions' as to the anomization of economic and social functions (p. 320). Suicide rates are an indicator of only the costs of economic and social progress. With industrial and urban progress have come 'sorrows and deprivations both more intense and more numerous' (p. 315). But, 'In comparisons between today's style of life and former times ... we must take joys and satisfactions into account as well as sufferings' (p. 314). And these too, Halbwachs asserts, have become more intense and more numerous.

IN SUM

In sum, while Halbwachs's and Durkheim's work show strong resemblances, their utilization of suicide statistics as a social indicator of the consequences of the economic development and urbanization of Europe in the nineteenth and twentieth centuries led them to fundamental differences in theory, research procedures and methodology, and in their evaluation of the significance of the rising rates of suicide. Durkheim's evaluation of the pace and mode of social and economic change was negative; Halbwachs's analysis led him to an evaluation that, on balance, was favorable. It is evidently not accidental that Durkheim's concluding chapter is entitled 'Practical Consequences' and presents his ideas for a fundamental reorganization of society to achieve a new moral discipline, while in contrast, Halbwachs's concluding chapter is confined to the clarification of prevailing definitions of suicide and summaries of the theories and researches he has presented in the preceding chapters.

EPILOGUE

The dates are important. One wonders in hindsight whether in 1897 Durkheim was fully justified in uttering a pessimistic cry of alarm based upon the continuously rising rate of suicides in the nations of Europe. In hindsight, one wonders too whether, in 1930, on the eve of the Great Depression which would be followed by a second World War, Halbwachs was fully justified in allaying our apprehensions. 'We shall ... have to wait several years,' he wrote (p. 70) 'to observe whether the suicide rates in different countries continue to converge as they have done continuously in the course of the fifty-five years' from 1856–60 to 1911–13.

Have the rates of suicide continued to increase in the nations of the world since 1927? If so, do they show a maximum limit appropriate to each nation which it cannot surpass? Have the suicide rates of diverse nations of the world been converging toward a uniform level and are they now giving evidence of leveling off at a rate appropriate to a new stage of civilization? Would this mean that our societies are indeed attaining worldwide a social equilibrium indicative of the emergence of a new moral constitution binding upon individual members who shall thus be well integrated into a stable moral order?

We do not know. We await a third volume in the trilogy of works on the causes of suicide that would dare address such questions, a third phase of the same research, conducted in the same spirit, a necessary supplement, complement, and indispensable corrective to the other two.

Harold Goldblatt

Foreword to the French edition

Halbwachs strongly desired to take up again the question that
Durkheim addressed thirty-five years ago and, we make so bold as
to say, treated brilliantly, in the collection* the latter founded. The
present work, *The Causes of Suicide*, is the successor to Durkheim's
book, *Suicide*.

Our first intention had been simply to bring Durkheim's work
up to date, indicating in a supplementary chapter, or in an
Introduction, the points at which new data published during a
third of a century confirmed his conclusions or put them in
question. Halbwachs gradually felt compelled to undertake new
research, pose new problems, and present the facts from another
perspective.

Eventually he found that an entirely new book was needed. In
sociology, as in the sciences generally, the work of analysis is never
completed. As Durkheim noted, historical observation is an
essential means of sociological inquiry and, in this case, important
new events since Durkheim's work in 1896 had to be taken into
account. Nevertheless, Halbwachs has shown here that the
profound disturbances and adaptations in European societies
throughout this long period were of a kind like those that
Durkheim led us to anticipate. Most new data about suicide are
subject to essentially the interpretation he proposed.

Quantitative methods and procedures of analysis have, of
course, greatly developed since Durkheim's time and had done so
appreciably by the time Halbwachs took up his inquiry into
suicide. Substantially, Halbwachs finds that more exacting modes
of quantitative analysis also lead to results largely confirming
Durkheim's interpretations.

However, these verifications did not suffice. Halbwachs went on
to examine related matters closely. Accordingly, he extended the

Travaux de l'année sociologique – Tr.

field of observation to other societies, to other periods, and to other details. Analyzing Durkheim's facts anew and in greater depth, he introduced recent theories as well as new facts into the domain of his inquiry. He was thus able to determine the extent to which particular theories proposed by Durkheim must be completed, modified, or even abandoned. Where necessary, he proposed his own theories. Halbwachs has executed a work that is positive and new.

This work presupposes a knowledge of Durkheim's book. The latter, however, requires knowledge of this one for it is the necessary supplement, complement, and indispensable corrective to the other. When making use of Durkheim's *Suicide*, it would be imprudent, unscientific, and absurd not to refer constantly to Halbwachs's *Causes of Suicide*.

This book brings the sociology of suicide up to date. The two books are two phases of the same research, conducted in the same spirit.

Marcel Mauss

Introduction

Suicides are numerous in Shakespeare's plays, and in the entire romantic theater. The spectator or reader finds no fault with that, undoubtedly because it is a convenient type of ending to which authors have long habituated us. The newspapers apprise us that suicides are rather frequent, that hardly any events are more banal or require us to be more blasé. Nevertheless, whenever a suicide is imposed on our attention we are astonished anew. For in this manner of taking leave of one's fellow men there seems to be a disconcerting mixture of free choice and of inevitability, of resolve and of passivity, of lucidity and of bewilderment.

Much has been written on this subject. A recent bibliography which cites no fewer than 3,771 works is nevertheless incomplete. Suicide has a place in ethics, history, literature, and art. Physicians, jurists, and theologians are concerned about it. It continues to provoke curiosity, to awaken sentiments of pity and terror, and to offer rich, paradoxical material for discussion. Do many facts exist which arouse deeper human interest and which the sciences of man have more reason to examine?

Though suicide is ancient, undoubtedly as ancient as humanity, its study did not advance much before the middle of the nineteenth century. At this time there occurred what happened in astronomy when the invention of perfected optical instruments disclosed to observers an entire order of facts, at least as old as mankind, whose existence had not been suspected until then. The invention and perfection of statistics, those instruments of modern measurement, was needed in order for suicide as a mass phenomenon to be born, so to speak, before our eyes, just as at a sufficient magnification a part of the sky which had appeared empty suddenly becomes filled with a multitude of stars.

Guerry, as far back as 1835, Etoc-Demazy in 1844, Lisle in 1856, and still others were pioneers in viewing and describing this phenomenon which had just come within range of our instruments of observation. Wagner in 1864, and especially Morselli in 1879, perceived its diverse parts and determined its phases with much more precision. These precursors deserve great praise. Morselli, for example, though commanding only very incomplete data, not extending beyond 1841–5 for the majority of countries, recognized, or at the very least glimpsed, the type of influence which not only sex and age exert on suicide but also religion, marital status, occupation, population density, the rural–urban difference, economic crises, etc.

Durkheim's work, however, was much more important and decisive. In 1897 he became the first systematically to interpret these facts in the manner we know.[1]

> It seems hardly possible to us [he wrote] that there will not emerge from each page of this book, so to speak, the impression that the individual is dominated by a moral reality greater than himself: namely, collective reality. When each people is seen to have its own suicide rate, more constant than that of general mortality, that its growth is in accordance with a coefficient of acceleration characteristic of each society; when it appears that the variations through which it passes at different times of the day, month, year, merely reflect the rhythm of social life; and that marriage, divorce, the family, religious society, the army, etc., affect it in accordance with definite laws, some of which may even be numerically expressed [it will then be understood that these collective conditions and institutions are] real, living, active forces which, because of the way they determine the individual, prove their independence of him, [that they are] realities as definite and substantial as those of the psychologist or the biologist.

On closing this work, more than one reader – especially readers of philosophy – must have felt that suicide no longer posed a problem and that henceforth its solution was known. Was it the dialectic or the statistics which carried conviction? Both, without one always knowing clearly what was argument and what was fact. Sometimes, through no fault of Durkheim's, the dialectic was more persuasive than the facts. This has been more than an inconvenience. The structure was not perceived to rest on foundations that in some places are unsound. How could it have been otherwise? There is no scientific work that new observations do not require us to revise and complete.

It was therefore useful to resume this study at the point where Durkheim had left it, first, with a view to comparing his results with statistics published since then. Durkheim depended on figures which only occasionally went further back than 1840 and which never go beyond 1890–1. These data are of very unequal value. In Prussia, one of the most important countries in this respect, the statistics of suicide are almost complete only after 1883. In England they begin in 1856, in Italy only in 1864. Figures for the German Empire as a whole are lacking until after 1881. There are reasons to believe that in a number of countries the tabulations have been improved and completed during the latest periods, decade by decade. It is no exaggeration to say that data on suicide at our disposal since 1890 are at least as valuable and as numerous as those with which Durkheim worked. We can therefore verify his observations and state them precisely, ourselves benefiting from more detailed statistics. What the data from these last thirty or forty years teach us in this respect will be realized by referring to Chapters 8 to 10 of our book. Here we study problems addressed by Morselli and Durkheim in the framework they chose. If we possibly improve upon their solution to these problems, it is because we have the advantage of coming after them and of commanding a field of observation more extensive both in time and space.

Especially important, however, is the progress that methods of statistical elaboration have been making for some time past. We are no longer satisfied with calculating averages, proportions, or percentages. An American sociologist, John Rice Miner, recently expressed surprise that such modern statistical procedures have not yet been applied to the study of suicides as calculations of deviations, indices of correlation, dispersion, etc. We have embarked upon this course. The procedures we have used cannot be criticized as having treated these imperfect statistical data like rigorous physical observations. However, they are sufficiently empirical, sufficiently mathematical to render almost the same services.

We were immediately led by them to fix our attention on an aspect of suicide that, while neglected, seems to us quite important. The study of suicides has usually been confined up to now to tabulation of the increase or decrease in their number or proportion, much as one follows variations in the temperature of a feverish patient. Is suicide increasing? Can one forecast whether it will increase further? On this point, it is already clear that observations pursued over a longer span enable us appreciably to rectify Durkheim's conclusions and forecasts. That, however, is by no means the whole of the research. It may not even be its essence. The number of suicides in a region is a completely relative datum which is not illuminating or fully meaningful until several more or less proximate regions are compared. Do suicide rates converge in the principal countries of Europe and, within a given country, in different regions or provinces, and in large, medium, and small cities? At what rate and exactly to what extent? We have been able to discover just this by means of relatively simple calculations.

Interest in such a research derives, first of all, from the fact that the number of suicides can be considered a sort of thermometric indicator which informs us of the condition of the mores, of the moral temperature of a group. It does not suffice to depict the customs, beliefs, and modes of existence and behavior observable in a region. Such a description, unaccompanied by quantitative data, remains imprecise and leads only to uncertain conclusions. If, on the contrary, the distribution of suicides is, or tends to become, more homogeneous in one country than in another (or, within a country, in a group of provinces) one is entitled to assume that a certain moral uniformity is in process of realization in such a category, province, country, or continent. Considered from this point of view, however, the theory of suicide proper presents a rather new form. The environments constituted by regions are complex. However, rather simple traits that lend themselves to measurement are tabulated there. Examples are the density and mode of association of the population and the predominance of the urban or rural style of life. When suicides are studied in a regional framework they are related to factors of precisely this type. Neither Morselli nor Durkheim has stressed the influence of the city or of the countryside on the number and distribution of voluntary deaths, possibly because this was not easy for them to study. The reader who refers to the first and most extensive part of our study will see that variations in suicides are explained most clearly by transformations in the style of life so defined. We are far from misunderstanding or underestimating the importance of family sentiments and religious practices. These, however, are bound up in a totality of customs and type of social organization from which they partially draw their strength and from which they cannot be separated. We call that a style of life. We depart from Durkheim only in replacing the family and the religious group by more comprehensive social milieux of which they are but an aspect.

However, at several points this difference in method has led us to results that differ from his.

Durkheim summarized his explanation of suicide in this manner: 'Suicide varies in inverse proportion to the degree of integration of religious society, domestic society or the family, and political society or the nation.'

Though Durkheim was the first to prove it, Morselli had in fact already indicated that unquestionably married people kill themselves less often than do the unmarried. The family protects against suicide, especially when it includes children. He added that the continued growth of suicides in the course of the nineteenth century is explained by the weakening of bonds of every kind which keep the members of a family group united. However, he has not proven that the family of like composition is less protective today than formerly. He was, undoubtedly, unable to do so, because the social milieu of which the family is a part was transformed at the same time, with the result that one cannot study the influence which the family exerts on suicide in isolation from that of the milieu. The finding placed by Durkheim beyond doubt is, notwithstanding, no less essential and, as we have shown, can actually be confirmed by other statistics which specifically deal with the number of the suicide's children. Up to the present, however, it does not have as much significance as he attributed to it.

The earliest of the statistician's researches drew attention to the relatively small number of suicides which are committed in Catholic groups. Catholics kill themselves much less often than do Protestants. Durkheim placed great emphasis on this fact. We know how he explained it. 'Protestantism's inclination to suicide is related to the spirit of free inquiry.' Free inquiry, however, results from the disturbance of traditional beliefs.

> The greater concessions a religious group makes to individual judgment, the less it dominates lives, the less its cohesion and vitality .... The superiority [or rather the inferiority] of Protestantism with respect to suicide results from its being a less strongly integrated church than the Catholic church.

Father Krose S. J., who has published the best study of suicide since Durkheim, believes that Catholicism deters one from killing oneself because it inspires fear of punishment beyond the grave. He also attributes a powerful preservative quality to the Catholic religion as such. As for us, we agree that in many cases religious beliefs and practices do deter Catholics from committing the mortal sin of self-murder. The statistics, however, have actually very little to teach us about that. Nothing can be inferred from a comparison between two countries such as Italy and Germany because they differ in many other respects than religion. Besides, very few nations indicate the religious persuasion of their suicides. Prussia and Switzerland are almost the only ones that do. Now, in Prussia, most Catholics and Protestants differ in national origin, the Protestants being Prussian and the Catholics, Poles. Or they differ in style of life, the Catholics being more numerous in the country, and the Protestants in the cities or in regions most subject to urban influences. Do Catholics in Prussia infrequently commit suicide because they are non-Protestants or because they are Polish or rural? As we shall see, a more detailed analysis of Swiss statistics leads to the same conclusion. Up to now, it has not been possible to isolate the religious factor and to measure its influence. This remains a problem and we do not have even an inkling of how it could be solved. There are grounds for believing that national sentiments become stronger on occasions when the country is in danger. The experience during the last war confirms observations made up to now since, in most countries, many fewer have been victims of suicide than in times of peace, among both sexes and all ages of the civilian population, as well as among servicemen. This is also true of revolutions and political crises: we have been able to show that all the events that brought parties into conflict in France from 1872 to 1913 are reflected in the suicide curves. We have particularly studied the period 1899–1904 from this point of view, month by month, because in no other period in France, possibly during the entire century, is this type of influence more plainly revealed. Is it true, however, as Durkheim says, that 'these facts are susceptible of only one interpretation; namely, that great social disturbances and great popular wars rouse collective sentiments, stimulate partisan spirit and patriotism, political and national faith, alike, and concentrating activity toward a single end, at least temporarily cause a stronger integration of society'? War does more than overstimulate national passions. War transforms society profoundly, slackening or paralyzing some of its functions and creating or developing others. In particular, it simplifies the structure of the social body and greatly reduces the differentiation of its parts, as Spencer said. Are suicides not less numerous at least partly because a more even pace of life in a more uniform social milieu means that there are fewer collisions and frictions between individuals, that is, fewer occasions for discontent and despair? This would also be true of revolutions, however, and perhaps even of periods of political agitation when, to external appearance, there has been no change in the structure of the social body. The functions, undoubtedly, remain the same and continue to hold sway. Tradesmen, workers, officials and peasants remain in place. However, their thought is elsewhere. Their lives, familial, professional, and friendship, continue, but with much more automatism and much less involvement of self. All activity that is not political in character finds itself, therefore, likewise reduced. We conclude that the decrease in suicide during such periods can be explained in more than one way since, at the same time that national or party passions are more active and more extensive, the life of society becomes simplified and presents fewer occasions for conflict and instability.

Durkheim truly saw that suicide results from social causes. Does not each of the groups among which people are distributed tend to produce annually the same number or the same proportion of voluntary deaths? However, he considered only the mainsprings of collective life in society. When they sag, he said, man loses all the reasons he had for living. The individual becomes discouraged and despairing, or even exasperated, and turns his fury against himself for such reasons as that he does not have a wife and children to whom the double bond of affection and duty unite him; that he does not find support or regulation within a group of people who accept the same dogmas and practice the same religion; or, finally, that he is not distracted from his egoistic preoccupations and is not elevated above himself by great political or national interests. On first or even on second glance, this is a paradoxical theory, for one ordinarily seeks the causes of suicide in an entirely different direction.[2]

> Suicides due to the desire to atone, to avoid the disgrace of punishment, to escape illness, suffering, old age, to not survive a loved one: husband, wife, child, friend, master, to prevent or to expunge an outrage, to avoid disgrace, to avoid falling into the hands of the enemy; suicides due to disgust with life, committed on command. To these let us add: the inclination to astonish, desire to be spoken about, fit of insanity, idiocy.

The two lists of motives from which these are drawn are quite old since they relate to the Roman epoch. However, the reasons for suicide are still enumerated in nearly the same manner now.

According to Durkheim, these particular, individual motives are pretexts or occasions but not causes. The individual whom nothing binds to life any longer will find everywhere reason to end it, but this reason does not explain his suicide. Similarly, when one leaves a house which has several exits, the door through which one passes is not the cause of one's leaving. There had first to be at least an obscure desire to leave. A door opens before us but had it been closed we could always have opened another. Shall we say then that the unfortunates who commit suicide are impelled towards their death by forces whose nature they do not understand and that the motives they give to explain their act in no way enter into their decision? Durkheim appears indeed to have gone that far because there was, in his view, an abyss between the great collective forces, and motives or circumstances. He attributed causal power only to social factors. Undoubtedly, in order for this power to become active it must indeed descend into the world of individual proceedings and it can only penetrate there on the occasion of worry, suffering, and discouragement. However, while, similarly, one must indeed make use of an instrument to kill oneself, the causes of the choice of instrument are not to be confused with the causes of suicide. Likewise, according to Durkheim, the causes which explain the number and distribution of motives are not to be confused with the true causes of suicide: much more of chance and caprice enter into the former.

We will oppose two arguments to this sharp distinction between the motives and the causes of suicide. Durkheim's thesis would be plausible if no relationship existed between the effect of such motives and the results of disturbance to collective sentiments. This, however, is by no means the case. When one reviews the diverse particular motives for suicide, one sees that people only kill themselves following or under the influence of an unexpected event or condition, be it external or internal (in the body or in the mind), which separates or excludes them from the social milieu and which imposes on them an unbearable feeling of loneliness. This, however, is also the effect one experiences when, as Durkheim put it, one ceases to be 'integrated' into one of the groups which constitute the framework of society. There is, therefore, no essential difference between what he calls motives and causes. When to the emotional impoverishment of a bachelor is joined declassment or dishonor of the bankrupt, moral isolation to illness or desperation, two conditions of like nature become superimposed. The forces which are combining their influence are of the same type. Hence, there is no reason to exclude some from an explanation of suicide and retain others.

On the other hand, however, Durkheim believed that those circumstances that are invoked as motives of suicide are individual, not only because each of them affects an individual, but because their number and distribution do not depend at all on the particular structure of the group in which they are produced. To be sure, human nature considered in its organic aspects is nearly the same everywhere, and presents nearly the same varieties of temperament in diverse groups. If motives result only from the diversity of temperaments, it would follow that motives are everywhere the same and there would be no grounds for taking them into account to explain variations in the number of suicides. However, even were the diverse human organic types indeed distributed in the same proportions in all groups, which is itself debatable, circumstances and motives are certainly related to the organization of society. A priori, one can assume that events such as reversals of fortune, troubles and disappointments of a career, and even those conditions one groups under the rubric of boredom or disgust with existence are produced more frequently in a more complex society where individual situations change more often and more rapidly, where the rhythm of life is more rapid, and where individuals more often risk finding themselves unadapted to their milieu. Of course, at first, when each particular case is considered separately, one is not aware of this. Taken all together, however, facts that are called occasions or motives for suicide are only an aspect or an effect of group structure and style of life.

Thus, suicides are always explained by social causes. These, however, sometimes present themselves as collective forces, properly so called, such as family and religious customs, or great political and national currents, sometimes in the form of more or less numerous individual motives distributed in varying fashion depending on the degree of complexity of the society itself. It is not within our grasp, however, to separate habitual family or religious ways from other considered group ways of existence with which they intersect in a more or less closely-woven network. What would the warp be without the woof? How distinguish what in the fabric's strength comes from the one and what from the other? No more can we observe separately each of the totality of particular circumstances and motives of suicide. They are like so many ambushes placed in the path of the living, as they are concealed. What then is the reason for this surprising increase in suicides which has continued for more than a century? Is it the disruption of traditional groups? Is it the inevitable multiplication in a more complex society of opportunities for individual misfortune and suffering? We do not know what share must be allotted to each of these two types of causes. Durkheim confines himself to consideration of the weakening of the traditional bonds which formerly constrained and sustained people. If this were the only cause of the increase in suicide we would recognize in it then not only an evil but an absolute evil. For if they disappear, nothing replaces these traditions; society gains nothing in exchange. For this reason, a cry of alarm must be uttered. If, on the contrary, however, suicides are increasing particularly because social life is becoming complex and because unusual events which expose people to despair are becoming more common, suicides, while still an evil, are perhaps a relative evil. As a matter of fact, there is a degree of complexity which is the necessary condition of a richer and more intense social life.

Durkheim's accomplishment was to cover the phenomenon of suicide fully and to propose an explanation for it which might be completed and amended but whose principle seems quite unassailable. It is entirely natural that we, possessing new sources, have been able to push further ahead in the paths he has marked and possibly to open new ones. It was, however, important to indicate at the outset of our study at what essential points we agreed with him. We shall wish, in concluding, to call attention again to two problems that he touched upon at a time when no one commanded sufficient information to resolve them. These are studied in our last two chapters.

Durkheim believed that economic crises exert an influence on the trend of suicides precisely because they are crises. He even distinguished crises of prosperity and crises of depression. Both, it seemed to him, caused an increase in voluntary deaths because they trouble the normal course of economic life. We have been able to compare the movement of prices and the movement of suicides in Germany from 1880 to 1914, that is, in a country and during a period where industrial and commercial activity became outstanding, and we have found that suicides diminished during the phase of prosperity and increased, not only at the moment of crisis, but during the whole phase of depression. One cannot construct a theory from a single observation, even tested under the most favorable conditions. However, we have shown in our conclusion the sense in which this relationship could be interpreted.

The idea that all suicide results from mental trouble is still very widespread. We have been able to criticize Durkheim for blocking consideration of this question a little too quickly through depending on data that was too old and incomplete. He seems to have particularly ignored the existence of the illness named manic-depressive psychosis, characterized by alternating phases of excitation and depression. According to certain physicians, this would be one of the most frequent causes of suicide. The clinical observations analyzed by Dr Charles Blondel in his book *La Conscience morbide* have enabled us to understand the nature of these troubles a little better. This is the reason we have examined the psychiatric thesis anew in our penultimate chapter. We have placed it after all the statistical study, rather than before it, like Durkheim, because it was important to establish the influence of social factors before replying to those who question it.

We have not proposed a definition of suicide at the outset: in a study which rests principally on official statistics we were indeed obliged to accept the categorization of facts as presented to us. Despite recent interesting researches we have alluded to, there seems to us no grounds for enlarging this definition in such a way as to include attempted suicides. As a consequence, we had to examine closely the validity of the data. Our chapter on sources is short, too short for our taste. Such as it is, however, it assembles indispensable information which may be adequate for safe guidance.

A bibliography is appended in which we have included only those works on suicide published since Durkheim's book that we have made use of, not including official publications mentioned in the course of our study. Bayet's book, *Le Suicide et la morale* is almost the only French work cited. This is a remarkable book, very thoroughly documented, and we have often had occasion to refer to it, although the author has only studied how opinions of suicides have varied in popular and cultivated milieux in France since the Gallo-Roman epoch, according to law, literature, newspapers, etc.

We must express our gratitude to all those who sent us various recent statistical publications on suicide, in particular to Mr Nicefero, professor at the University of Naples; to Corrado Gini, director of the Central Institute of Statistics of the Kingdom of Italy; to Dr Zdanèk Ullrich of the University of Prague; to J. R. Cowell, of H. M. Stationery Office in London; to Mr Gernet, professor at the National University of Moscow; to Marcel Mauss, director of the École des Hautes Études at Paris; to Georges Dumas, professor at the Sorbonne; and to Mr Becker, chief of the Office of Statistics of Alsace-Lorraine.

chapter 1

Methods of enumerating suicides in European countries

There is much discussion of suicide statistics, and with reason. These materials are collected by agents and compiled by administrators who very often do not take into account the difficulties of their tasks. It would not be worth the trouble to devote much, or even a little time to the study of these figures if we could not know their sources or what those who first wrote them were able to learn, to understand, to perceive, and to establish, or in what form they have been transmitted to the statistical bureau whose publications we read.

Here, even more than in other areas of quantitative research, one must not fear to take the time for such examination.

We must note at the outset that suicides are not registered in the same manner in all countries.[1] To get our bearings, we shall distinguish four procedures that can be used for this purpose either separately or in combination. We shall then examine the methods followed by the most important European countries.

1. The suicide can be noted in the registry office on the occasion when the dead person is inscribed on the death register. Sometimes the cause of death, and hence the suicide, is mentioned in the register itself. Often, however, as in Germany for example, it is not. Here, after the particulars that are inscribed in the register, the official at the registry office then asks the cause of death for the purpose of statistical information, and indicates it on cards (*Zählkarten*) which are transmitted to the central statistical office. This, as we shall see, is what is prescribed in Prussia.

2. That suicide was the cause of death can be shown on the documents of the official proceedings, etc., which have both a medical and police character: the declarations of physicians who visit the dead are of this type, as are those of physicians who have treated them (the certificate of the death visit or the certificate of death, for example, in Bavaria). In Switzerland the two methods

are combined: a statistical card established by the official in the registry office is transmitted to the physician who indicates the cause of death on it. Sometimes the physician is then permitted, or may even be required (as in Schleswig-Holstein), to perform an autopsy on the corpse.

3. Suicides can be recognized simply by the reports or official proceedings of police agents or superintendents. In this case, it happens that the official must comply not only with strictly police regulations and public orders but also with directives that make him a veritable statistical official. This is the case in Prussia, where they are required to complete forms containing a rather large number of questions which are transmitted to the Bureau of Prussian Statistics.

4. Finally, suicides can be ascertained and recorded by the judicial administration: either by the courts (as in Spain, England, and Sweden), when suicide entails penal sanction, or (as in France) by the public prosecutor, undoubtedly because it is considered to be in every way contrary to law and order.

We shall now show how suicides are enumerated in various countries, beginning with those in which they are most numerous.

To begin with, here is a table which will permit us to identify the contribution of each country to the total number of suicides actually recorded. In the period 1901–5 an average annual number of 57,621 suicides was totalled for 23 countries. Of these, 20 European countries alone contribute 75 per cent of the total. The remaining quarter are distributed between the United States (7.9 per cent); Japan (16.3 per cent); and Australia (0.8 per cent).[2] The 42,231 European suicides are distributed as shown in Table 1.1.

Thus, Germany and France alone account for half the European suicides.

We shall begin with Germany and shall show how the principal states of the Reich have compiled and actually do compile their suicide statistics.

Prussia alone accounts in 1896–1900 for 59 per cent of all the suicides in Germany. Prussian statistics on suicide are among the oldest. They begin in 1816. Until 1868, one depended on the death and burial registers kept for Catholics and Protestants by the priests and pastors, and for Jews and dissenters by the state administration. Hence certain discrepancies.[3] Since 1 October 1868, on the occasion of each suicide police officials in cities and provinces must fill out a form consisting of fifteen questions. These forms are sent directly to the Bureau of Statistics, which is thus enabled to have them completed, if need be, by those same

Table 1.1 *Suicides in Europe* (*1901–5*)

	Number of suicides annually	Percentage of total for Europe
Germany	12,437	29
France	8,926	20.6
Holland, Belgium, Switzerland	2,003	4.6
Italy	2,095	4.8
Austria-Hungary[4]	8,117	18.7
England, Scotland, Ireland	3,803	8.8
Sweden, Norway, Denmark		
Finland	3,896	9
Spain	1,200	2.8
Romania, Serbia, Bosnia,		
Bulgaria	754	1.7
Total	42,231	100

officials and to obtain from them all necessary clarifications. This reform was undoubtedly enacted earlier, for between 1866 and 1867 there is a very sharp increase, not only in the absolute number, but in the proportion of voluntary deaths.[5] There was a new reform in 1883. From this date on, the Bureau of Statistics compares the police forms with the 'death certificates' instituted by the officials of the civil registry and, if there is ground, holds an inquest.[6] Now here are the figures obtained:

1882 following the old method 5,072
1883 following the old method 4,984
1883 following the new method 6,171

Or an increase of more than a fifth due solely to the reform in enumeration. The result of this is that suicide statistics in Prussia are undoubtedly much more precise after this date. But it is not easy to compare the new figures with the data prior to 1883. We note that the essential table published by Durkheim (*Suicide*, p. ·153) on the distribution of suicides by religious persuasion in Prussian provinces is compiled with the help of figures from 1883 to 1890, that is, after the reform in question.

The kingdom of Saxony has long been considered the record country for suicide. In 1890–1900 it is outstripped by Schleswig-

Holstein, and exceeds Brandenburg by only a little. Counted there, moreover, is an absolute number of suicides only equal in 1896–1900 to 11.2 per cent of the total voluntary deaths in Germany. Not until after 1830 was this type of death enumerated there. Here is the procedure. Suicides are recorded, on the one hand, in the church registry (under a special heading: only sex and age are distinguished); on the other hand, on lists prepared by police officials which contain more details: profession, marital status, mode of death, etc. The raw data are the death certificates (*Leichenscheine*) which must be delivered to the district physicians. Whenever there is doubt about the cause of death the officials are required (*streng verpflichtet*) to conduct an inquest. Until 1902 these district physicians themselves analyzed the certificates and reports. Since 1902 the forms have been centralized in the Bureau of Regional Statistics of Saxony. The forms compiled by the civil registry and by the police are compared (as in Prussia), the necessary corrections are made, and the definitive statistics are compiled.[7]

Suicide statistics in Bavaria date from 1884. From then on, less than a third as many voluntary deaths were counted there as in Saxony. This may explain why they were not concerned with registering them until later. This country includes in 1896–1900 only 7.4 per cent of all those produced in Germany. In Bavaria, contrary to what happens in Prussia, the district physician was the one who, until 1923, drew up the list of causes of death in his district, using the required death certificates. These lists or reports which, moreover, concerned only the civilian population were consolidated for the kingdom by the Bureau of Statistics. The Minister of War communicated to the same Bureau reports compiled by the army on suicides of soldiers. We note an interesting circumstance: if the suicide did not die within three days, but only later, no suicide was deemed to have taken place. We do not know whether this rule is still maintained. Since 1923 every case of suicide in Bavaria has been enumerated like other causes of death, that is, the individual form which the district physician must fill out for every case of death carries, along with the others, questions specifically concerning the suicide: manner of suicide, motive, etc. Suicides of soldiers are now enumerated in the same manner. If the district physician is not the one who compiles the special list of suicides, the result is that the forms are delivered to the Bureau of Statistics, that is, suicide statistics are now centralized.

Württemberg since 1846, Baden since 1830, and Oldenburg since 1854 have been continuously registering a number of suicides which in 1896–1900 were equal to 7.4 per cent of the

German contingent (that is, as many as in Bavaria). We recall that, although the Grand Duchy of Oldenburg was a very small state in which not even an average of 100 suicides a year was produced, it was the only one to have published for 1871–85 suicide statistics by age and by marital status. From these it was found that the unmarried and the widowed of both sexes killed themselves more often than did the married. Durkheim verified and specified these findings with French data.

Not until the close of 1880 did all the German states, without exception, have statistics on suicide so that it was possible to publish statistical totals for the whole Reich. The Imperial German Office of Statistics, powerfully organized and having a numerous staff of technicians at its disposal, consolidates the data collected by the various states. It may be assumed that it has succeeded in introducing into the various parts of the Empire uniform and elaborate methods of delivery and of control. The German suicide statistics indeed seem to be one of the best sources at our disposal.

In France, suicide statistics have been compiled by the Administration of Criminal Justice (since 1827).[8] In cases of violent death, the burial could not take place until after an official report had been drawn up by a police officer assisted by a medical expert. These official reports are transmitted to the public prosecutor who can initiate a new examination or order a judicial inquest. Statements indicating sex, age, marital status, nationality, and profession of the suicides, as well as the mode of suicide and the motives, are administered by deputies in the statistical department of the Ministry of Justice, which consolidates them and annually publishes tables summarizing all these findings in the *Comptes généraux de l'administration de la justice criminelle en France*. According to Father Krose, 'official French suicide statistics have, from the beginning, been very complete and very reliable.' We shall see, further on, that there is no reason to believe that any considerable number of suicides is concealed in France. It undoubtedly seems a little unusual for the task of compiling enumerations of this type to be entrusted to magistrates and officials of the Ministry of Justice, for no more than the physicians have they been prepared for it by schooling or a special apprenticeship.[9] But, as in Prussia, the brute fact of suicide is established, after all, on the testimony of physicians, by means of police inquests.

French suicide statistics have existed for a century without the introduction of any important reform. Let us note, however, that before 1892 the public prosecutors sent to the Ministry of Justice an individual form on each suicide. After this date the Ministry received only tables. Thus, suicide statistics were decentralized to a certain extent. The Central Agency is confined to being a ministerial bureau. Had it been, instead, an office of statistics, properly speaking, commanding technical personnel prepared for its task, the decentralization of suicide statistics would have been regrettable. It is indeed in the direction of centralization of suicide statistics that one would wish the French organization to evolve. However, by dint of handling even an imperfect instrument, one may learn to make better use of it. A certain continuity and conformity with traditions becomes established such that one can assume the French data have equal validity from one region within the nation to the next, and from one period to the next, and can be compared amongst themselves.[10]

Let us add that in *L'Annuaire statistique de la Ville de Paris*, which begins in 1880, one finds detailed information on suicides in Paris (and in the department of Seine) by wards and by months.

We are ill-informed on the organization of suicide statistics in Austria and in Hungary. The data are drawn from death registries (where the cause of death is indicated). Father Krose says that the figures relating to the crown lands of Hungary are very incomplete.[11] Austrian statistics on suicide are very old, having existed since 1819. But at first (until a date we do not know) the death registers were kept by the priests. Now Father Krose (*Der Selbstmord*, p. 102) writes,

> Until 1872, the number of suicides [in Austria] increases only slowly: there are no abrupt and unexpected rises. This same year, the publication of the health statistics required by the Superior Council of Hygiene begins, permitting completion of the data drawn from the registers kept by the priests. Now the number of suicides increases from 1,677 in 1872 to 2,463 the following year, or nearly 50 per cent. Undoubtedly, the 'Crash of Vienna' in 1873 can explain a small part of this increase. But it must result principally from the greater accuracy of enumeration since it continues in the following years.

One can assume that Austrian statistics on suicide are more accurate after 1872.[12]

In England, as in Spain, suicide carries penal consequences: attempts at suicide are considered an offense. That is why, as in France, the judicial administration publishes in *Judicial Statistics* the number of attempts at suicide as well as the number of suicides. Special officials, the coroners, examine the corpses of the suicides. It is from their reports that these enumerations are compiled. They cannot have been very accurate at the outset. That is why publication of these figures, begun in 1838, was interrupted in 1841. It was resumed in 1866. On the other hand, the statistics on the causes of death published in the *Annual Report of the Registrar General of Births, Deaths, and Marriages* indicated the number of suicides and their characteristics in more detail.[13] There must therefore be a liaison or collaboration between the administration of justice and the registry office. But we are not told under what conditions it is prescribed.[14]

In Italy until 1864 information on suicides was to be had only for the northern part of the country: Lombardy, Piedmont, and Liguria. Since 1864 suicides have been tabulated by the registry office from certificates of the physicians charged with examining the bodies of the deceased. A recognized statistician, L. Bodio, directed and supervised the preparation of these data, published first in the *Movimento dello stato civile* (with the *Confronti internazionali*), then, after 1881, in the *Statistica delle cause di morte*. The annuals published by Italian cities are an equally valuable source. It must be noted that since Morselli the Italians have studied suicide continuously, their statistical data particularly, and that they are better placed than we for judging the methods in use amongst themselves.

In some cantons in Switzerland suicide statistics are very old. But figures are to be had for the whole country only since 1876. They are included in the statistics on the causes of death, that is, the statistics are enumerated by the registry office, we do not know exactly under what conditions. In Belgium, causes of death have been recorded since 1850, but it is only following 1866 that physicians must certify them. At each death an official report must be filled out by an experienced person, or by somebody else in his absence.[15] Only 6 or 7 per cent of the deaths cannot be classified.

In Sweden, suicide statistics go back to the middle of the eighteenth century. But the early statistics are drawn only from the registers of death kept by the pastors. Later, two other series of tables were published: some were drawn up from judicial documents, the others from autopsy certificates (*Gesundheitscollegium*). There are important differences between these three sets of data.

In Norway, we do not know how the numbers included in the statistics of the causes of death are obtained: probably by the registry office.

Father Krose tells us that in Denmark since 1836 the enumerations of suicides have been made with great care under the direction of excellent statisticians. They seem to have relied on the reports of the 'medical police.'[16] (We do not know from what period.)

In Spain, according to Father Krose, 'the authorities try seriously to compile exact statistics of suicide, contrary to what is often, mistakenly, supposed.' On the occasion of each suspicious death, and also in the case of an attempted suicide, an inquest is ordered by Criminal Justice. The official charged with the inquest must fill out an individual form which includes quite a large number of questions. But the very same Father Krose adds that, precisely because suicide carries penal sanctions, one must attempt to conceal it in Spain more than elsewhere, and that the authorities themselves are more accommodating in this respect.[17]

Father Krose wrote in 1907 that in the United States the official statistics confined themselves to showing the number of suicides in the year immediately preceding the census. Thus, 31.8 per million were found in 1859 (census of 1860), 33 in 1890, and 45 in 1900. Statistics compiled at such intervals are clearly uninstructive. According to Krose, more complete and more reliable data are obtained by some states where a well-organized administration of statistics has been enumerating suicides for a rather long time: Massachusetts in particular (average proportion per million: 71.4 from 1859 to 1863, 60.5 from 1866 to 1870, 91 from 1880 to 1893). In Rhode Island, the proportion from 1880 to 1893 was 84. Several other states in the Union have published some figures. Altogether, the proportions indicated by the states are considerably higher than the results of the censuses would have allowed us to predict. Von Mayr reproduces the average number and the annual proportion of suicides in America for the period 1901–5: 4,548 suicides or 140 per million inhabitants. But the inquiry deals only with the Registration Area, which was not the same during all five years. In 1906 and 1907 it consisted of hardly half the population of the Union.[18]

In Australia, one is in command of continuous data on suicides in the seven united provinces since 1871, for Victoria and Southern Australia since 1868. The proportion of voluntary deaths in Victoria passed from 104 in 1868–70 to 117 in 1871–6 and 95 in 1896–1900. For Australia in its entirety it rose to 124 in 1896–1900, to 125 in 1901–5.

Suicide statistics in Japan go back a little further than 1885. Krose enumerates the following proportions: 159 in 1886–90, 179 in 1891–5, 179 in 1896–1900. But von Mayr gives a proportion of 185 for 1896–1900 and of 201 for 1901–5. This corresponds to a total of 9,355 suicides for 1901–5, almost as many as in France.

According to Krose, all the European states were publishing suicide statistics in 1907 except Portugal, Turkey, Bulgaria, and Greece.[19] Only very incomplete and discontinuous data were to be had from non-European states except for Australia, Japan, and, of later years, the United States.[20] We have no indication of the methods of enumeration of suicides in these three countries. In what follows we shall make hardly any use of their statistics.

This very short, very incomplete review of the methods adopted in a certain number of countries at least teaches us that the great difficulty everywhere must be to assure oneself that the physicians, the police officers, and the registry officials have properly researched, discovered, declared, and registered every suicide. Whether they are transmitted to the Ministry of Justice as in France, or to a central statistical bureau as in Germany, the accuracy of the statistical enumerations depends on this initial operation. These difficulties must be nearly the same in both places. We shall therefore confine ourselves to the procedure adopted in France.

We read, in the *Dictionnaire encyclopédique des sciences médicales* (Dechambre et Lereboullet, 1889, pp. 585–7):

> a circular of 24 December 1866 requires the verification [of the declaration of death] by a physician or by a sworn-in health officer . . .. Despite these requirements, verification of death is unusual except in the large cities. It hardly exists in rural communities.

In the large cities, physicians from the registry office call at the dwelling place of the deceased. Elsewhere, people are satisfied with the declaration of the physician who has cared for the deceased during his illness, or of the family physician, or, sometimes, with the family's declaration. When it concerns someone who has died on a public thoroughfare, death is verified in the cities by the police superintendent; in the country by the gendarmerie.

These few lines contain almost all we know of the verification of death in France. Let us add, however, that in the *Statistique du mouvement de la population en France* (published by the *Statistique générale de la France* since 1925), one finds, for 1926, the figures shown in Table 1.2.

Table 1.2   *Number of deaths verified by a physician*

Total	Verified by a physician	Not verified	No indication
707,806	511,667	123,093	73,056

That is, 72.5 per cent of deaths have been verified by a physician, 17 per cent have not, and for 10.5 per cent we do not know whether they have been verified or not. We can assume that a quarter or more of the deaths have escaped all control.

This is a large proportion, but is it certain, or even probable, that this last quarter contains a considerable number of voluntary deaths? If we had to defend the thesis that it is quite difficult to conceal a suicide, we could say the following: suicide takes place out of doors as well as at home, in both the cities and the countryside.[21] If it takes place out of doors, even in the immediate environment of the house, the chances are very good that strangers or neighbors will learn of it. Why should they remain silent? Let us suppose that it takes place at home where strangers do not intrude, where the members of the family have the time and sometimes the ability to feign an accident, a sudden death, a short illness, etc. Who will prevent them? One must imagine, however, that suicide provokes an entirely different reaction in the family from a simple death, even a sudden death. It is by no means an ordinary event, and it is difficult to prevent the disturbance it causes in the family group, for one or more of its members, from spreading outside and beyond the home. It is the kind of brutal and grievous shock which paralyzes abilities, prevents thinking, and unchains a veritable social and superstitious terror. One is unprepared, one finds oneself in an entirely new situation for which one lacks any habitual reaction. At such a time, how can one give evidence of self-composure, decisiveness, self-mastery? How should one not make any confused gestures, not cry out, not call, not look for help, in no way share with others an emotion one feels too weak to bear alone? To imagine and to realize a staging, certain preparations are needed. That, however, presupposes that the next of kin have been forewarned, that the suicide has been decided upon in concert with them, that is, that impossible conditions have been precisely fulfilled. A person who wishes to kill himself does his best to hide his intentions from his relatives and his friends, for fear they will dissuade him by their prayers or put physical obstacles in his way.[22] They must therefore be taken by surprise. One does not kill oneself in a casual manner. Rather, one excuses oneself, inwardly or in a letter they will later read beside the remains, not only for the grief caused them but also for the scandal to which, as we well know, the suicide exposes them. Moreover, whoever is prepared to leave life voluntarily is, most often, already more than half separated from his group, and dead to society. He lacks sufficient strength to concentrate on the act he is about to accomplish as well as actually to accomplish it. Once he has decided to seek reasons for his final step only within himself the social aspect of death disappears from view. Let us repeat that even should the relatives of a person who has just killed himself have the time to recover, to reflect, to deliberate, and to understand one another, if there are several of them, they may judge it prudent to verify a fact which always risks being discovered subsequently and which they may not even temporarily be able to conceal. Even if they are sure of the physician's willingness, can they know that the mayor will not order an inquest, that neighbors, friends, will not be astonished by so sudden and mysterious a disappearance, that some unforeseen accident will not render all their precautions futile? Even though they have placed themselves in the most favorable position, if a poisoning has occurred of which no visible trace appears externally, are they not by that very fact exposing themselves to the greatest risk? And if there are visible traces, to what extent will the physician consent to ignore them and remain an accessory?[23]

Here, in effect, are some of the arguments we could develop. However, we also know well what the rejoinder might be: We must expect people who have a major interest in concealing an act committed by someone in their group to use every means to succeed. In certain cases, no motive will be strong enough to divert them from it. We must expect even more that such intense sentiments will not be experienced by the representatives of society who verify it, and besides, that the verification itself is often difficult. When a person kills himself outdoors, one must undoubtedly reckon with the curiosity and indiscretion of strangers, and with the spitefulness or the ill-will of neighbors. The former, however, may be indifferent and the latter may obey a sentiment of fellowship which sometimes unites inhabitants of the same neighborhood or even of the same village against the law. It has been said that for a long time most of the drowned persons in England were considered to be victims of accident, probably because the police accepted the false declarations of neighbors and friends of the suicide so as not to put into effect the procedure of felo de se. When legal proceedings are not instituted there remains the sanction of opinion which one attempts to avoid at all costs. When the suicide takes place at home family solidarity comes into play with much more force. This may perhaps explain why the unmarried and even the widowed appear to kill themselves more often than do married people, and married people without children more often than do married people with children. The public becomes more involved, and the family does not shelter them like a screen. It is a question of avoiding a kind of dishonor which overtakes all the relatives. How should they not unite? It is objected that the proportion of suicides remains constant over a long span of years in the same country and in the same region. Is this not because there is no longer any change in the force of those sentiments that arise and maintain themselves in groups which keep the same structure and that they hold sway from one year to the next with equal intensity? The constancy of suicides could result from the constancy of forces which aim at concealing suicides. These forces increase when religious sentiments are added to family sentiments. May not fewer suicides be enumerated among Catholics than among other persuasions because the relatives transfigure his act from fear lest a kinsman not be buried in sacred ground and, with perhaps the indulgent complicity of the church, indulge in a pious lie to save face? After all, one never knows whether the guilty person may not have repented at the last moment. It is true that suicide cannot always be concealed. But favorable circumstances are not lacking. Even when the physician from the registry office calls, as is required in the big cities, he is often a man who is a little overworked and, above all, is preoccupied with simply filling an administrative function. He casts a glance at the deceased, of whom he ordinarily sees only the face, and asks what illness he died from in order to know what he must write on his questionnaire. What pressing motive would commit him to insist on more? Very often, however, especially in the past, people were satisfied, and are satisfied, with the declaration of any physician whatever and of the relatives themselves. What guarantee can be given? Undoubtedly the more timid and the more prudent relatives will be restrained by the fear of risk. However, the preoccupation with avoiding scandal is very strong. Also, what does one risk? If discovered, one has an excuse quite ready. One has obeyed sentiments which everyone understands and which, in themselves, are respectable. The physician can invoke the like when he does not retreat behind a somewhat narrow interpretation of professional secrecy. That many suicides could be concealed is very evident since a large number have been. Is it not true that every reform in statistical procedures leads to enumeration of a larger number? And who could say that the means of uncovering all of them have finally been found?

Thus, we remain in uncertainty. It serves no purpose to say that, after all, even if some of the suicides escape us we know by far the greater number. For the study of this phenomenon depends upon variations and differences which are sometimes minimal.

It would not be the first time that apparent laws had been formulated because a systematic error, always reproduced in the same circumstances, regularly falsified our observations.

chapter 2

A means of appraisal: the study of the modes of suicide

There may be a way to tell whether certain types of systematic concealment, related to the particular mode of suicide, accidentally falsify the statistics. This recognition would reduce errors in them even if it did not guarantee their accuracy in every respect.

Guerry is one of the first authors to point out that the proportions of the various means used to commit suicide are quite remarkably constant from one year to the next. His observation has been confirmed by every statistician who has studied this aspect of suicide after him. Durkheim wrote on this subject:

> The relative frequency of different modes of suicide remains invariant for a given society over a very long period .... Each people has its style of preferred death, and the order of these preferences is very resistant to change. It is even more constant than the total figure of suicides.

However, he perceived this problem only in passing. The choice of the means of death seemed to him to depend on social causes independent of those which determine suicide. Study of the modes of death could not therefore teach us anything about suicide itself. Legoyt expressed the same opinion as early as 1881 in his book, *Le Suicide ancien et moderne*.

However, even if the execution and the choice of means represent only an external and superficial aspect of voluntary deaths, they are objective facts. These very ones are the most objective, the most accessible to the senses, in suicide. Although there is every ground for mistrust when we are presented with tables of motives, because these are the interpretations of observers or witnesses, the statistics on modes of execution cannot arouse the slightest doubt. One may not have enumerated all the suicides. At least one could not be deceived about the means chosen by the suicide to kill himself.

'Suicide,' said Goethe, 'is an act so unnatural, so contrary to human nature, that, once decided upon, the person relies for its execution principally on the nature of things.' The weight of his own body is what will make him fall from a high place, or suspend him from the end of a rope, or, sometimes, impale him on a sharp-pointed weapon. It is the resistance of the rope which strangles him; the impenetrability of the water which prevents the air from arriving at his respiratory tract, the brute force of the bullet, the sharpness of the steel, the chemical action of the poison, the toxicity of the gas, which mutilate, ravage, and destroy his organism. Here, only the diverse properties of matter intervene.[1] Now, these are self-evident, directly observable, in contrast to human thoughts and sentiments. They are things. But the first rule of sociological observation, as Durkheim has shown, is to treat social facts as things, that is, to apprehend them in their tangible form. It is the only way to set out from data whose reality and whose very nature escape all discussion. Will it be said that what will be attained thus is what is most superficial and of least interest? But how does one know this? In any case, it is a point of departure. Every step taken on this terrain will be certain. All parts of reality are interrelated, but everything will escape us unless we succeed in taking hold of one of its parts, a hold that can no longer be denied us.

But is the instrument, the mode of execution, truly part of the suicide? Durkheim seems to have doubted this. He criticizes statisticians for usually devoting a chapter to the study of the means, as if there were no relationship between the means and the act. But that is exactly what is unknown, and the question can only be settled following examination. To be sure, the idea is rather widespread that of the two phases of the act of suicide, the decision and the implementation, only the first counts. Once death is decided upon the person would be relieved of a burden, as if everything were settled. The choice of means comes later, but as the suicide will be effected in any case, the act will not be modified by it. The act will remain what it was at the outset: the will to put oneself to death. On the contrary, however, it is quite possible for the choice of means to be an element in the decision, and perhaps it is so in the majority of cases. Besides, as we shall see at once in the next chapter, only when the act has been accomplished is one certain that the decision was firm, that is, only after the means have been chosen. Plenty of suicides do not take place, are not accomplished simply because the means have been badly chosen.

Since every suicide results from the collaboration of decision and means, has one the right to neglect the latter?

In a table reproduced by Morselli, Farr showed the number of suicides executed in England from 1858 to 1876, year by year, distinguishing them according to the mode of execution. For an almost constant proportion of voluntary deaths (from 65 to 70 per million) in 16 out of 19 years there were 3 suicides by firearms; in 18 out of 19 years there were 6 to 7 suicides by poisoning; in 18 out of 19 years there were 25 to 30 suicides by hanging, etc.[2]

We shall give some examples of the constancy of the distribution of suicide. Instead of multiplying tables we shall calculate for each mode of suicide the mean of the numbers corresponding to a series of years, the deviation between the number for each of these years and this mean, and the mean of these deviations (that is, their arithmetic sum divided by their number).* We shall take a simple example first. Let the average proportions of the diverse modes of suicide per year, per 100 suicides, and for four successive periods in Prussia be as shown in Table 2.1.[3]

Table 2.1   *Suicides in Prussia*

	Per cent suicides				Proportion of suicides per million inhabitants
	Hanging	Firearms	Sidearms	Drownings	
1869–72	60.8	10.2	4.2	19.7	128
1873–6	60.3	11.1	3.7	18.6	143
1877–82	61.4	10.7	2.9	18.4	184
1883–90	60.3	11.1	2.8	19	201

The number of suicides increased between the first and last period by 56 per cent but, as one immediately sees, the proportions of diverse means employed for putting oneself to death hardly changed at all. Of 100 suicides, an average of 61 hanged themselves in the four periods. The sum of the differences between the figure for each period and the average is equal to 2 or

*Or the mean of the deviations of the annual frequencies of suicides from the mean of the annual frequencies – Tr.

0.5 on the average for each period. 0.5 is to 61 as 0.8 is to 100. This is an extremely weak degree of variation. It would scarcely be raised if, instead of periods, we had compared successive years. The same calculation for firearms gives an average difference of 1.3 or a degree of variation of 3 per cent, and for the drownings of 2.25 per cent. The same is not true for sidearms (degree of variation: 16.2 per cent). Here, however, the numbers are much smaller. Moreover, they decrease continuously between the first and last periods. In fact, as we shall see, although the numbers corresponding to the modes of suicide remain very close from one year to the next over extended periods, it is noticeable that changes are always in the same direction.

Let us now examine diverse modes of suicide in several countries, year by year.[4] Variations will naturally be greater because of accidental causes. However, except when the number of cases concerned is small, we shall see that they remain confined within rather narrow limits.

Here, first of all, is England where, according to an opinion long given credence, a large number of suicides are allowed to escape enumeration. This is one of the European countries where hangings are fewest. Hanging is considered to be an 'ungentlemanly' act, the least aristocratic mode of suicide. It may be held in indifferent esteem because this type of capital punishment was long inflicted on highway robbers and bandits. However, from 1867 to 1874 a little more than a third of the English suicides hanged themselves: 371 per thousand. The deviations of the annual figures from this average are small: 5.6 on the average, or 1.5 per cent. Poisonings, much less numerous, yielded a proportion of 90 to 100 per thousand suicides during the same period.

In France from 1866 to 1875 people hanged themselves a little more often: an average of 449 hangings per thousand suicides. A maximum was enumerated in 1870, a minimum in 1872. In the other eight years these figures are confined between 430 and 460 per thousand, 43 and 46 per cent. That is an average deviation of 2.8 per cent for the ten years and, for the eight, of only 1.5, as in England. The number of drownings is smaller (a little more than a quarter of the suicides). It varies a little more, by 3.1 per cent, on the average: still a rather small deviation.

In both England and France rarer modes of suicide naturally lend themselves to wider variations. Suicides by firearms are fewer than one-twentieth of the total in England. The variation is 12.9 per cent. In France, suicide by suffocation or asphyxiation is a little more than one-twentieth of the total. The variation is 15.2 per cent. But if one restricts himself in both instances to only half the years, these latter two proportions are nearer the average. These deviations decline to 7.3 and 3.9.

This last deviation is equal to that found in Prussia for the thirty-five-year period from 1874 to 1908 by calculating the average proportion of men who hang themselves: a relative deviation of 3.9 per cent. This concerns 2,500 male suicides by hanging each year. Men hang themselves in Germany more than in France or England (nearly two-thirds of the total of suicides). However, in the course of these thirty-five years, the proportion of hangings diminished. If we divide this series of years, which is too long, into three periods of 12, 12, and 11 years, we ascertain that the proportion of suicides who hang themselves in Germany passes from 65 per cent to 64, then to 58, or three relative deviations of 1.26, 1.87, and only the last (since the proportion drops the most) of 3.2 per cent. Thus, the variations appear to be very small from one year to the next.

Let us, similarly, enumerate the proportion of women in Prussia who commit suicide by drowning each year during the same period. Prussian women hang themselves less frequently than do the men, but they drown themselves much more frequently. It is so, moreover, in all European countries. The number of drownings is less than 500 each year, although they comprise 37 per cent of the suicides. That is because women, as we know, kill themselves much less frequently than do men. Given this number, which is but a fifth of the preceding, one could expect these annual variations to be greater. In fact, they rise to an average of 7 per cent. But here again, thirty-five years is too long a period. During the course of it this proportion has clearly declined: from 40.5 in the first ten years to 34 in the last ten. This downward movement stands out from 1885 onward. In the first ten years, the deviation represents only a variation of 4.1 per cent, a slight variation if one takes account of the smaller number of cases. The proportion oscillates between 39 and 43 per cent.

But here are still smaller numbers. In Saxony during the eight* years from 1881 to 1890 the proportion of suicides by hanging has been, on the average, 62.8 per cent, almost the same as in Prussia. But the number of cases concerned is much smaller than in Prussia. The average deviation shows, however, an average variation of 3.2 per cent, which is not very great. In Italy in the same period only 15.8 of every 100 suicides per year hanged themselves. The Italians, as we shall see, prefer poison or the revolver to the rope. This yields about 200 suicides by hanging per year, a much smaller number than even in Saxony. The average variation in this small number of cases is 5.7 per cent. But here

Sic – Tr.

too, even though only eight* years are concerned, the proportion increases between the first three years and the following seven* from 14.6 to 16.2 per cent. If the average deviation is calculated separately for the first three and the last seven, one finds two equal variations at 1.14 and 4.4 per cent: the proportion oscillates between 14.4 and 14.7, then between 16 and 17. But the most remarkable example is again found in Prussia, where men very rarely poison themselves. During the twenty years from 1875 to 1894, poisonings represent 2.6 per cent, on the average, of all male suicides, a hundred per year. Now, the deviations from the average, for each of these years, are so small that one finds an average variation of only 0.8 per cent (setting 2.6 = 100).

Thus, the constancy with which the same modes of suicide are reproduced from one year to the next, within the same country, is entirely surprising. It would be easy to show by the calculation of probabilities that, while for 2,500 suicides per year the average variation scarcely exceeds 1.5 per cent, when a much smaller number of cases is concerned, somewhat higher variations of 4, 5 and 6 per cent or more are entirely in the same range and can only be explained by accidental circumstances. The effects of these accidents are more marked when small numbers are concerned because they only imperfectly counterbalance one another. They nonetheless remain accidents.

This constancy, remarkable as it may appear, is not, however, absolute. Continuous changes sometimes occur with the effect, in the long run, of reducing or increasing the importance of one or another of the means to which one resorts in order to attain death. Now, these changes might themselves result from the accuracy with which suicides that are accomplished by such means are enumerated, that is, from success in concealing a larger or smaller number. If the choice of mode of suicide did not present any regularity whatever, we would naturally not be able to observe such changes. That is why it behooved us to establish at the outset that, in general, and in the majority of cases, everything happens as if each of these different means of killing oneself could only be employed within the same country a limited number of times, the same (proportionately) from one year to the next. One had to be assured of the existence of the rule to be in a position to notice exceptions.

We say that changes or exceptions to this rule lead one to ask oneself whether all the suicides have indeed been registered or, more precisely, whether the category of suicides that is varying (poisonings, immersion, etc.) has been adequately enumerated. However, the lack of exceptions does not confer the right to

Sic – Tr.

conclude, from the modes of suicide being always partitioned similarly in a given country, that all the suicides have been enumerated. This clearly limits the reach of our appraisal. Suppose that a category of suicides committed in such and such a region, or by members of the same religious persuasion, or by people of the same social class, should in fact be more poorly registered than others because they succeed in concealing a large number. There is no reason whatever for the modes of suicide to be distributed otherwise in the group which succeeds in concealing a large number of suicides than in the totality of suicides. Suppose that the Catholic group, in a country where religions are mixed, appears to produce fewer suicides than average for the country but that, in reality, this difference is explained by the fact that Catholics conceal a large number of their suicides. Nothing indicates that the choices of Catholics will not incline, on the average, towards the same modes of death as the choices of Protestants. The suppression of part of the Catholic suicides will not, therefore, alter in any way the proportional partition of the modes of death, which will remain the same for those that are left as if they had not been suppressed.[5]

If, therefore, we find irregularities, variations from one year to the next in the partitioning of the modes of death within a given country, we cannot conclude from this that one group is more successful at concealing a larger or smaller number of its suicides than some other. Rather, we must then ask ourselves whether suicides accomplished by a particular instrument, or by a particular means, have been accurately enumerated for the totality of the groups, whether concealment has not systematically affected some particular mode of death.

Father Krose has, in fact, researched whether some among the diverse modes of death might be better concealed than others. How to determine them? He places in this category only suicides by drowning as well as those by asphyxiations because, he says, they can be passed off as accidents. Thus, in England the police have for a long time usually assumed that drownings were not suicides. This would explain why the proportion of suicides in this country has passed from 16.3 per cent in 1858–64 to 22.7 per cent in 1889–93. This last number corresponds fairly exactly to the average proportion of suicides by drowning, or 21.6 per cent, for 16 states in 1887–93 (see below). True, one always drowns himself outside his own home, in the open, if not in public, while half the people who hang themselves do so indoors. But when one pulls from the water the body of a drowned person whom one has not been able to observe at the moment he threw himself in, nothing prevents one from supposing that he fell in by accident, because he was drunk, or took a false step, or that he was thrown in by someone. Here, everything undoubtedly depends on the readiness of the police or the gendarmerie to accept the explanations of relatives, the statements of neighbors and of friends. In sum, suicides by drowning can be hidden more easily, not because one is able to conceal the drowning itself, but because, in this case, several explanations are possible and because the police see nothing inconvenient in accepting the one which, in the eyes of public opinion, is the most honorable for the drowned person. This is not true of other modes of suicide for which there is no alternative: if the hypothesis of a crime is improbable, one will not hesitate to conclude that a man whose body bears the marks of a revolver bullet, or who has been found hanging from a tree, or who has swallowed poison, has put himself to death. Hence, this time it is the mode of death itself which must be hidden. That is not easily accomplished, but can be, more or less. We are rather surprised, for example, to meet in the English statistics an exceptionally high number of suicides by thrusting or cutting weapons: 18.2 per cent instead of 5.7 per cent, on the average, for 14 countries, England included. Only in Scotland would there be almost as many. Spain, which comes next, does not exceed 7.3 per cent. Even Japan, the country of hara-kiri, remains average, along with Switzerland and Sweden. Now in England, suicides accomplished with firearms are likewise few in number: their count is 9.3 per cent instead of 14.4 per cent, the average in 16 countries. The count is even less in Scotland, as well as in Norway, Denmark, and Saxony. But most of the other countries very clearly exceed the average.[6] Shall we say that the revolver leaves external marks less visible than the razor which cuts the throat, or the dagger, or the knife? And, enumerating in England an exceptionally high number of poisonings, 12.7 per cent instead of 5.8 on the average for 15 countries (only Sweden exceeds England in this respect and only Scotland and Spain approach it), shall we conclude that, for rather natural reasons, one most often hesitates to conceal a suicide by poisoning? Thus, England would present us with rather a good portrait of a country where are hidden, or, indeed, where have long been hidden, all the kinds of suicide that lend themselves to it, the suicides by drowning, first of all, then those which leave the fewest external marks, so that the voluntary deaths which are the most difficult or which one hesitates the most to conceal would occupy here a more conspicuous place.

But the following objection can be raised to Father Krose. If such a mode of suicide is rare in a given country, it can be imputed, not that it is easier to give it the appearance of an accident, or to hide it from the representatives of the law, but, more simply, to the customs, traditional preferences and repulsions in such a region within the national group. Regarding the diverse means to which those who put themselves to death have recourse, Goethe writes,[7]

> Hanging oneself is hardly an attractive idea because it is an ignoble death. It is acquiesced in more willingly in England because, in this country, from youth on one sees more than one person hang without this punishment's being exactly dishonorable.

He intends to say, of course, that hanging is not reserved there especially for those guilty of crimes so low that the baseness of the misconduct would become attached to the penalty which punishes it. However, in England from 1846 to 1850, 35 to 37 per cent of the suicides hanged themselves; fewer than in France, more than in Italy. But after 1874 this proportion diminishes. It is no more than 27.7 per cent in 1889–93 (27.5 per cent in Scotland) instead of 47 per cent, on the average, for 16 countries including these two. Must we believe that this decrease in the number of suicides by hanging is more apparent than real, given that, in the same period, the number of suicides who drown themselves has increased, perhaps because they have been registered more accurately? But the proportion of suicides by hanging decreased from 37.4 in 1867–74 to 27.7 in 1889–93, that is, by 9.7 points. That is much more than the proportion of suicides who drown themselves has increased, since the latter gained only 3.1 points. They are, therefore, far from counterbalancing one another.[8] The proportion of suicides by poisoning increased 2.3 points in the same interval, and the proportion of suicides by firearms 4.7 points. Even if the increase in the number of suicides by drowning is partly due to their being registered more accurately, one can scarcely deny that people hang themselves less often, and that they poison themselves and have recourse to firearms more often. It is impossible to distinguish in these changes what should be explained by the fact that less is concealed and what by the slowly changing customs and preferences of the English as to the mode of suicide.

Of course, we do not understand very well at first glance why the English, contrary to what Goethe believed he observed, show an increasing aversion to hanging themselves. But let us refer to one of the rare tables which show the classification of modes of suicide by profession. It was compiled by E. Lisle from French data for the period 1836–52 and reproduced by Morselli and by Krose. Even though a little old, it remains rather instructive. It shows that the agriculturists and the country workers (who alone account for over one third of all suicides) hang themselves more than the suicides grouped in twenty-six other categories. The only exceptions are the herdsmen and foresters (*Waldarbeiter*) who come first in this respect and who, living in regions covered with trees, do not have to exert any great effort of the imagination to find alongside of them a means of killing oneself. Of 100 peasants who commit suicide, 42.3 hang themselves. Workers in the textile industry follow them closely, undoubtedly because they are still half immersed in the agricultural class. But metal workers choose this style of suicide only 27 times in a hundred, tailors 20 times, merchants 27 times, clerks 18 times, etc. On the other hand, peasants resort more rarely than the others to firearms and much less to poison. Especially so than metal workers, who kill themselves with firearms, on the average, 18 times per hundred, with poison more than $4^1/_2$ times per hundred. These findings can be confirmed by observing the difference between modes of death in the cities and in the country. Morselli has reproduced the following figures for Denmark: of every 100 suicides in 1845–56, the proportion of those who hanged themselves was 56 in Copenhagen, 69 in the other cities, 79 in the countryside, and, from 1863 to 1873, 77 in Copenhagen, 78 in the other cities, 84 in the countryside. In Italy during the year 1877, of 100 suicides, the count is only 8 hanged in the cities, and 27 in the countryside. According to a table reproduced by von Mayr, in Bavaria during the years 1904, 1905, and 1906 the proportion of suicides of this type was 32 per cent in the cities, 54 per cent in the countryside.

Now, England is becoming more and more urbanized and industrialized. The rural population of 1850 still comprised 50 per cent of the entire population; this proportion fell in 1871 to 35 per cent, in 1911 to 22 per cent.

It is, therefore, natural to assume that if the proportion of suicides who hang themselves in England has decreased,* that is to be explained by these conditions and not by the fact that the number of desperate persons who drown themselves was enumerated more accurately here.[9] In almost all the other European countries the proportion of drownings strongly decreased during the nineteenth century (contrary to what happens in England). However, a little earlier or a little later the proportion hanged also diminished in Denmark after 1871, in Norway since 1876, in Sweden since 1878, in Belgium since 1870, in France since 1866–70, in Italy since 1871, in Prussia since 1877–82, in Bavaria since 1857–71, in Saxony since 1857–66, in Württemberg since 1870–9, in Switzerland and in Austria since a

*A typographical error in the original reads 'increased' – Tr.

period we cannot determine. All these countries entered into industrial life, into the era of great cities, later than England. But they were ultimately caught up in the same evolution. During the same period, the proportion of suicides by hanging declined. This is no illusion but a reality.

It is no less true that the continuous increase (though at a decreasing rate) of voluntary deaths by drowning in England is a unique and strange phenomenon. This is the only European country to produce it.[10] There is no doubt that the proportion of this type of suicide in Prussia from 1869 to 1900 scarcely changes. France, however, provides the most perfect contrast with England in this respect. During thirty years, the proportion of drownings in England increased from 100 to 140; in France it diminished from 100 to 87 during the same interval.[11] It is still possible that this fact is partly explained by the growing accuracy of the enumerations in England. But the decrease in suicides by hanging, much more rapid in this country than in the other states, suffices to account for it.[12]

We shall depend on English suicide statistics in several of the following chapters. That is why we have examined at some length the thesis that, while concealment might be less there today, the English have always succeeded in keeping hidden an important part of the voluntary deaths that it was possible to pass for accidents, particularly suicides by drowning. But absolutely nothing, it seems to us, shows this thesis to be justified. Until there is evidence for it, English suicide statistics will merit as much credence as all the others.

We might now leave the study of those external circumstances that the Germans call the technique of suicide. The narrations of drownings, hangings, and asphyxiations enumerate facts that differ. They turn up in compilations of curious and terrifying anecdotes. The portrayer of customs, the scholar in search of the teratological case, the medical expert and the psychiatrist may find here food for thought. In a *Bibliographie du suicide* published recently by Rost, the author mentions no fewer than 2,300 books, articles, and pamphlets devoted to varied means of killing oneself. As for us, we could hasten to forget that they concern hangings, drownings, and asphyxiations, because all of these details might distract our attention from the relationships which exist between the social fact of suicide and its causes. This fact consists in the voluntary disappearance of a certain number of members of the group. What interests us is the volition to disappear, and the reasons which explain it, not the external, more or less picturesque forms in which the disappearance clothes itself.

We must, however, again form an idea of the totality of ways and means which lend themselves to suicide in different countries of Europe. Until now, our attention has been fixed on England because the proportion of suicides by drowning greatly increased there during a thirty-year period. We were able to ask whether this increase was entirely illusory, the result of enumerating this type of voluntary death with ever-increasing accuracy. The same question, however, can be posed for other countries.

That within a given country the proportion of voluntary deaths hardly changes from one year to the next is a fact no less established and no less remarkable than that it does vary from one country to the next. The former can be explained by traditional, local preferences and aversions. However, suicides by drowning are least numerous in the very place where this style of suicide appears easiest to conceal or disguise. Why should systematic concealment not be at least a partial explanation? If we could establish that, on the one hand, the proportion of voluntary deaths by drowning varies very little, varies even less than the proportion of other modes of suicide, and that, on the other hand, what variation does occur appears to result from national or local customs and dispositions, we could discard this cause of error at least, one which, moreover, risks being among the most serious.

We shall therefore study from this point of view diverse countries which differ or resemble one another in language, traditions, and degree of culture, taking into account their geographic proximity. If we find that the modes of suicide are distributed in analogous proportions in countries that are most similar and nearest to one another, this will be reason to assume that the distribution results from nation-wide circumstances and conditions.

We have extracted (see Table 2.2) from a table reproduced by Father Krose (*Die Ursachen*, p. 73) data relating to nine countries:[13] these countries are listed from top to bottom in their order from north to south. We have likewise computed the average proportion of these modes of suicide for sixteen* countries (last line), including, in addition to the nine, Bavaria, Württemberg, Austria, England, Scotland, and Japan.

Proceeding from north to south, we immediately notice that the proportion of suicides by hanging decreases very regularly, while, with one or two exceptions, suicides by firearms increase. The fact which particularly interests us, however, is that, of all the modes of voluntary death, the proportion of suicides by drowning varies least. Let us calculate the relative deviation (arithmetic sum of the deviations in relation to the mean, multiplied by 100 and divided

* *Sic* – Tr.

Table 2.2   *Modes of suicide*

Number of suicides per hundred who killed themselves

	By hanging	By drown-ing	By fire-arms	By cutting or piercing weapons	By poison-ing	By jump-ing	By asphyx-iation	By being run over or tram-pled	By other or unknown means
Norway	65.6	17.2	7.8	4.7	3.1	—	—	—	1.6
Denmark	73.4	13.7	5.8	1.5	4.2	0.7	—	0.5	0.2
Prussia	58.6	18.6	13	2.3	4	1.3	0.2	1.8	0.2
Saxony	61.8	18.8	10.9	1.9	3.4	1.1	0.1	1.7	0.3
Belgium	49.2	24.9	15.5	1.9	2.2	0.8	1.2	3	1.3
France	43.5	26	12.5	2.4	2.2	2.7	8.8	1.4	0.5
Switzerland	43.3	23.5	19	5.3	3.8	1.7	1.4	1.7	0.3
Italy	16.7	23.2	25.4	4.1	7.4	10.9	4.6	3.5	4.2
Spain	18.3	17.5	35.7	7.3	9.2	7.4	2.2	1.5	0.9
Average for 16 nations[14]	47	21.6	14.4	5.7	5.8	3.2	2.3	2	2.1

by the number of suicides of each species) for these different categories. One finds 34.5 for suicides by hanging, 43.5 for suicides by firearms, 40 for poisonings, and only 17.6 for drownings.[15] As one proceeds successively from north to south in the collection, the proportion of drownings certainly tends to diminish, despite some exceptions. We shall see whether this diversity can be explained by local conditions. In every instance, this mode of suicide is subject by far to the smallest of all fluctuations in amplitude. Now, this one would be the easiest to conceal. This is a major reason for assuming that, in this respect, the enumerations are, on the whole, about right.

Let us bring together now the countries nearest to one another and in which the principal modes of suicide are distributed nearly alike. We can group them in four totals (Table 2.3).

The six countries we discarded would not have entered into any of these categories.[16] Sweden is linked to Norway and Denmark only by the relatively small number of desperate persons who drown themselves there: 15.4 per cent on the average, as in the latter two countries. This proportion is actually higher in Norway; then comes Sweden, and only then Denmark. Is this aversion to water, common to the three northern countries, explained by the fact that the temperature is lower there than elsewhere during the greater part of the year? Perhaps. It is a fact that people drown

Table 2.3   *Countries where modes of suicide are distributed alike*

| | Of every 100 suicides, how many killed themselves | | | | |
	By hanging	By drowning	With fire-arms	With thrusting weapons, etc.	By poison-ing
Norway and Denmark	69.5	15.4	6.3	3.1	3.6
Prussia and Saxony	60.2	18.7	11.9	2.1	3.7
Belgium, France, and Switzerland	45.3	24.8	15.7	3.2	2.7
Italy and Spain	17.5	20.3	30.5	5.7	8.3

themselves more often in the southern countries. Morselli noticed earlier that there are fewer drownings among the Slavic portion of the Austrian population, as well as in Russia. But while Sweden follows the example of the northern countries in this respect, she comes closer, on the other hand, to France and to Belgium in the average number of desperate persons there who kill themselves by hanging or by means of firearms. Sweden shows, moreover, an abnormally high number of poisonings, 14.2, that is, many more than in Spain itself. Bavaria appears to be partly dominated by the influence of the Midi: fewer suicides by hanging than in Prussia or in Saxony and much more recourse to firearms there than in these two other German countries. Württemberg is close to Bavaria in this last trait. England and Scotland resemble Italy and Spain where, as we have seen, very few hang themselves and many poison themselves. However, England and Scotland are very plainly distinguished by the small role firearms play there and by the astonishing predilection they show for sidearms: 18.2 per cent of English suicides have recourse to them. This proportion was surpassed even earlier, as long ago, at least, as 1858. Finally, there is much self-hanging and more self-drowning in Japan than anywhere else, while firearms are hardly ever used there. Thus, all of these countries, particularly England, are distinguished from all others in their choice of truly unique modes of death. This is the reason they do not lend themselves to the comparison we wish to make. Let us return to the four categories we have formed by grouping the nations which differ in this respect by more or less closely resembling one another. They are not equally homogeneous. To measure these degrees of resemblance, we can compute within each category the arithmetic sum of the differences between the proportions indicated in the table for the countries included in each group. Let us indicate simultaneously the corresponding differences between two consecutive groups of nations.

Sum of differences in the distribution of modes of suicide:

Between Norway and Denmark	17.6
Between Norway–Denmark and Prussia–Saxony	19.3
Between Prussia and Saxony	6.5
Between Prussia–Saxony and	
Belgium–France–Switzerland	26.9
Between Belgium and France	10.3 (or 2.7)
Between Belgium and Switzerland	15.8
Between France and Switzerland	13.7 (or 6.3)
Between Belgium–France–Switzerland and Italy–Spain	55.2
Between Italy and Spain	22.6

In France, there is an exceptionally high number of suicides by asphyxiation.[17] If they were distributed proportionally between the five modes of suicide distinguished above, the sum of the differences between Belgium and France, and France and Switzerland, would take the values shown in parenthesis.

We see that the differences between groups of nations are larger than the differences among countries included within each group, much more pronounced even if the Norway–Denmark group is discarded. Prussia and Saxony, that is, the largest part of Germany, on the one hand, and Belgium, France, and Switzerland on the other, constitute two groups within which the choice of modes of suicide does not vary much from one country to the next. As to Italy and Spain, they come much closer to one another in this respect than to other groups. Likewise, nowhere are there more pronounced differences than between these southern countries and all the others. The instruments and means of suicide are plainly distinguished here. They express accurately national peculiarities, of temperament perhaps, of customs at least. To kill themselves, the inhabitants of these transpyrenean and transalpine countries use firearms and poison especially, the Spaniards even more than the Italians. They throw themselves from the tops of high places much more often than the suicides of other countries (in this respect the Italians exceed the Spaniards a little). Does a chivalrous spirit, especially among the Spaniards, a sense of the dramatic or of the aesthetic, turn them from hanging themselves, and make them prefer forms of death more shattering and less ugly? That has been said. Perhaps it should rather be noted that firearms and poison are also instruments of murder, and there is still no country in Europe where more homicides are counted at present. There remain the Scandinavian countries and Denmark. Profound and inexplicable differences in the choice of modes of death are enumerated between Sweden and the two other countries, but also between Denmark and Norway. Denmark, above all, offers a singular distribution of modes of suicide. Of all the European countries, this is the one where people hang themselves most often by far, and where, by far, they drown themselves least often. Denmark and Norway resembled one another more closely in 1835–45 in both of these respects, but have since followed an opposite evolution. Concerning Denmark, one could ask whether all the suicides by drowning are enumerated accurately or whether this country has not acquired the habit of putting all such cases of voluntary death into the tally of accidents.

Thus, it is possible to distribute the majority of nations into a few groups comprising neighboring countries among whom many similarities exist and who resemble each other as to the modes of death chosen by those who commit suicide. To be sure, there continue to be differences between them in this respect, though rather reduced, and undoubtedly such as would be found were the diverse regions within a single country compared with one another. This is the proof that the choice of modes of suicide is explained in these countries by the play of constant forces, both physical and social simultaneously, in any case natural, and that variations in this respect ascertained from one country to the next are not at all caused by unequal genuineness in their statistics.

As for countries which do not enter such categories or else represent complex totalities, they comprise nonhomogeneous populations, like Austria and Hungary before the war, and Switzerland. They belong simultaneously to several groups, or else, like England, they occupy an unusual situation and present a distinctive type. One could have expected that these countries would not have recourse to the same instruments or means of death as the others. These countries are exceptions that confirm the rule.

To summarize, the astonishing regularity that one ascertains in the distribution of modes of suicide from one year to the next teaches, first, that even if a person should have the capacity to halt his organic evolution by a free decision, at least in the choice of means that he employs for leaving life, he is guided by forces that do not depend on him: there are only a certain number of exits and the number of those who, each year, can pass through one of them appears indeed to be fixed in advance. On the other hand, these forces or these causes, while not the same in all countries, do not result solely from national conditions. There are undoubtedly complexes of traditions and of customs in Europe, corresponding to different geographic zones, which explain why the preferences

•of diverse groups of states or of nations have a bearing for certain modes of suicide rather than for others. Is the nature of suicide, as such, affected by this, independently of its implementation? Possibly. Durkheim said that the causes which impel toward a certain mode of suicide are not the same as the causes which lead to killing oneself. However, the modes of suicide vary according to whether one passes from cities to countryside, and from countries where homicides are frequent to others. They also vary in a slow but continuous manner within a given country insofar as a new type of civilization is gaining ground there. Modern detailed statistics might teach us that a relationship exists between the choice of mode of death and the causes of the suicide. Just as each social group has its own suicide rate, so it might have its preferences for a particular mode of death. Study of means and instruments especially illuminates the genuineness and accuracy of the statistics which interest us. It has often been said that in England, and undoubtedly in other countries as well, people tended to conceal voluntary deaths which were most suited to concealment, particularly suicides by drowning. However, we have shown that the great increase in the proportion of suicides of this type in England appears to be explicable by the decrease in the number of desperate persons who hang themselves. This last fact is certain. It is in accord with the industrial and urban evolution of Great Britain. Except perhaps for Denmark, there are no indications that the statistics of the other countries on drownings are any more incomplete than on the other modes of suicide. It is the proportion of voluntary deaths by drowning which by far varies least, on the average, from one country to the next. It is not everywhere exactly the same, and the other modes of suicide also vary in proportion from one country to the next. Since these variations are produced simultaneously in neighboring and similar states, they appear to result from traditions and customs which are common to them. Also, self-drownings are continuously diminishing in many countries. However, other ways of death, some formerly unknown, are attracting a growing number of desperate persons. They are more familiar and more certain. Their diffusion is partly explained by the development of great cities. A new type of civilization is influencing people's thinking. It is therefore natural that one sees certain traditional modes of suicide slowly recede. Hence, we have every reason to strengthen our conviction that in the majority of European states the statistics of suicide are not being falsified at all by systematic errors affecting the modes of death that are most easily concealed.

Moreover, even should the absolute figures found in the

statistics of a particular country indeed be affected by a cause of error which tended to reduce all of them in the same ratio, that would weaken the bearing of international comparisons. At the least, we should be able to compare the figures and the countries with one another. A ratio calculated between two values that are equally inaccurate can, in fact, be correct.

chapter 3

Attempted suicides

We must call attention first of all to a collection of very interesting researches done quite recently in Italy on attempted suicides. Until now it was not judged useful or even possible to study attempts.[1] Most countries did not enumerate them. Earlier, Morselli had regretted not having much more data on this topic. From certain very limited investigations in the first half of the nineteenth century it was found that attempts were fewer than committed suicides: but the relationship between these two orders of facts was extremely varied from one locality to another. Moreover, attempts were not enumerated officially except where, as in Spain and England, the penal code provided sanctions, if not against the suicide, at least against those who attempted it. The very existence of these penal sanctions, however, allows us to assume that the majority of attempts remained unknown.[2]

Now in the same year, 1924, Mario Bachi and Leoncini were able to study attempted suicides from the annual municipal statistics of Florence in 1900–15 (Leoncini), of Florence in 1900–24, of Milan in 1916–23, and of Rome in 1920–2 (Mario Bachi). Then, too, in 1914 Massarotti had published the findings of an investigation, done in Rome on suicides attempted or committed in 1906–12, from enumerations he had made by examining the local newspapers for this period. Of these works, that of Bachi gives evidence of the greatest rigor, and is both the most penetrating and the most precise. We shall draw primarily upon him.

We can say that, in general, there is a perceptible relationship between committed and attempted suicides: both increase or diminish simultaneously. If eleven different observations are averaged (in addition to the three Italian cities, Brussels, Buenos Aires, and Budapest), 164 abortive attempts are found per 100 committed suicides. Does it follow that these suicides always represent the same proportionate number of attempts, particularly for the two sexes?

We have long known that women kill themselves less often than do men. Esquirol, one of the first investigators, found a relationship, based only on fewer than 200 cases, between the suicides of men and of women that, on the whole, has been subsequently confirmed: 30 women per 100 men. This ratio is not the same in all countries, and it varies from one period to another. Usually, however, it remains confined within rather narrow limits. In a table in which Morselli shows its value at diverse periods for 28 states, the ratio varies in 47 out of 54 instances between 21.8 and 33.4 female suicides per 100 male suicides. Table 3.1 gives some more recent data.

Table 3.1   *Number of female suicides per hundred male*

	1881–5	1891–5	1901–5	1909–13	1914–18	Post-war
France[3]	26.1	27.7	30.4	30	—	39 (1919–20)
Germany	24.5	25.1	27.3	31.8	43.1	57.8 (1919–20)
Austria	26.1	29.2	29.1	29.9	43.5	43.3 (1919)
Italy	23.6	23.5	26.5	35.5	38	—

These ratios (except in Italy in the first two periods) are a little higher than immediately prior to 1870. Moreover, they increase from one period to the next, even if one does not take the war and the aftermath of the war into account (notably in Germany and in Austria where economic distress very plainly influenced the trend in female suicides). This proportion is higher in England between 1881 and 1913: 33 to 35 women per 100 men. As early as 1863–7, women killed themselves much more often in England than in the other countries (36.5 women per 100 men). Likewise, 37.2 female suicides per 100 male suicides were counted in the United States in 1919. The proportion is very high in Russia, where in 1925 there were 48.5 female suicides per 100 men.[4] But women appear to approach the level of men in this respect, especially in the Asiatic countries such as Japan (from 55 to 63), and even to exceed them, as in British India where, in 1907, 171.4 female suicides were enumerated per 100 male suicides.[5]

We recall these figures only to give an idea of the difference that exists between women and men with respect to suicide. Though in general very marked, the difference is not astonishing. However, it is one of those cases where, a priori, one might pause and find good reasons why women kill themselves less often than do men.

We do not know what we would be told by a statistic compiled from one or two thousand or so novels published during the past fifty years. We might find that women put themselves to death as often as or more often than do men. The fact, once established, however, has not lacked for explanations.

> It is easily understood [Morselli writes] why the masculine sex produces more suicides. Life's difficulties, above all those which result from the struggle for existence, put the man to a more severe trial. While the woman's nervous system is more impressionable, she is more flexible and knows better how to adapt herself. Renunciation and patience are feminine virtues while ambition is proper to the male. Obstacles and resistance of every kind disturb him more profoundly than his mate, especially since he is more capable than she of thinking about them vigorously and of imagining their consequences. Add that he has more willpower and force of character ...

Durkheim did not especially study this problem. But he remarks in passing that since suicide has social causes, and since women and men do not occupy the same position or exercise the same functions in society, it appears very natural for the tendency to suicide not to be equally strong in both sexes.

But, interestingly enough, the Italian works we have been discussing lead to nothing less than calling into question the fact itself, which seemed so clearly established. In fact, while women do commit suicide less often than men, there is no evidence that they do not attempt suicide as often. Let us, therefore, examine these new statistics. We learn that 'the average number of attempts, successful and unsuccessful, per each committed suicide, is: in Milan, 2.6 for the men, 4.9 for the women; in Florence, 2.1 for the men, 3.7 for the women; in Rome, 2 for the men, 4.5 for the women.' That conspicuously reduces the distance between the two sexes.

We shall reproduce a table (Table 3.2) borrowed from Bachi, *noting that the attempts include successful attempts, that is, committed suicides.*

These data are of unequal value. One of the last two depends on Spanish figures which are small in number and suspect, the other was obtained by an examination of six local newspapers for a two-year period. This, for obvious reasons, is a quite undependable method. In any case, one can indeed conclude from their comparison that the difference between the two sexes, while very marked as regards committed suicides, diminishes very greatly as regards attempts. The difference disappears, even in Rome, for both periods, while in Milan it falls to 8 per cent. As for the other

Table 3.2   *Proportion of suicides by women per 100 men*

	Suicides attempted	Suicides committed
Milan (1916–23)	91.9	51.1
Florence (1900–15)	71.7	40.7
Rome (1920–2)	100.6	49.4
Rome (1906–12)	98.2	40.9
Buenos Aires (1899–1913)	54.2	?
Monaco (1903–9)	55.4	38.9
Budapest (1900–8)	82.8	38.2
Brussels (1901–6)	51.1	29.1
Spain (Bodio)	38.3	32.1
Six Italian cities (1893–4)	31.6	26.0

cities, the extent to which attempts at suicide there have escaped the investigators is unknown.

Since women attempt to kill themselves almost as often as do men, though they succeed less often, should we assume that the inclination to suicide is very nearly as pronounced in the one sex as in the other? Why, however, do suicides that are attempted by women much more often end in failure? According to the Italian authorities, the reason is that, contrary to men, most women use imperfect means to commit suicide which leave more possibilities for escaping death.

Before taking up the attempted suicides, let us first study from this point of view the suicides which have been completed. We have calculated the figures in Table 3.3 from the *Rapport sur l'administration générale de la justice criminelle en France*.

As we see, there is little or almost no equality except in the proportion of men and women who arrange to have themselves run over like Anna Karenina or the hero of *Fort comme la mort*. Women have used poison more ever since, and undoubtedly before, Madame Bovary. They throw themselves out of the window more often. These numbers, however, are quite small. Compensation occurs precisely between the two largest proportions of suicides. 65 per cent of the men and 65.9 per cent of the women kill themselves by hanging or drowning. Men, however, more often hang themselves, while women more often drown. Judas Iscariot acts according to rule when, after having thrown down the betrayal money in the temple, he goes off and

Table 3.3   *Mode of suicide by sex in France, 1913, 1919, and 1920*

	Hang- ing	Drown- ing	Fire- arms	Side- arms	Poison- ing	Jump- ing	Asphyx- iation	Being crushed
	Percentage of suicides who killed themselves by							
Men	43	24	17.6	2.6	1.1	3.0	3.9	2.7
Women	27.4	38.5	6.2	1.6	3.5	5.8	12.2	2.9
Differences	− 15.6	+ 14.5	− 11.4	− 1.0	+ 2.4	+ 2.8	+ 8.3	+ 0.2

hangs himself. Of course, Jocasta also hangs herself. Oedipus, having torn the door from its hinges, finds her 'hanging by a braided rope.' The reason is that she has committed an unforgivable crime and, for a woman, there is no death more atrocious and ignominious. However, it was Shakespeare who, in *Hamlet*, fixed the prototype of feminine suicide in indelible strokes. We shall return to this. Alongside of these traditional methods are others more modern: 25 per cent of the men and 18.4 per cent of the women have recourse to, respectively, firearms and asphyxiation. Asphyxiation, however, is reserved for women, firearms for men. That is, while the mechanism of the revolver rarely misses its objective and operates in a few seconds, the chemistry of oxygen and carbon develops reactions more slowly. Moreover, as in France, the latter mode of suicide is more often allied with poisoning among women in every country.

Table 3.4 shows some proportions in Bavaria.[6] As before, we show the positive and negative differences in the proportions of men relative to women.

The signs of the differences are the same for every category and the difference between the proportions of suicides by hanging is of the same order as in France. But in Bavaria suicides by asphyxiation are very few in number. Then, too, the number of

Table 3.4   *Mode of suicide by sex in Bavaria, 1904, 1905, and 1906*

	Hang- ing	Drown- ing	Fire- arms	Side- arms	Poison- ing	Asphyx- iation	Being crushed
	Percentage of suicides who killed themselves by						
Men	50.6	13.4	26.5	3.7	2.2	0.2	1.9
Women	34.3	45	5.2	2.6	6.3	0.8	2.2
Differences	− 16.3	+ 31.6	− 21.3	− 1.1	+ 4.1	+ 0.6	+ 0.3

men who drown themselves is almost half as low again in Bavaria as in France. This explains the very high proportion of women who drown themselves and the large difference between the proportion of men and of women in this respect. That proportion alone almost compensates for the apparent difference between the two sexes in suicides by hanging and by firearms. These are more numerous among men in Bavaria than in France. In sum, women in both countries prefer less brutal but less prompt modes of death. In Prussia the differences are in the same direction and of comparable size, although men and women hang themselves more often there than in Bavaria and use firearms much less often. Bavaria comes closer to the southern and Catholic peoples in this last characteristic, and also in having more homicides.

Let us consider one of these, Italy, in its entirety. (The Italian findings shown above only pertained to two large Italian cities.) Table 3.5 shows how the four most important modes of suicide were distributed there fifty years ago.

Table 3.5   *Mode of suicide by sex in Italy, 1868–77*

| | Percentage of suicides who killed themselves by | | | |
	Hanging	Drowning	Firearms	Poisoning
Men	16.8	24.7	30.8	4.9
Women	17.6	50.3	3.4	7.5
Differences	+ 0.8	+ 25.6	− 27.4	− 2.6

The number of male suicides by hanging is extremely low in Italy. The two sexes do not differ in this respect. The compensation is established between the voluntary deaths by drowning, which are very numerous among women who commit suicide, and the deaths by firearms, which are almost exclusively reserved for men. Here again, men are found to have recourse more often than women to styles of suicide which offer the least chance of surviving.

Finally, Table 3.6 shows the same proportions for England, also as of fifty years ago. As in France, Prussia, and Bavaria, women in England hang themselves and have recourse to firearms less than do the men. But they poison themselves much more often than in the other countries. Elsewhere, the figures corresponding to poisonings are low. Here, they are high for both sexes, but especially so for women.

Table 3.6 *Mode of suicide by sex in England, 1865–73*

| | Percentage of suicides who killed themselves by | | | |
	Hanging	Drowning	Firearms	Poisoning
Men	41.8	14.9	6.3	7.3
Women	28.8	31	0.2	15.9
Differences	– 13.0	+ 16.1	– 6.1	+ 8.6

Examining now the proportions reproduced by Bachi for attempted suicides, successful or unsuccessful, we find very surprising figures. In Rome from 1920 to 1922, 72 per cent of the women who attempted to kill themselves were self-poisoned, compared to only 36 per cent of the men. Inverse proportions are found for the use of firearms: 4.7 per cent for women and 35 per cent for men. The corresponding figures, still for Rome, from 1906 to 1912 are rather similar: poisoning, 56 per cent of attempts by women, 39 per cent of attempts by men: firearms, 27.5 for men, 2.2 for women. In Florence from 1910 to 1922 one finds: poisoning, from 65 to 69 of the attempts by women, from 28 to 32.5 of the attempts by men; firearms, from 23 to 29 for men, and from 2.5 to 7 for women.

We are reproducing all these figures exactly for the following reason. The proportion of suicides attempted with firearms by men and women corresponds very closely to those found for committed suicides in Italy (Table 3.5): 30.8 for the men, 3.4 for the women. But the proportion of suicides attempted by poisoning is unrelated to what we have found for committed suicides: 7.5 for the women; 4.9 for the men. The divergence is so considerable that, for a moment, we believed Bachi was mistaken and that in Rome in 1920–2, for example, the number of suicides attempted by poisoning had been 7.2 for women and 3.6 for men, instead of 72 and 36. However, a little further on he writes: 'Three-quarters of the women choose poison, undoubtedly because of the ease with which they can procure it.' That these figures are accurate must therefore be assumed.

They are plausible. We are told, in fact, that 'The ratio of attempts (successful or unsuccessful) to committed suicides is, on the average: in Milan, 2.6 for men, 4.9 for women; in Florence, 2.1 for men, 3.7 for women; in Rome, 2 for men, 4.5 for women.' Hence, if there are 450 attempts by women in Rome per 100 committed suicides (included in the attempts), and 72 per cent of the attempts (successful or unsuccessful) are by poisoning, that makes 324 attempts by poisoning. From this subtract 7.5 suicides *committed* by poisoning, leaving 317. There remain 133 attempted plus committed suicides by means other than poison. As there are 100 committed suicides, 33 attempts have failed. We must therefore assume that nearly 90 per cent of the women who have unsuccessfully attempted to kill themselves used poison.[7]

If we put aside suicides attempted and committed by poisoning, 36 attempts per 100 suicides committed by other means remain. Therefore, only a little more than one quarter of the other attempts miscarry. Women who poison themselves can be saved nine times out of ten, while those who have recourse to other means escape death only two-and-a-half times out of ten.

Poisonings predominate among prevented attempts because obvious but inconsequential gestures are not registered at all. The public's attention is not really aroused until the implementation has begun. When a woman acts as if to cut her throat with a knife that is snatched from her, or when she declares 'I am going to throw myself into the water' and is stopped midway, or at the river's edge, she is not said to have attempted to kill herself. This is not quite true when one poisons oneself. But even so, how often must one not refer to feigning rather than to attempts, to unconscious feigning, to hysterical, morbid, or deliberate feigning, that is, to attempts at blackmail rather than at suicide?

Having classified attempts at suicide by age groups, Bachi explains the exceptionally large proportion of attempts relative to committed suicides among children of both sexes below fifteen years of age by the fact that 'feigning has an important role among young people.' But what role does feigning play among women? Let us consider male adults over fifteen years of age in Milan. As one passes, by five-year intervals, from one age to a higher one, the number of attempts corresponding to a committed suicide diminishes with surprising regularity from 4.5 between fifteen and twenty years of age, to 1.6 between fifty and sixty. Same regularity in Rome for women as for men. We assume that, as they become older, 'people who attempt to commit suicide have more serious reasons for dying and put their plans into execution with more firmness.'

Study of the modes of suicide by age and sex (we are considering only committed suicides) teaches us that, as their years accumulate, both women and men choose more certain methods or instruments. In England in 1858–72 female suicides by poisoning or hanging (per 100 suicides of each sex and age category) were distributed as shown in Table 3.7.

Table 3.7   *Female suicides, England, 1858–72*

Women who killed themselves by	15–20 years	20–25 years	25–35 years	35–45 years	45–55 years	55–65 years	65–75 years
Poisoning	24	25	20	19.5	14.5	9	7.5
Hanging	11.5	15	20.5	29	37.5	41	41.5

Thus, from twenty years of age on, with increasing age women poison themselves less frequently but hang themselves more. The same is true of men (provided they do not hang themselves more often from twenty to twenty-five years of age than from twenty-five to thirty). The same result is found in Switzerland from 1881 to 1890. Denmark is distinguished from all other countries by very high proportions of suicides by hanging and very low proportions by drowning and poisoning. Female suicides are distributed as shown in Table 3.8. It is the same for men: poison, 5, 2.3, 1.8; hanging, 63, 81.5, 86.8.

Table 3.8   *Female suicides, Denmark, 1896–1905*

Of every 100 women who commit suicide in each age category	from 15 to 35 years of age	from 35 to 55 years of age	from 55 to 75 years of age
Poison themselves	17.5	7.1	2
Hang themselves	32.1	63.4	67.9

That the mass of female attempts at suicide by poisoning is attributable to young women can be assumed. But the psychologists would undoubtedly be quite perplexed were we to ask them what portion of these attempts can be explained by feigning, failure of firmness of purpose and of courage, ineptness, or incompetence.

Nothing resembles a genuine suicide more, on the surface, than certain feigned suicides, nor a feigned suicide than certain genuine suicides. But are the actors themselves any better situated in this respect than the spectators? Let us reread in *Hamlet* the tale of Ophelia's death.

> There is a willow grows aslant a brook,
> That shows his hoar leaves in the glassy stream;
> There with fantastic garlands did she come
> Of crow-flowers, nettles, daisies, and long purples

That liberal shepherds give a grosser name,
But our cold maids do dead men's fingers call them:
There, on the pendent boughs her coronet weeds
Clambering to hang, an envious sliver broke;
When down her weedy trophies and herself
Fell in the weeping brook. Her clothes spread wide,
And, mermaid-like, awhile they bore her up;
Which time she chanted snatches of old tunes,
As one incapable of her own distress,
Or like a creature native and indu'd
Unto that element: but long it could not be
Till that her garments, heavy with their drink,
Pull'd the poor wretch from her melodious lay
To muddy death.

Had she instinctively grasped the reeds along the bank, had anyone arrived unexpectedly in time to pull her out, could she have said whether she had slipped by chance, whether she had sought death, whether she had accepted it, whether her aberration had been partially feigned? Does one ever know whether he is totally committed to the supreme gesture? The person who has decided to end matters may feel bound by a pledge to himself. Or he may even be obeying an irresistible logic. But he is never certain whether, at the last moment, he will be disposed to carry out a pledge of this sort, or whether he will not feel his logic was mistaken. As for the most desperate persons, is not reaching out one's hand to retain life when it is leaving one an organic reaction, or even a cry from the deepest and clearest powers of one's being? There is, to be sure, no common measure between those who, firmly resolved to die, take necessary precautions so that one shall be able neither to stop them before they have attained their objective, nor to restore them to life, and those who merely wish to flirt with death and do not boldly challenge it. Only the first should be labeled 'self-violent.' Only they deserve the cruel but pathetic and moving punishments that Dante reserves for them in the mournful forest. The place of the others will be at the entrance to the circles of hell among those who do not know how to come to a decision and who, as a unique punishment, have been deprived forever of the hope of dying.

However, there is an undoubtedly important group of unfortunates between the conscious or unconscious feigners and the genuine suicides, those who have lacked neither will nor courage but only opportunity or capability. Only if the majority of unsuccessful attempts by women were attributable to this group would one have the right to conclude that the inclination to suicide is almost as well developed in both sexes.

Comparing now diverse professional groups, we learn that, in general, there are proportionately more completed suicides among the wealthy and leisured classes (professionals and tradespeople) than among workers, domestics, etc.

Table 3.9   *Suicides in Prussia, 1883–90*

	Per million people in each profession, 14 years of age or more
Domestics	28
Clerks, workers, wage earners, etc.	54
Independent laborers	67
Private officials	82
Persons of independent means, pensioners	114
Public officials	150

According to Prinzing, the proportion of suicides in Prussia from 1883 to 1890 in the various professions was as shown in Table 3.9. But here too the differences are much less marked when it is a question of attempts. The last (professionals and tradespeople), says Bachi, succeed in committing suicide more frequently than the first (workers, domestics). After quoting a phrase from Durkheim, 'One can say that misery protects,' Bachi adds: 'But it protects not because the members of humble classes less often attempt to kill themselves but because they more readily survive their attempts.'

The case of the military must be observed a little more closely. Since the studies by Wagner and Morselli, soldiers are known to be much more inclined to kill themselves than is the civilian population. The literature on this is very abundant. According to Krose, a proportion of 670 suicides per million soldiers is found in the German army from 1878 to 1888, while the proportion for the male civilian population aged twenty to twenty-five years is 360 suicides. The difference is almost 2 to 1. Table 3.10 shows, per 100 military suicides, the percentage attributable to officers, non-commissioned officers, and privates, as well as the proportion of men in each category.

Earlier, Durkheim noticed that the non-commissioned and the re-enlisted kill themselves more often than the other members of the army. He saw in the suicides of soldiers a particular instance of what he called altruistic suicide which, contrary to other voluntary

Table 3.10   *Suicides in the German army, 1878–88*

	Number included in each category per 100 soldiers	Number of suicides per 100 military suicides
Officers and officials of the army	6	7.1
Non-commissioned officers	13	26.5
Privates	81	66.4

deaths, would result from the man's no longer possessing sufficient individuality. 'Excessive individuation,' he said,[8] 'leads to suicide but insufficient individuation has the same effects.' Now,

the first quality of a soldier is a sort of impersonality not to be found anywhere in civilian life to the same degree. He must be trained to set little value upon himself, since he must be prepared to sacrifice himself upon being ordered to do so. Even aside from such exceptional circumstances, in peacetime and in the regular exercise of his profession, discipline requires him to obey without question and sometimes even without understanding. For this an intellectual abnegation hardly consistent with individualism is required.

As in inferior societies, savage clans, and primitive tribes, the soldier is detached from his own self. The principle of his conduct is external to himself. That is why he

kills himself at the least disappointment, for the most futile reasons, for a refusal of leave, a reprimand, an unjust punishment, a delay in promotion, a question of honor, a flush of momentary jealousy or even simply because other suicides have occurred before his eyes or to his knowledge.

That is also why the members of the army who most often kill themselves are those who have been subjected to the most prolonged training and whose military spirit is strongest.

Ten years before Durkheim, Tarde had also proposed several solutions to the most 'enigmatic problem raised by military suicide.' First of all, the barracks are 'as sudden and powerful an emancipation from religious and traditional prejudices as the school has been for the child.' In the second place, 'it is no mystery to anyone that the enforced idleness of regimental life favors intemperate habits.' Finally,

is not the military milieu the one where one rubs shoulders, where social life presents exceptional, even excessive intensity, where, consequently, the electric influence of example is propelled with most force and speed? Here, there is no act of despair, as there is no act of heroism, which does not find imitators.

These somewhat unmethodical explanations had to be recalled after Durkheim's systematic explanation. Thus, one can see the extent to which sociologists have been concerned with this fact. As for Bergson, shortly after the appearance of Durkheim's book he told us: 'It may not be necessary to search so far. Actually, it is very well understood why soldiers, especially old soldiers, kill themselves more often than do other men: they are bored.'

This last explanation is simple and, of course, not entirely incorrect. However, Bachi proposes one that is even more simple and has the merit of resting on indisputable facts. Soldiers commit suicide more than do members of the civilian population because they do not fail at it. In fact, the proportion of committed suicides by firearms or hanging – the two modes of execution which succeed most often – is much higher among them. In Milan, 88 military suicides out of a hundred from 1896 to 1913 killed themselves by these means. The proportion is 80.7 per cent for factory workers, 60.9 per cent for white collar workers, 57.7 per cent for students, and only 32 per cent for craftsmen. On the other hand, however, von Mayr indicates that, according to a study by S. Rosenfels, only 30 attempted suicides (not followed by success) were counted in the Austrian army from 1883 to 1891 per 100 committed suicides.[9] He calculates that there were only 48 attempts per 100 suicides in the Prussian army in 1905–6. We recall that 111 attempts are counted per 100 suicides in Florence in 1902–7 and that very similar numbers are found in Milan in 1916–23, and in Rome in 1906–12 and 1920–2.

We can conclude from these researches and findings that suicide has a technical aspect that must not be neglected when taking up certain problems. Does it necessarily always follow that there are grounds for enlarging the definition of self-murder henceforth to include all attempts to put oneself to death, whether or not they have succeeded? To be sure, it would seem to matter rather little whether the suicide was accomplished, provided one could be assured that the subject had truly intended to kill himself. We could, however, see two serious objections to such a change in method. First, it is much more difficult to enumerate attempts than suicides. In fact, the number of cases on which these observations depend is rather limited. (For example, there were 2,232 attempts and suicides in Florence from 1900 to 1915, while

8,612 committed suicides took place in France in the single year 1922.) It is easier to conceal an attempt than a committed suicide. Moreover, and above all, one never knows whether these attempts correspond to any firm intentions to put oneself to death or to what extent there has been feigning, simple impulsiveness, or both. Nothing proves intention, nothing proves that the victim had known that his act *had to* produce death, if not the indisputable fact that he carried it out to the end.

chapter 4

The distribution of suicides in Europe

Morselli and Durkheim noted earlier that every nation has a suicide rate of its own which remains constant, or almost so, for many years. In other words, comparing various countries, the proportion of suicides in the population varies two-, three-, or four-fold, or according to some other ratio. Over long periods, the numbers of their suicides increase or decrease. However, on ranking countries in order of increasing proportions of suicides, they are found to remain at nearly the same rank.

Table 4.1 was compiled to show for 11 European countries annual suicide rates per million inhabitants from 1836 to 1925, that is, over a span of ninety years. (They are by five-year intervals except for the last two: 1911–13 and 1922–5.) These are the same countries for which Durkheim presented suicide rates for only three periods, from 1866 to 1878 (Table III in his book, p. 50), and almost the only ones for which we command data that is continuous since 1836. For the reasons we shall give, we were eager to extend our observations over as long a period as possible.

This table must be read with caution. To begin with, the populations of the countries are very unequal and have varied unequally in the course of the century. Alongside of France, Italy, England, and Prussia, which in 1911–13 numbered respectively $39^1/_2$ million, 34 million, 36 million, and 40 million inhabitants, are found others such as Belgium, Sweden, and Norway, whose populations attained respectively only 7, 5, and $2^1/_2$ million people. Now, while from 1835 to 1913 the population in France increased by almost 34 per cent, and in Italy by 60 per cent, the rate of increase in Prussia was 135 per cent, and Sweden and Norway saw the number of their citizens double.* It was inadvisable to discard these small countries, however, because the population and the conditions of life there are more

* That is, increase by 100 per cent – Tr.

Table 4.1 *Average number of suicides per year in eleven European countries per million inhabitants*[1]

	1836–45	1846–55	1856–60	1861–5	1866–70	1871–5	1876–80	1881–5	1886–90	1891–5	1896–1900	1901–5	1906–10	1911–13	1922–5
Italy	29	29	29	29	30	35	41	49	50	57	63	63	78	84	86
Belgium	50	61	61	46	66	70	94	107	119	129	119	124	142	139	137
England	62	64	67	65	67	66	74	75	79	89	90	103	110	100	110[2]
Norway	107	107	94	85	76	75	72	67	67	65	55	64	(56)	57	60[3]
Austria	45	48	55	64	78	106	162	162	160	159	158	173	187	201	293
Sweden	66	69	57	76	85	81	92	97	118	144	151	142	(150)	178	148[4]
Bavaria	65	72	85	78	90	89	127	136	137	135	134	140	150	166	152
France	80	98	110	124	135	144	168	194	216	241	238	228	245	252	229
Prussia	104	112	121	118	142	119	167	202	200	205	195	203	205	214	221
Denmark	222	259	284	270	277	244	267	248	261	249	220	227	(204)	182	147[5]
Saxony	167	224	244	263	293	268	383	379	323	321	305	325	315	326	344
TOTAL	997	1,143	1,207	1,218	1,339	1,297	1,647	1,716	1,730	1,793	1,728	1,792	1,842	1,899	1,927
Average	91	104	110	111	122	118	150	158	157	163	157	163	167	172	175

homogeneous, and they are sometimes more interesting, than the large countries. In any case, their various peculiarities complete the European picture and enrich it with new characteristics. We shall take into account as necessary the size of these nations at various periods.

It must not be forgotten, on the other hand, that the largest among these countries include very diverse regions whose suicide rates, as we shall see, are sometimes very unequal. We could have distinguished northern from southern France, western France from the south, northern from southern Italy, German-speaking Austria and Bohemia from the diverse and very heterogeneous parts of Prussia. However, even aside from the fact that data referring to national subdivisions are not always easy to find, a country's suicide rate remains meaningful even if it does result from quite different regional figures. After an overall view, we propose to go into details and examine regional suicide rates in the most important countries.

Finally, we are not forgetting that these suicide rates are calculated in relation to the total population of both sexes and all ages. The proportion of sexes varies little. But the composition of the population by age category is not the same in all countries. Now, it is a well-known fact that, in the male population at least, the suicide rate increases very regularly with age. Table 4.2 is a table from Krose which shows the proportion of male suicides by age:

Table 4.2   *Suicide rate per million men of the same age*

Age	Prussia (1883–90)	Baden (1891–1900)	Denmark (1896–1900)	France[6] (1887–8 and 1891)	Italy (1899–1901)
10–15	31 ⎫			23 ⎫	
15–20	179 ⎬	94	80	144 ⎬	72
20–5	360 ⎫				
25–30	324 ⎬	344	285	262 ⎫	
30–40	441	360	365	350 ⎬	132
40–50	683	597	706	516 ⎫	
50–60	868	850	969	711 ⎬	176
60–70	952	890	1,109	919 ⎫	
70–80	982	1,098	1,206	1,035 ⎬	225
80 or more	1,044	1,403	952	987	223

This also holds true for women, except that their suicide rate is higher from 20 to 25 years of age than from 30 to 40, though lower than after 40 years of age. Hence, if a population contains a very high proportion of men and women over 60 years of age, the proportion of the total suicides that is produced by the older classes will be higher. This is the case in France when compared with Germany. The population of France is older on the average. Of the inhabitants over 15 in 1910, 17 per cent in France were over 60 and 11.7 in Germany. Let us suppose that the suicide rate, calculated in relation to the population over fifteen years, is found to be the same in Germany as in France. One would have to say that, in spite of this apparent equality, more men and women in a given age category kill themselves in Germany than in France. And that is not all. For the suicide rate is calculated over the total population, including children below 15 years of age (who commit suicide only very rarely). Now, in 1910 equally, the population below 15 years of age represented 25 per cent of the total in France and 33 per cent in Germany. If the same proportional number of suicides is found in France and in Germany, this implies a population more strongly 'disposed to suicide' in France than in Germany. People kill themselves more often, therefore, in the latter country than in the former. The impact of each of these causes reinforces that of the other to falsify the comparisons one might make by depending on a suicide rate calculated for the totality of the population. None of this is unique to France or Germany. In 1910 the Austrian population below 15 years of age represented 36 per cent of the total, and the population over 60 years of age, 7.2 per cent of the total over 15 years of age. This population was likewise very young. In 1920, the English population below 15 years of age comprised 28 per cent of the total: it was almost as old as the French population. Hence, in a population which is growing, an apparently stationary suicide rate is actually increasing. In a population which is not growing, a suicide rate that appears to be increasing may actually be stationary.

One might think that it would be more correct, then, uniformly to calculate the suicide rate in relation to the population from 15 to 60 years of age. But aside from the fact that this would still not entirely eliminate the element of confusion referred to, one must note that age categories do not correspond to well-defined social realities. For example, in a given country the totality of men from 20 to 30 years of age does not constitute an independent group. The suicide rate calculated in relation to the total population is an indicator, at once moral and demographic, that retains its distinctive value. It will suffice to recall that an increase in the suicide rate does not necessarily result from an increase in moral and social disequilibrium and that it may simply be caused by the fact that the population of the group considered is growing older. It will be entirely otherwise, of course, if the suicide rate inceases in a population with a high birthrate. Finally, in a population which is growing rapidly it is possible for the suicide rate to increase strongly while appearing to remain stationary or to increase only a little. France, Germany, and Italy, respectively, may offer examples of these three cases at present.

We turn to Table 4.3, which is compiled from the previous table. When these countries are ranked in order of the size of their suicide rates at diverse periods, it is not difficult to discover from comparisons of their serial numbers that they group themselves in three categories: low rates: Italy, Belgium, England, and Norway; average rates: Austria, Sweden, and Bavaria; high rates: France, Prussia, Denmark, and Saxony. Of course Norway has a high rate at the beginning and a low rate at the end, while Austria is the opposite. But let us compare the serial numbers of the two periods 1866–70 and 1901–5, which are located neither at the very beginning nor at the very end. We find that there are, indeed, transpositions from one period to the next but within each category. No country has passed from one category to another except Belgium–Sweden.

This is all the more noteworthy in that the proportion of suicides increased unequally in these three categories: from 1836–45 to 1911–13 the average increase was 73 per cent in the low-rate countries, 225 per cent in the countries of average rates, 98 per cent in the high-rate countries. The finding from these figures is that countries in the first category (low rates) are lagging. But the countries of average rates have taken more than two steps forward, while the high-rate countries have taken only one. The distance between them was very great, for it still exists.

Will it disappear? It would, according to one hypothesis, were there a maximum rate of suicide that no society could exceed but which all approached more or less rapidly. But does a limit of this type exist? This is certainly one of the most important problems that could be raised and that the most extended observations in time and space at our disposal could permit us to resolve.

In 1879 Morselli wrote: 'In civilized nations of Europe and America, suicide increases regularly and continuously at a greater speed than the population and mortality until the beginning of the nineteenth century.' Only two nations seemed to him to be exceptions: Norway and Dalmatia. Was this a premature generalization? Let us not limit ourselves only to increases in population. The eleven countries included in our table comprise,

Table 4.3 (compiled from Table 4.1)

Serial number in Rate of increase[7]

	1836–45	1861–5	1866–70	1886–90	1901–5	1911–13	1840–63	1863–87	1887–1913	1840–1913
Italy	1	1	1	1	1	2	—	62	78	189
Belgium	3	2	2	5	5	4	16	105	16	127
England	4	4	3	3	3	3	5	22	26	62
Norway	9	7	4	2	2	1	-26	-27	-18	-87
Austria	2	3	5	7	7	8	42	150	26	349
Sweden	6	5	6	4	4	6	15	56	51	170
Bavaria	5	6	7	6	6	5	20	76	21	155
France	7	9	8	9	10	10	55	75	16	215
Prussia	8	8	9	8	8	9	14	70	7	105
Denmark	11	11	10	10	9	7	22	-3	-44	-22
Saxony	10	10	11	11	11	11	58	24	2	95

in 1840, 117 million inhabitants, and in 1911–13, 206 million or an increase of 76 per cent. In the course of the same period of a little more than seventy years, the average of the suicide rates in these same countries went from 91 per million inhabitants to 172, or an increase of 90 per cent. Thus, the suicide rate rose more rapidly than did the population. However, let us break down these trends. In the first half of this period, from 1840 to 1877 (or thirty-seven years), the average suicide rate in these eleven countries increased by 64 per cent while the population grew by 36 per cent. Those are the only facts that Morselli could know. But from 1877 to 1912 (or thirty-six years) the average suicide rate rose only 14 per cent while the population increased 30 per cent. This time the growth in the suicide rate was much slower than the increase in the number of inhabitants.

It is, therefore, not demonstrated, as is sometimes believed, that the proportion of suicides increases in a continuous and unlimited manner. Let us view the eleven countries from this perspective. For each of them we show in Table 4.4 the suicide rate in the first period, 1836–45, and in the last, 1911–13. The numbers in italics correspond to the maximum. When the maximum occurs between the two periods, we so state.

Table 4.4   *Suicide rates in eleven countries*

	1836–45			1911–13
Italy	*increase from*	29	to	*84*
Belgium	*increase from*	50	to	139
			(max.: 142 in 1906–10)	
England	*increase from*	62	to	100
			(max.: 110 in 1906–10)	
Norway	*decrease from*	*107*	to	57
			(min.: 55 in 1896–1900)	
Austria	*increase from*	45	to	*201*
Sweden	*increase from*	66	to	*178*
Bavaria	*increase from*	65	to	*166*
France	*increase from*	80	to	*252*
Prussia	*increase from*	104	to	*214*
Denmark	*decrease from*	222	to	182
			(max.: 284 in 1856–60)	
Saxony	*increase from*	167	to	326
			(max.: 383 in 1876–80)	

Thus, the maximum comes at the outset, or not far from the outset, in two countries, Norway and Denmark. It occurs in the interval between these two periods in three other countries: Belgium, England, and Saxony. It is found at the end in only six countries. Furthermore, in three of these six countries, Sweden, Bavaria, and France, the suicide rate after the war is clearly below what it was in 1911–13. We have discarded the war years. As we shall see, the suicide rate dropped considerably during them in all the belligerent countries and even in several neutral ones, for example, Sweden. But we can assume that by 1922–5, a period whose mean occurs almost five-and-a-half years after the war, these nations had almost recovered their equilibrium. The suicide rate continues to mount in Italy, Saxony, and Prussia. The curves continue to rise as if there had been no break in continuity from 1913 to 1922. But in Sweden, Bavaria, and France, the curves fall again as if the maximum had been exceeded. In England, itself, where the last period includes the years 1923–6, the suicide rate is again found at the same level as sixteen years earlier. Everything happens, in short, as if eight of the eleven countries studied have left a maximum behind them which varies greatly from country to country and which is proper to it. Thereafter, the rate falls more or less below the maximum and, in every instance, never exceeds it again.

About 1880, two countries attracted particular attention because of the extraordinarily high number of their inhabitants who killed themselves there. Morselli then wrote, 'The homeland of *Hamlet* is the classic country for suicide surpassing all the northern countries in this respect.' He noticed that the proportion of suicides there had increased in the thirty years from 1835 to 1865 by 56 per cent. This rising trend seemed to stop then but it resumed very quickly and Morselli did not doubt that these figures would be exceeded. Consider the maximum ratios enumerated in Denmark between 1856 and 1880: 284, 277, 267; and the ratios enumerated in the same period in Sweden: 92 (1876–80); in Norway: 94 (1856–60); in Finland: 79 (1876–7). The deviation was considerable. Moreover, it is worth noting that Schleswig-Holstein, which was still part of Denmark, does not attain the maximum in 1856–60: 284 for this country.[8] The rate in this period is 208 for Schleswig and 173 for Holstein, which is much more than in Prussia (121) and a little more than in Mecklenburg-Schwerin (160). Denmark's rate at this time equals two-and-a-half times the general average for the eleven countries. But from 1876–80 to 1911–13 it declines in the ratio of 100 to 68, and then in the more recent interval 1911–13 to 1923–6 in the ratio of 100 to 81, for a total ratio in forty-five years of 100 to 54. This is exactly half of the maximum attained earlier. In 1922–5 Denmark's rate coincides exactly with Sweden's rate in 1921–4, which in forty-five years increased in the ratio of 62 to 100. To be sure, it remains higher than Norway's figure, which diminished by a fifth in forty-five years. But let us consider Schleswig-Holstein, linked to Prussia in 1867. From 1871–80, exactly as many people killed themselves there as in Denmark, and in 1891–1900 many more (319 against 235). Besides, Schleswig-Holstein never loses its position in suicide rates at the head of all the Prussian provinces. If, as Morselli believes, it distinguished itself early in this respect because of the Danish influence, one must regret the departure of the dukedom's inhabitants from 'Hamlet's homeland' to Werther's just when the horizon around Elsinore's terraces brightened.

While Saxony retains an honorable rank in the statistics of suicide, since it clearly has remained the country where the suicide rate is maximum in all periods, it may not have reached the height that in 1876–80 might have been expected of it. Arriving at once in this period at the considerable rate of 383, it has not maintained itself at this peak nor regained it. (The next highest rate of 261 would only be attained by Denmark in 1886–90 and Germany in 1926, and by the exceptional rate for France of 260 in 1913.) To be sure, with 344 in 1922–5 Saxony is not very distant from its maximum, but it fell in 1896–1900 as low as 305. This is, indeed, a limiting case permitting formulation of the hypothesis that each country lends itself to a maximum suicide rate which, once attained, cannot be exceeded.

We can now state this hypothesis more precisely and show its reasonableness by examining the right side of Table 4.3. Here we have shown the rate of increase (and of decrease) in the proportion of suicides in our eleven countries for three periods which are consecutive and almost equal (23, 24, and 25 years). We have marked the highest rate of increase or decrease for each country in italics. Let us confine ourselves to the rate of increase. This, it will be noticed, occurs in Saxony and in Denmark during the first period, in six countries during the second (1863–87), and in only two countries, Italy and England, during the third. Let us also note that the rates of increase which occur during the second period are relatively very high. The average rate of increase at three successive periods was 27, 89, and 23, or, setting the first number equal to 100: 100, 330, and 85. Moreover, except for Italy, these are all large nations. We could conclude from these observations that Norway and Denmark attained, and Saxony came closest to, their maximum rate of suicide during the period 1840–63; that Belgium, Austria, Sweden, Bavaria, France, and Prussia were only a little distance from their maximum at the end of the second period, and undoubtedly attained it during the course of the third. Only for Italy and England, for whom a certain range of attainment could still open up, is this not the case. (The latter might still rise to it towards the end of this last interval.) These hypotheses correspond well to the most extended period of observation yet offered to the attention of statisticians. Unfortunately, the end of this period is obscured by the war and its aftermath, so that we still do not know whether the increase in suicides after 1918 is explained solely by their decrease during the course of the war or is the first phase of a new period of ascension.*

> The suicide rate [said Durkheim], to a much higher degree than the death rate, is specific to each social group, where it can be regarded as a characteristic index. It is even so closely linked to what is most fundamental in each national temperament that the order in which different societies appear in this respect remains almost exactly the same at very different periods.

This is almost (with a few exceptions) what does indeed emerge from the previous study. But if the diverse European countries that we are comparing in our table do indeed pretty much keep their rank from one period to the next, do they also maintain their distances? In other words, do the divergences between these countries in their contingents of suicides that one notices at the beginning of the period tend to diminish? And to what extent? Let us assume, as Durkheim believed, that the rate of suicide in a group is linked to its diverse social characteristics. If what we will call the degree of convergence of these suicide rates could be measured precisely at diverse periods we would succeed in determining whether there is or is not progress towards uniformity for the totality of these countries.

In what follows, we shall apply a method of calculation which statisticians have used for some time with a view to measuring *dispersion*. What is dispersion? Given a series of numbers, one can calculate the average. But a given average can represent a series of very proximate numbers as well as a series of numbers very distant from one another. Dispersion represents the greater or lesser distance of terms in a series in relation to one another and in relation to their average. This is how it is measured. First calculate the positive or negative deviations of the diverse terms of the series from their mean. Compute the arithmetic sum of these deviations (that is, without taking account of + and − signs). Multiply this sum by a hundred and then divide it by the sum of the numbers in

*See, in this regard, Gabriel Deshaies, *Psychologie du suicide*, Paris, Presses Universitaires de France, 1947, pp. 43–9 – Tr.

the series. We shall call the result of these computations the *coefficient of dispersion*.[9] The greater the distance of the terms of a series from one another, the larger it is.

True, such a calculation may seem artificial because the terms of each series here, that is, the eleven suicide rates corresponding to each period, refer to countries which are very unequal in population. If we wish to take account of the difference in population, we must see to it that each country is counted as many times as it includes, for example, a million inhabitants.[10]

We obtain, in that case, what we shall call the *adjusted coefficient of dispersion*. We have, however, calculated the simple rate of dispersion as well as the adjusted rate of dispersion, for each is of interest in its own right, depending on whether one's attention focuses upon countries considered as indivisible national unities or upon the European unity of which they represent unequal fractions.

We show in Table 4.5 the coefficients we have found for each of the periods distinguished in Table 4.1.

All in all, as is seen, the two coefficients of dispersion, both simple and adjusted, vary in the same direction and at the same times. They increase in the first phase from 1836–45 to 1861–70, that is, during about thirty years. They decrease during a second phase from 1866–70 to 1911–13, that is, during more than forty years. The rates of increase and decrease may be represented by setting the maximum equal to 100 in both series. We then find that the simple coefficient has risen from 88 to 100 and declined from 100 to 63, while the adjusted coefficient has risen from 81 to 100 and declined from 100 to 79.5.

We had at first calculated these numbers only since 1860, ascertaining that the two coefficients decreased continuously from one five-year period to the next (with but one exception: from 1871–5 to 1876–80). In 1871–5 Prussia's suicide rate, which is greatly superior to the average in every period, again descends abruptly to its level, to rise very strongly again in the following period. We shall see that this drop is explained by the exceptional circumstances in which Prussia (and Germany) found itself in the aftermath of the war of 1870–1. On the other hand, Austria's suicide rate increases on this occasion by more than 50 per cent, which, as we have seen (p. 19), must be explained by a profound transformation in the methods of enumeration of suicides. These two reasons sufficed to account for the exceptions pointed out. Everything seemed to indicate that, increasingly, the suicide rates in the different countries were converging.

But on going back to earlier periods it appeared that, on the contrary, from 1836–45 to 1856–65, the dispersion or the inequality in the suicide rates from country to country increased.

Table 4.5   *Coefficients of dispersion of suicide rates in Europe*

	Simple coefficient	Adjusted coefficient[11]
1836–45	48 ⎫ 49	35.1 ⎫ 37.3
1846–55	50 ⎰	39.5 ⎰
1856–60	53 ⎫ 53.8	42.5 ⎫ 42.5 ⎫
1861–5	54.6 ⎰	42.5 ⎰ ⎬ 42.7
1866–70	54.1 ⎫ 50.5	43.1 ⎫ 40.1 ⎰
1871–5	46.8 ⎰	37 ⎰
1876–80	48.4 ⎫ 48	42 ⎫ 42 ⎫
1881–5	47.5 ⎰	42 ⎰ ⎬ 40.3
1886–90	43.2 ⎫ 41.9	41.5 ⎫ 41.1 ⎰
1891–5	40.5 ⎰	40.6 ⎰
1896–1900	38.3 ⎫ 38.1	38.2 ⎫ 37.8 ⎫
1901–5	37.8 ⎰	37.3 ⎰ ⎬ 40.1
1906–10	34.5 ⎫ 34	33.5 ⎫ 34.5 ⎰
1911–13	33.5 ⎰	35.4 ⎰
1922–5	40.1	38.3	35.4

That is explained by the fact that, at first, all the suicide rates were very low (except in Denmark and Saxony) and, especially in Prussia, France, Saxony, and Austria, had not taken the advance that they were to keep for a long time.

What remains, then, is this: let us choose the period 1856–65 as a point of departure. (Morselli and Durkheim considered only two or three periods beyond this – see the tables reproduced by Durkheim on pp. 47 and 50 which only go to 1872 and 1878.) In the ten quinquennial periods which follow, the dispersion of the suicide rates continuously decreases. Moreover, this decrease seems to accelerate from one decennial period to the next (see the figures in the second and fourth columns in Table 4.5). Table 4.6 shows the percentage rates of decrease.

Table 4.6   *Rate of decrease in suicides*

	1861–70	1871–80	1881–90	1891–1900	1901–10
Simple coefficient	– 6	– 7	– 13	– 9	– 11
Adjusted coefficient	– 6	+ 5	– 2	– 8	– 9

It is true that the coefficients of dispersion again rise in the period 1922–5 to the level at which they were in 1891–1900. But this is explained by the war of 1914–18 and its aftermath. During the war, suicide rates dropped very sharply in the belligerent countries and also in the others. They rose again in 1922–5 but unequally, faster, for example, in Prussia and in Saxony than in England, Belgium, or France. We shall therefore have to wait several years to observe whether the suicide rates in different countries continue to converge as they have done continuously in the course of the fifty-five years which precede the war of 1914.

We can confirm these results with other observations.

We compiled the Table 4.7 from a recent work published by Enrico Ferri. These data refer to seven nations, of which only four appear in our previous table: namely, Italy, Belgium, France, and England. (Some slight differences will be noticed between these numbers calculated from Ferri's figures and those which appear in the previous table for the nations.) Two others do not appear there: Ireland and Spain, both countries with extremely low suicide rates. Finally, though Prussia and Saxony are not found here (any more than the Scandinavian nations), data relating to Germany as a whole, published only since 1891, have been reproduced here. Short though the period considered may be, it is of interest because it includes the war years.

Here are the simple coefficients of dispersion that we have found for these periods.

1891–5	56.5 }	55
1896–1900	53.5 }	
1901–5	52 }	50.5
1906–10	49 }	
1911–15	51 }	48.7
1916–20	46.5 }	
1921–5	50.5	

It will be noticed that during the war (especially after 1916) the suicide rates decreased very perceptibly, except in Spain, and that the coefficient of dispersion dropped during this time. It rises after the war. That is because the enumerations of the suicide rates were completed more rapidly in some countries than in others. The coefficient of dispersion is clearly larger in all these periods than in the previous test because fewer countries are being studied and because two of them have a particularly low suicide rate. But on the whole the results are in the same direction.

John Rice Miner published a table showing the proportion of suicides in 19 states (9 of which are not included in Table 4.1, namely: Ireland, Scotland, Finland, Holland, Australia,

Table 4.7[12] *Suicide rates in different European countries (Enrico Ferri)*

	1891–5	1896–1900	1901–5	1906–10	1911–15	1916–20	1921–5
Italy	54.6	61.7	64.5	81.9	82.5	70.4	83.6
France	242	240	232.1	247.6	230.2	178.1	229
England	91.3	97	103.2	110.1	96.5	82.6	102
Germany	218.3	209.9	220.6	217.8	217.4	177.1	224
Belgium	134.8	130.2	129.8	142.2	133.1	133.4	135
Ireland	28.5	27.4	32.5	35.7	33.9	24	33.5
Spain	(66)	(66)	(66)	66.4	55.1	71.9	57
TOTAL	835	832	848	902	848	735.5	864.1
Average	119	119	120	129	120	119	124

Massachusetts, Japan, Switzerland, and Serbia; Austria is missing) for the two periods 1871–5 and 1896–1900, and for the year 1913. We calculated from these data (which we are not reproducing) the three simple coefficients of dispersion which follow:

1871–5	55.8
1896–1900	53.9
1913	43.8

Here again, we find that the suicide rates tend to converge, although largely different countries are concerned (almost half did not appear in Table 4.1) and three are very distant from Europe. They pass 100 to 79, while in our first test they declined from 100 to 72. The change is a little slower from 1871–5 to 1896–1900: from 100 to 96.5 (instead of 100 to 82), but it is more rapid from 1896–1900 to 1913: from 100 to 81 (instead of 100 to 87.5).

More up-to-date is a table published in the *Handwörterbuch der Staatswissenschaften* (4th edition, 1925), which gives us, for six periods, the suicide rates of 20 nations (though only of 7 nations for the first period, and of 18 for the second and fifth). We notice that these periods are not the same as in J. R. Miner's table, and so this one presents an entirely new observation. We are reproducing the table as is (see Table 4.8).[13] We have only replaced the numbers given for France in the last two periods, 145 and 140, with the correct numbers, which are much higher. In the last two columns we compare the ordinal numbers of diverse countries ranked in decreasing order of suicide rates for the two periods 1881–5 and 1911–13 (the brink of war).

Table 4.8   *Suicides per million inhabitants (the nations are ranked by decreasing suicide rate in 1911–13)*

	1841–5	1881–5	1901–5	1911–13	1914–18	1919–22	Rank order in 1881–5	Rank order in 1911–13
Switzerland	—	233	232	239	208	214[14]	2	1
France	85	194	228	252	175[15]	222[15]	4	2
Germany	—	211	212	220	173	212	3	3
Austria	46	162	173	201	221	238	5	4
Hungary	—	84	176	194	146	256	10	5
Japan	—	146	201	187	188	185	6	6
Denmark[16]	230	248	227	182	175	136	1	7
Sweden	66	97	142	178	129	140[17]	9	8
United States[18]	—	—	139	161	150	118[19]	—	—
Belgium	56	107	124	139	—	129	7	9
Australia	—	98	125	128	116	107	8	10
New Zealand	—	—	147	126	117	122	—	—
England (and Wales)[20]	—	75	103	100	85	96	11	11
Finland	38[21]	39	55	99	91	99	16	12
Italy	—	49	63	84	79	76	15	13
Holland	—	53	64	63	60	61	14	14
Scotland	—	53	60	57	47	52	13	15
Norway	106	67	64	57	44	47	12	16
Spain	—	25	21	48	61	46	17	17
Ireland	—	22	33	36	—	28[22]	18	18

Since data are lacking in the majority of these countries for the first period, we have taken the next (1881–5) as the point of departure. On the other hand, we have discarded the United States and New Zealand, for which we do not have figures for 1881–5 (the number of states in the first country to which the rates shown refer seems to have greatly increased from one period to the next).* Five periods and eighteen nations remain.

*From 3 states in the Death-Registration Area in 1880 to 26 in 1911. See *Vital Statistics of the United States*, 1950, vol. 1, p. 14 – Tr.

The comparison of ordinal numbers deserves our attention for a moment, for it concerns a large number of countries whose situations are different. One will note that this series of nations is cut into two categories by the line which corresponds to New Zealand, where there are fewest figures. From one period to the next, no country has passed from one category to the other. Within the first category two countries have clearly changed rank: Denmark passed from first to seventh and Hungary from tenth to fifth. All the others keep their respective ranks except France, whose suicide rate, at first below Germany's, appears to exceed it at the end. This, as we have indicated, is an illusion. Were the proportion of German suicides calculated in relation to the population over fifteen years of age, it would be much higher than the French rate for this last period as well. There are only small changes in the second category (lower rates): Finland and Italy gain (or, if one prefers, lose) several ranks. People commit suicide a little more often here. In Norway and Scotland suicide rates increase less than elsewhere. But it is only a question of two or three ranks gained or lost. In the series as a whole, 6 of the 18 countries keep exactly the same rank, 8 others only lose or gain by one or two.

We have shown above the rate of increase in the proportion of suicides for nine of these countries in periods which are very close to each other. Table 4.9 shows how they have increased in the other nine.

The strong increases were produced exclusively in the European countries. The average rate of increase is also, we recall, very clearly exceeded in France, Germany, Austria, Sweden, and Italy. It is almost attained in Belgium and in Germany. The suicide rate decreased in Norway and Denmark.

Table 4.9   *Percentage rate of increase from 1881–5 to 1911–13*

Finland	133	Japan	25
Hungary	130	Holland	19
Spain	81	Scotland	6
Ireland	64	Switzerland	2
Australia	30	The 18 countries	27

We calculated the simple and the adjusted coefficients of dispersion for these five periods (Table 4.10). The war period included, these coefficients drop continuously. They clearly rise again in the four years following the war: we have given reasons for this, and observed that this rise appears much smaller if, instead of keeping to the period 1919–22, one takes the next one: 1922–5. The few years which follow the war are entirely exceptional. But from 1881–5 to 1911–13, that is, in only thirty years, the simple coefficient drops from 100 to 84, and the adjusted coefficient from 100 to 88.

Table 4.10   *Coefficients of dispersion of the suicide rates*

	Simple coefficient		Adjusted coefficient	
1881–5	54.5		40.9	
1901–5	49 ⎫	47.5	37.5 ⎫	36.7
1911–13	46 ⎭		36 ⎭	
1914–18	41.6 ⎫	44.8	35.4 ⎫	38.5
1919–22	48 ⎭		41.6 ⎭	

chapter 5

The distribution of suicides in France

We have said that international comparisons are always suspect where suicide is concerned. We were interested to show with a wide range of observations that differences between European countries are always found to diminish from one period to the next. So, too, do differences between some countries outside of Europe. This is one way of measuring convergence among the customs, beliefs, and institutions of diverse peoples. Such an evolution must be explained by the convergence and growing similarity of these countries and peoples during the nineteenth century and up to our own times. Now, however, we can research the same problem with statistical data which is much more uniform and more reliable, namely, the extent to which suicide rates in diverse regions converge within large countries.

Father Krose reproduced the suicide rates in France for three periods, not by departments, for these are too small in area, but by provinces or groups of provinces. Let us first note that the ranks occupied by these diverse provinces, ordered according to their suicide rates, have hardly varied for the three periods considered, that is, during fifty years. There is, to begin with, the collection of five provinces or groups of provinces where people commit suicide most frequently (more than 60 suicides per million inhabitants in 1827–43; more than 100 in 1856–60; and more than 160 in 1872–6). These are: Ile-de-France and Orléanais, which clearly come out on top at these three periods; Flanders–Artois–Picardy and Champagne; then Provence and Normandy. (The map prepared by Durkheim for the period 1878–87, p. 396, shows the same thing.) Then comes the aggregation where the suicide rate is average: Poitou–Angoulême, Alsace and Lorraine, Burgundy and Franche-Comté; Anjou–Maine–Touraine; Lyonnais–Dauphiné; Berry–Nièvre–

Bourbonnais. There are displacements within this aggregation, but without any groups leaving or entering. Finally, there is the aggregation where the suicide rate is low: Britanny and the central and southern provinces (except Provence), all of whom keep nearly the same rank. This method of dividing France into a number of parts, each of which includes five departments, may seem a little artificial. Before employing it ourselves we prepared a map of France on which the departments are distinguished according to their suicide rates in 1872–6 (the rates for this period are reproduced by departments in Morselli). If we classify the rates in five categories, very low (VL), low (L), medium (M), high (H), and very high (VH), here is what we find for the departments included in each group:

Ile-de-France–Orléanais: VH: Seine, Seine-et-Oise, Seine-et-Marne, Eure-et-Loir; H: Loiret.

Champagne: VH: Aube, Marne; H: Meuse; M: Ardennes, Haute-Marne.

Flanders–Artois–Picardy: VH: Aisne, Oise; H: Somme; M: Nord, Pas-de-Calais.

Provence: H: Bouches-du-Rhône, Vaucluse, Basses-Alpes; L: Hautes-Alpes; VL: Var.

Normandy: H: Eure, Seine-Inférieure; M: Calvados; L: Manche, Orne.

Anjou–Maine–Touraine: H: Indre-et-Loire, Loir-et-Cher; M: Sarthe, Maine-et-Loire; L: Mayenne.

Burgundy–Franche–Comté: H: Côte-d'Or, Yonne; M: Doubs, Jura, Haute-Saône.

Alsace-Lorraine: M: Meurthe-et-Moselle, Vosges.

Lyonnais–Dauphiné: M: Ain, Drôme, Rhône; L: Isère; VL: Loire.

Poitou–Angoumois: M: Charente, Charente-Inférieure; Deux-Sèvres; L: Vienne; VL: Vendée.

Berry–Nièvre–Bourbonnais: M: Saône-et-Loire; L: Allier, Cher, Indre, Nièvre.

Guyenne: M: Dordogne, Gironde; L: Lot-et-Garonne; VL: Aveyron, Lot.

Languedoc Oriental: M: Gard; L: Ardèche; VL: Hérault, Lozère, Haute-Loire.

Limousin–Auvergne: L: Puy-de-Dôme, Haute-Vienne; VL: Cantal, Corrèze, Creuse.

Brittany: L: Finistère; VL: Côtes-du-Nord, Morbihan, Ille-et-Vilaine, Loire-Inférieure.

Gascony: L: Landes; VL: Basses-Pyrénées, Hautes-Pyrénées, Gers, Tarn-et-Garonne.

Languedoc–Roussillon: VL: Ariège, Aude, Haute-Garonne, Pyrénées-Orientales, Tarn.

Savoy: VL: Haute-Savoie, Basse-Savoie.
Alpes-Maritimes: M.
Corsica: VL.

The separation between three categories of 'provinces' seems very clear. In the northern and eastern region extending to Besançon, Dijon, Orléans, Blois, and Tours to the south and to Rouen, Evreux, and Chartres to the west, suicide rates fall between Very High and Medium. The second is the entire region between Orléans, Tours, and Clermont-Ferrand, southward in the great valley of the Loire (Berry, Nièvre, Bourbonnais), the entire western region of France included between Tours and Bordeaux, and Alsace-Lorraine and the whole valley of the Rhône. Here suicide rates fall between Medium and Low or Very Low. Rates are uniformly Low or Very Low in the third: Auvergne and Brittany, the entire region bordering the Pyrenees, the upper valley of the Garonne above Agen, and all of the Languedocian country watered by the Aude, the Tarn, and the Hérault. Provence and Normandy are the only exceptions. Hautes-Alpes, a department where suicides are very rare in 1872–6, has been included in Provence along with regions where people frequently kill themselves, namely Avignon, Digne, and Marseilles.

In Normandy, there is a marked contrast between Eure and Calvados (the western border of the great suicidogenic zone occupying the entire north of France) and Manche and Orne. This will later become attenuated, however. It might have been better to link Mayenne (included in Anjou–Maine–Touraine) with Brittany and, further south, Vendée (included in Poitou–Angoumois). It might have been equally appropriate to study separately Pas-de-Calais and the north where the suicide rate has remained low relative to all other departments in the north and east. Finally, Aveyron and Lot seem linked to Tarn and Tarn-et-Garonne rather than to Gironde and Dordogne. They belong to the compact mass of southern and central departments in which suicide rates fall to the lowest level. It would have been better to link Charente and Charente-Inférieure with Gironde and Dordogne, with which they constitute a kind of advance bastion of suicide in southwestern France. Apart from these reservations, the mode of classification adopted by Krose, Morselli, Wagner, Kayser, and Dufau is less arbitrary than it seems to be.

For the three periods 1827–43, 1856–60, and 1872–6, we kept these same categories and reproduced the figures shown by Krose (see Map 1). We have calculated the proportion of suicides in France by provinces for the periods 1884–92, 1893–1900, 1901–8, 1910–13, and 1919–20 (see Map 2). (The *Compte général de l'administration de la justice criminelle en France* has published figures for the war period retroactively but only in aggregate, without distributing them by departments.)

Map 1   *Suicides in France in 1872–6 (per million inhabitants)*

Table 5.1 shows for each period the average suicide rate in France and the coefficients of dispersion of the provincial rates of suicide. During the course of the eighty-five years from 1835 (the median of the first period) to 1919–20, the two coefficients diminished from one period to the next without exception. The decreases of the simple coefficient from 1856–60 to 1872–6 and from 1884–92 to 1893–1900 are both so small that they amount to no decrease. The dispersion in suicide rates does not seem to decline continuously. The two coefficients drop rather sharply from 1893–1900 to 1901–8 and from 1910–13 to 1919–20, that is, on the two occasions when the average suicide rate itself drops. The highest rates seem to drop the most, thus approaching the aggregation of the rates. We are unable to say before 1856–60 when the dispersion decreased, or when it did so most rapidly.

Table 5.1   *Suicide rates in France*

	Proportion of suicides per million inhabitants	Coefficient of dispersion of the provincial suicide rates			
		Simple coefficient		Adjusted coefficient	
1827–43	68	51			
1856–60	111	42.5 ⎱			
1872–6	152	42.3 ⎰	42.4	42.5	
1884–92	216	40.6 ⎱		40.5 ⎱	
1893–1900	240	40.5 ⎰	40.5	38.2 ⎰	39.3
1901–8	234	35 ⎱		32.1 ⎱	
1910–13	252	34.5 ⎰	34.7	30.5 ⎰	31.3
1919–20	215	30.9		24.3	

Let us relate to these findings those arrived at from the European data (Table 4.5). From about 1893 until 1911–13, the simple coefficient is nearly the same in Europe as in France. From 1876 to 1892, the adjusted coefficient is very close in both (equal to 40 or 42) but drops a little faster after this in France than in Europe: in 1911–13 it is 30.5 in France and 34.5 in Europe. Around 1893, indeed since 1872–6, the dispersion of suicide rates in European countries and French provinces was equal, but after that, diminished faster in France. It even diminished further during the war and the two post-war years. We calculated for France before 1876 only the coefficient of simple dispersion. In 1856–60, this coefficient is clearly lower in France than in Europe: 42.5 instead of 53. That the degree of dispersion from 1872–6 to around 1900 should be found equal in eleven European countries and twenty French provinces is, in any case, very remarkable.

We show in Table 5.2 the rate of these variations for Europe (from Table 4.5) and France (from Table 5.1). The simple coefficient of dispersion, we recall, measures the degree of uniformity within a group of nations or provinces assumed to be equal in population. On this measure, the suicide rates after 1876 become equalized more rapidly in Europe than in France. The adjusted coefficient of dispersion takes into account the unequal population of nations or provinces, and not only measures the tendency towards uniformity more accurately among nations or provinces, but among equal groups of inhabitants within them. On this measure, the dispersion decreases more rapidly in France than in Europe.

Table 5.2   *Variations of suicide rates in Europe and France*

	Europe	France
Decrease in the simple coefficient of dispersion		
1836 to 1911–13	from 100 to 70	from 100 to 68
1871–5 to 1911–13[1]	from 100 to 71.5	from 100 to 82
1875–80 to 1911–13	from 100 to 69	
Decrease in the adjusted coefficient of dispersion		
1871–5 to 1911–13[1]	from 100 to 96	from 100 to 72
1875–80 to 1911–13	from 100 to 84	

Map 2   *Suicides in France in 1911–13 (per million inhabitants)*

In 1879 Morselli wrote that

Guerry was the first to notice the difference in suicide rates between northern and southern France. Dividing the country into five regions, North, Center, East, West, and South, he found that in 1827–30 their suicide rates formed a decreasing series, with the North (Picardy, Artois, Normandy, Lorraine, and Ile-de-France) coming at the top, and the South (Guyenne, Gascony, Languedoc, Roussillon, and Corsica) at the bottom. French statisticians such as Brierre de Boismont, Lisle, Legoyt, and Blanc, and Germans, such as Wagner, Oettingen, and Frantz, have confirmed Guerry's observation for other periods. This finding is thus one of the most certain that suicide statistics have obtained.

The numbers in Table 5.3 were taken from a small table compiled by Morselli. On calculating coefficients of convergence, we find for the successive periods: 37.5; 31.2; 29.5. This completes our observations on the period prior to 1872.

Table 5.3 *Number of suicides per million inhabitants, France*

	Brierre de Boismont (1835–43)	Wagner (1856–60)	Morselli (1872–6)
North	130	168	237
East	63	95	139
Center	53	73	126
West	48	70	95
South	42	68	93
Average	67	95	104

However, a more precise idea can be formed of the variations in the suicide rate in these regions during these thirty-five years. Let us set equal to 100 the average suicide rate in France for each period or, more precisely, the average of the suicide rates of the five regions. Table 5.4 shows the relative numbers. Thus, from 1835–43 to 1856–60, the East and the North converge while the Center, West, and South remain in place; from 1856–60 to 1872–6 the Center clearly converges toward the North and the East (which are themselves closer to one another) while the South falls further and further behind. However, this division is rather artificial. The central region is not what geographers customarily call by this name since it includes departments such as Eure-et-Loir, Loiret, and Yonne, which are ordinarily linked to the Paris basin. On the other hand, the North does not contain Aube, whose suicide rate is high, and does include Orne and Manche, where it is low. As a result, the distance between the North and the Center is less.

Table 5.4   *Suicide rates in five regions of France*

	1835–43	1856–60	1872–6
North	194	177	169
East	94	100	100
Center	79	77	90
West and South	67	72.5	67

Let us therefore repeat this comparison with somewhat different categories by separating groups of departments we have already studied. We will include: 1. in the North, the groups Flanders–Artois–Picardy, Ile-de-France–Orléanais, Champagne, and Normandy; 2. in the East, Alsace, Lorraine, and Burgundy; 3. in the Southeast, the group Lyonnais–Dauphiné, Provence, Savoy, and Alpes-Maritimes; 4. in the Center, the groups Limousin–Auvergne and Berry–Nièvre–Bourbonnais; 5. in the West, Brittany, and the groups Anjou–Maine–Touraine, Poitou–Angoumois, and Guyenne; 6. in the South, Languedoc Oriental and the group Languedoc-Roussillon. We calculated the average suicide rate and the corresponding relative numbers for each region at each period by setting equal to 100 the average of these suicide rates period by period (see Table 5.5).

Let us focus on the table of relative numbers. By calculating them we have assumed that the average suicide rate always remained equal to 100. That is, we eliminated whatever variations might appear in the general average (on the 'total' line). The relative positions of the diverse regions, in suicide rates, are retained at different periods. Let us put the post-war period aside provisionally. We notice at once that the deviation of the high suicide rate in the North from the average diminishes by half from start to finish (going from 208 to 152 relative to 100). Meanwhile, the low suicide rate in the South is almost the same in 1910–13 as in 1856–60 (since in setting 56 equal to 100, the average becomes 178). Hence, with respect to deviation from the average, there is no change in the South for half a century. On the other hand, the deviations of suicide rates in the East, the Southeast, and the West remain substantially the same. In compensation, the suicide rate

Table 5.5   *Average suicide rates in France, by region*

	1827–43	1856–60	1872–6	1884–92	1893–1900	1901–8	1910–13	1919–20
North	125	185	239	323	352	328	351	259
East	59	100	145	213	247	243	277	240
Southeast	69	84	130	205	230	226	248	188
West	48	76	110	156	182	187	201	205
Center	33	61	95	130	152	163	175	175
South	26	52	69	104	117	122	132	126
Total	60	92.5	130	188	214	212	230	198

Relative Rates : 100 = average of the suicide rates in each period

	1827–43	1856–60	1872–6	1884–92	1893–1900	1901–8	1910–13	1919–20
North	208	200	184	172	167	154	152	130
East	98	108	112	113	116	114	120	121
Southeast	114	90	100	109	108	106	108	95
West	80	83	85	83	85	88	88	104
Center	56	66	73	69	71	77	76	88
South	44	56	53	50	55	57	57	64

in the Center, which is very far from the average, rises very perceptibly, passing from 56 to 76 relative to 100. Thus, the initiative for convergence comes above all from the North, where the rate of increase in suicides clearly diminishes, and from the Center, where it accelerates.

In order to give a better account of these movements we prepared two maps of suicide in France corresponding to the two periods 1872–6 and 1911–13 on which the departments are distinguished by different shadings according to whether the suicide rate is very high, high, average, low, or very low (Maps 1 and 2).* What do they teach us?

To begin with, regions covered by the same shading are remarkably extensive. Durkheim, because he was preoccupied with establishing that suicide is not spread by contagious imitation, had prepared a map of suicides in France for 1887–91 by districts.† Despite its many subdivisions and enclaves, the same fact becomes evident here too. However, the category of department suffices to call attention to vast regional uniformities. We then find that, in 1911–13, 9 departments are included in the group with very high suicide rates (Champagne, Ile-de-France, Eure, and Calvados). All are contiguous. Eight departments of the Center and South, similarly contiguous, all have very low suicide rates. The departments with average suicide rates are grouped principally in two contiguous zones, one of which, extending towards the southeast, includes 12, and the other, to the west, includes 7. Only 5 departments are isolated in this respect like islets surrounded by other departments in which people do not kill themselves nearly as often. The same is true to a possibly higher degree in 1872–6. During this period,‡ the suicide rate in 18 contiguous departments in the Center and the South is very low.

It would be tempting to seek the cause of this distribution of suicides over great homogeneous zones in the geographic structure of France. One fact above all strikes us when we study the map of suicides in 1872–6, namely, that departments where suicide rates are very high, high, or average, succeed one another in more or less broad bands following the course of great rivers and their principal tributaries, while suicide rates in the mountainous regions are low or very low. There are exceptions, of course, but it is worthwhile examining a little more closely the extent to which this relationship can be verified.

*Pages 78 and 80 – Tr.

†*Suicide*, p. 394 – Tr.

‡That is, the number of contiguous departments in the Center and the South with very low rates diminished between 1872–6 and 1911–13 from 18 to 8 – Tr.

Of the Paris basin, Vidal de la Blache said,[2]

> The ridge of Cambrésis and the slopes of Artois separate
> Flanders from the Parisian basin. Thereupon one enters a great
> region, the coordinates of whose principal contours are the
> Ardennes, the Vosges, and Massif Central, and Armorica,
> revealing a unity of structure which despite many irregularities
> remains engraved upon the earth .... The Parisian basin, which
> is appreciably larger than the Seine river basin, is bounded by
> the Meuse, the Ardennes, the entire northern loop of the Loire,
> and the tributaries of the Manche between Caen and Boulogne.
> This region (a quarter of France) is distinguished from all the
> others by the convergence of rivers, the subsidence of
> intermediary ridges, and the diversity of landscapes. It thus
> fulfills best the conditions for bringing people closer together
> and inspiring in them a reciprocal sentiment of solidarity.

Now, this region corresponds quite precisely to the extensive dark
patch which overlays departments having high or very high
suicide rates in 1872–6. Let us review the various parts of this
region. Flanders is excluded: the suicide rate is only average in the
North and in Pas-de-Calais, while it is high in Aisne, next to Oise.
It is average in Ardennes, which is excluded, high in Meuse, which
is a component. It is high in Côte-d'Or (the source of the Seine),
Aube, Yonne, Loiret, and Loir-et-Cher (at the upper bend of the
Loire), but low south of the last two departments. That is, the rate
declines as soon as one crosses the boundary of the basin going
south. It is very high in Eure (to the south of the Seine estuary),
average or low more to the west. It is very high in Seine-Inférieure
and high in Somme (tributaries of Manche between Caen and
Boulogne which are part of the basin). Haute-Marne is the only
exception in the two periods. As in Vosges, the suicide rate here is
only average. This marks the eastern boundary of the great
suicidal zone. Nièvre marks its southern boundary even more
clearly. The two contiguous departments, Yonne, to the north,
and Nièvre, to the south, account respectively for 218 and 94
suicides per million inhabitants.

Champagne includes Meaux and Château-Thierry in its historic
boundaries. This province is almost entirely hidden by the dark
patch which covers the regions most exposed to voluntary deaths.
However, people do not commit suicide equally throughout
Champagne. Let us refer to the map of suicides by districts
reproduced by Durkheim for 1887–91. The average suicide rate
then for all of France is 220. However, it is more than double, over
500, in the group of five districts of Champagne: Meaux, Château-
Thierry, Reims, Épernay, Arcis-sur-Aube. (These form a solid

block with 9 districts of Ile-de-France in which the suicide rate is likewise very high.) In six other districts of Champagne, all contiguous with the preceding, namely, Nogent-sur-Seine, Troyes, Bar-sur-Aube, Vitry-le-François, Châlons-sur-Marne, and Rethel, the suicide rate is between 400 and 500: still very high. In five others it is between 300 and 400, namely, Sens, Joigny, Tonnerre, Vassy, and Sainte-Menehould. Finally, it is only 200 to 300 in the district of Chaumont and 100 to 200 in the district of Langres. Langres, Chaumont, and Vassy (from south to north) are the three districts of Haute-Marne.

How are these differences to be explained? Though Champagne is 'a geographic region that is extremely well demarcated and its unity long recognized,' Vidal de la Blache distinguishes between northern Champagne, that is, Reims, whose destinies 'are tied to the great Picardy region' on its border, and southern Champagne, which has its political center at Troyes and is connected by passes through the Auxois with Burgundy and the southeast. In fact, the intervals between the suicide rates of Reims, Épernay, and Troyes are almost as great as between Troyes and Chaumont. The rates in 1872–6 were 380 for Marne, 285 for Aube, and 142 for Haute-Marne. Instead of examining the features of all of these regions in detail we shall quote this description, again from Vidal de la Blache:

> Between the sources of the Seine and the Marne, over a length of sixty kilometers, stretches one of the driest, most heavily wooded and most secluded regions in France. The inhabitants call it the Montagne. Its plateaux have place only for meager crops, sheep grazing, and above all, immense oak forests.

Now the district of Langres, in which the suicide rate is the lowest in Haute-Marne, is found on this plateau.

The district of Château-Chinon in Nièvre, further to the south, has a very low suicide rate because it covers another part of the Morvan mountains.

> The Morvan is one of those isolated regions which evoke in the vine grower and farmer of level ground the idea of a barren life. Retail trade, which governs the mode of living and daily relationships, is lacking here. There are only very narrow ravines or valleys between the ridges .... 'A backward country of frozen lands, a wolf country,' said one of its inhabitants.

Suicide rates drop sharply at the southeast boundary of the Paris basin because here the streams have their source and the mountainous region begins.

Upon descending towards the southeast, we go from the Paris

basin into the valleys of Savoy and the Rhône. We first traverse Côte-d'Or, where the suicide rate is high. In this department, however, the districts of Semur to the west and Beaune to the south have fewer than 200 suicides per million inhabitants (south of the plateau of Langres and the mountains of Côte-d'Or), while the districts of Châtillon-sur-Seine and Dijon have more than 200 (the Seine and the Saône valleys). Departments of the Saône and the Rhône valleys, in which the suicide rate is medium-high, succeed one another continuously on the left bank between the rivers and the alps. Isère, where it is low, is the one exception. In the district of Vienne, the only part of this department bordering the Rhône, it is average. From Châlon-sur-Saône to the Rhône, the suicide rate in Vienne, Valence, Montélimar, Orange, Avignon, and Arles, on the left bank, stays within 200 and 300 per million inhabitants. This is not true of the right bank in the Gier valley where the Rhône comes closest to the Loire and the Center canal passes through. Here, the rate is as high only in the districts of Lyon and Saint-Étienne. From Mâcon to Nîmes, the suicide rate is always lower than 200. The mountains of Charollais, Mâconnais, Lyonnais, Vivarais, Gerbier-de-Jonc, and the first slopes of the Cévennes are here. In the mountainous part of Isère between the Rhine and the Rhône the suicide rate at Grenoble is below 200; at Annecy, Chambéry, Briançon, and Saint-Jean-de-Maurienne, it falls below 100.

The suicide rate is very low throughout the region of the Massif Central: in almost the whole department of Loire (except at Saint-Étienne), at Roanne, and Monbrison, in Haute-Loire, Cantal, Lozère, Aveyron, Corrèze, and Creuse. The rate remains below 90 in Puy-de-Dôme and Allier, where it is barely enumerated. It rises again in Cher and Nièvre, with a minimum in the district of Sancerre. The Loire, from Orléans to Angers, just after it enters onto the plain, flows past an uninterrupted series of districts in which the suicide rate rises from 200 to 300, while, to the south, in Cher, Indre, and Vienne, it hardly exceeds 100 to 105.

Thus, in the whole of the part of France we have just studied, suicide rates which are high or above average are encountered in the great river basins and in the broad valleys, while the low rates are found in the mountainous regions. The picture is not as simple in the south and west, however, for although this type of relationship is still manifest there, it is often obscured.

According to Vidal de la Blache (pp. 307–13), the peninsular region of Poitiers, Le Mans, Alençon, and Caen, which is reached by going west, is another primary mountain range. Though less extensive than the Massif Central, it is still considerable and it projects France into the Atlantic Ocean.

One has the impression, from its approaches, of entering into a very distinctive region which often recalls the Massif Central by the nature of its rocks, but whose harshness is attenuated by the mildness of its climate and its slope. What name would designate it appropriately? To call it Brittany would be improper for it also includes Cotentin, Bocage normand, a part of Maine and of Anjou, and the Vendée portion of Poitou. Even 'Armorique,' though often applied to it, would be inaccurate for this old Celtic word implies contact with the sea, whereas the region is much more inland and rural than maritime. 'The West' ... is still the phrase which seems most capable of expressing what is common to these lands and peoples who, except for the seamen, though little involved in outdoor life, are hardly more involved with one another .... The West is a compact mass where relatively uniform conditions of existence reign over an area of more than 60,000 square kilometers.

This region coincides exactly with a zone in which the average suicide rate is very low. The average suicide rate was 79 in 9 departments: Finistère, Côtes-du-Nord, Morbihan, Ille-et-Vilaine, Manche, Orne, Mayenne, Loire, and Vendée. In the 7 adjacent departments of Calvados to Charente-Inférieure it was 176.6. Besides Brittany, the zone includes Cotentin (Manche), Bocage normand (Orne), part of Maine and of Anjou (Mayenne), and part of Poitou (Vendée). If only the distribution of suicides is being considered, it cannot be delimited otherwise.

Let us examine suicide rates in this region in more detail by districts (La Blache, pp. 333–4).

Brittany draws upon outside influences throughout a coastal area increasingly parcelled into small holdings. At the same time, however, she rejects them because of an internal structure in which two zones are juxtaposed: a maritime zone, l'Armor, that is open to the world, and an interior zone that is remote and withdrawn .... The general slope of the shore and its numerous indentations ... combine with the movements of the tides, so greatly to extend the breadth of the zone that it is a linguistic confusion to call it a coastline. Here is no simple line of contact between earth and sea but rather, all along the peninsula, a band varying in appearance from the point of view both of nature and man.

This contrast is clearly reflected in the distribution of suicides, which are more numerous in coastal than in interior districts. (The suicide rate is from 100 to 200 per million inhabitants in the coastal districts at Paimbœuf, Saint-Nazaire, Lorient, Quimperlé, and Quimper, on the Atlantic, and at Brest, Morlaix, Lannion,

Saint-Brieuc, Avranches, and Valognes, and from 200 to 300 at Cherbourg.) Vannes and Châteaulin are exceptions. Though on the coast, the former extends deep inland. (Between the Vilaine and the Blavet are granite ridges and arid wastelands.) The latter borders the ocean only at the peninsula of Crozon. The lowest rates of suicide are in the interior. Hardly anyone ever kills himself in the interior except at Rennes and Montfort in the Vilaine valley. The hills of the region are 'hardly a mountain. Nevertheless, one's impression is the same as in the sternest solitudes of high places. They are in fact the ruins of a mountain chain at earth's earliest ages that now is worn down to the roots.' (The districts of Châteaulin and Guingamp are here.) On the site of the Black Mountains in the Pontivy district, and in the Central Forest, the legendary Broceliande* of the Round Table romance is a vast, solitary forest-land, once extensively covered by great oaks, but now covered only sparsely by endless woods (the districts of Ploërmel, Loudéac, and Guingamp). Thus, in Brittany, 'solitary, savage spaces rather than true mountains cause the real separation between the regions of the interior.' On the other hand, bordering the sea are the 'coastal currents, the combined action of winds and rains, and the interior channels which penetrate inland between the lines of reefs and the coast' (p. 336). These routes serving the movement of people explain the contrast between the coast and the interior, and why people kill themselves less often in the latter and more often in the former.

Stendhal wrote in 1835:[3]

> A minister of the interior who wished to fulfill his duties ... would have to ask for a grant of two millions a year to bring up to the level of instruction of other Frenchmen those living in the fatal triangle extending between Bordeaux, Bayonne, and Valence. In these lands the people believe in sorcery, are illiterate, and do not speak French. It goes without saying that priests are all-powerful in this fatal triangle. Civilization extends from Lille to Rennes, falling off towards Orléans and Tours. It is at its most brilliant south of Grenoble.

Of Stendhal's fatal triangle, let us retain only the side that joins the two summits: Bordeaux and Valence. This line rather clearly separates the south, as far as the Rhône, from the rest of France. As we have seen, suicide rates are lowest in this region. In particular, there is a deep furrow marked by the departments of Haute-Loire, Lozère, Aveyron, Tarn, Haute-Garonne, and Ariège, where the average for suicides in 1872–6 was only 49, or, if Hautes-Pyrénées is included, 46. In no other part of France is this

*An enchanted forest in Arthurian literature – Tr.

minimum met again; it is lower than the suicide rate in France in 1827. Let us note at once that what we are calling a furrow is, on the contrary, a succession of almost continuous heights from which Lot, Aveyron, Tarn, and Ariège descend westward, and, southeastward, Gard, Hérault, and Aude. Elsewhere the course of the Garonne is clearly indicated from source to estuary by a succession of districts with suicide rates which are higher (from 100 to 200): Saint-Gaudens, Muret, Toulouse, Castelsarrasin, Moissac, Agen, Marmande, La Réole, and Bordeaux, as well as the valleys of the Gard, Hérault, and Têt. This is true as well along the shores of the Atlantic and the Mediterranean. Although in this entire vast region there are only two districts, La Réole and Bazas, where the suicide rate is higher than 220, greater differences with respect to suicide are always enumerated in this region than one might suppose at first glance: the proximity of the sea or of major rivers, on the one hand, and of mountains, on the other, appears to play the same role here as elsewhere.

Perceptible rates of suicide are enumerated in two remaining groups of departments, northwest and southeast of this zone, namely, Aunis, Saintogne, Angoumois, Périgord, and all of southern Provence from Avignon to Marseilles to Nice. The first group corresponds to the valleys of the Sèvre Niortaise, the Charente, and the Dordogne: there are more voluntary deaths in the two northern districts of the Deux-Sèvres (Melle and Niort on the Sèvre Niortaise) than at Parthenay or Bressuire. More people kill themselves at Angoulême on the Charente than at Poitiers. On the other hand, the departments of Basses-Alpes, Vaucluse, and Bouches-du-Rhône, in Provence, whose suicide rates cluster about 200, delineate very precisely the courses of the Durance and the Rhône. Rates are much lower in Hautes-Alpes to the north and in Alpes-Maritimes to the south. Here again, the influence of the rivers appears to be dominant.

This study of the distribution of suicides in France by departments and districts has therefore led us to a very clear finding. Suicide rates increase in the great river valleys and along the coasts. They diminish in mountainous regions, in humid plains latticed by pools, and in the solitudes of forests. Does this mean that in this respect people are under earth's direct influence, that geographic structure suffices to explain their unequal attachment to life? We believe not. The tendency to suicide varies in diverse human groups. It is a social fact. Now a social fact cannot be explained by a physical fact such as the structure of the earth or the geographic shape of a country. The geographic fact therefore interests us only to the extent that it is an indicator of social characteristics that we cannot apprehend directly. We may assume, for example, that communications are difficult in a mountainous region, houses and groups of houses are dispersed, the more sedentary inhabitants conserve family and religious traditions here better than elsewhere, etc. These are just so many social characteristics that must be known to account for the tendency to suicide as it is manifested in diverse human groups. Of course we do not at all mean to conclude from the fact that people circulate more freely in one place than another or that groups of diverse origin or social situation, etc., intermingle and enter into more frequent contact, that their traditional beliefs are weakening or, further, that they are undergoing, in addition, repercussions from economic or political crises. All that we may rightfully assume is that if suicide rates are continuously unequal in mountainous regions and in the valleys of great rivers, the social causes explaining suicide exert their influence unequally in these two places.

It is true that the opposition we have shown to account for the difference between suicide rates in adjacent regions appears not to explain the great contrasts between, for example, the West and the Paris basin, or between the North and the South. These divergences have always been profound and, as we shall see, continue to exist. People seem clearly more attached to life in the Rhône than in the Seine valley and, likewise, although to a lesser degree, in the Midi than in the West. Here again, however, it is possible for the geographic method to show us how to search for the social causes that explain contrasts extending to the largest divisions of national territory.

According to Morselli, that suicides were minimal in the Center and the South and maximal in the North must be explained by the ethnic differences between these two populations. After criticizing this thesis, Durkheim wrote (pp. 92–3),

> Our country is known to be divided morally as well as
> ethnologically into two parts as yet not wholly combined. The
> peoples of the Center and the Midi have retained their own
> temperament, a characteristic way of life, and for this reason
> resist the ideas and manners of the North. If the people of the
> North commit suicide more than those of the Midi, it is not
> because they are more predisposed to it by their ethnic
> temperament, but simply that the social causes of suicide are
> more specially located north rather than south of the Loire.

He added,

> for historical reasons the provincial spirit and local
> traditionalism have remained much stronger in the Midi, while

in the North the need of facing common enemies, a closer solidarity of interests and more frequent contacts have brought the peoples together and blended their history much sooner.

Vidal de la Blache, from another point of view, writes (p. 376),

> Cultural similarities have united the South of France but have never formed it into a political whole. This shortcoming is a historical fact not unknown to geography. Relationships between the Mediterranean Midi and the Atlantic Midi are distant. Though it would seem possible for at least the plains of the Garonne to have become a unified political domain, that outcome appears never to have been realized.

And he notes that the evolution of the river system has made little progress, especially in Gascony.

> Between Gascony and the Pyrenees there sprawls a great fragmented plateau which a network of tributaries and smaller streams has yet to unify. Rivers unrelated to one another flow between deep embankments.... For a long time there were no permanently secure routes across these jagged banks. This region has not found the means to constitute itself a political unity. It lacked a common center. Toulouse and Bordeaux, although situated on the same river, have lived separately, each within its own sphere of activity.... Much more restricted spatially than France as a whole, the South presents divisions which are more enduring.

Thus, geographic study of the regions where people scarcely think of forestalling natural death always reveals the same order of characteristics: obstacles to human movement, fragmentation of land holdings, absence of those great permanent currents of collective life which, traversing the vast basins, flow down river valleys into which powerful tributaries hurl themselves, and lack of political unity and a common life. A different aspect of the same geographical idea is presented by the comparison of northern and eastern France with the west. In the north and east a rural population clusters around the church tower of the small town or village. Here is a 'small society accessible to general influences.' The west is a country of scattered farms and hamlets where 'people live in isolation through long rainy seasons having contact with the external world only on festivals or fair days.... The country dweller in Lorraine, Burgundy, Champagne, and Picardy is usually a villager, while in the west he is a peasant' (p. 311).

Although the distribution of suicides remains on the whole very similar from 1872–6 to 1911–13, there have been general and local changes everywhere. The northern zone where suicides are the most numerous stretches from west to east: Calvados and Haute-Saône are included at the latter period. That is, the northern suicidal zone extends from Belfort to Caen, covering the Ardennes to the north. At both periods, however, it collides against the barriers of Haute-Marne, Nord, Pas-de-Calais, Orne, and Manche. To the south, Loir-et-Cher and Indre-et-Loire ceased to be part of it (for there the suicide rate increased much less quickly). Suicide rates are lower in the entire west than the average for France, except in Vendée. The zone of very low suicide rates is narrower in the south: in Loire people kill themselves with moderate frequency, as in neighboring Rhône (Saint-Étienne and Lyon). Suicides in Lot and Gers are as numerous as in Lot-et-Garonne and Landes since the influence of the coast of Aquitaine extends towards the interior. The influence of the Mediterranean coast makes itself felt in Pyrénées-Orientales, Aude, and Hérault. In each of these southern departments suicides are proportionately less rare and the suicide rate, though still very far from average, comes a little closer to it. In the region extending south of the line between Manche and Jura only two patches are entirely dark: Charente-Inférieure and the group of two departments of Provence: Bouches-du-Rhône and Var. (The suicide rate in the valley of the Durance, Vaucluse, and Basses-Alpes increased in much smaller proportions.) There are as many suicides in Var in 1911–13 as in Seine and Seine-et-Oise, and more than in Bouches-du-Rhône.

How shall these variations be explained? Are they related to population movements? Although the number of inhabitants may not have changed appreciably in France during this period, certain regions became more populated while others lost some of their inhabitants. For example, if the population of each province in 1876 is set equal to 100, we find in 1911 for the Ile-de-France–Orléanais, 150; for Flanders, Artois, and Picardy, 117; for Anjou–Maine–Touraine and for Provence, 108; and, on the other hand, for Burgundy–Franche-Comté, 90; for Gascony, 91; for Languedoc-Roussillon, 93; for Savoy, 93; for Normandy, 94. Now the suicide rate increased more in Burgundy–Franche-Comté and in Gascony, in which it almost doubled, than in Ile-de-France–Orléanais (an increase of 6 per cent) or in Flanders–Artois–Picardy (an increase of 50 per cent). We must examine more closely whether the rate of increase in suicide rates has slackened where the population has increased, and conversely.

For each department we calculated relative numbers representing their suicide rates in the two periods 1872–6 and

1911–13 by setting equal to 100 the average of the departmental suicide rates in each of these two periods. These numbers measure the deviation of the suicide rates from that average at each period. Let us first consider the twelve departments with the largest population increases from 1872 to 1911. We find that in 9 departments the deviation of the suicide rate from the mean remained stationary or decreased. Table 5.6 lists those in which the rate decreased (that is, where the increase slackened noticeably).

Table 5.6   *Decreases in the suicide rate*

	Percentage increase in population	Suicide rate in relation to the mean set equal to 100	
	from 1872 to 1911	1872–6	1911–13
Seine	72	267	146
Bouches-du-Rhône	45	135	132
Seine-et-Oise	44	258	178
Meurthe-et-Moselle	38	103	102
Pas-de-Calais	35	98	99
Rhône	29	111	82
Finistère	21	72	58
Seine-Inférieure	10	160	158
Gironde	12	81	82

Exceptions are: Nord, Haute-Vienne, and Morbihan, where the population increased by more than 12 per cent, and the deviation of the suicide rates from the mean increased likewise. However, the deviation from the mean for the totality of the 12 departments with the greatest increase in population went from 100 to 87, compared with 100 to 82 in the 9 departments.

Finally, let us consider the 20 departments whose populations decreased the most from 1872 to 1911. With but five exceptions, the suicide rates there are below the mean. Now, we find that in 16 of these departments the negative deviation of the suicide rates from the mean has diminished very perceptibly. In fact, the average rate of suicide in these 16 departments, relative to the average for all the departments set equal to 100, went from 71 to 96, that is, the negative deviation diminished in relative numbers from 100 to 14. The suicide rates therefore increased more rapidly than for France as a whole from one period to the next. In three others, the deviation remained constant. In only one did it increase. For the totality of 20 departments where the population decreased the most, the deviation from the mean went in relative numbers from 100 to 35.

How shall these two facts be explained? One might assume that there is a limit to the increase in suicide rates. This limit is nearly attained in departments where people kill themselves most frequently. It is therefore natural for the increase in suicides to slacken. The limit is more distant in the others where the suicide rate is much below the average. It is understandable that the increase in suicides is accelerating in such departments. Moreover, we may further assume that the migrants to the former departments (which enclose most of the very large cities) originated in departments that are more resistant to suicide, and bring with them traditional and preservative traditions which they maintain temporarily in their new environments. This would explain their restraining role. Conversely, we may assume that departments which are becoming depopulated lose the youngest part of their population, which is least given to suicide, so that their departure raises the proportion of voluntary deaths. Finally, we might assume that small cities and peasant groups, in departments which are losing population, are losing a very large part of their resources, that traditions are being disturbed there without anything to replace them, and that their economic life is becoming more difficult, while in departments which are becoming more populous, the standard of living is rising.

These are so many hypotheses. Each of them may be realized in one or another instance and we are in no position to choose among them. The fact indicated is what is essential. This helps us to understand why suicide rates tend to converge in the diverse regions of France. The rate of increase in suicides slackens in regions which are becoming populous and in which the proportion of suicides was highest. The rate accelerates in regions which are losing population and in which the proportion of suicides was lowest. Hence it is natural that disparities between regions are lessening and that the suicide rates are converging.

chapter 6

The distribution of suicides in Germany, Italy, and England

It would be interesting to research the distribution of suicides in other countries in a similar way, but for most of them we do not command data that are sufficiently continuous and detailed. The statistics of Germany, Italy, and England, however, are sufficiently reliable for us to calculate the coefficients of dispersion of their suicide rates. These additional measures will permit us to verify the general results we arrived at for France and for Europe, and even outside of Europe.

The distribution of suicides in Germany[1] in 1891–1900 is shown in relation to the population by districts (*Kreise*) on the map drawn by Father Krose.[2] We observe that the regions of Germany in which people kill themselves most frequently (more than 276 suicides per million inhabitants) are arranged from east to west in three short though rather large parallel bands. Included in the southernmost band is most of Silesia, on the two banks of the Oder, and especially on the south side (minus the Oppeln district),[3] the entire kingdom of Saxony, and the duchies of Saxony (Jena, Weimar, etc.) up to Hesse-Cassel. Further to the north, another band extends in a wide patch over the greater part of Brandenburg (limited by the Spree and hardly touching the Oder on the north), over the province of Saxony, and over the entire duchy of Brunswick (to the Weser). The third embraces all of Schleswig as well as Lübeck and Hamburg. Bremen is connected to it a little further to the west, like an islet. Thus, the region with the most frequent suicides in Germany is included between the Oder and the Weser. But Hanover, Mecklenburg, southern Brandenburg, Anhalt, Hildesheim, and Göttingen are not part of it at all. In contrast, the lowest suicide rates (less than 125 per million inhabitants) are found, going east, in Posnania, Pomerania, and most of West Prussia (except the Danzig region), going west, in Westphalia and the Rhine province, and going south, in Lower Franconia, Upper Palatinate, and Lower Bavaria.

This distribution has hardly changed since the middle of the nineteenth century. In 1849–58 the regions in which the highest suicide rates are found are the kingdom of Saxony, first, followed by the district of Berlin, the province of Saxony, Brandenburg, and Silesia. In 1903–13 the order is the district of Berlin, the kingdom of Saxony and Brandenburg (same rate), the provinces of Saxony, Schleswig-Holstein (which does not appear in German statistics until 1871–80, in the second rank) and Silesia: taken two at a time, they have not changed ranks at all.[4] As to the regions where the suicide rate is lowest, proceeding from the minimum, they are in 1849–58: the Rhine province, Westphalia, Posnania, West Prussia, and Bavaria; in 1903–13: Posnania, Westphalia, West Prussia, and the Rhine province; then East Prussia, with Bavaria almost on the same rank. Württemberg, Baden, Hanover, Pomerania, Hesse-Nassau, and Mecklenburg-Schwerin kept their intermediate position from one period to the next (see Map 3).

Map 3   *Suicides in Germany in 1903–13 per million inhabitants*

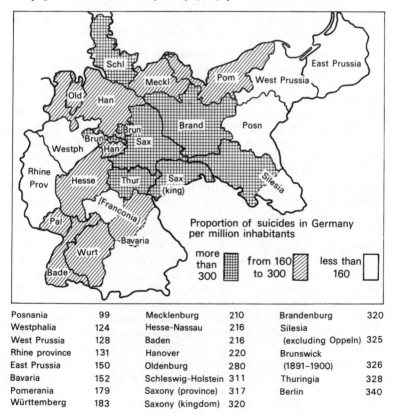

Posnania	99	Mecklenburg	210	Brandenburg	320
Westphalia	124	Hesse-Nassau	216	Silesia	
West Prussia	128	Baden	216	(excluding Oppeln)	325
Rhine province	131	Hanover	220	Brunswick	
East Prussia	150	Oldenburg	280	(1891–1900)	326
Bavaria	152	Schleswig-Holstein	311	Thuringia	328
Pomerania	179	Saxony (province)	317	Berlin	340
Württemberg	183	Saxony (kingdom)	320		

Father Krose reproduced numbers showing the suicide rate for the periods 1849–58 and 1871–80 and the year 1900 for 14 Prussian provinces (only 12 in the first period) in Table XX, p. 88, and for 11 German states other than Prussia in Table XXV, p. 100. We eliminated the province of Hohenzollern, whose absolute numbers of suicides is insignificant, and four states, Brunswick, Thuringia, the Hanseatic cities, and Alsace-Lorraine, for which suicides are not shown for the first two periods. We calculated the same average rates for the period 1903–13 for the same provinces and states from tables published annually in the *Statistik des Reiches*.[5] These numbers enable us to find for each period the average suicide rate of these twenty provinces and states and the coefficients of dispersion (Table 6.1).

Table 6.1   *Suicide rates in Germany*

	1849–58	1871–80	1891–1900	1903–13
Average suicide rate	128	178	209	219
Coefficient of dispersion	35	32.3	30.3	28.2

As we see, the degree of dispersion of the suicide rates, already very low in the first period, diminished continuously and perceptibly from, in relative numbers, for instance, 100 to 81. This amounted to a coefficient of dispersion equal to 32.3* in 1871–80 in Germany, to a coefficient clearly higher in France in the same period, 43.5, or a ratio of 100 to 134. (Recall that the degree of convergence is the inverse of the coefficient of dispersion.) We add that 7 states or provinces out of 17 had a suicide rate superior to the average in the first period, 8 out of 20 in 1871–80, 9 out of 20 in 1891–1900, and 9 out of 20 in 1903–13. The distribution of the suicide rates of diverse regions around the average also tends to become more regular.

Let us examine the proportion by which suicide rates increased during the past sixty years within each Prussian province (the general increase being 68 per cent for Prussia) and in each of the German states. We find a very rapid increase in the Rhine province (162 per cent) and in Westphalia (111 per cent), where voluntary deaths were, and still are, the fewest. (Suicide rates in Posnania and West Prussia increased only moderately during this time, by 51 and 66 per cent.) The increase continues to be very rapid in Baden (96 per cent), in Württemberg (83 per cent), in Bavaria and Hanover (80 per cent in each), countries where it is rather rare for people to kill themselves. In the kingdom of

---

* In the original 3.23, a typographical error – Tr.

Saxony, where more people killed themselves in 1849–58 than in all of Germany, the increase in the suicide rate is lowest (30 per cent). Saxony's rate is now exceeded only by Berlin and Brandenburg, whose increase is average, 61 and 70 per cent. These indications suffice. The increasing convergence of suicide rates is explained principally by the rapid or very rapid increase of suicides in regions where it was the least widespread and the much slower increase in regions where it was most widespread. (The exceptions are few: East and West Prussia, Pomerania, and Posnania.)[6]

A line may be drawn across Italy from a point on the coast of the Adriatic Sea, situated halfway between Ravenna and Ancona, to another point on the coast of the Tyrrhenian Sea, halfway between Ostia and Gaeta. The number of people situated west of this line who are determined to put themselves to death is, of course, fewer than in Germany or France, but is almost as many as in Austria and Sweden, and almost as many as in France and Germany forty years ago. A lower but reasonable rate of suicide, such as is appropriate to a people caught up in the stream of modern life. East of this line, on the other hand, as well as in Sicily and Sardinia, the proportion of voluntary deaths is extremely low, though not as low as or below that in Russia. In 1827–43 suicides in a few provinces in the south of France (Gascony, Languedoc) were also scattered. Italy, though quite closely related to the European countries in this respect, is again far behind them.

The suicide rate in 16 Italian provinces is found in Father Krose for two periods, 1864–76 and 1894–1900, and in Mario Bonsegna for the period 1905–14.[7] The finding is that during these three periods, the line of separation described above between provinces having high and those having low suicide rates has not moved. There have been some changes of rank within the first group. In 1905–14 Liguria (Genoa) moved to the head of the list: this long black belt seems to be a continuation of the dark band of Provence. Interrupted by Tuscany, it covers as well all of Latium (Rome), which occupies the second rank. Piedmont, with an almost equal suicide rate, comes immediately after it. In 1864–76 Emilia (Parma, Modena, and Bologna) outdistances the others: Piedmont was then in the fifth rank. Today Emilia comes immediately after Piedmont: then come Tuscany and Lombardy, which have hardly dropped one rank, while Veneto and Umbria have not budged: they end the series of provinces included in the first group. In the second, Basilicata, Calabria, and Sardinia have insignificant numbers of suicides in 1864–76 so that their rank in this period can be ignored. In the following two periods Sardinia, Sicily, and Campania head the list of the second group, and the

four other provinces (Basilicata, Abruzzo, Apulia, and Calabria)
follow them a little at random. Badly adapted to modern life, their
names evoke a past of savagery and brigandage.

As before, we calculated the average suicide rate for Italy for the
three periods, and the coefficient of dispersion of the numbers
corresponding to each province (Table 6.2). By setting the
coefficient of dispersion equal to 100 in the first period, we find
that it falls to 90 in the second, and to 77 in the third.

Table 6.2   *Suicide rates in Italy*

	1864–76	1894–1900	1905–14
Average suicide rate	30	60	77
Coefficient of dispersion	41.5	37.5	32

Table 6.3   *Proportion of suicides in Italian provinces in relative numbers*

	100 = rate in the 1st period In the 2nd period	100 = rate in the 2nd period In the 3rd period
Liguria	215	149
Latium	246	120
Piedmont	240	137
Emilia	159	100
Tuscany	203	112
Lombardy	170	132
Veneto	186	137
Umbria	185	137
Marches	190	105
Sardinia	(390)	117
Sicily	229	134
Campania	181	139
Basilicata	160	188
Abruzzo	207	134
Apulia	200	134
Calabria	234	126

In the first period 9 provinces out of 16 have a suicide rate superior to the average; in the second, 6, and in the third, 8. In 1864–76 suicides are so rare in the provinces of the second group that the average is extraordinarily low. The increase in suicide rates from one period to the next in different provinces is represented in Table 6.3 in relative numbers. The provinces are ranked in order of the decreasing size of their suicide rates.

The increase from the first to the second period in the proportion of suicides for the whole kingdom is 97 per cent, while from the second to the third period it is 31 per cent.

We find that the averages of the growth rates between the first and the second period are: for the first five provinces (high rate), 112.6 per cent; for the next five (medium rate), 83 per cent; for the last six (low rate), 102 per cent. From the second to the third period, the averages of the growth rates are, respectively, 24, 21, and 42.5 per cent.

Thus, during the second period the suicide rates mount, above all in the high- and low-rate provinces and much less in those occupying an intermediate position. In the third period the suicide rate mounts in the same proportions for the high- and medium-rate provinces, but much less than in the low-rate provinces.

Table 6.4 *Proportion of suicides in England per million inhabitants*[8]

	1861–70	1872–6	1920–6	Rate of increase from 1st to 3rd periods (per cent)	Rank order in the 1st period	2nd period
London	80.9	85.70	118	46	2	1
Southeast	82.7	85.34	113	36	1	2
South central	61.3	67.09	100	63	6	7
Southwest	57	55.82	98	72	9	9
West central	56.9	64.39	99	74	10	8
East	59.8	68.43	110	85	7	
North central	76.8	79.89	110	44	3	3.4
Northwest	65	69.45	102	56	4	6
Yorkshire	62.2	72.07	104	67	5	5
North	57.3	65.49	84	46	8	10
Wales	31.6	42.06	76	140	11	11

In sum, these suicide rates appear less dispersed than in France at corresponding periods, but more so than in Germany. England brings us a surprise.

Krose reproduced a table in which Morselli showed the suicide rates for the two periods, 1861–70 and 1872–6, in eleven regions. We calculated the suicide rates in the same regions for the period 1920–6[9] and so were able to compile Table 6.4.

We calculated simple and adjusted coefficients of dispersion of these suicide rates, obtaining the results shown in Table 6.5. (We

Table 6.5   *Dispersion of suicide rates in England*

	Suicides in England			Relative numbers		
	1861–70	1872–6	1920–6	1861–70	1872–6	1920–6
Average suicide rate	63	68	101	100	108	160
Simple coefficient of dispersion	16.8	13	8.7	100	77	51.5
Adjusted coefficient of dispersion	15	10.7	7.8	100	71.5	52

also show the average suicide rate for all of England.) These coefficients of dispersion are very low when compared to those found in France, Italy, or even Germany. The adjusted coefficient of dispersion in France in 1910–13 is 30.5, or double the adjusted coefficient found in England in 1861–70. In Germany the simple coefficient in 1903–13 is 28.2, or more than double the simple coefficient in England in 1872–6. Table 6.6 permits us to compare the four countries we have studied.

Might these great differences have been due to the fact that the groups of counties formed by Morselli were too few? We calculated the simple coefficient of dispersion of the suicide rates in the 44 counties in 1920–6 in order to have a standard of comparison. Instead of 8.7 for the eleven groups of counties we found 11.1, which is about the same order of magnitude. (We recall that in Germany we compared 21 provinces and states and, in France, 20 groups of departments.)

We must therefore assume that the tendency to suicide is much more uniform in the English counties than in the French departments, the Italian provinces, or the German states and provinces. England would be more homogeneous, and conformity to customs and beliefs greater here than in Germany, and evidently greater in Germany than in France or Italy.

We prepared a map of suicide in the various counties of England and Wales for the period 1920–6. Without going into as

Table 6.6   *Simple coefficients of dispersion (relative numbers in parentheses)*

	1872–6	42.3 (100)
France	1893–1900	40.5 (96)
	1910–13	34.5 (81.5)
	1864–76	41.5 (100)
Italy	1894–1900	37.5 (90)
	1905–14	32 (77)
	1871–80	32.3 (100)
Germany	1891–1900	30.3 (94)
	1903–13	28.2 (87.5)
	1861–70	16.8 (100)
England	1872–6	13 (77)
	1920–6	8.7 (51.5)

much detail as in our study of suicides in France, we will indicate the general observations suggested by it.

Demangeon says:[10]

> The British relief map is characterized both by separation into small parcels and low elevation. It juxtaposes in a small territory parcels both high and low in elevation. This frequent contact and repeated distinction between highlands and lowlands is unique to this country. A source of local contrasts, it multiplies the small natural units and distinctive regional characteristics.

Will we find as much contrast here as in France between the mountainous countrysides and the wastelands, where suicides are few, and the valleys and the plains, where they are frequent? It must be noted that, because of the intensive industrialization of England, the same counties sometimes contain both mountainous regions and very numerous industrial establishments. However, some contrasts are very quickly revealed.

Wales has the fewest voluntary deaths. The average suicide rate in England in this period is 104, but drops to 78 in the south and to 75 in the north of this region. Now Wales (p. 177),

> a peninsula covered by mountains, belongs to the highlands of western Britain and is isolated, rugged, and savage. Aside from valleys which shelter trees and fields and coastal borders where there is fertile soil, it offers people only vast reaches of denuded wastelands.

Wales makes one think of French Brittany, but is harsher and more savage. It used to be more isolated than it is today. In 1870 the suicide rate was 40, or only 60 relative to the average, set equal to 100, instead of 74 fifty years later, in the period we are studying. To find a lower rate one would have to turn to Scotland, which counted 33 voluntary deaths per million inhabitants in 1871–5 and 66 in 1920–6, and it must be still lower in the Scottish highlands since two-thirds of Scotland's inhabitants are crowded in the lowlands around Glasgow and Edinburgh.

Let us travel to the north of England. Suicide rates are low in all the mountainous counties of Cumberland, Northumberland, and Durham. They rise in proportion as one descends into Liverpool and Manchester, the industrial and commercial region of Lancashire that the Pennine chain separates from Yorkshire. An agglomeration of five million people lives here: the suicide rate equals the average for England, and remains almost the same further south in Cheshire, where industrial activity is also considerable. To the east, in the North Riding and West Riding of Yorkshire[11] (Middlesbrough, Leeds, Halifax, and Sheffield), and towards the south in Nottinghamshire, is another region where dense agglomerations are grouped around mills and factories. Here, too, the suicide rate is higher than or equal to the average. In none of these counties is it possible to distinguish the mountainous parts from the lower plains. The most dense settlements are in the foothills, with densities diminishing further up.

None of this holds true of the East Riding of Yorkshire and Lincolnshire, to the north and south of the Humber on the east coast. Here the suicide rate clearly drops. This region is entirely covered with 'wolds' (forests and woods) and 'fens' (marshes).[12] The Lincolnshire Wolds run along their western border. Great industrial centers are not encountered here. These counties are too far west to be influenced by Manchester and Sheffield and too far north to be influenced by London. They contrast sharply with Norfolk and Suffolk. One encounters this on descending southeast to the extensive peninsular hump which projects between the Wash and the Thames. Here is where suicides are the most numerous (128 and 122 per million, while the average is 104). Demangeon says (p. 219):

> Great plains, almost unrelieved, slope gently towards the North Sea. This is East Anglia, the country of large-scale farming, the only one in all of Britain to resist extension of the sheepherding economy and conquest by grass. Fields of wheat often cover half of it.

On these cultivated plains the population is rather dense around Norwich and Ipswich and nothing there impedes the movement of people. 'Towards the south, the more the covering of glacial clay becomes thinner and less continuous, the more one sees the pleasing country landscape of the "moors" (heathlands and lands of furze) and the woods of Essex that Constable and Gainsborough painted' (p. 221). Simultaneously the suicide rate clearly diminishes, even dropping below the average.

Now we reach the estuary of the Thames and the region situated to the south of London. Here, 'the rise of urban life is due not to the earth but to the sea. The peninsula of Kent advances toward the continent. Further west, the estuary of Southampton opens a route towards the Midlands.' It is the sea that has formed all these towns on the border of the Channel, in Kent, Sussex, and Hampshire. London has made satellites of them, however.

> Crowds fleeing the great city find refuge in all the coastal towns, even the ports, during the summer months, and in the interior towns all the year round. Pressed against one another, here and there to the point of touching, they form a zone of luxury and elegance, like an esplanade for amusements or sports. From a ship which hugged the coast one would see a procession of them from Kent to Dorset.

Now this is one of the regions where suicides are most numerous, as frequent as, or more frequent than in London. Suicides are much fewer in Surrey, which is near London but far from the sea. In this county there are woods, barren soil, and humid lowlands intersected by hills (the 'downs').

A map showing the distribution of lowlands, plains, hills, and mountains in the part of England bounded by Manchester and Birmingham to the north, Cambridge and London to the east, and Wales to the west, aids remarkably in understanding the map of suicides in the same region. Immediately after the region south of London that we have just discussed, sailing along the Channel coast, one arrives at Dorset, where the suicide rate is low, 92, below the average of 104. From there, going north, one crosses Wiltshire, where it drops even further, to 78; then Gloucestershire, Oxfordshire, and Berkshire, where it remains low (90, 85, and 95): a white patch, very clearly delineated. Now Dorset is covered with hills; the Cotswolds traverse the region of Gloucester and Oxford, 'limestone plateaus between the valleys of the Severn and the Thames.... There are urban centers (rural towns) only in the deep valleys which enclose them at the edge of the plains.' Finally, in Wiltshire and Berkshire run the Marlborough Downs. Further on, in Buckinghamshire (suicide rate, 102) and in Bedfordshire (82), extend the massive and chalky slopes of the Chiltern Hills. On the map the regions where people kill themselves least correspond to the white trails of the hills and slopes.[13]

In the long peninsula to the southwest where England ends

> There are two thoroughly different regions: to the west is the plateau of primitive rocks growing progressively thinner as one advances to the sea. To the east is a low plain, a true extension of the English plain .... By virtue of their irregular plateaus, Devon and Cornwall (suicide rates of 87 and 106, respectively low and average) belong to the mountain range of the ancient west. By virtue of its plain, Somerset (a rather high rate of 112) recalls the countryside of the Midlands. (Worcestershire, 106; Warwickshire, 100; Leicestershire, 110.)[14]

We have completed the full tour of England. The center remains to be explored, especially that part of the English plain called the Midlands which is bounded on the west by the Welsh mountain range, on the north by the Pennine range, and on the south by the chalky coast of the wolds. Here we find that suicide rates are lower in the grazing regions than in the farming country.

> If one excepts the moors and the woods of certain rocky districts in the counties of Warwick and Stafford (suicide rates of 100 and 97, a little below the average of 104), the Midlands enclose soil which is hard to plough but excellent for grain.

All during the nineteenth century, however, England continued to turn to grass, to pasture, above all in the more coastal and humid west, while the east is more continental, drier, and warmer.

> In the plains bordered by the counties of Leicester, Rutland, Northampton, Huntingdon, and Bedford (toward the east Midlands) one still sees vast cultivated fields of corn and barley worked and harvested by machines. One already senses their proximity to the eastern counties which are devoted to cereal plants [*ibid.*, p. 210].

The average of the suicide rates in the four counties rises to 115.[15]

> Everywhere else in the west, however, the exploitation of the land is dominated by the pastoral tendency. Permanent pastures cover more than half of the total extent of Leicester, Warwick, Shropshire, Worcester, and Gloucester, representing more than double the agriculture. The fields are immense grasslands, pastured or mown. The arable surface in

Staffordshire dropped 70 per cent between 1794 and 1912. The land put to grass more than quadrupled.

The average of the suicide rates in these counties drops to 103 (to 102 if Leicester, which straddles these two regions, is excluded). In Stafford, in particular, it falls to 97. These grazing regions are rich. It is an abundant land 'in a country fortunate beyond all others.' There are farms, picturesque villages, and towns throughout the length of the valleys. To be sure, the towns are of ordinary dimensions. One has only to compare two maps showing the distribution of British towns in 1801 and 1921 to find that while the large towns to the south, east, northeast, and north of London increase, they hardly do so to the west.[16]

> In the Midlands is an entire swarm of old, small, market towns, formerly fought over by Danes and Saxons, whose names recur often in the history of warfare: Stafford, Warwick, Worcester, Nottingham, Bedford, Leicester, Derby. The past persists in the characteristics of their appearance and still resists the severe leveling of the present [*ibid.*, p. 281].

The region is relatively sheltered by the nature of its economy, which holds people to the soil. Holdings are small parcels in a series of rather isolated valleys. This is what distinguishes them from the aggregate of counties grouped to the south, east, and north of London. Indeed, it is toward this tranquil west of pleasant, fruit-bearing gardens and fresh and verdant plains that the aristocratic element of the great English metropolis turns, far from the bustle to the east.

This represents only a rough sketch of what a study of the relationship between the distribution of voluntary deaths and the structure of the soil in England could be. Such as it is, it confirms and gives precision to findings we have been led to by the same study pursued in France. To be sure, one could have expected that, in a country as industrialized as England, geographic influences would be nullified by the fact that in many regions people have imposed the mark of their activity on the soil. For example, the Pennine chain spreads over the entire north of England, covering part of Lancashire and Yorkshire and descending very far south. Suicides, however, remain at an average level. That is because the whole region from Newcastle to Liverpool and Manchester is also populated by industrial establishments. Coal seams crop out in these mountainous counties, so that the presence of mountains, though ordinarily a sign of dispersion and an obstacle to the circulation of people, is here both cause and indication of their concentration and multiplies social relationships. Elsewhere, few people kill themselves in regions traversed or intersected by hills, coasts, cliffs, moors, grasslands, or grazing lands. More people kill themselves in the lower plains and in the open country where extensive fields of cereal foods are grown.

We showed a less than average rate of increase in suicides from 1872–6 to 1911–13 in departments of France whose population increased most rapidly, and a more than average rate of increase in the most depopulated departments. Is this the case in England? Let us consider the two periods 1870–6 and 1920–6. We formed a group of twelve counties[17] whose suicide rate was above average in 1872–6 and whose population increased during the next fifty years from 69 to 380 per cent while the average increase in the English population as a whole was 64 per cent. The average increase in suicide rates in these counties from one period to the next was 25.5 per cent, instead of 58 per cent for England as a whole.[18]

We formed a second group of 14 counties whose suicide rate was equal to or lower than the average and whose population either increased much less than the average for England as a whole, or diminished: 7 counties increased from 6 to 40 per cent, 7 diminished from 2 to 32 per cent. The average increase in their suicide rates was 81 per cent, instead of the 58 per cent for England as a whole, that is, a 70 per cent increase in the departments where the population increased little and a 90 per cent increase in the departments where the population decreased. Thus, the law we formulated is truly verified.

chapter 7

The distribution of suicides in cities and countryside

In studying how suicides are distributed, we have thus far confined ourselves to regional or political divisions, that is, to nations, or to states, provinces, counties, and departments within a given nation. Might the same problem not be posed, however, within each of these divisions by relating suicide rates to the urban and rural population and to the population of large, average, and small cities, that is, to the size and density of human settlements? Suicide is widely believed to be especially evident within the great urban centers, while the countryside is subjected to the influence and contagion of the large cities. What shall we think of this?

Father Krose studied the relation between population density and suicide rather closely, arriving at essentially negative results. However, population density must not be confused with degree of agglomeration. In Table XXI of his book he ranks 22 countries according to their population density and frequency of suicides in 1891–5. From these data we calculated the average effective distance between these two rankings:[1] the opposition being measured by 11, the independence by 5.5, we find an average distance equal to 6.3, that is, no correspondence. Note particularly that France ranks 10th in population density and 2nd in suicide, and Germany, respectively, 6th and 4th. He similarly compares 71 small states and large electoral districts in Germany for 1891–1900. We calculated the average distance between the two rankings, by density and suicide rate, for these also. The opposition being measured at 35.5, the independence at 17.75, we find an average distance equal to 19.70: no trace of correspondence. This, however, we repeat, is not at all surprising. It is the population of the cities and the countryside which we would have to compare with respect to suicide.

Father Krose has indeed done this, but by comparisons which could not lead to findings. Defining communities of more than 2,000 inhabitants as urban, he ranks 19 European states by the proportion of their total population which is urban and by their suicide rates. The opposition between these two columns is 9.5; the independence is 4.75, for an effective average distance of 5.52. The result is again negative. The same thing happens if these countries are ranked by the proportion of their total population in cities of more than 50,000, and by their suicide rates: opposition, 9.5; independence, 4.5; average effective distance, 5.15. There is no correspondence. The reason for this is that each country in a given period has a suicide rate appropriate to it which, while partly due to the size of the urban population, also reflects the influence of other and possibly more important factors. In any given country, however, there may be a very strong difference between the suicide rate in the countryside and in the cities, especially the large cities.

Hardly anything has been published up to now on urban and rural suicide rates, other than very fragmentary information. A table reproduced by Morselli gives relative suicide rates in the cities, assuming the rural suicide rate equal to 100:[2] Prussia (1849–1856–1858): 184; Saxony (1859–63): 146; Italy (1877–8): 227; Belgium (1851–5 and 1858–60): 181.[3]

Table 7.1   *Urban and rural suicide rates in France*[4]

	Per million inhabitants		Relative urban suicide rate (100 = rural suicide rate)
	urban suicides	rural suicides	
1866–9	202	104	195
1870–2	161	110	146
1873–6	217	118	184
1884–7	268	171	156
1891–2	287	194	148
1897–1902	260	186	140
1905–11	264	215	122
1919–20	219	192	114

It would have been of greater interest, though hardly possible at the time Morselli wrote, to observe the evolution of this relationship in a large country over an extended period. French statistics show annually the absolute number of suicides in cities and in the countryside (communities smaller than 2,000 inhabitants). Neither Krose nor Durkheim used these figures. We calculated the suicide rates in French cities and countryside and their ratio for the largest possible number of years to compile the statistics shown in Table 7.1.

The figures in the third column show that the distance between urban and rural suicide rates was very great at first (over nine-tenths), but diminished steadily, falling to a seventh.[5]

The rural population in France is known to have decreased greatly since over a half century ago. We were curious to discover whether the decrease in the distance between urban and rural suicide rates was proportionate to the decrease in the rural population (Table 7.2).

Table 7.2   *Urban and rural suicide rates in France*

Urban suicide rate (100 = rural suicide rate)		Rural population (100 = urban population)	
1873–6	184	1881	187
1897–1902	148	1901	144
1919–1920	114	1921	116

There is certainly a very strong correspondence between these series. They appear to support the proposition stated previously that suicide increases in regions or groups whose population is diminishing, and conversely. However, the question again arises whether this is because the group with diminishing population loses those of its members who were the least inclined to suicide, or because it is more fully open to influences coming from the group which is growing.

In Sweden, if the proportion of rural suicides is set equal to 100, the rates for the cities[6] are as follows:

1821–30	315
1851–60	225
1881–90	230
1911–15	168
1922–3	124

The distance between city and countryside diminished continuously and much more rapidly than in France.

Lastly, we compiled the Table 7.3 on suicides in Czechoslovakia in 1920: the population figures are from the census taken on 15 February 1921. All calculations are ours.

Table 7·3　*Suicides in Czechoslovakia in 1920*

	Population of cities of more than 10,000 inhabitants (percentage of the total population)	Suicide rates in		Total	Ratio of the suicide rate in cities over 10,000 inhabitants to the rate in other municipalities[7]
		cities over 10,000 population	the other municipalities		
	1	2	3	4	5
Bohemia	22.5	432	280	320	154
Moravia	22.2	310	192	218	162
Silesia	15.8	330	136	167	242
Slovakia	11.1	290	70	94	415
Russia (Subcarpathian)	11.1	314	60	87	522
Czechoslovakia	19.1	378	198	233	190

The numbers in column 2 are seen to be much closer than those in column 3: the coefficients of dispersion are 11.5 for cities of more than 10,000 inhabitants (3.5 if Bohemia and Prague are discarded) and 48 for the other municipalities. On the other hand, the suicide rate in the 'other municipalities' diminishes extremely rapidly as one goes from provinces where the urban population is largest to where it is smallest. Finally, the distance between urban and rural suicide rates increases even more rapidly as one goes from regions where cities are numerous to where they are few. Large cities do indeed appear to influence the suicide rates in the surrounding region and in proportion to size.[8]

This is especially noticeable in the province of Bohemia, which alone accounts for almost half of the Czechoslovakian population (more than $6^{1}/_{2}$ of $13^{1}/_{2}$ million inhabitants). Calculating for this province the ratio of the suicide rate in cities over 10,000 to the rate in the other towns, assumed equal to 100, yields the following results:

1919	302
1920	154
1923	132
1924	122
1925	116
1926	122

An almost continuous tendency seems to have developed during this eight-year period toward equalization of the suicide rates of the large cities and the towns in Bohemia.[9]

One of the salient facts of modern times is the appearance of large cities of over 50,000 and 100,000 inhabitants. Do people in very large cities kill themselves more often than those in average-size cities? Does this difference diminish from one period to the next?

Comparing the suicide rate in very large cities to the rate for an entire country is inaccurate. Father Krose enumerated suicide rates in a number of large cities. In Paris, for example, there were 315 voluntary deaths in 1896–1900 per million inhabitants, while for France as a whole there were only 238 during the same period. Setting the suicide rate in France equal to 100, the relative Parisian suicide rate then equals 132. But if we set at 100 the suicide rate in the region constituted by Aube, Eure-et-Loir, Marne, Seine, Seine-et-Marne, Seine-et-Oise, and Yonne, in 1893–1900 this rate rises to 460 and the rate for Paris falls to 68. Relative to the proportion of suicides in Seine-et-Oise in 1896–1900, or 490, it falls to 64. Relative to the same proportion in Seine, it reaches only 68. The same is true of Vienna and Austria: if the suicide rate in Austria is

100, the suicide rate in Vienna in 1896–1900 is 190. However, comparing Vienna and Lower Austria, Vienna's rate is 110. Compared to Prussia, the rate in Berlin would be 146, but comparing Berlin to Brandenburg, Berlin's rate would be 94 – always in relative numbers, that is, representing Brandenburg's suicide rate by 100. The relative rate for Berlin when compared with the district of Potsdam is 83. Comparing Hamburg in 1896–1900 with Germany, the relative suicide rate is 152, but comparing it to Schleswig-Holstein, 97. The rate for Munich is nearly the same when compared to Bavaria, 145, or to Upper Bavaria, 148. The comparison of Nuremberg with Bavaria, however, would give 181, and with Middle Franconia, 134. The comparison of Breslau with Prussia would give 194, but with the extended district of Silesia, of which it is the judicial seat, 132. Frankfurt's relative suicide rate is 174 when compared with Prussia, 158 when compared with the district of Wiesbaden. Cologne's rate is 160 when compared with the Rhineland and 146 when compared with the district of Cologne. Compared to Württemberg, Stuttgart has a rate of 134, but 100 when compared to the district of Neckar. For Hanover, if compared to Prussia, it is 138; compared to the district of Hanover, 131.[10] London in 1872–6 had a suicide rate relative to England of 122. (According to annual figures published by Morselli, the rates for 1865–70 and 1871–6 were, respectively, 132 and 128.) In 1920–6, its relative rate was 114. Compared to the group of counties including Surrey, Kent, Sussex, Essex, and Middlesex, London had a suicide rate equal to 90 in 1872–6 and to 109 in 1920–6.[11]

There appears to be less difference between the suicide rate of the great cities and the others when only a limited region is considered. This may be true not only because the large city manifests the characteristics of the region to which it belongs but also because the region has experienced the influence of the big city for some time.[12] Moreover, the numbers just cited do indeed indicate that, with some exceptions, capital cities especially, more people kill themselves in large than in medium-size cities. *La Revue hongroise de statistique* published a table which has enabled us to calculate the proportion of voluntary deaths in Germany from 1920 to 1923 inclusive: 225 in cities of 15,000 to 30,000, 238 in cities of 30,000 to 50,000, 225 in cities of 50,000 to 100,000, and 278 in cities over 100,000, or, respectively, 100, 106, 100, and 124. Forty-five years earlier, in 1876, Morselli had reproduced these suicide rates in Germany: 195 in cities below 20,000, 236 in those between 20,000 to 100,000, and 313 in those over 100,000. The second and the last can be represented by 100 and 132. Although the gap has narrowed, cities with over 100,000 inhabitants always have a higher suicide rate than the others.[13]

Table 7.4   *Suicides in large Italian cities*[14]

	Average suicide rate[15]		Relative difference between the city and the province[16]	
	1896–1900	1901–1914	1896–1900	1901–1914
7 large cities (where the distance between the urban and provincial rates is maximal)				
Naples, Milan, Catania, Venice, Turin, Padua, and Bologna	176	199	272	237.4
		(an increase of 13%)	(a diminution of 12.5%)	
8 large cities (where the distance between urban and provincial rates is average)				
Rome, Genoa, Florence, Leghorn, Bari, Pisa, Brescia, and Perugia	141	171	187	182
		(increase of 21%)	(diminution of 2.5%)	
5 large cities (where the distance between urban and provincial rates is minimal)				
Ferrara, Lucca, Modena, Alexandria, and Ravenna	92	125	95	119
		(increase of 36%)	(increase of 25%)	

These facts are too fragmentary to answer the second question, whether the difference in the suicide rates between large cities and smaller ones tends to lessen. After much searching we finally succeeded in obtaining two tests. The second is more important in every way, but we reproduce the first because it concerns a country, Italy, whose urban population is increasing very rapidly, and which is also the only one for which we possess suicide figures on an important number of large cities.

From a table compiled by Mario Bonsegna we have taken the suicide rates in the 23 largest cities in Italy and compared them with the suicide rates in the provinces of these cities for two consecutive periods lasting almost twenty years: 1896–1900 and 1901–14. In Table 7.4 we have classified them by size in three categories. Recall that the suicide rate for the whole of Italy increased between the first and second periods from 61.7 per million inhabitants to 73.3, or by 19 per cent. The increase was clearly less in the 7 large cities of the first group: the distance between the cities and the provinces diminished in almost exactly the same ratio. The average suicide rate increased almost three times as much in the 5 large cities of the third group, and the distance between these cities and the provinces increased almost in the same ratio. Finally, the increase in the average suicide rate in the second group almost equals that for all Italy and the distance between the cities and provinces has diminished very little.

The explanation of these variations most certainly lies in the unequal population of these cities. Each of the first seven has more than 148,000 inhabitants. (Naples with 564,000 inhabitants and Milan with 491,000 are the two largest in Italy.) The average size of these cities is 275,000 inhabitants; in the second group, 152,000; and in the third, less than 60,000 or 70,000. Only Rome, Genoa, and Florence in the second group exceed 200,000 inhabitants. In the third, only Ferrara attains 87,000 inhabitants. Thus, in provinces where the largest cities are found (and where the suicide rate is highest), the distance between city and province clearly tends to diminish. It is as if the influence of these large cities tended to establish a common moral level throughout the region. Local conditions do not at all explain this phenomenon since, except for Padua and Venice, both of which are in Veneto, the cities in the first group are distributed in different provinces. Five cities are found in the north (Piedmont, Lombardy, Veneto, Emilia) and two cities in the south (Naples and Sicily). In other large, though smaller, cities where the suicide rate was lowest and increased the most, the distance between city and province becomes greater in this respect. One's impression is that when a city begins to grow it soon differentiates itself plainly from the surrounding region as to proportion of voluntary deaths. Only when it has become very large and its suicide rate has become very high does the increase in suicides in the city tend to slacken, while increasing more rapidly in the surrounding region, probably influenced by the urban agglomeration.[17]

Map 4 *The distribution of cities in England in 1921 (according to Demangeon's map,* Iles Britanniques, *p. 218)*

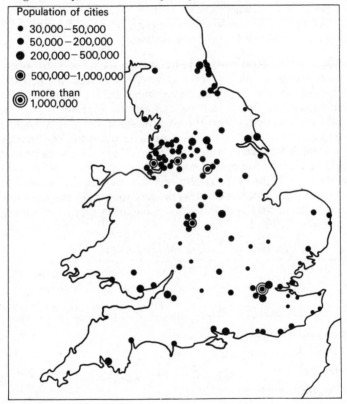

Population of cities

- 30,000–50,000
- 50,000–200,000
- 200,000–500,000
- 500,000–1,000,000
- more than 1,000,000

This Italian test covers only a rather limited period. The effect of large cities cannot be best observed in Italy, but unfortunately, neither in Germany nor in England are we shown in detail the progress of suicide in the large urban agglomerations.

It is possible, however, to isolate this type of influence in England by an indirect method. Demangeon says:

More than two-thirds of the inhabitants of the United Kingdom live in cities. Nowhere else in Europe is a like proportion to be

found, and nowhere else was it formed so quickly. Only
England went from 50 per cent urban in 1851 to 78* per cent in
1911.[18]

Now, the new cities particularly are built on coalfields in wild, and
barren country, in mountains, forests, and marshlands. Let us add
that

the modern city is only one of a series. It belongs to a group, to
a constellation. There are the cotton cities of Lancashire, the
wool cities of Yorkshire, the iron cities of the Midlands, and the
coal cities throughout the northeast.

If on Demangeon's map of England showing the distribution of
British cities a line is traced from Newcastle to Liverpool,
Liverpool to Birmingham, Birmingham to Nottingham, and
Nottingham to Newcastle, the majority of England's large cities
would be included within the quadrilateral (see Map 4). Another
group to the south and to the east of London are the 'parasite'
cities which revolve around the capital. Two sets of counties can
easily be formed to cover these two zones, plus two others, one to
the southwest, the other to the east, comprising almost all of the
rest of England. We researched the distribution of suicide rates in
these zones at fifty-year intervals, calculating their coefficients of
dispersion (Table 7.5; Map 5).

Table 7.5   *Distribution of suicide rates in England*

	Average suicide rate		Coefficient of dispersion[19]	
	1870–6	1920–6	1870–6	1920–6
1st group (Liverpool, Newcastle, Birmingham, etc.)	69	106	15.2	4.9
2nd group (London, Surrey, Kent, etc.)	83	113	16.8	5.6
3rd group (Plymouth, Oxford, etc.)	58	94	15.2	9.1
4th group (Norfolk, East Riding of Yorkshire, Cambridge, etc.)	69	107	12.9	12
England (total)	66	104	13	8.7

*In the original, 70 per cent, but compare note 18 – Tr.

Map 5 *The distribution of suicides in England in 1920–6*

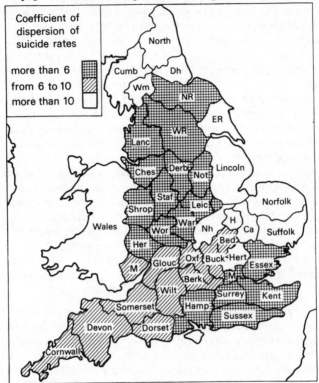

Proportion of suicides by county per million residents

1st group		2nd group		3rd group	
Worcester	106	London	118	Oxford	85
Warwick	100	Surrey	108	Gloucester	90
Stafford	97	Kent	114	Wiltshire	78
Shropshire	120	Sussex	124	Berkshire	95
Leicester	110	Hampshire	113	Dorset	92
Nottingham	104	Essex	100	Somerset	112
W. Riding of				Devon	106
Yorkshire	106			Cornwall	87
N. Riding of				Buckingham	102
Yorkshire	112			Middlesex	94
Lancashire	102			Bedford	82
Cheshire	99	4th group			
Hereford	100				
Rutland	111				
Derbyshire	95				

4th group			
Norfolk	128	Northampton	130
Suffolk	122	Durham	79
Lincoln	93	Northumberland	90
E. Riding of		Cumberland	88
Yorkshire	92	Westmorland	124
Huntingdon	102	Monmouthshire	79
Cambridge	108	North and South	
Hertford	111	Wales	77

Let us set the coefficient of dispersion for each group and for England in the first period equal to 100. In the second period it is 67 for England. For the first two groups (which contain the large majority of cities and the large cities especially) it falls to, respectively, 32.3 and 33.34; for the last two groups, where cities are fewest, to 59.9 and 93. Thus, in regions where cities make their influence most plainly felt, suicide rates converge much more quickly and tend toward a norm, while elsewhere these same coefficients of dispersion are very close to the average or exceed it. A fact worth noting is that in the north, where the industrial cities crowd against each other, and in the region south and east of London, where cities line the sunlit coast of the English Channel or group themselves in a ring around the outskirts of London, and are not simply industrial suburbs, a similar influence seems to make itself felt to the same extent, since, in both instances, the distance between the proportion of voluntary deaths has diminished by exactly two-thirds. Undoubtedly, some of them relieve London of industrial work: 'In Essex, at Silvertown, Stratford, Ilford, etc., there are workshops of mechanical engineering, chemical factories, refineries, and metallurgical factories.' Others

> join together with London to fulfill the functions of a great capital: arsenal and defense cities like Woolwich, Chatham, and Sheerness on the Thames, Dover on the Strait, Portsmouth on the Channel, and Greenwich with its observatory.... Still others are auxiliaries and branches of the great Thames port: naval stations of the capital, Queenborough, Port Victoria, Harwich, and Dover, where one embarks for Belgium, the Low Countries, and northern Europe: Dover, Folkestone, and Newhaven, where one embarks for France, and Southampton, where one embarks for France, North America, and South Africa.

There are also the vacation cities of seaside resorts and of sport: 'Cities of the moors and woodlands, like Epsom and Tunbridge Wells; innumerable coastal cities linked to London by rapid trains, Leigh, Southend, Margate, Ramsgate, Hastings, Eastbourne, and Brighton.' This whole coast is naught but the summer residence of part of London's population. This region is in sharp contrast to Lancashire or Yorkshire, where factory chimneys rise at all points on the horizon. Urban life seems to have extended its influence throughout both, however, to have almost entirely effaced local differences, and to have raised or lowered custom to the same uniform level everywhere. Fifty years ago people killed themselves more often in this corner of London than around Birmingham, Manchester, or Newcastle: 100 in the latter region, 112 in the former. Now the corresponding figures are 100 and 106. Perhaps this inequality expresses the difference between a purely industrial, urban population and one where diverse elements intermingle. In any case it has noticeably diminished. Most important is that these two regions, which are alike only in the predominance of cities, have converged in the extent of their urbanization. One finds in both a vast zone throughout which life is a burden to the same number of people.

Table 7.6 *Population density by region in England*

	Population in thousands	Area in square kilometers	Density per square kilometer
1st group (Liverpool, Newcastle, Birmingham, etc.)	14,115	35,312	400
2nd group (London, Surrey, Kent, etc.)	9,757	18,117	539
2nd group (London excluded)	5,273	17,814	295
3rd group (Plymouth, Oxford, etc.)	3,493	29,515	118
4th group (Norfolk, East Riding of Yorkshire, Cambridge, etc.)	2,148	21,315	100

Both the diversity and the internal homogeneity of each of these zones appear very plainly when their population density is calculated (Table 7.6). The population density in two of the ten counties in the first group, Shropshire and the West Riding of Yorkshire, is very low: 70 and 83. By contrast it is extremely high in Lancashire. Densities in the seven other counties vary between 570 in Warwickshire (Birmingham) and 220 (Worcestershire). The extremes in the five counties of the 2nd group (excluding London) are 497 (Surrey) and 192 (Sussex). In the nine counties of the 3rd group densities vary between 231 (Gloucestershire) and 90 (Dorset). Finally, densities vary in the six counties of the 4th group between 152 (East Riding of Yorkshire) and 57 (Huntingdonshire), averaging exactly 100. We have shown that the proportion of suicides varies least from county to county within the urban industrial group. Suicide rates here have converged the most rapidly over a fifty-year period. These counties are also distinguished by the extremely high population densities. A density close to this in 1919 is found in Germany only in the Saar (397). Not in the province of Saxony (311), nor in the province of the Rhine (276), nor in Westphalia (222) does the density come close to this.

We know that when several countries are ranked in order of their suicide rates and population density there appears to be no relationship between these two rankings. Here, however, we do find a clearly higher proportion of suicides in the first two groups, which contain more cities and where the population is denser than in the other two. In the industrial group in the north, however, though the density is greater, the proportion of suicides is lower than in the south (London excluded), the group with the heavy urban population. In the eastern counties, on the other hand (Norfolk, etc.), the suicide rate is higher but the density lower than in the western counties (Oxford, etc.), while a very clear relationship exists between population density and what may be called the dispersion of suicide rates. Suicides are distributed a little more uniformly in the first group where the density is higher than in the second (London excluded), and with clearly greater uniformity in the second than in the third, whose density is still lower, and a little more uniformly in the third than in the fourth, whose density is a bit lower still. Moreover, from the first to the second, as from the third to the fourth, the differences in these two respects are small. What is salient is the contrast between the counties which include the majority of the cities and the others as to: 1. the size of their suicide rates; 2. their distribution; 3. the rate at which the rates converge (among counties within the same group); 4. the population density.[20] This is indeed an important finding. We were able to establish this in England, though it might have been difficult to do so elsewhere because in no other country has the local concentration of industry advanced further.

Let us summarize briefly the conclusions to which these first researches have led us.

1. How do voluntary deaths vary in eleven European countries during the eighty years from 1834–45 to 1911–13? Except in Denmark and Norway the proportion of voluntary deaths increased greatly. In the majority of countries, however, · the maximum suicide rate appears to have been attained before the end of the period, to have fallen since then to a greater or lesser degree, and in no case to have risen above this level. We can assume that each country bears a maximum figure of suicides which is peculiar to it and which it does not exceed. There is no

evidence, therefore, that the growth of this phenomenon is unlimited, though the limit is different in each country.

2. How are these suicide rates distributed nationally? Do national differences remain constant or do they tend to converge or to diverge? We have found that the divergence between these countries in proportion of suicides at first increased, from 1836–45 to 1866–70, but afterwards diminished for forty years, that is, until 1911–13. This rise and fall can be measured by the simple coefficient of dispersion: 88 to 100 followed by 100 to 63. In any case, suicide rates in these European countries converged continuously for more than 60 years, except during the last war. This observation is confirmed by other tests extending over a shorter period but relating to different or more populous countries.

3. In France, the divergence between twenty provinces or groups of departments diminished continuously from 1872–6 to 1911–13 as measured by the numbers 100, 73.

4. When suicide rates in France are studied by departments and districts on the one hand, and by the geographic structure of the country on the other, suicide rates are found to increase in the great river valleys, along the major rivers, and along the coasts. They diminish in mountainous regions and wherever the movement of people seems less intensive. They are highest in the Paris basin, a highly centralized, well-defined natural region; very low around the mountains of the Massif Central and in the Midi (west of the Rhône to the Atlantic), where the not-well-developed river system offers no encouragement to the movement of people. Suicide rates are lower in the west, where the 'peasants' are more dispersed, than in the east, where villages multiply and the population is more agglomerated.

5. In France too, the increase slackens from 1872–6 to 1911–13 in the regions in the path of settlement, where the proportion of voluntary deaths is highest, and accelerates in the regions which are losing population or where this proportion is lowest. This law is also verified in England.

6. The divergence between the suicide rates in the Prussian provinces and the German states, very low from 1849–58, diminished continuously and very perceptibly until 1903–13 from, in relative numbers, 100 to 81. In the 16 provinces of Italy, an equal divergence diminished still more rapidly between 1864–76 and 1905–14 from, in relative numbers, 100 to 77. In England, the divergence between the suicide rates for 11 groups of counties, much weaker than even in Germany, decreases very strongly from 1861–70 to 1920–26, in relative numbers from 100 to 52 (adjusted coefficient of dispersion). Uniformity of customs, to the extent that

the suicide rate is an indicator of it, therefore appeared to be greater in England than in Germany, and in Germany than in Italy and France. These countries rank the same if ordered by the speed at which each achieves a common level of customs.

7. In England, as in France, there is a very clear relationship between the distribution of suicides and geographic structure and appearance. People kill themselves less often in regions traversed or intersected by hills, coasts, moors, and grasslands than in lowlands and counties where cereal fields extend. The suicide rate always remains rather high in mountainous regions where coalfields crop out.

8. In France in 1866–9 people kill themselves almost twice as often in cities of over 2,000 inhabitants as in the countryside. This difference diminishes steadily and very rapidly until 1919–20. If the suicide rate in the countryside is always represented by 100, the rate in the cities falls between the former period and the latter from 195 to 114.

9. Suicides are proportionately more numerous in large than in medium and small cities. If the large cities are compared, not with the entire country, but with the more limited region surrounding them, this difference tends to diminish from one period to the next. Especially is this true of the largest cities where suicide rates are highest.

10. In England from 1870–6 to 1920–6 the tendency to suicide has become much more uniform in the two zones where the majority of cities are concentrated (between Newcastle, Manchester and Birmingham, and in the southeast zone south of London) than in the two much less urban zones of the east and west. We also note that the social density (number of inhabitants per square kilometer) is much greater in the first two zones, and that the population has increased much more rapidly there.

Since Durkheim was so insistent on the social causes of suicide it is surprising that he did not grapple with the influence of urban life on the distribution of suicides except indirectly, as a digression. The reason is that he was mainly preoccupied with establishing that imitative contagion does not suffice to explain the distribution of voluntary deaths. He opposed Tarde's theory of the role of imitation in social life and assertions by Guerry and several other authors attributing the high number of suicides in the Ile-de-France and Champagne groups of departments to the influence of Paris. He cited certain precise details: for example, that more people kill themselves in the district of Meaux than in Seine, at Pont-Audemer than at Rouen, at Toulon and at Forcalquier than at Marseilles. He might likewise have noted that in 1870–6 this type of death was more frequent in all counties surrounding London than even in London. These, however, are only exceptions which it is possible to account for either by the demographic composition of the population of the capital cities, or by the fact that people originating in all parts of the country intermingle here.

However, in a country where cities grow and multiply, urban civilization exerts an influence beyond the limits of the city. In general, social habits become modified without imitation taking place. Durkheim himself distinguished two types of influence. 'Two or more contiguous departments,' he wrote, 'showed an equally strong tendency to suicide' without imitation. And again,

> This diffusion within a single region may well spring from an equal diffusion of certain causes favorable to the development of suicide, and from the fact that the social environment is the same throughout the region. To be assured that imitation causes the spread of a tendency or idea, one must see it leave the environments of its birthplace and invade regions not themselves calculated to encourage it.*

It is certainly not merely by chance that two or more neighboring departments of an entire group of contiguous counties are socially similar but rather because of the influence of social causes which have created this milieu: for example, by contributing a large number of new social uniformities, by mass displacements from one region to another, and by growth in the density of population over an extended area. There is no need to assume contagion or imitation if a uniform suicide rate tends to be established in several places. However, as contacts become more frequent among the large cities, which are rather closely related to one another anyway, as well as to the region which surrounds and separates them, the differences between them naturally become attenuated, as do even those between cities and countryside. That is because all these elements, large, medium, and small cities, and country towns, are now contained in a total system whose bases of operations and organic centers are to be found in big cities. At the same time, the diverse parts have a common tendency to reunite across the distances separating the most populated region. More precisely, the total system (rather than any particular part) puts a common stamp on the most concentrated parts of the population and on the smallest and most scattered communities within a given region. The railroads, the mail and telegraph, the telephones, the branch offices of banks and of large stores are not extended and expanded from large and medium cities to small localities because the latter have imitated the neighboring cities

Suicide, p. 133 – Tr.

and borrowed these institutions from them. They have not imitated; rather they have been assimilated, which is very different.

The imitator is, in fact, always more or less of a borrower. We take whatever mode of acting or thinking we imitate from another and adapt it to ourselves. Hence, one can remain oneself while imitating. In a genuine imitation, properly so called, one almost always does remain oneself. On the one hand, one chooses what one borrows. On the other hand, one adapts it to oneself, incorporates it into oneself. An imitated act dissolves in the substance of our volition. A thought taken from another intermingles with our other thoughts. Imitation (always understood in the narrow, that is, the precise sense of the term) always supposes on the part of the imitator that the path has been totally or half paved. It gives people the means of developing dispositions or of manifesting qualities and capabilities which were latent. They are often novel and always capable of numerous variations and personal nuances. The assimilation of a small social unit by one or more larger social units results in annexation of a small town, a small half-rural locality into an urban current of life. There, it is seized and carried along, not selecting what it reproduces, for all of it is confined within the totality of enveloping institutions, customs, and beliefs. It is not free to commit itself half way. It does not borrow, for what is borrowed is altered in a certain manner by the addition to it of oneself. The small social unit is obliged to give itself totally, not to a unit of the same nature as itself, differing from it only in degree, but to a totality of which both units are only parts. One style of life, uniform or tending toward uniformity, is substituted for another over the entire extent of a vast region.

Thus, a group of migrants from very different regions blend into a new group, lacking a past or traditions of its own, to form an urban civilization which they have not brought with them, which is not the result of a compromise between the customs and ways of different lives. Neither does it originate at the center of a mass extending to outer limits like an inflammation created around a center of infection which invades the whole organism. But as soon as certain conditions of size and social density are given, it manifests itself in the group like an attribute inseparable from the others. Of course, these conditions are not the only ones to make their influence felt. The same proportions of voluntary deaths are not found in groups of given size and density in Germany and England. Each nation has up to now shown tendencies which are peculiar to it, which result from its customs, its ancient institutions and its total history. Notions, both simple and confused, of race and climate, that is, of physical factors, have a place only in a physical science. However, one may attempt to translate so-called differences of race and climate into social terms. It is probably not enough for all the members of a group to be of the same origin, have the same traditions, have remained relatively homogeneous, or be the product of well-defined cross-breedings and intermixtures, or, lastly, to have long kept the same religious, family, and economic customs, for the group to provide a hold equal to the temptation of voluntarily quitting life. What is more and more salient within the nation is the difference between urban civilization and its opposite. The rural style of life favors and maintains regional diversities; the urban levels them, and does so at a high level, for the urban style of life normally seems to bear a higher suicide rate.

chapter 8

Suicide and the family

Statisticians have continuously improved their capacity to make increasingly precise observations. By so doing they have steadily improved their ability to illuminate the influence of marital status on tendencies to suicide.

Because sociology often appears to discover truisms, justice is not always rendered it. Durkheim, following Morselli, showed that marriage protects against suicide and that people who have children kill themselves less often than do married people without descendants. To many, this is a commonsense truth that it scarcely requires a large array of figures to rediscover. However, one probable proposition is generally opposed by another which seems equally obvious. There is, therefore, just as much scientific merit in determining which of two probable opinions corresponds to reality as in engendering an entirely new truth. That, truly, is crossing the boundary separating scientific knowledge from common knowledge.

According to current opinion, said Durkheim, the unmarried man has an easier life than the married man. Since marriage brings with it all kinds of burdens and responsibilities, married people may be expected to commit suicide more often than the unmarried. This opinion has been defended by certain authors, particularly by A. Wagner.[1]

Morselli was to our knowledge the first to maintain the opposite opinion. This is especially noteworthy because the statistics he commanded were not very elaborate. He found, even without controlling for age, that proportionately fewer married than unmarried men kill themselves in France and Italy. To be sure the reverse was true for women, while in Prussia and Saxony the reverse was true for men as well as for women. Morselli then had the idea of using census data to calculate the proportion of suicides in relation to the adult population only. He drew up a table for 89 nations and several periods which very clearly showed a higher suicide rate among widowers than among the unmarried. With one or two exceptions, married people had the lowest proportion of voluntary deaths. The deviation was slight: in France, for example, suicide rates of married and unmarried people were expressed by relative numbers of 100 and 112 (for the widowed by 196). This fact was general.

Morselli also observed that this difference between the unmarried and the married was smaller for women than for men, often disappearing among the former. He arrived 'at the unexpected finding that widowerhood entails fewer disadvantages for men than widowhood for women, and that being unmarried reinforces the tendency to suicide among men but not among women.' Durkheim corrects Morselli on the first point for forgetting that everywhere widows are twice as numerous as widowers. He shows (p. 192) that 'in passing from marriage to widowerhood, man loses more than woman.' As to the second point, however, he expresses (p. 179) what Morselli had glimpsed, though with greater force and precision: 'The coefficient of preservation of married persons by comparison with unmarried persons varies with the sexes. In France, it is men who are in the favorable position.' Among the unmarried, men are less protected than women.

The elder Bertillon had shown that in France marriage was such a protection against suicide that it thwarted the influence of age and reduced the suicide rate of elderly people by about half. As we have shown, suicides increase with age. Morselli noted that, if only age mattered, the unmarried, who on the average are younger than married people, would have killed themselves less often. In sum, it was well understood before Durkheim that the influence of age must be eliminated in order correctly to compare the suicide rate of unmarried and married people and the unmarried related to married people of the same age. However, the data did not permit this.

Durkheim's contribution to the study of this aspect of suicide is fundamental, in the judgment of all statisticians who have worked in this field. He had the very fortunate idea of preparing a table in which voluntary deaths in France in 1889–91 are distinguished by age and marital status. That is, the suicide rates of married in relation to unmarried, and of widowed in relation to unmarried, are shown distinguished by sex and by age.[2]

This table is essential. We are reproducing it in slightly different form (Table 8.1) to facilitate subsequent comparisons with other data.[3]

Table 8.1   *Suicides in France (1889–91)*

Annual suicides per million inhabitants of each age group and marital status (relative numbers)

Age[4]	Men				Women				
	Husbands	Unmarried	Widowers	Unmarried Widowers	Wives	Unmarried Wives	Unmarried	Widows	Unmarried Widows	Widows	Unmarried
20–25	100	240	100	145	100	166	200	105	100	160
25–30	100	320	100	337	100	95	222	261	100	84
30–40	100	277	100	247	100	112	153	250	100	61
40–50	100	286	100	212	100	135	161	158	100	101
50–60	100	275	100	188	100	146	135	131	100	102
60–70	100	278	100	183	100	151	119	162	100	77
Total	100	280	100	218	100	134	167	178	100	97

Table 8.1 continued   *Suicides in France (1889–91)*

Proportion of suicides in each age group and marital status in France, in Seine and in the provinces (1889–91) (relative numbers)

Age	Men (provinces)					Women (provinces)				
	Husbands	Unmarried	Widowers	Widowers	Unmarried	Wives	Unmarried	Widows	Widows	Unmarried
20–25	100	225	161	100	139	100	182	146	100	125
25–30	100	354	362	100	97	100	190	245	100	78
30–40	100	292	254	100	115	100	136	235	100	58
40–50	100	330	222	100	154	100	154	157	100	98
50–60	100	307	182	100	169	100	130	128	100	102
60–70	100	307	180	100	170	100	114	156	100	73
	Men (Seine)					Women (Seine)				
	Husbands	Unmarried	Widowers	Widowers	Unmarried	Wives	Unmarried	Widows	Widows	Unmarried
20–25	100	380	—	100	—	100	306	—	100	—
25–30	100	201	240	100	83	100	318	286	100	110
30–40	100	199	210	100	95	100	180	239	100	75
40–50	100	121	180	100	67	100	164	133	100	123
50–60	100	118	201	100	58	100	129	116	100	111
60–70	100	96	186	100	51	100	109	135	100	80

This table must be read as follows. The two halves of the table (men and women) are symmetrical. The numbers in the second and third columns show in relative numbers the proportion of suicides by the unmarried and the widowed, setting equal to 100 the proportion of suicides by the spouses. (The numbers in the third column were all calculated by us.) The numbers in the fifth column show the proportion of suicides by the unmarried, setting equal to 100 the proportion of suicides of the widowed.

We calculated the totals in Table 8.2 from the preceding table for the provinces and Seine (1889–91).

Table 8.2   *Suicides in Seine and provinces by sex and marital status*

	Married	Unmarried	Widowed	Widowed	Unmarried
Men (provinces)	100	300	227	100	140
Men (Seine)	100	185	203	100	71
Women (provinces)	100	151	178	100	89
Women (Seine)	100	200	182	100	100

Durkheim also reproduced statistics from the Grand Duchy of Oldenburg (the principalities of Lübeck and Birkenfeld included). These gave for 1871–85 the distribution of suicides by age for each category of marital status considered separately. Oldenburg was the only place where such particulars could be found for this period.

He drew two general conclusions from these tables.

After the age of 20, married persons of both sexes benefit from a coefficient of preservation relative to the unmarried. This coefficient is higher than indicated by Bertillon and advances with age. It reaches maximum between the ages of 25 and 30 in France and between 30 and 40 in Oldenburg. Then it decreases until the last period of life, when it sometimes rises slightly.

It varies with sex.[5] In France, men are favored and the distance between the sexes is considerable. The reverse is true in Oldenburg.

Durkheim carefully researched the ratios of widowhood to marriage and presented his data in an entirely new light. In France, married men are better protected than married women, and widowers better than widows, as compared to the unmarried.[6] In Oldenburg, however, the opposite is true of both married men and widowers. Does a relationship exist, then, Durkheim asked himself, between the tendency to suicide in marriage and in widowhood? To test this, he carried the analysis of these figures further and calculated separately the suicide rate for each age group and marital status in the provinces and in Seine. He found that in the provinces, as for the whole of France, the married man was better protected than the married woman, and the widower than the widow. In Seine, however, the reverse was true. These differences were important. It is sometimes said that while married people have troubles, the unmarried have the cankerworm of boredom. The latter is certainly more fatal than the former. Unmarried men and married women may both suffer from boredom more in the provinces than in Paris. Married men and unmarried women, whatever their age, may also feel the full effect of all their troubles and cares in Paris, while neither group experiences them as much in the country. In every instance it was possible for Durkheim to conclude that with respect to suicide each sex behaves in widowhood as in marriage. Suicide is more frequent among widows when resistance to the temptation to end themselves is weaker among married women. This teaches us that widowhood is not an incurably bad condition. The dispositions of widowers and widows vary with the moral state of married people of the same sex in a given country. Whichever sex profits most from the matrimonial state suffers more when single, but is more hardened to resist suicide, just as if it had stocked up on vigor during marriage and retained the *élan* it had captured then.

Durkheim did not limit himself to more precise determination of the divergences between the suicide rates of the married, the unmarried, etc. He proposed completely original interpretations of these facts. Morselli explained what he had glimpsed with reasons such as the following: 'Marriage calms the passions, is a prop in the struggle for existence, subjects life to regulation, augments the restraints of work, and raises the social and moral level of the spouses.' Women are less protected against the tendency to suicide than are men because, 'after marriage, the woman more often than the man sees her illusions take flight.' Besides, unmarried women find fewer reasons than men for quitting life voluntarily. 'Celibacy presents many advantages to compensate for the sorrows of youthful love, the solitude which weighs on elderly people, the shattered illusions. Besides, pregnancy and child-birth expose the wife to diverse nervous and mental troubles.'

Durkheim located himself at another vantage point, though without discarding this style of reasoning entirely. According to him, 'the immunity to suicide which married people generally present is due among women entirely, and among men largely, to the influence of the family circle, of the children, rather than of the conjugal society or of marriage as such.' He was very impressed to learn that in France married women without children kill themselves more than do the unmarried of the same age. That is undoubtedly because marriage brings the childless woman fewer general benefits than it does her spouse. (This may be for the reasons Morselli invoked, or other analogous ones.) If she does not lose by marrying, she gains less than he. On the other hand, 'childless widows commit suicide less than do childless husbands.' His wife's death does not increase the husband's suicidal tendency because, however long the marriage lasts, it restrains this tendency only feebly.

It was essential to verify that collection of impressive propositions. None of the publications on suicide appearing since Durkheim's book disproves them. We hope to bring some facts to their support.

Father Krose reproduces the table Durkheim compiled, in the book to which we have repeatedly referred. After comparing it with the table of suicides in the Grand Duchy of Oldenburg (1871–85), he writes, 'The principal' finding of Durkheim's investigation is plainly confirmed by the Oldenburg statistics. This is all the more remarkable because it concerns a population which, in size and structure, is entirely different from the French population.'

When Durkheim was studying this problem, Swedish statistics of suicide also existed, classified by age and marital status. These, however, combined the unmarried and widows in one category, and were therefore unusable. Krose reproduced these particular Swedish figures for 1891–4, distinguishing the widows and the unmarried. Since then they are to be found in von Mayr for the periods 1891–1900 and 1901–7. Confining ourselves to the figures for the longest period, 1891–1900, we calculated the same relative numbers as before.[7] Von Mayr reproduced tables for Denmark, likewise presenting the same distinctions and combinations (he forgot to indicate for what period; each of the age categories includes only five years), and for Norway, from 1881 to 1900, or twenty years (age categories: from 15 to 25 and by ten-year intervals thereafter, but from 55 to 75 at the end).[8] We calculated the same relative numbers for these two tests also, but are not reproducing them to avoid misuse of the tables. With regard to the distribution of suicides by age and marital status, these countries seem to occupy a position intermediate between France and Switzerland. We reproduce in Table 8.3 only the averages of each column of relative numbers (suicide rates of the unmarried in relation to the married, etc.). These averages of numbers calculated for each age category, following Durkheim's method, are valid comparisons with averages calculated similarly for other countries. Since we shall confine our attention in what follows to four clearly-differentiated tests – France, Switzerland, Oldenburg, and Hungary – it will suffice to annotate parallels and peculiarities suggested by these Danish and Scandinavian statistics.

Table 8.3 *Scandinavian countries: proportion of suicides (in relative numbers)*

		Married	Unmarried	Widowed	Widowed	Unmarried
Sweden	Men	100	270	273	100	110
(1891–1900)	Women					
		100	220	215	100	84
Norway	Men	100	235	302	100	82
(1881–1900)	Women					
		100	170	189	100	98
Denmark	Men	100	259	219	100	95
(?)	Women					
		100	237	246	100	97

Thus, as in France,* married people of both sexes kill themselves less often than do the unmarried. In Sweden, this divergence is almost the same as in France for the married men but much larger for the married women; in Norway it is lower for the married men, almost the same for the married women; in Denmark it is not much lower for the married men (equal to that in Switzerland, as we shall see)† but much larger for the married women. As in France, the married men are favored more than are the married women. Widows of both sexes kill themselves more often than do married people and also than the unmarried (except that in Sweden widows kill themselves as often as the unmarried). Only in Sweden is Durkheim's law verified: the married man being better protected than the married woman, the widower is more sheltered than the widow (as compared with the unmarried). True, there is hardly any difference in this respect in Denmark, and the divergence between widowers and widows is low in Norway. As we shall see, the type of suicide distribution by marital status most closely resembled by these three examples is the French.

*The comparisons are with the total line in Table 8.1 – Tr.
†The comparison is given in Table 8.8 – Tr.

Elsewhere, Krose reproduced Swiss statistics of suicides by age and marital status for 1881–90 which had escaped Durkheim's attention.[9] 'The total number of suicides in these four investigations,' Krose concludes, 'was 6,756 in Switzerland, 2,736 in Sweden, 1,369 in Oldenburg, and 25,474 in France, or more than two-thirds of the total. The French figures therefore have the most weight.' The Swiss statistics for 1881–90 are as shown in Table 8.4.

Table 8.4   *Switzerland (1881–90): proportion of suicides per million inhabitants of each category (in relative numbers)*[10]

	Per hundred married suicides							
	Men		Women		Men		Women	
Age	Single	Widowers	Single	Widows	Widowers	Single	Widows	Single
20–29	135	143	194	—	100	95	—	—
30–39	195	259	144	142	100	75	100	102
40–49	172	273	126	188	100	63	100	67
50–59	156	253	82	120	100	61	100	68
60–69	148	187	102	146	100	79	100	70
70–79	190	196	163	185	100	97	100	88

This chapter was completed when we found in von Mayr's *Statistik und Gesellschaftslehre*, p. 323, similar data for Switzerland from 1891 to 1900 and from 1901 to 1905. We calculated the numbers shown in Table 8.5 from the data of 1891 to 1900, arranging them in the form of the above tables. We are not using the data of 1901–5 as the number of suicides is too small.

By calculating from the data of 1881–90 the average of the numbers in each column for the first five age categories (from 20 to 69 years), we obtain the figures in Table 8.6.[11]

Thus, as in France, the married of both sexes kill themselves less often than do the unmarried. However, the difference is much less than in France: for every 100 married suicides we find, respectively, 161 unmarried men and 127 unmarried women, instead of 280 and 167 as in France.* Married males are more favored in this respect than wives, as in France. Both widows and widowers kill themselves more than do married men, as in France. However, they kill themselves more often than do the unmarried, as well, contrary to what Durkheim observed in France, where the unmarried clearly kill themselves more often than do the widows.

*Table 8.1 – Tr.

Table 8.5 *Proportion of suicides in Switzerland (1891–1900) (relative numbers)*

	Men		Women		Men		Women	
					Per hundred married suicides			
Age	Unmarried	Widowers	Unmarried	Widows	Widowers	Unmarried	Widows	Unmarried
20–29	189	219	189	(590)	100	86	100	32
30–39	222	333	160	205	100	67	100	78
40–49	203	282	174	220	100	71	100	83
50–59	154	201	118	120	100	77	100	98
60–69	150	241	80	164	100	62	100	49
70–79	167	188	82	91	100	88	100	89

Table 8.6 *Averages for age categories from 20 to 69 years*

	Married	Unmarried	Widows	Widows	Unmarried
Men	100	161	222	100	75
Women	100	127	149	100	68

(The average difference in this respect between widows and unmarried women is very low in France: there, widows who are between 25 and 40 years of age, or over 60, kill themselves more than do unmarried women.) Compared to the unmarried, widowers seem to be more favored in this respect than widows (as in France). Durkheim's law is verified in every respect. The married man being more protected than the married woman, the widower is more protected: or, to be more precise, is less exposed than the widow.

This test is unusual in that marriage reduces the suicidal tendency less than in the other tests and that widowhood, far from reducing the suicidal tendency, appears to reinforce it relative to the unmarried. These two facts are probably related. Married people, who are less armed against suicide, lose their immunity entirely when they become widows and their prior habits do not equip them with the strength necessary to adapt to the new and, by contrast, painful condition.

We compiled Table 8.7 for Hungary from very recent data (*Revue hongroise de statistique*, July 1928). The figures in the first three columns are borrowed from this publication. We calculated all the others ourselves, as well as the last two lines (total), eliminating all figures of suicide which are too low or which correspond to a group of less than 2 per cent of all the suicides. In calculating the averages (total) of the numbers in each column, we have not taken account of the extremely high rates of widowers over 70 years (those between parentheses). This table corresponds to 7,155 suicides in absolute numbers, which is more than in Sweden, Oldenburg, and even Switzerland (6,576), or nearly a third of the 25,474 suicides studied by Durkheim in France.

Let us refer to the averages of the columns (total). As in previous instances, the married of both sexes kill themselves less often than do the unmarried.

However, contrary to what Durkheim observed in France, marriage protects women more than men, on the whole and in every age category except from 40 to 49 years. (Here 295 unmarried men commit suicide for every 100 married men, instead of 280 in France, while 320 unmarried women commit suicide for every 100 married women, instead of 167 in France.) Hungary resembles Oldenburg in this respect. The widows of both sexes kill themselves more often than do the married people, as in France. Also, as in France, they kill themselves less often than do the unmarried, especially the widows. Compared with the unmarried, widows seem more favored in this respect than widowers. (This is not the case in France.) Again, the law formulated by Durkheim is verified. The wife being better

Table 8.7   *Hungary (1923–5): suicides annually per million inhabitants by age and marital status*

| | Suicide rate relative numbers | | | | | | | |
| | | | | Men | | | | |
Age	Unmarried	Married	Widowed	Married	Unmarried	Widowed	Widowed	Unmarried
15–19	294	155	—	100	190	—	—	—
20–24	842	243	—	100	357	—	—	—
25–29	811	305	—	100	266	—	—	—
30–39	792	238	1,033	100	335	434	100	77
40–49	1,312	355	724	100	370	204	100	183
50–59	1,551	570	1,550	100	271	271	100	100
60–69	—	788	2,057	100	—	251	—	—
70 and over	—	146	(3,750)	100	—	(2,560)	—	—

Table 8.7 continued   *Hungary (1923–5): suicides annually per million inhabitants by age and marital status*

Age	Unmarried	Married	Widowed			Suicide rate relative numbers		
				Married	Unmarried	Widowed	Widowed	Unmarried
					Women			
15–19	240	112	—	100	215	—	—	—
20–24	453	117	—	100	388	—	—	—
25–29	490	155	—	100	316	—	—	—
30–39	394	105	153	100	375	146	100	257
40–49	299	120	205	100	249	171	100	146
50–59	587	156	242	100	375	155	100	241
60–69	—	181	321	100	—	178	—	—
70 and over	—	347	748	100	—	215	—	—
Total								
Men	930	350	1,340	100	295	290	100	120
Women	410	161	334	100	320	173	100	215

protected than the husband, the widow is better protected than the widower. The sole exception occurs in the age category from 40 to 49 years, where the widower is better protected than the widow. This corresponds to the exception noted above, for the same age category, where the husband is better protected than the wife. The exception therefore falls within the law which was verified by the four tests studied. Table 8.8 assembles the general results obtained in these four countries.

Table 8.8 *Proportion of suicides, by marital status, in four European countries (relative numbers)*

	France (1889–91)		Switzerland (1881–90)[12]		Oldenburg (1871–85)		Hungary (1923–5)	
	Married	Single	Married	Single	Married	Single	Married	Single
Men	100	280	100	161	100	174	100	295
Women								
	100	167	100	127	100	202	100	320
	Widows	Single	Widows	Single	Widows	Single	Widows	Single
Men	100	134	100	75	100	200	100	120
Women								
	100	97	100	68	100	208	100	215

In each of these tests, divergence between the suicide rate of the married and unmarried is greatest for the same sex for which the divergence between suicide rates of the widowed and unmarried is also greatest. That is, the sex which is best protected by marriage is also best protected (or least exposed) by widowhood.

The divergence between the married and unmarried in suicide, or what Durkheim calls the coefficient of preservation of the married, varies greatly from one country to another. In France and Hungary the rate for the men is very high and very similar in both countries while, for the women, it rises in Hungary to twice its level in France. Men are protected almost equally in Switzerland and Oldenburg, but women much more in Oldenburg than in Switzerland. In general, marriage abates the tendency to suicide, especially in Hungary, where both sexes have maximal protection. Its influence on men and women is weakest in Switzerland. France is plainly distinguished from the other countries in that the difference in suicide between the married and unmarried is much higher for the men than for the women.

Marriage does not exert the same degree of influence at each age. Examining the tables we have reproduced from this standpoint, the suicides and the suicidal drop out of sight completely and one thinks henceforth only of the vicissitudes of human life, of the joys and sorrows peculiar to each age which are reflected in these variations. In Hungary, married people 20 to 24 years of age kill themselves exactly three-and-a-half times less often than do the unmarried. They do not regain or exceed this proportion until 40 to 49 years of age. Married people in France also kill themselves almost three-and-a-half times less often than do the unmarried, but a little later, at 25 to 30 years of age. Also, marriage will never afford them as much protection as they have at this age (although the maximum at 40 to 49 years of age will be lower than a first maximum). Seine must be distinguished from the other provinces in France. Let us refer to the second part of Table 8.1, which borrows data from the table reproduced by Durkheim (*Le Suicide*, Table XXII, p. 196). What we have just said of the difference between unmarried and married men in France is true in the provinces, but not entirely so in Seine. As in Hungary, married people between 20 and 24 years of age (rather than those from 25 to 30) kill themselves almost four times less often than do the unmarrieds (100 per 380 unmarrieds* instead of 357 as in Hungary). However, contrary to both Hungary and the French provinces, where marriage protects men against suicide until the end of their lives, in Seine marriage protects men less and less after they are 25 years of age. From 25 to 40 years, the marrieds kill themselves only two times less often than the unmarrieds. From 40 to 60 years of age, this difference diminishes by three-quarters, and disappears entirely after the age of 60. In Paris and its suburbs married men over 40 are no more capable than unmarried of resisting the temptation to commit suicide when it comes. Rather than cavil about that a great deal, let us confine ourselves to the fact.

How do women behave? In Hungary, unmarried women of 20 to 24 years of age, 30 to 39, and 50 to 59 commit suicide much more than do married women. The difference is least from 40 to 49 years of age which, as we have seen, is the period when married men are better protected against suicide than are married women. It is difficult to explain this rather clearly-marked rhythm. Perhaps for women married 20 to 30 years who had children immediately, the period from 40 to 49 years of age represents a transformation or crisis not only physical but moral and familial.

In France† voluntary deaths also victimize more unmarried

---

*A typographical error in the original reverses these numbers – Tr.
†Table 8.1 – Tr.

women than married. The difference is stronger among those from 20 to 30 years of age (especially from 25 to 30). After 30 it diminishes sharply by more than half, remains constant at that level from 30 to 50 years of age, then diminishes continuously until it is only a fifth. This applies to the provinces rather than Seine, and always with the proviso that the suicide rates always favor the married over the unmarried women, and the difference clearly increases from 40 to 50 years of age, instead of decreasing as in Hungary. The immunity of the married woman to suicide is strongest between 30 and 70 when compared to the unmarried. Is this because unmarried women are becoming spinsters during this period while the married women's situation is not changing? Why then the decrease in Hungary? The Seine statistics produce an entirely different impression from those for the provinces. Here, the salient fact is that more than three times as many unmarried women 20 to 30 years of age kill themselves as do married women, an exceptionally high proportion. That is, the difference in Seine in the ratio between unmarried and married women 20 to 30 years of age is the same as between unmarried and married men in the provinces, and as between unmarried and married women in Hungary. However, this difference in ratio falls sharply after the age of 30, diminishing uninterruptedly from one period to the next in the ratio of 100 to 52 in Seine, while in the provinces the drop is only from 100 to 71. Hence, after the age of 50 there is no greater difference in Seine than the insignificant one found in the provinces at the same age. To measure the difference between the provinces and Paris, let us compare the maximal divergence for 25 to 30 years of age and the minimal divergence for 60 to 70 between the tendencies to suicide among unmarried and married women, first in the provinces and then in Seine. In the provinces it diminishes from 100 to 68 and in Seine from 100 to 34. However, the suicide rate of married women 25 to 30 years of age is lower in the provinces than in Seine: 64 per million married women instead of 103 in Seine. This exceptional difference is therefore due to the very high suicide rate among unmarried women of the same age in Seine, whose suicide rate is 328 instead of 122 as in the provinces. The conditions of life in Paris and its vicinity seem particularly conducive to suicide among unmarried women 20 to 30 years of age. Marriage protects provincial as well as Parisian women, especially those under 30 years of age, but progressively less and less in the years following.

This is also true of Switzerland, where the difference between married and unmarried women is greatest from 20 to 29 years of age; immediately thereafter it is more than cut in half, diminishes further from 40 to 49 years of age, and disappears after the age of

50.[13] This is not the case in Hungary, where marriage continues to be as strong an influence until the end, or in the Grand Duchy of Oldenburg, where it is more effective from 40 to 60 years of age than at any other time.

This leads us to distinguish two types of country (see the summary Table 8.8). France and Switzerland are examples of the first type. Here married men are better protected against suicide than married women because it is only married women under 30 who are genuinely protected. Hungary and Oldenburg are examples of the second type. Here married women are better protected against suicide than married men and marriage exerts its influence during the married women's entire life. If we set equal to 100 the difference between the suicide rate of unmarried women (who will kill themselves more) and of married women, we find the following relative differences between the unmarried men and the married:

France	168
Switzerland	126
Hungary	92
Oldenburg	86

These figures express what Durkheim calls the coefficient of preservation against suicide for the married men, assuming the same coefficient for the married women is set equal to 100.[14]

Durkheim believed that the higher suicide rate of unmarried people is explained less by marriage as such than by the family, or by the presence of children. Why, however, do French and Swiss married women find greater protection in marriage at 20 to 30 years of age than later? We might assume that until the age of 30, marriage as such protects these married women almost as much as it does the men, and that the matrimonial union itself brings them advantages which will later disappear. Or we might assume that having, or destined to have, but few children, between 25 and 30 is when children are most on their minds. We might entertain both assumptions. These, however, are simple hypotheses.

The first thing we must ascertain is whether married people produce fewer suicides if they have children than if they do not.

Morselli devoted only one or two pages to this question because at the time he was writing hardly any country except France separated the suicides who left children from the childless. Morselli confined himself to showing their number (perhaps he could not calculate their proportion, lacking data from the censuses on the number of marrieds who had children, etc.). He found that of every hundred married suicides in France from 1867 to 1876, 67.6 per cent left children and 32.4 did not, while of every hundred married women suicides the percentages were respectively 61 and 39. Thus, the presence of children seems to have bound the woman to life more than the man, for the proportion of married women having children who commit suicide, relative to men in similar circumstances, was 100 to 110.

Morselli 'concluded from these numbers that children protect widows against suicide more than widowers, and, among the married, protect the mother more than the father.' He also found that children seem to protect both widows and widowers against suicide a little more than the married of both sexes. Commanding only very imperfect data, Morselli could go no further. He had, however, shown the way.

In 1879 Bertillon published the following suicide rates for France for 1861–8 in an article, 'Les celibataires, les veufs, etc.,' in the *Revue Scientifique*. This time the suicide rates are calculated (in suicides per million) in relation to the corresponding population category.[15]

Married men with children	205
Married men without children	478
Married women with children	45
Married women without children	158
Widowers with children	526
Widowers without children	1,004
Widows with children	104
Widows without children	238

Let us set equal to 100 the suicide rates of married men and women with children. The suicide rates of married men and women without children are found to be 233 and 351. Thus, children lower the suicide rates of both married men and women but of married women much more than of married men. The ratio of 233 to 351 is 1:1.51. Children protect married women against suicide one-and-a-half times as much as they do married men.[16]

Durkheim attempted a higher degree of precision. He calculated what the suicide rates became for married people with children, without children, etc., when compared with unmarried people. He could not separate the marrieds and widows with children, etc., by age. However, the average age of the married men was 45 years of age, of the married women, 42; of the widowers and widows, 60. From Table 8.1, mentioned above, which he compiled, he drew suicide rates corresponding to these categories and calculated the following relative numbers (in pairs):

Married men with children	100
Unmarried men, 45 years old	290
Married men without children	100
Unmarried men, 45 years old	150
Married women with children	100
Unmarried women, 42 years old	189
Married women without children	100
Unmarried women, 42 years old	67

The suicide rate of the unmarried relative to that of the married without children is 94 per cent higher than relative to the rate of the married with children. This measures the extent to which the suicide rate of the married who have children diminishes relative to the unmarried. The suicide rate of unmarried women relative to that of married without children is 182 per cent higher than relative to the rate of married women with children. These two numbers clearly show that children protect married women much more than married men. If the same calculation is carried through for widowers and widows relative to unmarried men and unmarried women of 60 years of age, we obtain ratios of 34 per cent for the men and 76 per cent for the women. These indicate that children protect widows against suicide more than they do widowers.

Neither Father Krose nor von Mayr provides new data as to the effect of children in marriage on suicide. There have been no advances on this since Durkheim.

However, two statistical tables published quite recently, one in Hungary and the other in the Soviet Union, appear not only to confirm the findings of Morselli, Bertillon, and Durkheim, and make them more precise, but to measure the effect of the number of children.

In France, the suicides of married people who have children are distinguished from those who do not. Do families that have only one child, however, protect the father and mother against suicide in the same way and to the same extent as those with more children? Durkheim understood the importance of this question. 'This immunity' against suicide, he wrote (p. 198), 'increases with the density of the family, that is, with the increase in the number of its elements.'

For want of other data, he turned to the census of 1886, where he found 'the effective average of family households.' He showed that a rather close relationship exists between the proportion of suicides and family density, that is, the number of persons in each household. The resemblance between two maps of France which distinguish departments according to these two characteristics is not surprising, despite minor inconsistencies. Is such a relationship not easily explained by the calculation of the proportion of suicides in relation to the total population, including children under 15 who rarely commit suicide? That too would be saying that where children (who do not commit suicide) are most numerous the proportion of suicides in the total population is lowest, a tautology.* The two maps would therefore only be reproducing the same trait: the proportion of children under 15 in the total population. Had this been the case our entire study of the geographic distribution of suicides in France would prove nothing, since the regions enumerating the highest proportions of suicides would be those where children are the least numerous, that is, where the population which is disposed to suicide is relatively the most numerous. However, this is not so at all. Differences between departments in this respect are very small, while at the same time very large differences are found between rates of suicide.

Durkheim distinguished six groups of departments according to decreasing suicide rates. Opposite each of them he set the effective average of the households on the same date. Let us calculate the relative increase or decrease of these numbers from one group to the next (see Table 8.9).

Table 8.9   *France (from Durkheim's Table, p. 199)*

	Decrease in the suicide rate	Increase in family density	Increase in the number of households having more than two persons
From 1st to 2nd group	100–67	96.5–100	92–100
From 2nd to 3rd group	100–75	95.5–100	91–100
From 3rd to 4th group	100–73	96 –100	91–100
From 4th to 5th group	100–66.5	94 –100	88–100
From 5th to 6th group	100–50	96.5–100	94–100
From 1st to 6th group	100–12.5	83 –100	63–100

The three clearest diminutions in suicide rates are from the 1st to the 2nd group, from the 4th to the 5th group, and from the 5th

*Ce qui est trop evident – Tr.

to the 6th or, respectively, 33 per cent, 33.5 per cent,* and 50 per cent. Corresponding family densities only increase by 3.5† per cent, 6 per cent, and 3.5* per cent. Had the suicide rates been calculated relative to the population over 15, therefore, the differences between them would have been reduced by a fraction which is quite small but would nevertheless continue to exist. Hence Durkheim cannot be reproached with having neglected this cause of error.

Now, however, let us consider the number in each household larger than two members. This may represent the number of children.

This number varies a little more rapidly from group to group than does household size but, again, much less rapidly than do the suicide rates (see the last line of Table 8.7), for it increases by 37 per cent while the suicide rates diminish by 87.5 per cent. France's regions do not differ markedly in this respect and it is hardly possible to discover from these figures how many households have two or more children, or to what extent they contribute to the total of voluntary deaths.

There would seem then to be only one way of measuring the influence of the number of children on suicide. We need statistics showing the suicide rates among married people by the number of their children. These statistics do not exist. Those we are about to study, however, provide valuable indications and may be adequate.

Table 8.10 *Hungary (excluding Budapest), 1923–5. Percentage of suicides of each marital status and sex who have left the given number of children*

Number of children	Married Men	Married Women	Widowers	Widows
0	29.7 ⎱ 47.7	39.9 ⎱ 63.4	85 ⎱ 88.4	86.3 ⎱ 91.2
1	18 ⎰	23.5 ⎰	3.4 ⎰	4.9 ⎰
2	17.4 ⎱	16.9 ⎱	3.2 ⎱	4.7 ⎱
3	12 ⎬ 38.3	8.2 ⎬ 32.1	3.1 ⎬ 9.1	2.7 ⎬ 8.1
4	8.9 ⎰	7 ⎰	2.8 ⎰	0.7 ⎰
5	6.2 ⎱ 14	1.2 ⎱ 4.5	1.3 ⎱ 2.5	0.7 ⎱ 0.7
More than 5	7.8 ⎰	3.3 ⎰	1.2 ⎰	0 ⎰
Total	100	100	100	100

*Omitted in the original. See Table 8.9 – Tr.
†In the original, 4 per cent. See Table 8.9 – Tr.

Here, first of all, is a table for Hungary in 1923–5, compiled as shown in Table 8.10. Four categories of other than unmarried suicides have been distinguished: married men, widowers, married women, widows.

The number of suicides in each of these categories has been assumed to be 100 and the percentage shown are those who left no children, 1 child, 2 children, 3 children, etc.[17]

If we could assume that the married men who attempted suicide were entirely unconcerned about the children they would leave, the numbers in the first column would merely represent the percentage of households with no children, with one child, etc. It is immediately apparent, however, that the more children women have, the less often they kill themselves. Were this not the case, their numbers in each of the categories would be the same as for the corresponding men, or, on our hypothesis, the same proportion as for the households with no children. Or, since the presence of children does modify the tendency to suicide among the men, the same proportion as for one child. Instead of 32.1 for the sum of the next three lines, we would expect to find a higher number, exactly 50, and for the sum of the last two lines, not 4.5 but 18. The differences between the numbers reported in the table and these new numbers would therefore measure the influence exerted by the larger number of children. Indeed, a glance at the table suffices to indicate that the difference between men and women increases continuously among households having more than one child. The same is true of widowers relative to married men, of widows relative to married women, and, to a lesser extent, of widows relative to widowers.

However, there is no basis for the hypothesis that the frequency with which married men kill themselves is uninfluenced by the number of their children. The numbers in the first column certainly do not merely indicate the proportion of households of no children, one child, etc. They become smaller than these proportions very quickly, and at an ever-increasing rate. We cannot prove this directly because the Hungarian statistics do not show the distribution of households by size, but we can proceed comparatively. During the thirty years preceding the war the populations both of Hungary and Germany increased very slightly and in the same proportion. Hungary's birthrate is actually high, 28 births per 1,000 inhabitants, clearly higher than that of Germany and almost all European countries. Now, for Germany in 1900 we know the distribution of households by size.[18] Let us compare the figures in Table 8.11.

The proportion of married suicides in Hungary who leave no children is much higher than the proportion of two-person or childless households in Germany, which must be almost the same in Hungary. On the other hand, the proportion of Hungarians

Table 8.11   *Suicide and family size in Germany and Hungary*

Germany (1900)		Hungary (1923–5)		
Households consisting of	Per cent	Married suicides, leaving	Men per hundred	Women per hundred
2 persons	15.9	0 children	29.7	39.9
3 persons	18.2	1 child	18	23.5
4 persons	18.1	2 children	17.4	16.9
5 persons	15.6	3 children	12	8.2
6 persons	12	4 children	8.9	7
7 or 8 persons	13.7 ⎱	5 children	6.2 ⎱ 14	1.2 ⎱ 4.5
9 or 10 persons	4.7 ⎰ 20.2	Over 5 children	7.8 ⎰	3.3 ⎰
Over 10 persons	1.8 ⎰			
Total	100		100	100

who, on committing suicide, leave five or more children, is clearly lower than the proportion of households of 7 or more persons, that is, of 5 or more children, in Germany and, undoubtedly, in Hungary. The result of this comparison, if correct, would be that children likewise exert an influence on married men who are disposed to commit suicide. In that case, however, married women would be much more dominated by this motive for not killing themselves than we have stated.

We in France are accustomed to think that large families begin after four children. Consider Norway, which for the past forty years has had a birthrate very close to that of Hungary. (Its birthrate has gone from 31 per thousand inhabitants for 1881–5 to 26 for 1908–13.) Now, 23 per cent of Norwegian women who married at 18 or 19 years of age and were at least 40 years old in 1920 have had ten children. Families having twelve children are as frequent as those having six, families with thirteen are much more frequent than those with three, fourteen more frequent than those with one.[19] Women who married at 24 or 25 years of age will have had rather fewer children, but 27 per cent of them will have been mothers seven or eight times. Families of nine children are more numerous than five, eleven almost as numerous as one. We do not know whether the same is true in Hungary. Besides, our statistics include married women of all ages. Those not yet 40 have a smaller number of children, of course. However, the proportion of married women in Hungary who have more than six children is certainly not negligible. The figure of 3.3 per cent on the last line of the column of married women is obviously the aggregate of a series for households extending up to eight children, nine children, etc. The first term of the series must be smaller than the penultimate percentage of 1.2 for 5 children. The older the women and men concerned, the more striking is the progressive decrease in these numbers for, as we have seen, suicide rates increase with age.

Finally, Table 8.12 is a table whose entries were taken with slight modifications from a publication on suicides in Soviet Russia already cited.[20] We placed in parenthesis the figures which correspond to fewer than 60 suicides in absolute numbers and have not calculated relative numbers corresponding to fewer than 20 suicides. Surprisingly, we are not shown the suicide rate for men, nor for men and women combined, undoubtedly because the distribution of the total population among these categories was unknown.

The table is instructive despite its numerous and sometimes novel classifications in the statistics of suicide. The table shows the proportion of female suicides per 100 male suicides. In Russia in 1925, 48.5 women committed suicide per 100 male suicides. Whenever the numbers in a category rise above 48.5 we may assume that the women in that category are less protected against suicide than men, and conversely.

This is strictly true for married women, however, only because there are as many married women as married men. We do not know whether unmarried and divorced women are more numerous than men in the same marital status, or less. Durkheim recalled that widows are twice as numerous, in general, as widowers.

The married women whom we shall consider first include a little less than half of all female suicides: 1,593 against 1,837 unmarried suicides. We notice first of all that they are appreciably better protected against suicide than men in the same category (their percentage is below 48.5) when they have children, considerably much less so when they do not. This accords with Durkheim's observations that marital status, as such, protects the woman against suicide less than the man, and protects her to a greater extent (as with the man) when she has children.[21] However, Durkheim was inclined to believe that children protect the woman against suicide less than they do the man. The table seems to show that in Russia it is she who has the advantages.[22]

Table 8.12 *Soviet Russia (1922–4): number of female suicides per 100 male suicides in each category*

	Unmarried women		Married women living with husbands		Separated	Living as mistresses	Widows			Divorcees		Marital status not given	
	Without children	Living as mistresses	Without children	With children	Living as mistresses		Without children	With one child	More than one child	Without children	With children	Without children	With children
Moscow and Leningrad	61	—	100	32.6	—	—	(350)	(138)	(100)	83	—	—	—
Other cities	65	—	88.5	29.9	—	—	(480)	(158)	70	155	—	—	—
Country-side	52.5	—	75.4	32.9	—	—	117	150	67.5	84	—	59.5	49
Total	58.9	(110.7)	83.3	32	31.9	55.3	188	150	70	106	112	74	49

This is as true of Moscow and Leningrad as of the other cities and the countryside. (The numbers in the fourth column are very close.) On the other hand, the difference between married women without children and men,[23] already small in the countryside, decreases as one moves to other cities and disappears entirely in Leningrad and Moscow.

The ratio of suicides of separated women to suicides of separated men equals the ratio of suicides of women with children to suicides of men with children. True, not all the separated women have children. That, however, may be due to the separated men having a high suicide rate because they do not remain married as long as the women and thereafter no longer have a home.

Even assuming two widows to each widower, the ratio of childless widows who commit suicide to suicided widowers is sizeable, for they committed suicide almost as often as the widowers: the ratio of their suicides to the male suicides, divided by 2, equals 94. This ratio is noticeably less for widows who have one child (75, still assuming widows were twice as numerous as widowers).

The really interesting fact, however, is that for widows who have more than one child, the ratio decreases by over half. This is not an accidental finding due to small absolute numbers, for the number of widows with more than one child who commit suicide is 170 and, in addition, the same decrease is found at Leningrad and Moscow as well as in other cities and rural communities.

We next turn to the married women who commit suicide. The Russian statistics distinguish between married women who have one child and those who have more than one. The proportion of married women with one child who commit suicide to men in the same category is 50 per cent, while for married women with more than one child it is 25 per cent: as in the case of widows, the ratio decreases by exactly half. The absolute numbers are higher: this time 315 married women having one child and 376 having more than one. These findings are shown in Table 8.13.

Thus, not only is the married woman better protected against suicide than the married man, providing the marriage is not reduced to the conjugal union and she has a child, but she is even better protected – exactly twice as well – when she has several children instead of only one. The same is true of widows. Using French data for 1861–8 and a table on suicides in French departments, excluding Seine, in 1889–91 that he had compiled from unpublished documents from the Ministry of Justice, Durkheim had shown that marrieds of both sexes, widows, and widowers all killed themselves more often if they did not have

Table 8.13   *Number of suicides by married women per 100 suicides of married men of each category*

	Childless	One child	More than one child
Moscow and Leningrad	100	47.5	23.3
Other cities	88.5	47.2	21.4
Rural communities	75.4	52	26.7
Total	83.3	50	25

children than if they did. The Russian facts tell us (what Durkheim foresaw but could not prove for lack of data) that there is an even more marked difference between households that have only one child and those that have several.

Both differences are a little larger in cities than in the countryside but are not substantial and can be explained by the fact that rural households have more children on the average than those in the cities.

The numbers in Table 8.13 are based on the assumption that the suicide rate of married men equals 100 in each category, that is, that one or more children exert no influence on them with respect to suicide. If this hypothesis is incorrect, as we believe we have shown it to be, the decrease in the suicide rate of married women with one child, and of married women with more than one child, would be greater (as we have already learned from the Hungarian table above).

It is unfortunate that married women who committed suicide were not classified in the table by the number of their children, for the Russian population must contain an exceptionally high percentage of large and very large families. During the thirty years from 1897 to 1926, the population in the Soviet Union's actual territory increased from 107 to 147 million, or more than 37 per cent. Its birthrate exceeded by far all those known in Europe.[24]

In sum, the more children the married man or woman has, the woman especially, the better protected against suicide. This surely explains, at least in part, a fact brought to light previously, namely that in Hungary and Oldenburg marriage is as influential in this respect for women of all ages (and for Oldenburg women even more from 40 to 60 years of age than earlier), while in France and Switzerland it is married women up to 30 years of age who commit suicide less than unmarried women: after that their immunity decreases sharply and very rapidly. The birthrate is higher in the first two countries than in the last two (especially higher in

Hungary than in France). Households therefore include more children in Hungary and Oldenburg. Assuming that in the less fecund households the children are born during the early years of marriage while maternities in the others are spaced at longer intervals over a longer period, it would follow that children protect a woman against suicide longer in countries with higher birthrates than in the others. This would explain why the influence of marriage is weakest and briefest in France, and strongest and most enduring in Hungary. Thus, the two parts of our study coalesce and corroborate each other.

The meaning of these findings must now be defined more precisely. We notice, first of all, that our observations pertain to several countries, but only for very short and very recent periods, thus providing a static description rather than a historical process. It was, of course, important to show at a given period that the family appeared to protect against suicide and that this was so in several very different countries. However, this would not entitle us to conclude that household groups of a similar composition were more influential formerly than today.

The preserving virtue of the family, if due principally to the number of children, could in fact only be weaker today, since the average number of children has diminished. Let us therefore compare France around 1830 and in 1900. The proportion of new marriages is the same but the number of living children per household has decreased, though much less than might be supposed: from 3 to around 2.2 or, in relative numbers, from 100 to 73, a decrease of 27 per cent. During this time, the proportion of suicides in France rose from 55 to 230, or from 100 to 420, an increase of 320 per cent. The first finding can therefore only explain an extremely small part of the second. In Germany, the average number of births scarcely varied during sixty years: it was 36.1 per 1,000 inhabitants in 1841–50 and still 36.1 in 1891–1900. The proportion of suicides, however, doubled from one period to the next. The changing integration of the family, meaning by this its average size, does not therefore explain the variations in the number of suicides.

Durkheim seems indeed to have been aware of this. Family density was the salient factor in his chapter on the influence of marital status on suicide. 'Where collective sentiments are strong,' he said (p. 201), 'it is because the force with which they affect each individual conscience is echoed in all the others, and reciprocally. The intensity they attain therefore depends on the number of consciences which react to them in common.' However, at the end of his book he recognized that 'the aggravation appearing in the

course of the century is independent of marital status.'
Nevertheless, he adds (p. 377), suicides have increased because

> changes have actually occurred in the constitution of the family
> which no longer allow it to have the same preservative
> influence as formerly. While it once kept most of its members
> within its orbit from birth to death and formed a compact
> mass, indivisible and endowed with a quality of permanence,
> its duration is now brief. It is barely formed when it begins to
> disperse. As soon as the children's first growth is over, they very
> often leave to complete their education away from home;
> moreover, it is almost the rule that as soon as they are adult
> they establish themselves away from their parents and the
> hearth is deserted. For most of the time, at present, the family
> may be said to be reduced to the married couple alone, and we
> know that this union acts feebly against suicide.... We certainly
> do not care less for our children but they are entwined less
> closely and continuously with our existence.

While this description may be accurate, we must recognize that
it lacks a statistical basis. Once we no longer consider the family's
composition but instead its spirit, customs, and sentiments, we
can no longer abstract it from the much broader social milieu
which environs it and whose evolution affects it. If the bond
attaching the family 'to the family house and ancestral field'
weakens, or if 'young people leave their natal family before being
in a position to establish one', should not the reason be sought in
changing economic conditions rather than within the household?
The advantage of the research by Morselli and Durkheim,
reviewed in this chapter, is that they concentrate on the form and
external structure of the family considered in isolation, thus
enabling us to discover very definite relationships between its size
and preservative influence. This is an abstract test leading to
certain but limited findings. Should we wish to go further, to
apprehend in all its richness the household's affective and moral
life, its functions and its customs, should we wish to trace its
evolution, we should have to examine it within the environing
urban or rural society. It would then, however, be impossible to
distinguish within this totality of customs what is specifically
familial.

Chapter 9

Suicide and religion

Adolph Wagner showed in 1864, though on the basis of rather limited statistical data, that Protestants commit suicide more than do Catholics. He declares that, being Protestant, this discovery displeased him and that he long hesitated over it, 'as he had great difficulty accepting it.' He had to acknowledge, however, that, whatever the reason, it was so. His observation was confirmed by Oettingen, Legoyt, and, above all, in 1879 by Morselli, who wrote that 'The Italians, Spaniards, and Portuguese, all purely Catholic nations, produce the fewest suicides. In exclusively Protestant countries such as Saxony, Denmark, and Scandinavia, the opposite is true.' This could be due to the influence of climate, race, or nationality. Morselli noticed, however, that in countries where the two religious persuasions coexist, the tendency to suicide diminishes proportionately as Catholics become more numerous. Of thirty-seven comparisons made on the proportions of Catholic and Protestant suicides in Bavarian, Prussian, Austrian, and Hungarian provinces, in Württemberg and in Baden, only four exceptions were found (Galicia, Bukovina, etc.). In thirty-three, Protestants committed suicide much more often that did Catholics.

Morselli observed something else that had escaped Wagner, Oettingen, and Legoyt, namely that the larger the proportion of Catholics in the population of a given country the less marked their advantage in this respect. The suicide rates are furthest apart in Prussia, where Protestants are the most numerous. If the suicide rate of Catholics is set equal to 100, the rate for Protestants is 322. In Bavaria, where the Catholic proportion is larger, it is only 276. In Austria, where Catholics are preponderant by far, the difference is still less noticeable: 100 for Catholics, 155 for Protestants. It seems that the suicide rate for the more numerous religious persuasion approaches that of the less numerous, and that a relative uniformity tends to be established.

The figures of Morselli, Legoyt, Wagner, and Prinzing, which Durkheim reproduced, sufficed to demonstrate that the number of suicides is not the same in diverse religious groups. As Prussian statistics between 1873 and 1890 no longer indicated the religion of the suicides, he had to limit himself to classifying Prussian provinces in four categories according to their proportion of Protestants and to reproducing the number of suicides per million inhabitants in each province, for the period 1883–90.

After 1890, Prussian statistics again indicate the religion of the suicides. This has enabled us to compile Table 9.1. We calculated the numbers in columns 8 to 11 ourselves. All others are reproduced from Morselli for the period 1849–55, and von Mayr for the period 1901–7. The numbers in column 8 are calculated from data reproduced by Krose for the period 1891–1900.

We will not stress the great increase in the suicide rate of Jews, which has quintupled in nearly fifty years. Durkheim had already noticed that while Jews killed themselves less often in the middle of the century than did Catholics, except in Bavaria, 'towards 1870 they begin to lose their ancient privilege.' Taking note of Krose's book, he wrote

> From facts which he borrows, particularly from a work by Rost ('Der Selbstmord in seiner Beziehung zur Konfession und Stadtbevölkerung in Baiern,' in *Historischpolitische Blätter*, XXX, Munich, 1902), it seems indeed to follow that the coefficient of preservation which Jews enjoyed tends more and more to diminish.[1] Although from 1844 to 1856, only 105 suicides annually were produced per million Bavarian Jews, the count from 1880 to 1889 was 115.8, and from 1890 to 1899, 212.4, which is a little more than the Protestants (210.2). In proportion as the Jewish population becomes assimilated to the surrounding population, it loses its traditional virtues without perhaps replacing them with others …. If we are to give their true significance to the preceding figures we must never lose sight of the fact that Jews live above all in cities and that urban life, in and of itself, impels toward suicide.[2]

The Prussian data confirm this forecast, since the suicide rate of Jews in Prussia almost sextupled in fifty years. They used to kill themselves as often as or even a little less often that did the Catholics. Today they clearly kill themselves more often than do the Protestants.[3]

Protestants always kill themselves more often than do Catholics (two-and-a-half times more), but the difference between the rates of the two persuasions has diminished noticeably since 1849–55, for at this period they killed themselves over three times as often. The decrease in the ratio between the rates of the two persuasions

Table 9.1   Suicides in the Prussian provinces by religious persuasion

	Number of suicides per million inhabitants of each persuasion						Ratio between the suicide rates of Protestants and Catholics[4]			Increase or decrease[5]		
	1849 to 1855			1901 to 1907			1849-55	1891-1900	1901-7	From 1849-55 to 1891-1900	From 1891-1900 to 1901-7	From 1849-55 to 1901-7
	Protestants	Catholics	Jews	Protestants	Catholics	Jews						
	1	2	3	4	5	6	7	8	9	10	11	12
East Prussia	{96.6			153	67	250	{311	226	229	{95.5	101	
West Prussia		31	33.3	213	53	141		370	406		108	101
Berlin	—	—	—	316	265	312	—	128	120	—	94	—
Brandenburg	165	—	—	294	303	518	144	106	97	73.5	91.5	67
Pomerania	102	—	—	177	188	292	—	123	94	—	76.5	—
Posnania	124	41.5	38	184	53	135	299	393	358	132	91	120
Silesia	153	58.5	31.2	356	133	236	259	268	268	104	100	104
Saxony	140	26.3	—	317	155	497	532	205	205	38.5	100	38.5
Schleswig-Holstein	—	—	—	294	334	719	—	86	88	—	102	—
Hanover	—	—	—	227	110	387	—	215	206	—	96	—
Westphalia	80	24.4	66.2	169	78	235	328	220	216	67	98	66
Hesse-Nassau	—	—	—	227	158	326	—	155	144	—	93	—
Rhineland	108	27.7	34.5	202	86	247	289	250	235	87	94	82
Prussia	160	49.6	46.4	252	101	294	322	265	250	82.5	94.5	77.5

has been 22.5 per cent. Moreover, we observe that the Protestant suicide rate increased in the period 1852 to 1904, that is, in fifty years, by 58 per cent, while in the same period the Catholic suicide rate rose 102 per cent. In the ten-year period 1895–6 to 1904 the Protestant rate rose only 2 per cent and the Catholic 8 per cent. These general findings are compiled in Table 9.2.

Table 9.2   *Number of suicides per million inhabitants of each persuasion*

	Catholics	Protestants	Jews	Ratio of the rates of Catholics and Protestants[6]
1849–55	50	160	46	320
1869–72	69	187	96	270
1891–1900	93	247	241	265
1901–7	101	252	294	250

Thus, in the twenty-year interval between the first two periods, the ratio of the Protestant to the Catholic suicide rate diminishes very rapidly, by 15.5 per cent. During the interval of more than twenty years separating the second and the third period, the ratio hardly changes (a decrease of barely 2 per cent). During the ten-year interval separating the last two periods, it diminishes again rather rapidly, by 5.5 per cent.[7]

Now let us examine the number of suicides which correspond to the diverse provinces (Table 9.1). Viewing the Catholics and the Protestants of diverse provinces, first separately, then comparatively, we asked whether with respect to suicide the two persuasions resembled one another more today than formerly. Calculating the relative deviation (or coefficient of dispersion) for the Protestants in 1849–55 and in 1901–7 (columns 1 and 4), we obtain 19.8 and 27.29. The same calculation for the Catholics (columns 2 and 5) gives us 29 and 36. Thus, from the outset suicide rates are much more dispersed, that is, unequal, among the totality of Catholics than among the totality of Protestants. However, during the fifty years this dispersion increased much more rapidly for the Protestants than for the Catholics (by 40 per cent and 24 per cent respectively). On the whole, if one considers all of the Catholic or Protestant religious groups in these provinces, one finds more differences as to suicides among Catholics than among Protestant groups, as if more distinct varieties were created because certain Catholic groups undergo the influence of Protestants and vice versa.

Let us ask now whether the suicide rates of Catholics and Protestants tend to converge in each of the provinces (columns 7, 8, and 9). In the first period, we have numbers only for 7 provinces which almost maintain in 1891–1900 the differences in the ratios between the suicide rates of Catholics and Protestants of 1849–55. The coefficient of dispersion, calculated for the first period, is equal to 22.5, and for the second, to 24.5. However, it increases from 1891–1900 to 1901–7, for the 13 provinces as a whole, from 34 in the second period to 47 in the third. Although as a result of this the deviation between the suicide rates of the two religions diminishes on the whole (see Table 9.2), the provinces become more and more differentiated. They show greater variety and on a chart are more variegated.

The tendency to suicide does not therefore vary only from one religious persuasion to another. It continues to vary from province to province. Is this because, as Morselli has said, minority persuasions vary in strength to the extent that they are distinguished from the majority? Let us rank these provinces according to their increasing proportion of Catholics relative to Protestants and let us also rank them according to the decreasing suicide of the Catholics. A certain correspondence is found between these two arrays. Contrast being measured by 6.5, independence by 3.25, correspondence by 0, one finds an effective mean deviation equal to 2. This, however, is only a slight correspondence. We cannot say that Catholics commit suicide everywhere in inverse proportion to their numbers.

Father Krose believed it necessary to take into account not only the number of Catholics but above all the way in which they are grouped. Let us examine the numbers in column 9 (suicide rate of Protestants assuming the Catholic suicide rate equal to 100). We find two provinces, Posnania and the Rhineland, have the highest proportion of Catholics (68 and 70 per cent). However, the difference between the suicide rates of Protestants and Catholics is much higher in Posnania than in the Rhineland (358 and 235 per 100). The proportion of Catholics and Protestants in Silesia and West Prussia is almost the same. However, the difference between the suicide rates of the two persuasions is also larger than in the Rhineland. The rate of suicide of Protestants in the Rhineland, clearly higher than that of Catholics, is lower than that of the Prussian Protestants. Poles are numerous in the eastern provinces of Prussia. The influence of race, if not of nationality, could strengthen the religious contrast there. However, Catholics form a more compact mass here than in the Rhine valley for this very reason. In Schleswig-Holstein, Pomerania, Brandenburg, and Berlin the proportion of Catholics is very low, and their suicide rate very high (higher than the average for Prussian Catholics).

That is because they are very dispersed. However, though the proportion of Catholics in Saxony and Hanover is scarcely higher, they have a moderate suicide rate. That is because there are Catholic concentrations within the Diaspora (Osnabrück, Hildesheim, Erfurt). Thus, the greater the concentration of Catholics the more they should distinguish themselves from Protestants in killing themselves less often. The more Catholics intermingle with believers in different religions the more the strength of their resistance to suicide should diminish.

It is not easy to measure the degree of dispersion of Catholics. However, a sufficiently accurate indicator of the consistency of religious groups can be found if we understand by that their exclusivism and the moral distance separating them. No statistician has used this until now. We shall see, however, that by relating it to suicide rates one arrives at a rather remarkable finding.

Table 9.3 has been compiled with the help of data reproduced in a work by Father Krose on the statistics of religious persuasions in Germany.[8] (He did not think of relating these figures to those of suicide.) We show here for each Prussian province in 1900, first, the proportions of Protestants and Catholics, second, the proportion of mixed marriages as a ratio of Catholic marriages (it suffices to divide these numbers by 2 to have the ratio of Catholics entering into mixed marriages to Catholics entering into Catholic marriages), third, the suicide rates per million inhabitants. These provinces are ranked in order of increasing proportions of mixed marriages.

A very clear correspondence is visible between the ratio of mixed marriages to Catholic marriages, and the suicide rate of Catholics. The opposition being measured by 6.5, the independence by 3.25, and the correspondence by 0, one finds as the average effective deviation, 0.6, that is, an extremely clear indicator of dependence. We have found none closer in the course of our entire study.

We have also calculated the number of mixed marriages per 100 Catholic marriages in Bavaria in 1900, and the number of suicides among the Catholics in 1870–99 (Table 9.4). The opposition being measured by 8, the independence by 4, and the correspondence by 0, one finds an average effective deviation of 1.75, that is, a certain degree of dependence. These findings are not as clear as in Prussia because the Catholic masses are more compact.

Moreover, in comparison with the Prussian figures, the total number of mixed marriages in Bavaria is very low, probably because this time the majority is Catholic and more opposed to them.

Table 9.3 *Suicide in Germany according to family religion and size*

	Number of Catholics	Percentage		Mixed Marriages per 100 Catholic marriages	Suicides per million Catholics	Rank order		Per cent children of mixed marriages	
		Protestants	Catholics			Mixed Marriages	Catholic Suicides	Protestant	Catholic
Posnania	1,280,172	30	68	4.3	49	1	1	56	44
West Prussia	800,395	46	51	15.4	56	2	2	46	54
Rhineland	4,021,388	29	70	15.6	72	3	5	47.5	52.5
Westphalia	1,616,462	48	50	17.6	64	4	3	45	55
East Prussia	269,196	85	13.5	24	70	5	4	52	48
Silesia	2,569,688	43	55	27.5	139	6	7	54	46
Hanover	338,906	86	13	47.5	104	7	6	59	41
Hesse-Nassau	530,541	69	28	65	140	8	8	57	43
Saxony	206,121	92	7	118	153	9	10	69	31
Pomerania	38,169	96.5	2	184	140	10	9	71	29
Berlin	188,440	84	10	320	225	11	11	75.5	24.5
Brandenburg	160,305	93.5	5	340	268	12	12	75	25
Schleswig-Holstein	30,524	97	2	465	362	13	13	76.3	23.7
PRUSSIA	12,113,670	63.29	35.14	27	93	—	—	56.5	48.5

Table 9.4 *Suicide and religious persuasion, Bavaria, 1870–99*

	Number of Catholics	Percentage		Mixed marriages per 100 Catholic marriages	Suicides per million		Ratio of Protestant rates of suicide to Catholic[9]
		Catholics	Protestants		Catholics	Protestants	
Lower Bavaria	671,678	99.04	0.88	1.2	47	233	495
Upper Palatinate	506,618	91.47	8.21	3.1	41	139	340
Middle Franconia	206,193	25.27	72.77	8.5	157	203	130
Lower Franconia	519,812	79.88	17.93	8.8	83	208	250
Swabia	609,250	85.37	13.93	9	97	208	214
Upper Bavaria	1,221,750	92.28	6.71	10	105	341	325
Upper Franconia	256,917	42.25	57.13	22.3	94	217	230
Palatinate	364,915	43.88	54.31	45.5	102	173	169
BAVARIA (total)	4,363,178	70.65	28.32	15	87.8	208.8	240

Table 9.5 *Protestant children and mixed marriages (Prussia)*

Proportion of	Relative numbers West Prussia = 100											
Mixed marriages to mixed plus Catholic marriages	100	112	149	166	268	336	515	668	855	875	960	
Protestant children born of mixed marriages	100	104	98	113	117	128	124	150	154	164	163	166

This ratio of correspondence can be interpreted in two ways: either by the fact that Catholic men or women who enter into mixed marriages become alienated from or leave their religious persuasion, and are less preserved against suicide, or that the number of mixed marriages measures the degree of disintegration of the entire Catholic group. Is it true, however, that a Catholic who enters into a mixed marriage becomes alienated from his religious group? We notice that in only two of the five provinces where Catholics are in the majority, Silesia and Posnania, do the majority (a very small majority) of children born of mixed marriages become Protestants. To be very precise, 49.9 per cent of all children born of mixed marriages in the five provinces are Protestants, against 50.1 per cent Catholics. In the four provinces where Catholics are only 10 to 28 per cent and which are separated from the preceding by a wide margin, the proportion of children born of mixed marriages is 65.5* per cent Protestant against 36.5* per cent Catholic, while in the last four, where Catholics represent less than 7 per cent of the population, the proportion of Catholic children born of mixed marriages is always appreciable: 73 per cent Protestant against 27 per cent Catholic.

We calculated for the eleven Prussian provinces and Berlin the ratio of mixed marriages to every 100 Catholic and mixed marriages combined. We expressed these proportions as relative numbers, setting equal to 100 the proportion corresponding to West Prussia (Posnania is a little exceptional). We calculated the corresponding relative numbers to represent the proportion of *Protestant children* born of mixed marriages in order to show another ascending series (Table 9.5).

As we see, the number of Catholics who contract a mixed marriage increases much more rapidly than the number of Protestant children born of mixed marriages. We may conclude that the majority of these Catholics, in any case, always maintain their relationships to their confessional group and are not necessarily alone in having a higher suicide rate. It must also be true of the entire Catholic group. The fact that 25, 30, 60, 95, 160 and up to 230 Catholics contract a mixed marriage, while only 100 contract a Catholic marriage, cannot fail to weaken the group. Such disturbances repeatedly compromise its equilibrium and slowly slacken its resiliency. It is not surprising that relations of Catholics to the Protestant milieu increase henceforth and the spiritual distance separating the two religious persuasions diminishes. The number of mixed marriages appears to be one of the best indices of the degree of integration or disintegration of the Catholic groups that are dispersed or concentrated in various

*Sic – ed.

Prussian provinces. The Catholic suicide rate increases in proportion to its mixed marriages, showing that Catholics are preserved against suicide to the extent that they live closely related, having few contacts and a minimum of relationships and material exchanges with other religious persuasions.

How may these facts be interpreted?

First, however, they may be challenged. Are not suicides less numerous among Catholics because a great number of them are concealed? 'The church's refusal to cooperate in the funerals of suicides,' said Legoyt, 'a refusal observed rigorously in rural areas in Catholic countries, is a serious reason for the relatives to conceal the cause of death.'[10] However, this passage follows purely hypothetical remarks, for which no evidence is given, on the reasons one may have for concealment. It would be rather extraordinary if the administration in a mostly Protestant country like Prussia were to accept the declaration of Catholics without verification.

The Church's refusal of ministrations at the funerals of the suicides is in fact a grave sanction for every believing Catholic. We recall the priest's declaration at Ophelia's funeral:

> Her obsequies have been as far enlarg'd
> As we have warrantise: her death was doubtful;
> And, but that great command o'ersways the order,
> She should in ground unsanctified have lodg'd
> Till the last trumpet; for charitable prayers,
> Shards, flints, and pebbles should be thrown on her:
> Yet here she is allow'd her virgin crants
> Her maiden strewments, and the bringing home
> Of bell and burial.

When Laertes asks him, 'Must there no more be done?' the priest replies,

> No more be done:
> We should profane the service of the dead
> To sing a requiem, and such rest to her
> As to peace-parted souls.

Thus does Shakespeare scruple about staging a suicide's funeral. However, we are no longer in the sixteenth century and the Church has substantially mitigated its former severity. Bayet traced this evolution, calling attention to many facts which increasingly resulted in hesitation on the part of the priests to apply the canon law in this matter.

No official text indicates what procedure parish priests shall

follow in case of suicide …. The canons all assume that suicide
is not presumed …. Even if there should be a public scandal,
the Church assumes that insanity [merely presumed] is a
sufficient excuse …. The parish priests are advised in all
doubtful cases to which a favourable interpretation can be
given to use indulgence and to accord a Christian burial.

Bayet concluded from much evidence that 'The Church has
mastered its power to refuse ecclesiastic burial to suicides. *The most
general* usage is to accord it to them.'[11]

In Paris and the large cities, the 'suicides' plot' has been done
away with. Doubtless all of this only applies in France. Father
Krose, who was well placed to know the practice in Germany, does
not even allude to this type of objection.

We shall therefore grant that Protestants commit suicide more
than do Catholics. Two explanations why have been proposed.
They appear to be clearly antithetical. According to Father Krose,
Catholics obey the religious commandment which proscribes felo
de se. Durkheim objects that one could not then understand why
Protestants, who also believe in the hereafter, are not restrained
by the same fear. According to him, Catholicism deters from
suicide, not because of any particular dogma, but because the
Catholic Church creates a close community of life and thought
among all its members, by the uniformity of its rites and beliefs
and the importance that it attaches to public worship. Thus, the
faithful feel themselves to be members of the same body, and the
bonds which attach them to their group also hold them to life. The
Church's effect upon the faithful does not differ from that of the
family over its members.

This unique thesis is Durkheim's particular contribution to the
study of the relationship between religion, or religious persuasion,
and suicide. For him, details of dogmas and rites are secondary.
What is essential is that the Catholic Church is a society, more
'integrated' than the other religious groups. We shall wish to
show, however, that one arrives at rather different conceptions
depending on how the term 'integrated' is construed.

Is the Church, or the religious body, a purely religious
community whose entire being and consistency derive from
practices and beliefs common to its members? If so, there may be
no radical opposition between Durkheim and such Catholics as
Father Krose.

Durkheim rejects the idea that the horror of suicide is explained
by fear of the hereafter. He asks why suicide is so frequent among
Protestants, who also fear this, and why 'Judaism, the religion
with least inclination to suicide, is also the one in which the idea of

immortality plays the least role.'[12] However, Jews do not occupy a place apart in society merely because of their religious practices. They have customs, modes of thought, and traditional ways of being which are explained by their common origin, or by the idea they entertain of it, and by the historical circumstances they have experienced. That alone would suffice to tighten the unity of their group. There is no evidence that it is because of their attachment to their religious community as such that they do not kill themselves. The practices relating to worship are only a means for them to maintain the continuity and integrity of their race. Moreover, family sentiments are powerful enough in these milieux to be a sufficient explanation as to why Jews have appeared immune against suicide over long periods. They have lost their immunity because this spirit of family solidarity has changed. The extremely rapid multiplication of mixed marriages between Israelites and Christians does not primarily result from the weakening of religious beliefs among them. Rather, such marriages would not be possible at all if Jewish families were forced back upon themselves as much as formerly and did not allow their members more freedom. There is nothing here that cannot be expressed in purely secular terms except for customs of long standing that have some ties to religion. For the purpose of examining the influence of the religious group as such on suicide, then, it would be better to discard the example of the Jews.

The Protestants, too, like the Catholics, believe in the hereafter, in the Last Judgment, in the reward of the virtuous, and in the punishment of the wicked. Among the Protestants, however, the image of hell is much less concrete and sentient and certainly occupies a lesser place in the totality of their religious representations. The Church teaches that one who dies in a state of mortal sin will undergo, in a definite place, tortures of which corporeal sufferings here on earth give him a foretaste. Some theologians have been able to interpret the punishments and hell fire as symbolic punishments and fire. The teaching of the priests is categorical, however, and has not varied. The wicked are not simply annihilated after death. They do not experience merely moral sufferings. They will burn eternally. To be sure, the mercifulness of God is infinite. Neither the faithful nor the Church know who are the sinners whom He has or has not pardoned. However, it knows, it believes with all its might, that those whom it has not pardoned will certainly suffer in the flesh. The doctrine of the Protestant churches on the fate of sinners after their death is uncertain in still another respect. To be sure there are the elect and the damned. However, there are different opinions about the fate of the damned, and in many instances the burden of elucidating this mystery is placed on the faithful man himself. We must expect that such indefinite punishments will not inspire the same genre of fear among Protestants as among Catholics. It is only natural, therefore, that more of the latter, just as they are about to put themselves to death, should be arrested by the thought that doing this is a mortal sin, and that he who commits it will expose himself to eternal punishment.

We could, to be sure, assume without departing from the domain of religious representations that it is not only the fear of hell, thus imagined, which plays the sole or principal role. Catholics are also more convinced than Protestants that there is a communion of the living and the dead. For them, both the faithful who observe the prescriptions of the Church on earth, and those who live again after death in the abode reserved for the righteous, belong to the same identical society. Now, the gravest misfortune they can expose themselves to is exclusion from this community. Durkheim believed that the consistency and cohesion of the Catholic group is particularly strong. It would be weak were a person to belong to it only during his life, and not perpetuate himself after death. In Protestantism, on the other hand, the idea of a kingdom to come that prolongs earthly society certainly takes second place. The bonds which link the living to one another slacken to the extent that they are not included in a greater whole, for interest then centers on individual consciences and on the moral character of people. People are separated on earth, however, feeling interrelated and united only when they project their thought onto a supernatural society which envelops them. The spirit of free inquiry and of individualism necessarily weakens this mode of representation.

The idea that the society of the living and the society of the dead are but one is met again in primitive or savage societies. That it is the root of religion has been well shown by Robert Hertz.[13]

If there were nothing after death, society would lose all confidence in itself. Whenever one of its members dies, society experiences a sentiment of stupor as if made aware of its weakness, as if momentarily doubting itself. It recovers, however, and asserts that the deceased has not left at all, has joined his ancestors, that is, has done nothing but change location. He abides in society's bosom and is always subject to its power. 'When the souls of the deceased disembark in the land of the dead, their ancestors who have long resided there assemble and bid welcome to the new arrivals.'[14] However,

> those who die by violence or by accident, women who die of childbirth, those who drown or are struck by lightning, and

suicides, are often the object of special rites. Their corpses
inspire the most intense horror, one rids oneself of them in a
hurry. Their bones are never joined with those of other
members of the group who die properly and their souls forever
wander upon the earth, restless and miserable. Or, if they
migrate to another world, it is to dwell in a separate village,
sometimes even in a region entirely different from where the
other souls dwell.

That is because, even during their lifetime, these people had
ceased to belong to society. Society was obviously incapable of
protecting them against hostile forces though, as a rule, it is strong
enough to retain its members and to prevent death itself from
snatching them away. The belief in an invisible world which is a
continuation of this earthly world is at once the condition and the
expression of the unlimited confidence that the religious society
has in itself. Catholicism perpetuates amongst us a conception
which is at the heart of all religions, even the most rudimentary.

Durkheim's conception, however, could be developed in an
entirely different sense. He certainly had reasons for not
explaining the particular aversion Catholic groups manifest
towards voluntary death by the dogma of the future life. He
insisted on the external manifestations of the cult, on the
uniformity of Catholicism in gestures and ways of being and
acting, because he saw no essential difference between this style of
conformity and the totality of conventions towards which
members of any non-religious group are inclined. Religious
customs are indeed religious, but above all they are customs. Now
a group may be called 'integrated' to the extent that in it are
encountered traditional practices which are deeply rooted.
Catholic populations might then differ from all others, not by the
particular nature of their religious beliefs, but simply because they
are better preserved, more traditional. Religious customs would
be only part of these traditions and one would be attached to them
only because they are ancient. We would then have to say that
Catholics kill themselves less often than do Protestants because
fewer suicides are encountered in regions where the force of
customs and ancient traditions is greatest and because the latter
most often occurs in zones occupied by Catholics. If the religious
group is partly confounded with other social formations, villages,
or professional categories, that is, masses of people united by the
sentiment of an ethnic or national community, there is then no
ground or possibility of detaching religious practices from the
totality of collective practices with which they are interdependent
but which do not have a religious character. They define, not a

religious group, but what we may call a style of life or a type of civilization. We shall better understand why many religious practices have this character, and why it is difficult to distinguish which ones are due to religion and which to old popular customs, if we ask why Catholics dread being deprived of a Christian burial. The Church decreed this preliminary punishment at an early period, the only punishment that could be applied in this world to self-homicides, and maintained it through the centuries. From whence did it really come, however, and what are its distant origins? For the Christian Church did not invent it. Did the canonical law of the Middle Ages forbid burial in sacred soil to those who had put themselves to death because suicide was considered an unpardonable sin? Bayet has shown that the Church made no such decision until the end of the fourth century.[15]

> Not only did canonical law [in the fourth century] not punish suicide but the Church Fathers did not ask that it be punished. Saint Augustine nowhere calls for punishment of those who kill themselves. Was it a question of refusing Christian burial? Repeatedly, he insists on the idea that the absence of interment is a matter of indifference for the Christian. It is paganism to imagine that the resurrection could depend on interment. When a Christian dies it is for God to judge him. In this he is in accord with all the Fathers.

Why, however, did the Church change its attitude after the fourth century? The reason is that, born and first diffused in cities, Christianity spread into the countryside only tardily. Thereupon the common masses suddenly invaded the Church. 'Introduced into the mystical banqueting hall abruptly,' said Monsignor Duchesne, 'the common masses brought in practices with which it was quite necessary to come to terms, however shocking they might seem to persons of a more refined upbringing.' Now, according to Bayet, 'a horror of suicide and sanctions against those who kill themselves are only one item among all the disturbing elements that the common multitude brings with it.'[16]

That suicide aroused such censure in milieux where traditional customs are very strong and where the individual is heavily dependent on the group need not at all be explained by religious beliefs. The person who killed himself did not seek advice from those who surrounded him and who valued having rights over him. He showed total indifference towards his family, his relatives, and his village, which was like an enlarged family. He set a deplorable example. How should the community not have reacted with all its might against an act which undermined its faith in itself and which appeared to deride sentiments on which it depended? Desertion is the gravest crime one could commit in war. Similarly, a primitive society resents no offense more profoundly than suicide.

We can therefore assume that even before Christianity the common people in rural milieux did not pay to suicides the funeral respects to which other deceased had a right, and that this custom, in itself not at all religious, was, like so many others, adopted by the Church.[17] The Church put its own stamp on it, of course. When it came within the ordinances of religion it partly changed character. However, we can also assume that, though in new attire, it kept its traditional appearance and authority, and that, in refusing to allow a suicide interment in sacred soil, the priest leaned on a popular, purely secular sentiment of collective censure. A non-believer could be diverted from suicide by the dim fear of such a sanction without considering supernatural consequences or punishments beyond the grave. When, not long ago, the Church was stricter in this respect, was it the terror of hell or the fear of being buried 'like a dog' which restrained the desperate person? We can assert the one just as well as the other. If the custom of considering suicide to be an act rendering one unworthy of reposing in the cemetery was maintained, the religious idea may have lost salience. One values, above all, being buried appropriately.

This example shows that religious motives are sometimes intermingled in strange ways with those based on simple customs. Thus it is that Catholic and peasant milieux are often confounded. Conversely, Protestantism first took root in the cities. There were close relationships between the tenets of the Reformation and urban life. Febvre has shown that the wholesale development of cities of artisans and merchants in the Germany of the sixteenth century prepared the way for Luther's reforms.[18] In the modern period Max Weber, studying the occupational statistics of countries where religious persuasions are intermingled, found remarkable agreement that Protestants are proportionately most numerous among owners of capital, entrepreneurs, and skilled industrial workmen.[19] Protestants have a disproportionate share in technical personnel and higher commerce. Finally, it is primarily the skilled Protestant workmen who leave the small handicraft trades, while Catholics remain to become masters. Now, handicrafts are an industrial regime developed primarily in regions and periods when urban centers are restricted in size and play the role of local markets where the peasants come to sell and to buy provisions.

That Protestants should be proportionally more numerous in

Map 6   *Suicide and religion in Germany in 1901–7 (two maps)*

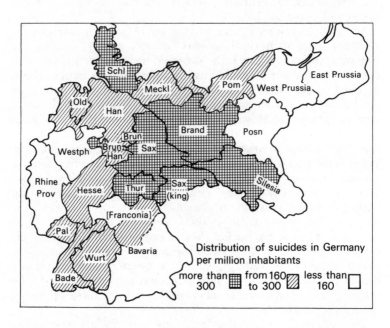

Distribution of suicides in Germany per million inhabitants

more than 300   from 160 to 300   less than 160

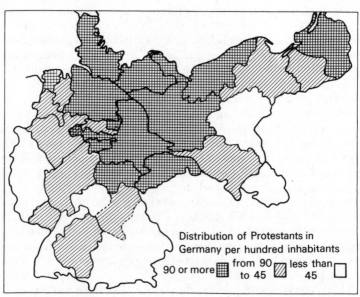

Distribution of Protestants in Germany per hundred inhabitants

90 or more   from 90 to 45   less than 45

the cities, and Catholics in the countryside, would not, of course, justify interpreting the statistics of religious persuasions as if the Protestant groups were all urban, and the Catholic groups rural. However, the type of civilization that we call urban can penetrate into the countryside. Moreover, there are cities, even large cities, which preserve a rhythm and habits of life more characteristic of rural milieux. It is a fact that Protestant villages in the Alsatian countryside are more oriented toward the cities than are the Catholic, and are influenced by communities of the same religious persuasion. The majority of the Catholic priests come from the country and have the traits and bearing of the peasantry. On feast and pilgrimage days, the churches are filled with peasants. The church itself is the center of the village. Its place is not among the great mansions which often overshadow it. It finds itself out of its element near the restless, populous streets of modern cities. The chapel is more like a place for reunion and conference, adapts better to popular districts and fits into the urban framework without difficulty.

Are the indicated differences in number of voluntary deaths among Protestants and Catholics to be explained solely by religion, or equally by the style of life, or what can be called the mode of civilization? Let us again, from this point of view, examine the statistics of suicide in Prussia by religious groups. We reproduce in Table 9.6 numbers drawn from the two preceding tables, but group the provinces in a different order.

Prussia as a whole has a suicide rate of 247 for Protestants and 92 for Catholics. However, Prussia's regions are quite different (see Map 6). First of all, the northeastern provinces contain a very large proportion of Poles. We owe to a German work published fifteen years before the period we are studying the following numbers, which are certainly too low.[20] In Posnania at this period there were 800,000 Poles out of 1,715,000 inhabitants; in West Prussia, 490,000 out of 1,408,000; and in East Prussia, 400,000 Poles and 145,000 Lithuanians out of 1,959,000 inhabitants. Almost all the Catholics are Poles while the Protestants are all Germans. Now, in this borderland region of German colonization, entirely covered by great rural domains, the Poles represent the peasant class, and the Germans the class which dominates and exploits the country through administration and commerce. These two elements living side by side are clearly opposite social types. The influence of religion cannot be studied here, for behind the religious groups are seen, on the one hand, the peasantry, and on the other, the tradespeople, public officials, managers, administrators, etc. It is also very probable that some of the German Protestants live in the

Table 9.6   *Suicides in the Prussian provinces, by religious persuasion*

	Per 100 inhabitants		Per 1,000,000 inhabitants		Protestant suicide rate (Catholic rate = 100)
	proportion		proportion		
	Protes-tants	Catho-lics	Protes-tants	Catho-lics	
Posnania	30	68	184	53	358
West Prussia	46	51	213	53	400
East Prussia	85	13.5	153	67	229
Silesia	43	55	356	133	268
Saxony	92	7	317	155	205
Pomerania	96.5	2	177	188	94
Brandenburg	93.5	5	294	303	97
Schleswig-Holstein	97	2	294	334	88
Hanover	86	13	227	110	206
Hesse-Nassau	69	28	227	158	144
Westphalia	48	50	169	78	216
Rhineland	29	70	202	86	235

country. This would explain why their suicide rate, though clearly higher than that of the Catholics, nevertheless remains lower than the average for all of Prussia.

Let us travel now to the western provinces: Hesse-Nassau, Westphalia, and the Rhineland. Catholics are as numerous there proportionately as in the northeast of Prussia. However, suicides are more frequent than among the Catholics of the east, and the difference in suicides between Catholics and Protestants is much less marked than in Posnania or West Prussia. Now, as in the eastern provinces, there are many peasants throughout this part of Prussia, but here the soil is more fertile and the rural population is richer. This is a more advanced agricultural region. Moreover, industry is located here. The great industrial agglomerations in the Rhine valley, and above all in Westphalia, concentrate a large working-class population which is primarily Protestant. The map of religious persuasions in Germany appears to show that, while the largest part of Westphalia is Catholic, the Ruhr region, Barmen, Elberfeld, and Dortmund, constitutes a Protestant island.[21] That the Protestant suicide rate should be much lower in Westphalia than the average for the Protestants in the whole of Prussia, 169 instead of 247, is remarkable. This is probably due to the fact that this population of Protestant workmen includes a large proportion of miners and blast-furnace workers who live in half-rustic working-class settlements around the mines. We notice from the statistics of suicides by occupation in Prussia that the mines and ironwork factories yield a particularly low proportion of voluntary deaths: 70 per million on the average in 1895 and 1907. This is much less than in the rest of industry (suicide rate: 172), and even much less than among the Prussian farmers (suicide rate: 135).[22] The influence of industry on the rural population of Westphalia appears to have been weak. Instead, the reverse is true. This population of workmen differs from industrial workers long settled in the cities in that a large number of them have probably left the peasant class only recently.[23] In any case, the contrast between Protestant industrial milieux and Catholic agricultural milieux appears rather marked, so that here again it is certainly unnecessary to invoke religious causes uniquely, or perhaps even principally, in order to explain why members of one religious persuasion kill themselves more often than do others.

A larger proportion of Catholics than Protestants is found in Silesia, which is clearly an industrial province. In general, both groups kill themselves more often than do Prussians of the same religious persuasion. The difference between their suicide rates is of the same order as in Westphalia. Here too, however, Poles are numerous: 800,000 out of 4,111,400 inhabitants, not counting 140,000 Wends and at least 50,000 Czechs. The Slavic part of the population is Catholic. A very large number of them undoubtedly work in the mines and factories, and this explains why the proportion of suicides is much higher among the Catholic Silesian Slavs than in the Polish agrarian communities of Posnania and the two Prussias. However, although they are industrial workers and more Germanized, the Silesian Poles remain in contact with the rural Polish groups because an entire part of Silesia is agricultural. They differ from the Germans, clearly, not only in religion but, even more, in style of life.

There remains the group of purely Protestant provinces of the center and the north: Pomerania, Brandenburg, Schleswig-Holstein, Hanover, and Saxony. The last two contain a slightly greater proportion of Catholics than the others, 13 and 7 per cent, most of whom are probably found in those parts of the provinces nearest to Westphalia and Hesse-Nassau, that is, in the most agricultural districts in Hanover of Hildesheim and Osnabrück, and in Saxony of Erfurt and Merseburg. In fact, the Catholic suicide rate is the same in Saxony, Hesse-Nassau, Hanover, and Westphalia. However, in the three provinces of Pomerania, Brandenburg, and Schleswig-Holstein, where Catholics represent only a very small minority (from 2 to 5 per cent), we are surprised to discover that they kill themselves more often than do the Protestants. Are we to assume that they lose their immunity entirely upon contact with Protestants? After all, they are still Catholics. We believe that the only reason why these Catholics, who are certainly from foreign countries, find themselves situated thus in the midst of a homogeneous Protestant mass is that, like all tiny religious minorities, they have high social rank and belong to the elite of the urban classes. They are more exposed to suicide for the same reason.

The Protestant population of this group of provinces is as much rural as urban, and is distributed among all the professions. There is nothing to prevent us from assuming that these German Protestants kill themselves more often in the city than in the countryside, in industrial milieux than in rural milieux. Pomerania is a country almost exclusively populated by peasants. A very great difference is found between the suicide rate of Protestants here as compared with Brandenburg: 177 in Pomerania, 294 in Brandenburg. True, this proportion is lower in rural Brandenburg than in urban, and very high in the cities. It is a fact that Protestants kill themselves much more often in these purely Protestant provinces than elsewhere. Is this because Catholicism does not exert any influence in purely Protestant religious milieux? We note that North Germans have always been settled in these provinces. These are not Slavic lands colonized by Germans, nor are they regions oriented toward western Europe, with which they have many traits in common, and which have been closely attached to Prussia only by historical circumstances and the rise of German industry. While they are the most Protestant regions of the Empire, however, they and the Empire have many other traits in common. National customs exist alongside rural or urban customs and explain why men are more or less firmly held to life. Each region has its own proper suicide rate. This is partly explained by its past, by the fact that its inhabitants have long lived closely related to one another in a cohesive historical and national community. That in these provinces the Prussians commit suicide, not only more often than do the Catholics, but also more often than the Protestants in other parts of Prussia, can be explained by causes other than their religion.

Study of the statistics of suicides by religious persuasion in Prussia leads us to the following conclusion: in the eastern provinces and in the provinces of the west, Protestants kill themselves more often than do Catholics largely because of the different types of occupation they pursue, and the contrasts in the urban or rural milieux in which they live. That people in the central provinces, where there are only Protestants, kill themselves more often than do other Prussian Protestants can be explained in large measure by the specifically German national character of these populations. They do not include the Slavic element, and have been influenced only recently by western civilization.

As we have shown, the proportion of suicides among Catholics increases in provinces where mixed marriages are most numerous. Our hypothesis explains this very well. Mixed marriages are, in fact, more frequent in cities than in the country. The more Catholics experience the influence of urban conditions of life, the more they kill themselves. It is not that those among them who really practice their religion become separated from it. We have seen, on the contrary, that Catholics who contract such marriages have their children brought up in the Catholic religion. They do not renounce their beliefs. However, from one type of civilization, the rural, they pass on to another, the urban: one which entails a larger number of voluntary deaths.

We know the distribution of suicides by religious persuasion for a small number of other countries. Let us see if the facts there can be interpreted in the same manner as in Prussia. In Bavaria, of 100 inhabitants 71 are Catholics and 28 Protestants. Now, Catholics commit suicide there almost as often as in Prussia: 88 suicides per million Catholics, instead of 93. Voluntary deaths are much less numerous among Bavarian than among Prussian Protestants, 209 per million instead of 247, but are three times as numerous as among Bavarian Catholics. Is this last difference indeed explained by religion? Do Protestants kill themselves less often in Bavaria than in Prussia because in Bavaria they are more subject to the influence of Catholics, who are in the majority there? Let us refer to Table 9.3, where these findings are reported by province. We notice immediately that in two provinces, Lower Bavaria and Upper Palatinate, the suicide rate of Catholics is very low (equal to only half of the average of the Catholics). It is even lower than in Posnania. There are no Poles in this part of Bavaria. However, this entire region is situated on the reverse or western side of the mountains of Bohemia. This is the Böhmerwald. Now, '70 per cent of the population of the Böhmerwald is devoted to agriculture; only 7 per cent is employed in the glassworks.' In Lower Bavaria, 99 per cent of the population is Catholic and almost exclusively rustic; the part of the population to which the very high Protestant suicide rate corresponds must be purely urban. Only Catholics are found in the Upper Palatinate, where 'the forest occupies 40 per cent of the surface.' The Protestants of the Upper Palatinate, who comprise 8 per cent of its population, commit suicide more than do the Catholics, but much less than do the Protestants of the other provinces. Although located primarily in the cities, they live in a milieu totally penetrated by rural influences. Ratisbon, the only large city of the Upper Palatinate, consists of only 45,000 souls. 'A third of its population is Protestant but only 40 per cent of the inhabitants earn a living from industry.' The two most southern provinces, Swabia (Augsburg) and Upper Bavaria (Munich) are situated in a mountainous region bordering on the Alps (Voralpen). The population here is sparse and primarily rural even in the vicinity of Munich. In Upper Bavaria, only 20 per cent of the population is engaged in industry. The Protestants, who constitute 8 per cent of the population, must be concentrated in Munich and engaged principally in commercial and industrial occupations.[24] This explains why they have a much higher suicide rate than the average for the Bavarian Protestants, or 341. This is a rate not attained by the Protestants in Brandenburg and exceeded only a little by those in Silesia. We are told that '94 per cent of the population in the Voralpen is Catholic. There are only 150,000 Protestants and they live exclusively in the cities.' In Swabia only 30 per cent of the population is engaged in industry. Protestants number 15 per cent in this province and must be very few outside the urban agglomerations.

In Middle Franconia, north of Bavaria, a quarter of the population is Catholic and the other three-quarters Protestant. The suicide rate is only a little higher among the Protestants than among the Catholics: in relative numbers, 100 for the Catholics but only 130 for the Protestants (instead of the ratios of 100 and 240 for all of Bavaria and 100 and 250 for all of Prussia). This is because the Catholic suicide rate in this province is twice the average for all Catholics in Bavaria. Now, Middle Franconia is the only Bavarian province that is clearly oriented toward industry. At Nuremberg, 56 per cent of the population is engaged in industrial occupations and 15 per cent (that is, more than in the other large cities of Bavaria) in commercial occupations. This is the most Protestant region and at the same time the most industrial: not an accidental coincidence. A good part of the Catholic minority must also be engaged in industry and live in more or less urbanized milieux. This explains why more people kill themselves here than elsewhere and why they do not differ much in this respect from Protestants.

The Bavarian Palatinate, which runs along the left bank of the Rhine, on the slopes of the Hardt, consists 44 per cent of Catholics, 55 per cent of Protestants.[25] At this time, Ludwigshafen hardly exists, and even though the neighboring Saar is developing its mining industry very rapidly, this region is still principally agricultural. The difference between the proportion of suicides among Catholics and Protestants is not high because rural influences penetrate the cities. However, in the Rhine valley the (Catholic) peasants have found fertile soil. Vine-growers, they are more affluent than the dispersed inhabitants of forests and peat-bogs in Lower Bavaria and in the Upper Palatinate (equally Catholic). They are clearly more exposed to suicide, at least twice as much.

That Protestants kill themselves more often than do Catholics, in every Bavarian province, can therefore be explained by the customs and dispositions of urban and rural milieux among which the members of these two religious persuasions are unequally distributed.

Table 9.7 shows how suicides are distributed by religious persuasion in another German state, the last, after Bavaria and Prussia, for which we possess figures.

Table 9.7   *Suicides by religious persuasion in Württemberg (1884–93)*

Districts	Per 100 inhabitants, number of Protestant	Catholic	Number of suicides per million Protestant	Catholic	Relative numbers Protestant suicide rate (Catholic rate = 100)
Neckar	85	14	184	182	100
Black Forest	74	25	148	122	122
Jagst	69	31	136	74	184
Danube	37.5	62	218	130	168

The Protestant suicide rate for the whole of Württemberg is 182 and the Catholic, 126. The ratio of these two numbers is 144 to 100, much lower than in Bavaria (240 to 100) or Prussia (250 to 100). At this period Württemberg is more populous than Bavaria, with 103 inhabitants per square kilometer instead of 71.5. It is also a more industrial region. In the Neckar and the Black Forest, which contain two-fifths of the Württemberg population, Catholics are a very small minority. What catches one's attention above all in Table 9.7 is that the suicide rates of the two religious persuasions are extremely close, even equal in the Neckar. Now, the population of these provinces is the most dense: 182 inhabitants per square kilometer in the Neckar and 99 in the Black Forest, compared with 80 and 74 in the other two provinces. Here is where industry is the most developed. In the Neckar valley 40 to 45 per cent of the inhabitants are employed in industry: spinning mills, weaving mills, and machine construction. Catholics commit suicide here as often as the Protestants, not, as Father Krose says,[26] simply because they are few in number and dispersed, but rather because they live in industrialized and urbanized milieux.

> The Black Forest and the Jagst [he adds] are also mainly Protestant, but the Catholics are not formed into little communities scattered about the whole district. The majority are grouped in very old Catholic regions that have been annexed with rather large Protestant zones into one administrative district. This is why they commit suicide less often here than elsewhere, less often even than in the district of the Danube where Catholics are a majority. It is true that the suicide rate is extraordinarily high at Ulm, in the Danube district, for Catholics as well as Protestants.

However, almost the whole population of Ulm is Protestant and does not exceed 50,000 inhabitants in 1885, while they number 465,000 in the Danube district. It is more likely that the Catholic suicide rate in the Jagst is so low because they are exclusively rustic, and that the Protestant suicide rate in the Danube is so high because they are all engaged in industry and commerce. Hence, in Württemberg, as in Bavaria and Prussia, when we venture into detail, rather than depend on averages for the totality, explanation of inequality in the suicide rates of diverse religious persuasions in terms of religion alone appears more problematic.

Now, these German statistics are nearly the only ones on which we can depend when we tackle this problem.[27] No enlightenment can be had from comparisons among countries, for there are many other differences between a country such as Denmark or Sweden and another such as Italy, besides religious persuasion.

The best way of establishing that not religion itself, but customs and style of life are what modify the tendency to suicide, would be to study the Catholics and Protestants separately, distinguished by trade or profession. Statistics which would permit making such comparisons are rather rare. Those we reproduce in Table 9.8 were compiled from figures obtained in Switzerland for the period 1881–90.[28] Not only cantons but districts are distinguished according to religious persuasion, economic character (industrial, agricultural, and mixed), and nationality. We have taken the figures in columns 1, 2, 4, and 5 from the table Krose presented, and ourselves calculated the relative numbers and distances.

Table 9.8 *Suicides in Switzerland, 1881–90*

Groups of districts	Population in thousands of inhabitants		Number of suicides per million inhabitants				Relative distance[29]
	Protestant districts	Catholic districts	Protestant districts		Catholic districts		
			Rates	Relative numbers	Rates	Relative numbers	
Industrial							
German	818	214	257	100	165	100	156
French	291	91	378	147	309	187	126
Total	1,108	305	289	—	208	—	144
Mixed							
German	457	296	228	100	116	100	197
French	115	70	429	188	151	130	284
Italian	—	96	—	—	66	57	—
Roman	11	—	153	67	—	—	—
Total	584	462	266	—	309	—	240
Agricultural							
German	111	108	209	100	74	100	281
French	47	99	414	198	88	119	470
Italian	—	43	—	—	82	111	—
Roman	11	23	213	102	88	119	242
Total	169	273	266	—	81	—	330
Swiss	1,861	1,040	280	—	132	—	212

We notice from the first two columns that there are 180 Protestants per 100 Catholics in Switzerland and 440 Germans per 100 Frenchmen. The Catholics are a majority in the agricultural districts (162 Catholics per 100 Protestants); in the mixed districts the two religious persuasions, though not balanced exactly, are distributed more equally (126 Protestants per 100 Catholics); finally, in the industrial districts, the Protestant population is by far the most numerous (365 Protestants per 100 Catholics). Thus, industry attracts and employs Protestants especially; agriculture, Catholics. We may assume that in industrial districts, most Catholics live in the rural areas surrounding the cities, and that in the agricultural districts, the Protestants prefer to group in the most dense agglomerations.

The numbers in the last column show that in every group of districts where the two religious persuasions are represented, Catholics kill themselves less often than do Protestants. This advantage is most apparent, however, in the agricultural districts where, if the Catholic suicide rate is set equal to 100, the rate for Protestants is 330. Protestants commit suicide there almost three-and-a-half times as often as Catholics. This finding concerns only a limited population (15 per cent of the entire Swiss population). Districts in which farmers and industrial workers are intermingled comprise 36 per cent of the total population. The difference here is still sizeable: as one passes from Catholics to Protestants the proportion of suicides varies in the ratio of 100 to 240: Protestants seek death voluntarily two-and-a-half times as often as Catholics. In purely industrial districts, however, this proportion only varies from 100 to 144; the Catholics remain better protected against suicide, but only a little better.

While Catholics of both nationality groups lose part of their immunity in urban and industrial milieux, French Catholics do so especially. German Protestants kill themselves a little more often here than in the countryside, and the tendency among French Protestants hardly changes. Table 9.9 shows this clearly.

Table 9.9   *Proportion of suicides per million inhabitants, Switzerland*

	Agricultural districts	Mixed districts	Industrial districts
German Catholics	74	116	165
French Catholics	88	151	309
German Protestants	209	228	257
French Protestants	414	429	378

The influence of the urban or rural milieu therefore appears to be the dominant one. Catholics in the countryside kill themselves so little, not because they are Catholics, but because they live in a rural, traditional milieu. It suffices to transport them to urban milieux for them to become remarkably similar to the Protestants. Protestants are brought to suicide not because they are Protestant but because they live in urban milieux, or are under the influence of these milieux. They may, like German Protestants, kill themselves less often when they are in the country. In that case, urban and rural influences are balanced in their group. Like the French Protestants, however, they too may happen to be accessible only to urban influences, even in the country.

The preponderant effect which city and country exert can be illuminated by still another method: industrial and agricultural occupations. The relative numbers reproduced in columns 4 and 6 show the ratios of suicide rates in French and German districts of each category. They are always higher in French than in German districts, but differences between Catholics of diverse nationalities, German, French, Italian, and Roman, are extremely small. Evidently there is a totality of very homogeneous, traditional customs here, a pure type of peasant civilization. The suicide rate is almost the same here as among Catholic Bavarians of the same period, as in Westphalia in 1901–7, as in Brittany and in the regions of France where, before 1880, people committed suicide the least (Provence, Languedoc, and the central departments). The difference between German and French Protestants in the industrial districts is more marked, from 100 to 147, but moderate. The suicide rate of French Protestants was the same as in the French regions where, at the same period, people killed themselves most often (Marne, Seine-et-Marne, Seine-et-Oise). The average suicide rate for German Protestants in these industrial regions is almost exactly the same as for the totality of German Protestants in 1901–7. There is a very strong difference between the German and French Protestants in agricultural districts, as opposed to the German and French Catholics in industrial districts: in both instances the French kill themselves almost twice as often as do the Germans. It is as if the French Protestants, even in the country, distinguish themselves from the Catholic peasants much more plainly than from the Germans, besides being much less numerous than the Germans, and as if the French Catholics in the cities lost their immunity entirely.

Were it religion which preserved the Catholics, viewed as a religious community, we would be unable to understand why they commit little suicide in the country while their propensity for it increases very rapidly in the cities. As we go from rural to industrial milieux, the suicide rate of German Catholics increases by 123 per cent, while the corresponding increase among the French Catholics is 250 per cent. Is not the influence of agricultural or industrial milieux dominant here? Shall we say that religion exerts all its preserving influence only when protected by a framework of peasant customs? In that case, however, why not attribute such power to the framework itself? Protestants living in the countryside are not influenced by the peasant milieu to the same extent because they do not become involved in it completely: in agricultural regions they represent divergent elements whose occupations and habits are oriented toward the cities and industry. Besides, the German Protestants, who comprise three-quarters of the Protestants living in Switzerland, kill themselves less often in the mixed districts than in the industrial districts, and still less often in the agricultural districts than in the mixed districts. Is this because their religious group is more uniform? Is it because the further they are from the cities, the more integrated? No. They are, however, a little less strongly influenced by the urban milieux to which they are attached without being steeped in them completely. There is only one rather weak difference between the suicide rate of German Protestants in the country and of German Catholics in the city. Were only religion operative here, we would have to say that the former are bad Protestants and the latter bad Catholics.

When the influences that nationality, occupation, and religion appear to exert on the multiplication of voluntary deaths are studied separately for all the districts, the following rates are obtained:

Protestants	280 ⎫	
Catholics	132 ⎭	213
Industrial workers	270 ⎫	
Agricultural workers	152 ⎭	178
Frenchmen	315 ⎫	
Germans	208 ⎭	152

The numbers to the right show for each comparison the ratio of the higher number to the lower set equal to 100. Let us first examine the first four categories. The difference between Protestants and Catholics is greater than between industrial and agricultural workers. Father Krose concludes from this that variations in suicide are not explained by economic and national characteristics. The main cause here is the difference in religion. However, the proportions of French and Germans among the Protestants and Catholics who are engaged in industrial and agricultural occupations are unequal. If differences within these groups of Catholics and Protestants, due to occupation and nationality, add to and reinforce one another, the distance between Catholics and Protestants will be greatest, without religion itself exerting a distinct influence. The religious group is therefore only the form in which a totality of people, having other characteristics, present themselves, and what is called religious influence only expresses the resultant of these characteristics. Thus, the Germans constitute 70 per cent of the Swiss Catholic districts, the French 30 per cent. They do not include 30 per cent of the industrial districts. Both the German and agricultural elements have little inclination to suicide. When these two tendencies combine, it becomes understandable why the proportion of voluntary deaths is so low among Catholics. Almost 60 per cent of the Protestant districts are industrial, and there are weighty reasons for assuming that the Protestants in mixed and agricultural districts prefer to engage in industrial occupations. However, only 25 per cent of the Protestant districts are French. We therefore find that the Protestant suicide rate is principally the result of forces impelling toward suicide people who are engaged in industry and are German. While high, it will be lower than if the Protestant group had included more Frenchmen. In fact, it exceeds the suicide rate of the industrial districts: 280 instead of 270. There is therefore no reason to attribute to religion as such what can be adequately explained by industrial or agricultural, urban or rural style of life.

In sum, that Protestants kill themselves more often than do Catholics is correct, as was observed by the first statisticians to study suicide. But why? Do differences in religion explain this fact. A priori, we immediately perceive reasons drawn from doctrine and rites, like those presented by the two religions, which could lead us to attribute the privileged situation of Catholics and their particular aversion to self-homicide to Catholicism as such. Father Krose reproduced the following passage extracted from a study of suicide by Osiander, a Protestant, published at the beginning of the nineteenth century:

> A faithful Catholic's supreme wish is to depart from this world fortified by the holy sacraments. As suicide would of necessity deprive him of this means of arriving at a blissful eternity, only a non-believing or strayed Catholic could kill himself voluntarily.

Another Protestant, J. L. Casper, wrote in 1846: 'I must admit that the sacrament of the confession and of extreme unction, without which the Catholic believer does not wish to leave the world, is certainly in many cases a weapon against suicide.' Adolph Wagner undoubtedly did not believe that the frequency of suicides among

Protestants was to be explained exclusively by religion. According to him, congenital, anatomic, or physiological differences existed between the Protestant and the Catholic: the two did not have the same brain or the same cerebral substance. In addition to this physical factor, however, protection was partly caused by the influence of religious practices and beliefs, especially the confession. Prinzing expressed the same opinion, adding that the fear of what would come after death can restrain even those who are not very devout. Father Krose also thinks that a firm belief in life beyond the grave, where the virtuous will be recompensed and the wicked punished, is the decisive motive turning the Catholic from suicide. The role played by confession is only secondary; it is not efficacious if one does not believe in an eternal life. That is why Protestants themselves find support in their faith when it is strong, and why it depends on the country or the province whether Protestants are more or less exposed to suicide and kill themselves more often in Germany than in England, Scotland, and Holland.

The shortcoming of this style of explanation is that there is no way of demonstrating whether it is right or wrong. We know that people have exposed themselves to certain death because they were assured of enjoying eternal bliss afterwards. There have been Christian suicides, voluntary martyrs.[30] If, to gain heaven, Christians have sought and endured torture unto death, why should not others, to avoid hell, bear evils they have not sought and resign themselves to life? It is logically absurd to commit suicide if one is a devout Catholic. Therein lies the whole question. Durkheim was right not to consider this type of motive, not at all because it could not exist or be strong enough, in many cases, to turn people from voluntary death, but because it takes the form of an individual sentiment which escapes all observation.

Durkheim sought the cause of the aversion that Catholics feel for suicide, not in dogma or belief, but in the form of their religious grouping. Catholics, according to him, resist the temptation to put themselves to death better than do Protestants because the society they are a part of is more integrated, that is, because the bonds which connect its members are rather tight. Of what does the type of influence which this group exerts on its members consist? Must we assume that the commandments of the Church have more authority over the faithful? Or does Durkheim indeed wish to say that life in common with people who think as do the faithful and observe the same practices is such a source of joy and comfort to them that it is distressing to leave it? Undoubtedly both, for the best way to become aware of participating in the same collective life is by performing the same duties. The difficulty does not at all lie here, but rather in the religious or non-religious meaning of the term 'integration'. Now, there is no doubt that the religious character of this association is foremost in his thought.

When, like Durkheim, however, one seizes upon practices external to religion in order to recognize the existence and to measure the cohesion of a religious group, it is difficult indeed to distinguish religious habits from other customs, as most often they form a whole which cannot be resolved into constituent parts. Is the peasant attached to his church because this is the location of the cult, or because to him it represents his village? Does he honor his dead and maintain their tombs because he thinks of the community of the living and the dead, of the future life, or because he preserves the remembrance of those who have preceded him, in his house, on his land, and through traditional attachment to what represents the past? Does suicide horrify him because it is an unpardonable sin, or because whoever kills himself is deemed peculiar and dies according to forms which are inadmissible in the rural community? To be able to distinguish what is and what is not truly religious, the religious group must not be intermingled with a non-religious society; its rites and ceremonies must not at all be bound up with traditional customs and festivals that are without any transcendental meaning. The first Christian communities may have been like this, composed of believers who practiced different occupations, usually lived in separate neighborhoods, and found themselves, on departure from the church, immersed in pagan surroundings. However, this is usually not the case among Catholic groups. When the Church does lack ties to a group outside the church, when Catholics outside the ritual are dispersed, living in contact with people of other religions or even irreligious people, then Catholicism ceases to offer protection against suicide, or offers less. The Catholic community therefore conserves its efficacious quality only when intermingling with a group not specifically religious. Is it then in the religious community, or in this latter group, that the Catholic must be strongly integrated, as Durkheim would say, in order to ward off the thought of voluntary death?

A religion such as Catholicism is more widespread in rural milieux for traditional reasons. It is the oldest religion, and the peasants who, as we know, were the last to convert to it at the beginning of the Christian era, will also be the last to separate from it. Historical circumstances in some countries have been able to counter natural tendencies inclining the rural population to conserve its traditional religious customs, and urban populations to prefer a new cult, possibly more consistent with their interests and style of activity. Father Krose admits without hesitation that Catholicism is imposed on us at birth, not at all in the name of the Church but because, until relatively recently, it was the state religion. The distribution of occupational groups in the German states is still reminiscent of Germany's political image at the time of the Reformation and the Counter-Reformation. The principle *cujus regio, hujus religio* did indeed make it necessary to adopt the prince's religion, but the reasons for his choice most often had nothing to do with religion. On the whole, Catholics are much more numerous in the rural milieux of Germany, while the majority of the Protestants are in the cities or in the regions that are most urban.

There are certain affinities between peasant customs and Catholicism. Protestantism, on the other hand, presupposes individualistic sentiments, a taste for initiative, and for this-worldly activities. These develop only in the urban milieux of commerce and industry. If each religion is well adapted to its style of life, we should expect both to afford equal protection to its members. This is not at all the case because the forces impelling toward suicide are engendered by these styles of life, and, as noted by Durkheim, are more numerous and undoubtedly more intense in the less well-organized or integrated milieux than in the others.

Urban societies are not organized, nor are peasant groups consolidated and perpetuated around religious concepts. The basis of their cohesion is not at all found there, but rather in a social structure composed of customs and institutions, some of which are traditional while others are more recent. There is no reason to perceive such groups only from a religious point of view. Though they also include religious practices, they are far more complex. While most of the members of these groups are Catholic, they share many other traits in common. This cohesion of tradition, rather than their religious cohesion, explains why less suicide is encountered here than in less conservative societies.

Moreover, as Durkheim notes, integration and cohesion are not the privilege solely of peasant classes. There is nothing to prevent customs in urban industrial milieux from becoming fixed traditions that are transmitted, or to prevent life from being quite as strongly organized here as elsewhere.

Moral conformity is perfectly consistent with the individualism commonly attributed to the inhabitants of a great Protestant nation such as England. Now, suicides are in fact few in England. We have tried to explain this apparent contradiction, since the English are Protestants. Durkheim said that this confirmed the rule, for 'the Anglican Church is indeed more strongly integrated than the other Protestant churches .... Many religious regulations are still enforced there by law …. Of the Protestant clergies, only the Anglican is graded.' These observations, though correct, do not suffice to explain why the English do not kill themselves more often than do Prussian Catholics. The truth is that religious conformity blends with the moral conformity which is so obvious a trait of English life. Despite the extensiveness of industrial and commercial development and the rapidity of urbanization, customs adapted to this style of life were established early in this country. The English succeeded by means of precise, traditional rules in constructing a civilization which simultaneously assures their material comfort and guarantees their moral calm. Religion, which is only part of this totality, is very well adapted to it: tradesmen, businessmen, clerks, and workers accommodate themselves to it perfectly, in just the way that, in Germany, the rural inhabitants, artisans, and that part of the urban population which is most imbued with traditional habits accommodates itself to Catholicism. It is the organization of morals in these two quite different cases which explains why English Protestants and German Catholics are equally protected against suicide, despite the difference in religion. Part of the reason the German Protestants are much less protected may be that their religious faith is weaker than that of the English churches. Their faith is less constant, however, because their religion is not well adapted to their style of life and, more generally, because that style of life is itself not well organized. Individual activity is not subject to traditions that are sufficiently strong and customs that are adequately rooted. A people can be capable of great collective works in the physical and industrial domain and yet be incapable, at the same time, of organizing its practical and moral life because its members are too lacking in individual initiative. This may be the case in the purely Protestant provinces of central Germany where the highest proportions of voluntary deaths are found.

Thus, it is certainly a bit premature to conclude that Protestants are especially exposed to suicide. German Protestantism presents particular traits just because it is German. Whenever religious influences vary by milieu we must guard against attributing to religion influences emanating from the milieu.[31]

chapter 10

Suicide and homicide

The previous research has led us to assume that an increase in suicides, wherever found, is related to the transition from one type of civilization to another. Italy offers us a really remarkable example of such an evolution. In 1875 first and second degree murders were still much more numerous than voluntary deaths. In that year only 922 suicides were counted here, as against 3,280 accusations of homicide. That is, the Italians killed others three-and-a-half times as often as they killed themselves. Now in 1913 the reverse is true. The number of suicides, now risen to 3,107, has more than tripled. Homicides diminished during this time by much more than half: the number of accusations of first and second degree murder fell to 1,389. More than twice as many Italians kill themselves as kill others. In forty years Italy has brought herself into modern civilization.

Is it quite true that suicide gains all that homicide loses? Several Italian authors, especially Morselli and Enrico Ferri, have maintained that suicide and homicide do in fact oppose one another consistently, forming two contrary currents, so that one cannot advance without the other receding. They saw in suicide and homicide

> two manifestations of a given condition, two effects of a given cause which sometimes expressed itself under one form and sometimes under the other, without being able to assume both at the same time. Suicide is a homicide transformed and attenuated.

Durkheim has examined and discussed this thesis at length (pp. 339–60).

Enrico Ferri recently reintroduced it in a communication to the XVIth Session of the International Institute of Statistics (Rome,

1925). He reproduced the number of verified suicides and of accusations of simple or aggravated homicide, annually, up to the most recent years, for seven nations: Italy, France, England, Germany, Belgium, Ireland, and Spain.[1]

Let us examine these tables rather closely, replacing those on which Ferri relied by relative numbers.

In Italy, suicides increased from 100 in 1861–5 to 265 in 1871–5 and to 295 in 1923, while homicides decreased from 100 in 1871–5 to 33.5 in 1911–15. On the other hand, we find that after the war homicides increased strongly from 100 in 1918 to 160 in 1919, 260 in 1920, and 270 in 1921 (the same as the figure for *circa* 1900), while, for their part, suicides increased.[2] We recognize that the war must be taken into account here and that, if anything, the criminological thesis is supported by the Italian experience taken in its entirety.

In France suicides increased from 100 in 1827–31 to 325 in 1911–15, while homicides decreased from 100 to 58. However, the homicide curve is very irregular. On the other hand, homicides increased between 1861–5 and 1906–10 from 100 to 140 while suicides did too, from 100 to 200. Whether there is opposition or parallelism depends on the starting or terminal points one chooses.[3]

In Germany, suicides remained stationary from 1891–5 until the war, while homicides diminished by almost a quarter. In Prussia, suicides and homicides decreased in a parallel direction from 1881–5 to 1886–90.

In England, suicides increased from 100 in 1856–60 to 150 in 1906–10. In the same period, homicides diminished from 100 to 22. True, on three occasions suicides clearly diminished at the same time that homicides diminished: from 1856–60 to 1861–5, from 1866–70 to 1871–5, and likewise from 1906–10 to 1916–20.

In Belgium, suicides increased from 100 in 1841–5 to 225 in 1906–10, which homicides diminished from 100 to 66. However, from 1861–5 to 1881–5 suicides and homicides nearly doubled (as Durkheim indicated, p. 347).

In Ireland, suicides increased between 1876–80 and 1906–10 from 100 to 194, while homicides diminished from 100 to 70. From 1876–80 to 1891–5, however, homicides clearly increased simultaneously with suicides.[4]

Durkheim observed that judging from what occurred in France in 1870 and Prussia in 1864, homicides increased during the war years, contrary to suicides, and, as in Prussia in 1870, always diminished much less than the other crimes. Such was not the case from 1914 to 1918. In every belligerent country the number of homicides diminished noticeably, even more clearly than suicides.

In any case there has been parallelism during the war period, not opposition, between variations in the number of homicides and the number of suicides.

The law formulated by Enrico Ferri does indeed admit of exceptions.

To be sure, this could be explained by the fact that Ferri considers different countries. As we have seen, there are indeed objections to international comparisons of suicide rates since the methods of enumeration of voluntary deaths vary from country to country. However, criminal statistics differ even more. This is why it is more valid to confine oneself to a single country.

Krose's book (*Die Ursachen*, p. 23) has a table in which are shown by states and provinces in Germany, the average number of suicides per million inhabitants from 1881 to 1900 and the average number of crimes in general, of severe injuries (*gefährliche Körperverletzungen*), and of thefts, from 1883 to 1897. We compared the rank order of these 33 states and provinces as to suicide and severe injuries. (For the entire Empire, they number about 110,000 per year.) This comparison led us to the following result. The maximum opposition is equal to 16.5 and the total independence to 8.25. A distance equal to 15.2 is found, which is very close to the number that would express the maximal opposition. This rather remarkable result supports Morselli's thesis to the extent that severe injuries result from homicidal intentions.[5]

This opposition, however, can result from there being either few suicides and many homicides or many suicides and few homicides. We know that there are more suicides among the Protestants than among the Catholics, and that there are more convictions for severe injuries among Catholics than among Protestants.[6] Let us therefore classify these states and provinces in several categories according to the proportion of suicides and severe injuries, and let us recall the proportion of Catholics and Protestants for each of them, in round numbers.

Let us add that there are many suicides and an average number of homicides in Silesia (distance: 5; 55 per cent Catholics and 43 per cent Protestants). In no region are both many suicides and many homicides to be found at the same time.

The first category (few suicides, many severe injuries) is seen to consist entirely of provinces where the Catholic population is in the majority, except for East Prussia. All the Bavarian provinces and both Prussias are here. The Bavarian provinces in which the distance between suicide and severe injuries is greatest are all in the east, that is, in contact with Catholic Austria, while those in which the opposition is less marked are in contact with the

Table 10.1 Suicides, severe injuries, and religious persuasion in Germany, 1881–1900 to 1883–97

States or provinces	Distance[7]	Percentage Catholic	Percentage Protestant	States or provinces	Distance	Percentage Catholic	Percentage Protestant
Few suicides, many severe injuries							
Lower Bavaria	31	99	1	Swabia	13	85	14
Upper Palatinate	27	91.5	8	Alsace-Lorraine	13	76	22
Posnania	25	68	30	East Prussia	10	13.5	85
Upper Bavaria	21	92	7	Middle Franconia	9	25	73
Rhine Palatinate	19	44	54	Upper Franconia	8	67	22
Western Prussia	18	51	46				
Many suicides, few severe injuries							
Kingdom of Saxony	31	5	94	Brandenburg	19	5	93.5
Schleswig-Holstein	29	2	97	Province of Saxony	19	7	92
Brunswick	27	5	94	Hanover	16	13	86
Berlin	25	10	84	Hesse-Nassau	14	28	69
Oldenburg	22	22	77	Mecklenburg-Schwerin	11	1	98
A small or average number of suicides and severe injuries							
Rhineland	9	70	29	Württemberg	3	30	69
Westphalia	9	50	48	Baden	2	61	38
				Pomerania	1	2	95.5

Protestant states of Württemberg and Hesse. Swabia, in contact with both Austria and Württemberg, occupies an intermediary situation. The Poles who represent the Catholic element in East and West Prussia are more numerous in the west. (This region will belong to Poland.) Matters are the same in Posnania. By virtue of the relationship between religion and nationality, the contrast between Catholics and Protestants is more marked in these provinces than in Hesse-Nassau. There are a few more Catholics in Hesse-Nassau than in East Prussia, but this province belongs in the second category.

The latter (many suicides, few severe injuries) includes all the states and provinces in which the very large majority, sometimes almost the totality of the population, is Protestant. Schleswig-Holstein and Saxony (kingdom) rank last (32 and 33) in severe injuries, 2nd and 3rd in suicides (Brunswick ranks 1st). Berlin also produces extremely few severe injuries (31st rank) but a rather high number of suicides (6th rank). All of these Protestant states, without exception, are part of a vast, compact, homogeneous mass.

The third and last category resembles the first in that suicides there are few, and the second in that there is no greater effort to kill or injure. This category includes one province in which Catholics are clearly in the majority (Rhineland), and another (Westphalia) where Catholics exceed Protestants by only a very little. This is the furthest extent of Catholicism in the north. The category also includes Württemberg and Baden, the furthest extent of German Protestantism in the south, between Catholic Alsace and Bavaria. These regions are intermediary between the preceding two categories, for in them are attenuated the strong tendencies to turn one's rage against others, observed in the first, and against oneself, characteristic of the second.

We do not intend in this analysis to draw any other conclusions than that two types of civilization are juxtaposed in Germany, corresponding geographically to the regions where the great Catholic masses are found, on the one hand, and on the other, the great Protestant masses. The violent instincts are allowed freer play in one, but attachment to life appears stronger here. In the other, corporal existence and integrity of others is better respected but voluntary death is more frequent.

There is a relationship between wounds and severe injuries, and homicides. However, the forms and degrees of criminality to which these two types of facts correspond must be distinguished as sharply, perhaps, as attempted suicides and completed suicides. Homicide is of interest to the extent that the killing is intentional. We reproduce Table 10.2 as much to permit the reader to inspect our calculations as because suicide statistics in France are rare by departments over a five-year period. The numbers in the first column were taken from a table published in the *Rapport sur l'Administration de la justice criminelle en France en 1895* by the Ministry of Justice, showing 'French departments in order of increasing degree of homicidal criminality measured by the annual average number of their premeditated murders, second-degree murders, parricides, and poisonings during the years 1891–5.' The numbers in the second column were calculated by us.

Table 10.2   *Homicides and suicides in France by departments (1891–5) (number of homicides and suicides per million inhabitants)*

Departments	Homicides	Suicides	Departments	Homicides	Suicides
Jura	2.9	204	Drôme	7.1	230
Indre	3.4	117	Manche	7.3	152
Vendée	3.6	93	Corrèze	7.3	129
Eure	3.7	480	Ain	7.3	192
Nièvre	4.0	178	Loiret	7.4	335
Saône-et-Loire	4.1	211	Lot-et-		
Lozère	4.4	70	Garonne	7.4	148
Hautes-Alpes	5.1	114	Cantal	7.5	72
Gard	5.2	154	Deux-Sèvres	7.5	214
Tarn	5.7	67	Savoie	7.6	80
Haute-Vienne	5.9	201	Eure-et-Loir	8.5	380
Meuse	6.1	288	Côtes-du-Nord	8.7	120
Cher	6.1	164	Tarn-et-		
Morbihan	6.2	108	Garonne	8.7	118
Isère	6.3	170	Loire	8.7	190
Haute-			Maine-et-Loire	8.8	255
Garonne	6.3	111	Hautes-		
Rhône	6.4	236	Pyrénées	8.8	72
Loire-			Ille-et-Vilaine	8.9	112
Inférieure	6.5	138	Pas-de-Calais	8.9	201
Ardèche	6.5	120	Nord	9.2	187
Landes	6.7	115	Charente-		
Vaucluse	6.8	276	Inférieure	9.2	257
Allier	7.0	140	Ariège	9.7	67

Table 10.2 continued   *Homicides and suicides in France by departments
(1891–5) (number of homicides and suicides per million inhabitants)*

Departments	Homicides	Suicides	Departments	Homicides	Suicides
Creuse	9.8	110	Ardennes	13.5	301
Puy-de-Dôme	9.9	132	Somme	13.5	370
Meurthe-et-			Loir-et-Cher	13.5	289
Moselle	9.9	245	Doubs	13.8	228
Gers	10.0	110	Haute-Marne	13.8	240
Sarthe	10.0	309	Seine-et-Oise	14.0	540
Lot	10.0	97	Pyrénées-		
Orne	10.1	204	Orientales	15.2	149
Basses-			Marne	15.6	472
Pyrénées	10.3	90	Oise	15.9	470
Dordogne	10.4	171	Haute-Saône	16.4	264
Gironde	10.5	192	Aude	16.4	131
Basses-Alpes	10.8	240	Calvados	17.7	270
Mayenne	11.4	132	Seine-et-Marne	19.0	530
Vienne	11.6	168	Indre-et-Loire	19.5	300
Seine-			Vosges	19.5	216
Inférieure	11.7	345	Charente	20.0	215
Aisne	11.7	460	Hérault	23.8	176
Finistère	11.8	118	Seine	24.4	500
Côte-d'Or	12.2	286	Bouches-du-		
Haute-Loire	12.6	79	Rhône	104.6	317
Haute-Savoie	12.6	116	Var	120.0	349
Aube	12.6	484	Alpes-		
Yonne	12.7	345	Maritimes	160	290
Aveyron	13.5	53	Corse	220	59

We have arranged these departments following the order of
their increasing rates of suicide and have compared the ranks they
occupy in these two classes. As there are 86 departments, the
maximum opposition is 43 and the total independence 21.5. We
find the average distance is 22. This very remarkable example of
total independence contrasts with the total opposition found a

little while ago in Germany. We bring this forward about France to reject Morselli's thesis. In our country, the number of suicides do not in fact seem to be in inverse ratio to the number of homicides. There is no relationship whatever between these two facts.

We shall classify these departments in categories as we have the German provinces and states.[8]

Many suicides, many homicides: rank above 70 in both series; Alpes-Maritimes, Var, (Basses-Alpes), Bouches-du-Rhône, Seine, Seine-et-Oise, Seine-et-Marne, Oise, (Somme), (Seine-Inférieure), (Calvados), (Aisne), (Aube), Marne, (Ardennes), (Loir-et-Cher), Indre-et-Loire, (Yonne), (Côte-d'Or), (Haute-Saône).

Many suicides, few homicides: distance greater than 40 between the two ratings; Eure, Eure-et-Loir, Loiret, (Nièvre), Saône-et-Loire, Jura, Rhône, Meuse, Vaucluse, (Haute-Vienne), Deux-Sèvres.

Few suicides, few homicides: rank below 20 in both series; Morbihan, (Ille-et-Vilaine), (Côtes-du-Nord), (Loire-Inférieure), Vendée, (Manche), (Allier), (Cantal), (Corrèze), Lozère, (Lot), (Lot-et-Garonne), (Tarn-et-Garonne), Tarn, Haute-Garonne, (Hautes-Pyrénées), Landes, (Ardèche), (Gard), (Isère), Hautes-Alpes, (Savoie).

Few suicides, many homicides: distance greater than 40 between the two ratings; Corsica, (Gers), Basses-Pyrénées, Ariège, Pyrénées-Orientales, Aude, Hérault, Aveyron, Haute-Loire, Haute-Savoie, (Finistère), (Vienne), (Mayenne).

In Germany, by far the largest number of states and provinces were distributed in the two categories where suicides and severe injuries were related inversely. Here, the opposite is the case: of the 66 departments above, 42 are grouped in the two categories where suicides and homicides are both numerous or both rare, and in only 24 do suicides increase when homicides diminish, or conversely. Of the 20* which remain unclassified, the majority undoubtedly resemble the last of the categories. In France, then, there is much more diversity in this respect. This explains why, relating facts of the same order, severe injuries and suicides, and homicides and suicides, we have found in the former instance a very strong opposition between them, and in the latter, almost total independence.

In France, the diverse groups counterbalance each other rather exactly because in two of them homicides and suicides oppose one another, while in the others they appear related. The most striking fact of all is that in no region of Germany did we find many suicides and many severe injuries occurring together, while in France many suicides and many homicides occur together in almost a quarter of the departments. We ordered the groups in

*In the original, the four previous figures are, respectively, 67, 42, 25, and 19 – Tr.

which there are many suicides, few homicides; few homicides and suicides; few suicides, many homicides in precisely this sequence because it corresponds to the spatial arrangement of these groups from north to south. The region with most indictments, that is, where people kill themselves and others most, corresponds to the Paris basin and the southeast coast of the Mediterranean, the zone where, as already indicated, the proportion of voluntary deaths is highest. Here is a mass of contiguous departments that are perfectly homogeneous in this respect. Finally, from the Eure to the Jura to the Rhône there stretches, like a kind of cross-belt, a line of departments in which people frequently kill themselves but seldom kill others. These departments resemble the Protestant provinces of Prussia in this respect. Then come, from Finistère to Savoie, the Breton regions, the center, the south (Garonne and Landes), and the Alps, the regions which appear most privileged since they escape both suicide and homicide. They are almost like Westphalia, the Rhineland, Baden, and Württemberg, that is, transitional countries where the currents of violence and depression neutralize each other or become attenuated. Within France, suicide is ignored along the borders of the Pyrenees, the length of the sandy coasts of the Mediterranean, at the extremity of Brittany, and in the narrow region between the Rhône and the Cévennes Mountains, where primitive and simple customs are perpetuated, but as in the German Catholic regions, first- and second-degree murders are on the increase.

In sum, the last three groups correspond rather well to those we have distinguished in Germany.

As we have observed, in no region of Germany are many suicides and many homicides both enumerated. This is not the case in France. Durkheim has not noticed this fact. He even wrote (*op. cit.*, pp. 351–2),

> If there are countries which accumulate suicides and homicides, it is never in the same proportions; the two manifestations never reach their maximum intensity at the same point. It is even a general rule that *where homicide is very common it confers a sort of immunity against suicide*. Spain, Ireland, and Italy are the three countries of Europe where there is least suicide.... *These are the only countries where the number of murders exceeds that of voluntary deaths*.... On the contrary, France and Prussia abound in suicides ... homicides there are only one-tenth as numerous.... The same proportions appear within each country. In Italy ... in France ... in Austria ...

In France, however, there are no fewer than nine departments which, on the average, are very high and equal in rank with respect to suicides and homicides, 78 and 78.2, while the nine departments where they kill others most frequently but kill themselves very little are of equal rank with regard to homicide, 78.5 on the average. The first group is not dispersed at random but constitutes two very homogeneous masses: Alpes-Maritimes, Var, Bouches-du-Rhône and Seine, Seine-et-Oise, Seine-et-Marne, Oise, Marne. Indre-et-Loire alone appears isolated, but is attached to the preceding group by nine other departments (indicated between parentheses). Though at a lower level with respect to suicide and homicide, these still rank high and rather close, on the average 71 and 65, and they form a totality similar to the others.

We may assume this is a recent development for, according to Garofalo, Quetelet believed he had established that 'crimes of passion increase in warm climates and decrease in cold climates.' Quetelet limited his observations to France. Despine, who believed that there is an inverse relationship between homicide and suicide, ascertained from French data that the maximum number of first- and second-degree murders coincided with the minimum number of suicides, and conversely. In 1872 Morselli, who held the same thesis, compared the proportion of criminal convictions with suicides by resorting to the Court of Appeals. We calculated the average distance according to the table he reproduced: the total opposition is measured by 13, the independence by 6.5; the average distance is found to be 9.5, that is, there is indeed opposition between the two facts. However, these regions do not array at this period with respect to crimes against persons in the same order as they do in 1891–5 (twenty years later) with respect to homicide. Thus, Paris (that is, the entire group of neighboring departments) is found among the three regions where crimes against persons are fewest. Today, the opposite is true. Also, the number of crimes against persons may not give an accurate idea of the tendency to homicide. In any case, neither Tarde in 1890 nor Durkheim in 1897 pointed out the existence of a group of departments in the Seine basin where one encounters at the same time both many homicides and many suicides.

Homicides are relatively few in number. In 1891–5 their annual total is on the average 12.4 per million while the proportion of suicides rises to 241 for the same number of inhabitants. For this reason it seemed useful to check the results from this period by making the same calculations for one more recent. We find in our notes the numbers of first-degree murders, second-degree murders and parricides, by departments, in 1910, 1911, and 1920. We calculated the average proportion of these crimes in relation to the population of the departments in 1911, comparing it with the annual proportion of suicides in all the departments in 1910, 1911, and 1913. The total opposition being always measured by 43 and the total independence by 21.5, an average distance is found equal to 23.5 (instead of 22 in 1891–5). Thus, the two facts still appear to be independent. As before, let us group in one category the departments where many suicides and homicides occur together.

Many suicides and homicides (1910, 1911, 1913, 1920): Bouches-du-Rhône, Var, (Alpes-Maritimes), (Vaucluse), (Basses-Alpes); Seine, Seine-et-Oise, (Seine-et-Marne), Oise, Somme, Seine-Inférieure, Eure, Calvados, (Aube), (Marne), (Haute-Marne); Haute-Saône, (Côte-d'Or); (Meurthe-et-Moselle); (Loire).

The ten departments where there are the most suicides and homicides (those whose names are not in parentheses) have ranks in the two series of 76.6 and 76.5, while the six departments in the south, where there are few suicides and many homicides, have an average rank with respect to suicide of 72. We find that as many departments are included in this category during this period as in 1891–5 and that they are nearly the same. Aisne, Loir-et-Cher and Indre-et-Loire are out because the number of homicides diminished there, but Haute-Marne, Meurthe-et-Moselle, Vaucluse, and Loire have entered. Indeed, at both times there is a compact group of departments in the Paris basin whose peculiarity is that the numbers of both suicides and homicides increase there at the same time. Another group where this is so is on the shore of the Mediterranean between the Rhône and the Alps. These two groups total almost a quarter of the French departments, but much more than a quarter of the population in France.

Durkheim, while asserting that 'if there are countries [or regions] which accumulate suicides and homicides it is never in the same proportions,' nevertheless recognized that 'sometimes suicide coexists with homicide, sometimes they are mutually exclusive.' The only way of reconciling these facts, according to him, was 'to assume that there are different species of suicide, some of which have a certain kinship with homicide while others repel it.' He distinguished egoistic from anomic suicide. The former would result from a state of depression and apathy produced by 'an exaggerated individuality.' The individual detached from society views himself as an end unto himself. How then would he allow himself to be carried away by violent passions which impel toward murder and which most frequently develop in a 'strongly integrated' society where collective sentiments are at their highest degree of intensity? 'Where social passions are animated, the person is much less inclined either to the sterile reveries or to the cold calculations' of egoism. Anomic suicide, on the contrary, is not at all explained by the apathy of the subject, but by the fact that individual passions no longer encounter social barriers. In a disorganized and demoralized society, human activity no longer knows rules. The individual collides with other people at the same time as with things: he is discontented with himself and with others. Then is manifested 'a state of exasperation and irritated lassitude which, depending on circumstances, can turn against the subject himself or against another person,' sometimes against both. Where this social instability appears, it explains why homicide and suicide develop in a parallel direction.[9]

This psychological distinction between the two species of suicide may be justified. All we can say is that we lack the data to recognize whether, in regions where first- and second-degree murders multiply, people kill themselves primarily from exasperation, while in the others they do so from apathy. On the other hand, the facts studied do seem to indicate that several sorts of homicide exist which are related to diverse states of civilization. These states of civilization of themselves entail an unequal development of suicide. This explains why homicides and suicides sometimes occur together and to the same extent, while at other times one excludes the other.

It is, first of all, quite remarkable that four departments in France are very plainly distinguished during the period 1891–5 from all others by the very high proportion of first- and second-degree murders produced there. While the average rate of homicides, for the others, is 10 per million inhabitants, and in Seine 24.4 at maximum, in Bouches-du-Rhône the count is 104.6, 120 in Var, 160 in Alpes-Maritimes, and 220 in Corsica. Italy is the only large European country where such figures are reached. Since these departments are neighbors of Italy and include a very large proportion of Italians, some naturalized, some not, this is naturally given as an explanation for the strong development of homicide here. Moreover, as we have seen, even first- and second-degree murders decrease very rapidly in Italy. We can also assume an increasing influence toward assimilation by France in regions where urban life closely unites people of different races and origins. This would explain why the number of homicides has diminished greatly in these four departments over the fifteen or twenty years (Table 10.3).

In this region, suicide and homicide may find favorable soil in two distant parts of the population living side by side with one another, that is, in two types of civilization which coexist without

Table 10.3   *Homicides per million inhabitants, France*

	In 1891–5	In 1910–11 and 1920
Bouches-du-Rhône	104.6	69
Var	120	50
Alpes-Maritimes	160	34
Corsica[10]	220	135

intermingling. The perceptible increase in homicidal criminality in several of the southern departments also may be explained by Italian emigration to Lot, Lot-et-Garonne, Tarn-et-Garonne, Ardèche, Gard, Isère, Savoie, and Gers. These have passed from an average rank of 28.5 to rank 53 in the series of departments arrayed according to the increasing proportion of first- and second-degree murders.

> The vendetta countries of Corsica and southern Italy [writes Tarde] can be considered islands of barbarism surviving in the midst of our civilization. Now, they form a perfect contrast to the entirely modernized countries, as much by an extremely high figure for punitive and sanguinary criminality as by the extremely low figure for sensual and stealthy criminality.

Enrico Ferri contrasted the civilization, or if one prefers, the barbarism, of the Middle Ages and modern civilization similarly: in the former, few suicides, many homicides; in the latter, the converse. In fifty years Italy will have passed from one age to the other.

In that case a certain number of French departments will still represent the social condition of the past in this respect, regardless of Italian influence. The best proof of this is, precisely, that the proportion of homicides there has not been increasing. In 1891–5 there were many homicides and few suicides in eleven departments (excluding Corsica and Gers, for reasons indicated above). From this first period to 1910–13 and 1920, the rank of these eleven departments went from 61 to 43. The average proportion of homicides there did not change perceptibly, however, rising from 128 to only 135, whereas first- and second-degree murders increased considerably in 1910–11 and 1920 relative to the average of 1895–8. (Of the years immediately following the first period, we have totals only for these.) The increase from one period to the next was 48 per cent (8 per cent for first-degree and 90 per cent for second-degree murders).

Homicides did not increase during this time in the departments in which few suicides are committed, undoubtedly because they result from stable conditions, for until now these regions have escaped forces linked to another type of civilization. Very primitive customs and the violent instincts undoubtedly retain their integrity in Basses-Pyrénées, Ariège, Pyrénées-Orientales, Aude, Hérault, Aveyron, Haute-Loire, Haute-Savoie, Finistère, Vienne, and Mayenne.

Matters are entirely different in the more developed regions where homicide and suicide increase simultaneously. On the whole, the thirteen departments of which they consist maintained their rank from 1891–5 to 1910–11 and 1920. But the proportion of homicides committed there rose from 14.7 to 21 per million inhabitants between one period and the next, that is, increased 43 per cent during fifteen or twenty years.

Thus, it seems that two currents of violent criminality develop simultaneously, one in the mountainous and dry regions, principally in the south, the other in a more northern climate on the banks of the Seine and on the Channel coast. The flow scarcely varies in the former, but rises rather rapidly in the latter. The first current is unaccompanied, while a strong suicidal current accompanies the latter as if the two were fed from the same source. How explain these two facts? Does invoking the climate suffice to account for the first?

> We know [says Tarde] that crimes against persons, that is, *crimes of passion*, are at their maximum, within a given country, in Spring if not in Summer ... the contrast clearly reveals that an indirect provocation is exerted by high temperatures on the maleficent passions.

Is the second explained by alcoholism, assuming that 'cold seasons and cold climates are when people become most intoxicated'? Must we believe that 'northern populations are as strongly impelled to crimes of passion by endemic and traditional drunkenness as are southern populations by their sun'? However, confining ourselves to France, how shall we explain the fact that an entire part of the south produces scarcely any homicides while Basses-Pyrénées, Ariège, and Aveyron are at the same level in this respect as Finistère, Haute-Savoie, Vienne, and Mayenne? Also, why is the multiplication of homicides only recent in the more northern departments? How does it happen that Nord, Aisne, Ardennes, etc., are below average in homicidal criminality and that first- and second-degree murders are almost unknown in Meuse?

Tarde, while contributing his share to this mode of explanation, prefers to invoke social influences. However, the very general observations to which he confines himself do not go very far. More interesting are the following bits of information that we owe to him (Tarde, *op. cit.*, p. 71):

> From 1826 to 1830, greed was thirteen times in a hundred the active determinant of crimes of first- and second-degree murder, poisoning, and arson. The proportion gradually rose to 20 per cent in 1856–60, then was brought down again to 17 in 1871–5, rising again in 1876–80 to 22 per cent. Conversely, fifty years ago love was the incitement to these crimes 13 times per hundred, but now no more often than 8 times per hundred.... Now, love cannot have diminished anymore than hate.... Therefore, it is greed which has made progress.

It is indeed in this manner that one must search. Perhaps, as Tarde goes on to say, civilization favors 'stealthy and sensual criminality' and discourages 'violent' criminality which proceeds from vindictive instincts, jealousy, hate, etc. We can do no more here than indicate problems that could be stated precisely and perhaps resolved only by an appropriate study of criminality.

We have been asking whether, as Morselli and Enrico Ferri maintained, homicide and suicide represent two alternative and complementary manifestations of the same inclination. This would have permitted us to explain why first- and second-degree murders are rare wherever voluntary deaths multiply, and vice versa. However, the fact itself has seemed to us inaccurate for, in more than a quarter of the French population, many homicides and suicides occur simultaneously. Of course, we have found regions in France where murder is frequent while suicide is infrequent, and others where people kill infrequently but commit suicide frequently. However, the former represent ancient and relatively primitive types of civilization where the inclination to murder exists alone and cannot be the source of nonexistent inclinations to suicide. The latter are to be found in an intermediary situation or one in transition. Primitive forms of homicidal criminality are no longer found there because the unpolished and simple customs of underdeveloped societies have disappeared. Suicides are already numerous there. The new forms of first- and second-degree murder, however, hardly appear there because the evolution of such regions is not yet entirely complete. Since an inclination to homicide such as develops in advanced groups does not yet exist, suicide cannot be its derivative. There remain the zones of urban civilization in which suicides and homicides are both very frequent. We have distinguished two of them. In the one which is entirely penetrated by Italian elements and influences, we may suppose that the same parts of the population are not at all inclined both to murder and to voluntary death. In the other, which, we repeat, includes almost a quarter of the French population massed in the Seine basin or in its immediate environs, the alternation between suicides and homicides does not exist, as both are simultaneously produced in large numbers. There is no evidence that they are similar people, of similar temperament, of comparable physical or psychic constitution, or that they are equally inclined to one or the other of these acts which are so different, even opposite, in every respect. Moreover, when each of two currents is flowing up to the brim, it cannot be said that one is diverting the content or a part of the content of the other.

chapter 11

The effect of wars and political crises: fluctuations in French suicides

Statistics on suicide in France enable us to follow the evolution of this phenomenon from 1827 to 1927, a period of 101 years, a century. No other country with a population as large as this has valid data on suicide that is as continuous.

To begin with, we observe that in the years preceding 1897, when Durkheim was writing his book, the statistical series as a whole showed a continuous ascent. The suicide rate rose from about 50 in 1827 to 100 in 1849–51, 150 in 1872–3, 200 in 1884, and 250 in 1894–5. In the thirty years which have elapsed since then, however, the rate has only risen to this exceptional level again in 1907, 1910, and 1912–13. During all other years the rate remained below this 1894–5 number until after 1927, as if it were a maximum that could not be surpassed.[1]

This finding emerges from Table 11.1 in which we have calculated the proportionate increase in the suicide rate in France from decade to decade.

Thus, the suicide curve clearly appears to have arrived at a plateau since 1890, and to have neither increased nor diminished in total since this date and throughout the war years.

Examining the successive points of this curve since 1890 in detail (Table 11.3), we notice at once a very clear drop during the 1914–18 war to a low in 1917, climbing again thereafter to the high where it had been in 1904. (We do not have figures for the years following 1927.)[2]

The numbers for the war years are incomplete. We are told in the report of the *Comptes généraux de la justice criminelle en France* (1919) that raw data for the statistics could not be gathered for 1914–18 in the following districts: Laon, Saint-Quentin, Vervins (or three-quarters of Aisne); Péronne (in Oise); Avesnes, Cambrai, Douai, Lille, Valenciennes (or the larger part of the Nord), Charleville, Rethel, Rocroi, Sedan, Vouziers (Ardennes), Briey, Montmédy, and

Table 11.1   *Increase in the suicide rate in France*

	Percentage increase
1827–36	+ 42
1836–45	+ 26
1845–54	+ 16
1854–63	+ 20
1863–72	+ 20
1872–81	+ 23
1881–90	+ 23
1890–9	+ 0.4
1899–1908	+ 0.4
1908–17	− 34[3]
1917–25	+ 42

Table 11.2   *Suicides per million inhabitants of each sex and each age group in England and Wales*

	1901–10	1914	1915	1916	1917	Number of suicides in 1917 per 100 in 1901–10
Men						
From 15 to 44	144	145	101	116	103	72
From 45 to 54	397	347	224	215	201	51
From 55 to 64	523	512	365	292	257	49
From 65 to 74	508	502	363	406	285	56
From 75 to 84	383	360	338	318	322	85
All ages	157	150	102	110	97	62
Women						
From 15 to 44	56	53	50	43	43	77
From 45 to 54	109	113	111	80	75	69
From 55 to 64	109	106	123	102	86	79
From 65 to 74	88	94	94	87	76	86
From 75 to 84	51	47	64	64	55	104
All ages	47	45	45	38	35	74

Saint-Mihiel. Now in 1913 the three departments of Aisne, Nord, and Ardennes combined contain 7.4 per cent of the total suicides. The proportion of suicides calculated in relation to the total population (estimated, taking into account war losses, at 39.8 millions in 1914, 38.8 in 1915, 38.2 in 1916, 37.6 in 1917, and 36.9 in 1918) is therefore a little below the real proportion. However, as we must also take into account the fact that all the mobilizable troops and a large part of the civil population of occupied regions were transported to the interior, it is unlikely that this proportion was affected by an error of deduction exceeding 4 per cent. The figures we are going to examine would therefore need only a rather small correction. Relative to 1913, the minimum in 1917 corresponds to a decline from 100 to 61.

In 1870 suicides diminished from 100 to 81. From 1913 to 1914 the suicide rate declined in exactly the same proportion as from 1869 to 1870. We must also not forget the wars began in July 1870 and August 1914. From 1914 to 1915 the rate declined again by almost as much, from 100 to 83. The declines of the next two years were equal and much smaller: each was from 100 to 96. The minimum occurred in France in 1917. The diminution in suicides occurring in Germany during the war was almost equal (taking into account that 4 or 5 per cent of the voluntary deaths in France could not be enumerated during this period): from 100 to 67.5 between 1913 and 1918. This time the minimum occurred in the last year of the war. There was a first minimum in 1915, followed by a rise in 1916.

Shown in Table 11.4 are the proportions of suicides during the war enumerated in the principal belligerent countries. Throughout, the suicide rate has clearly declined during the war period, and the rate of decrease is of the same order in all these countries: from 100 to 70 in England, from 100 to 66.5 in the United States (1915 to 1918), from 100 to 77 in Italy (1914 to 1917), from 100 to 66 in Austria (1914 to 1918), from 100 to 60 in Hungary (1913 to 1918) and, we recall, in France from 100 to 61, and in Germany from 100 to 67.5. The year when the enumeration is minimal is 1917 in France, England, and Italy. Enumeration is minimal in the conquered countries, Germany, Austria, and Hungary, in the year of defeat, 1918. Suicides increase very abruptly in the last two countries and the curve rises very high until 1919, undoubtedly because of their economic distress.

The figures just reproduced bring us the strongest proof that could be desired of the effect that war has on the suicide trend. How is it to be explained? According to Durkheim (*Suicide*, p. 208), 'great popular wars rouse collective sentiments, stimulate ... patriotism ... and national faith ... and, concentrating activity

Table 11.3 *Suicides in France from 1827 to 1927,* * per million inhabitants*[4]

Year	Suicides	Year	Suicides	Year	Suicides	Year	Suicides
1827	48.5	1852	102	1877	160	1902	224
1828	55	1853	95	1878	173	1903	225
1829	59	1854	102	1879	174	1904	226
1830	54	1855	106	1880	178	1905	239
1831	64	1856	115	1881	179	1906	235
1832	66	1857	110	1882	192	1907	254
1833	60	1858	108	1883	192	1908	239
1834	63	1859	107	1884	199	1909	245
1835	69	1860	111	1885	207	1910	250
1836	69.5	1861	120	1886	214	1911	244
1837	72	1862	128	1887	215	1912	254
1838	76	1863	122	1888	220	1913	260
1839	81	1864	120	1889	214	1914	210
1840	81	1865	130	1890	220	1915	172
1841	82	1866	135	1891	232	1916	166
1842	83.5	1867	131	1892	241	1917	158
1843	87	1868	146	1893	236	1918	167
1844	85.5	1869	140	1894	253	1919	213
1845	88	1870	113	1895	242	1920	217
1846	88	1871	124	1896	240	1921	228
1847	102.5	1872	146	1897	242	1922	229
1848	93	1873	153	1898	244	1923	222
1849	101	1874	155	1899	230	1924	231
1850	101	1875	150	1900	230	1925	234
1851	100	1876	158	1901	227	1926	232

toward a single end, at least temporarily cause a stronger integration of society.' While this explanation is not implausible and must undoubtedly be assigned a role, we must observe that the proportion of suicides has also diminished during the war period in the few neutral European countries for which we command data. Putting aside Spain, whose statistics are hardly

* In the original, 1925 – Tr.

usable, we reproduce in Table 11.5 the figures for four other neutral countries.

Table 11.4   *Suicides during the First World War (belligerent countries)*

	France	England	United States[5]	Italy	Germany	Austria[6]	Hungary[7]
1913	260	96	199	88	232	(209)	214
1914	210	91	215	89	218	269	204
1915	172	78	215	84.5	166	233	174
1916	166	77	185	69	173	225	155
1917	158	67	177	68.5	164	198	131
1918	167	74	152	72	157	177	128
1919	203	90	143	75	184	250	(239)

Thus, in all these countries suicides have likewise diminished during the war and, except for Switzerland, the decline has been even greater than in the belligerent nations: in Norway from 100 to 53, in Sweden from 100 to 55, in Denmark from 100 to 49, in Switzerland from 100 to 72. Now, the explanation that Durkheim proposed cannot be relevant here. To be sure, the great conflict which broke out in 1914 concerned every European country, but at no time was the integrity of the neutrals threatened. We have no alternative but to assume that other factors played a role without our being in a position to determine what they are. One would be tempted on first consideration to assume that the neutral countries developed a more intensive industrial, commercial, and financial activity, and to explain the diminution of observed suicides by their prosperity and exceptional profits. As we shall see, however, though suicides do diminish in periods of prosperity, they do so in a relatively small proportion: between such moderate decreases and this profound sag there is no connection.

Moreover, suicides do not reach their minimum in all belligerent countries at the same time. In 1918, the last year of the war, the number of suicides begins to increase again in the countries which are going to be victorious, but continues to decline in the others. Shall we assume that as the latter continue to exhaust themselves and come to feel the chill wind of defeat and of panic pass over them, to that extent patriotism and national faith become exalted and national integration strengthened, while on the contrary, they sag amongst the victorious countries just at the time when they are approaching the end and getting ready to

Table 11.5   *Suicides in neutral countries*

	Norway	Sweden	Denmark (the cities only)	Switzerland
1913	58	179	232	251
1914	—	—	—	—
1915	53	153	219	215
1916	38	132	165	204
1917	36	102	150	181
1918	30.5	99	119	197
1919	47	135	114	205
1920	48	147	139	226

make the supreme effort? Is it not among the conquerors at the moment of victory that the collective enthusiasm most closely unites the citizenry in a triumphant sentiment?

Creating unanimous passions, however, is not war's only effect. War also transforms the life and structure of the nation. While Spencer's views on the opposition between societies of the military and industrial types appear a little too schematic, it is nonetheless true that in many respects life is simplified and eased when one passes from the second of these types to the first. Does this not explain most, if not all, of the diminution in the number of suicides in time of war? War multiplies the barriers between nations. At the same time that it brings people of a given country closer together, it also separates them from one another in quite numerous ways. Not only are economic and professional activity partially paralyzed, but families who are deprived of some of their members bear witness to a diminished vitality. Fewer contacts are established among individuals, and occasions for shocks and particular conflicts less frequently present themselves. How should suicides not diminish?

This is only a hypothesis, but one which is not less acceptable, a priori, than the explanation proposed by Durkheim. In any case, it will enable us to take into account the fact that suicides also diminish in time of war in the neutral countries. For they, too, are separated from the European community. Hence, even though certain branches of their industrial production are stimulated, though their bankers handle a greater number of transactions and see their cash balances swell, they lack all of the vitality which previously came to them from their contacts and communications with other states. It is hardly possible for the level of such social interactions to decline in all the large European countries without declining within some small neutral states that are normally so closely related to them. We also understand from this hypothesis why suicides are at their minimum the last year of the war in countries which have been or are about to be conquered. At this time in fact is when their resources are most reduced and their life most simplified. They resemble a besieged city in which, at the point of surrender, the streets are deserted and silent, while the defenders and inhabitants husband their remaining forces, make the fewest gestures, and speak the fewest words. It is less the rhythm of collective sentiments and passions which are reflected in the suicide trend in time of war than the lessening degree of complexity of life and increasing simplicity of the social structure.

Another decline occurred during the period 1897 to 1927, less extreme, of course, than the one described above but very clear, just as prolonged, even more remarkable because it showed up during peacetime, and unique in that no other fluctuation of this type is found in France during the entire century. It begins in 1899, with the minimum occurring in 1902. Not until 1905 does the suicide rate come close to its level in 1899. To describe better the exceptional character of this variation, we calculated the sum of suicide rates (per 100,000 inhabitants) of every three consecutive years for 32 triennial periods from 1828 to 1922.

The increase during these hundred years is seen to be continuous and uninterrupted except for the two war periods, 1869–71 and 1914–19, and the decline, already referred to, of 1899–1904. *There is no other exception.*

There were, however, fluctuations during the course of the century, within the triennial periods, that our calculations have eliminated from Table 11.6. These must now be examined and measured in comparison with the fluctuations that interest us. Here is the list showing proportionate declines, and comparing them to the decline of longest duration, 1899–1902, whose value is also given:

1829–30	from 100 to 92
1847–8	from 100 to 91
1852–3	from 100 to 93
1862–3	from 100 to 95
1899–1902	from 100 to 92

Durkheim, confining himself to absolute figures, had already shown (*op. cit.*, p. 203) that the revolutions of 1830 and 1848 and the *coup d'état* of 1851[8] were accompanied by a decline in suicide.[9] As will be observed, this decline is obviously of equal depth in the three cases, and clearly smaller than the decrease in suicides during the war years.

Table 11.6 *France: increase in suicide rates*

Years	Suicides	Years	Suicides
1827–9	16	1875–7	46.5
1830–2	18	1878–80	52
1833–5	19	1881–3	56
1836–8	22	1884–6	62
1839–41	24.5	1887–9	65
1842–4	25.5	1890–2	70
1845–7	28	1893–5	73
1848–50	29.5	1896–8	72.5
1851–3	30	1899–1901	69
1854–6	32.5	1902–4	67
1857–9	32.5	1905–7	72.5
1860–2	35.5	1908–10	73
1863–5	37.5	1911–13	76
1866–8	41	1914–16	55
1869–71	37.5	1917–19	55
1872–4	45	1920–2	64.5

It therefore appears natural enough to assume that the decline of 1899–1902 falls within the same category as these. Let us always first ask ourselves whether some transformation or some event in the economic order which would account for it has not occurred at the same period. Durkheim had already observed that most economic crises are accompanied by a notable increase in suicides (p. 241). This is confirmed for the crisis of 1846–7 (an increase in the suicide rate of 16 per cent), for the crisis of 1864–6 (an increase of 8 per cent in 1865, and of another 4 per cent in 1866), for the crisis of 1873 (an increase of 5 per cent), for the crisis of 1881–2 (an increase of 7 per cent), for the crisis of 1890–1 (an increase of 6 per cent), for the crisis of 1907 (an increase of 8 per cent), at a time when the average annual increase, for the whole period 1847–1907, is equal to 1.9 per cent. Only the crisis of 1857 takes place in a year of decline, but this is immediately after a year of strong rise in suicides and, for all we know, may have begun as early as the end of 1856. Thus, suicides increase in times of crisis.

Now, there was an economic crisis in 1900. The period of depression lasted until 1904.[10] Suicides should have increased. They declined, however, because the economic crisis came up against a crisis of another nature which neutralized its effect.[11]

In fact, while suicides are so clearly declining in 1899–1904, France is going through an extremely serious and very prolonged political crisis. It opens in 1898* with the Dreyfus Affair and will not end until the victory of the radical party in the elections of 1906. This decline in suicides, which is prolonged over a period of almost six years, is as important as those in 1830, 1848, or 1853. We do not believe it possible to explain it by a cause other than this political crisis which, in its vicissitudes and outcome, actually resembles a revolution.

The Dreyfus Affair is an important test, almost unique up to now because it lasted for a long time, occurred in a great country and, unlike the Russian or German revolutions or the advent of fascism in Italy, whose effect on suicides is necessarily obscure, did not take place in a war or post-war period of monetary and financial crisis, famine, or economic distress.

It is therefore worthwhile to examine it rather closely, in detail, and as precisely as possible. Since we possess monthly suicide figures in France we shall relate them to the most notable political events occurring at the same time during this period. The reader will undoubtedly find more than one of these comparisons to be debatable or forced, and criticize us for wanting to rediscover in the suicide curve, at whatever cost, traces of all the contemporary political events. We believe that, actually, the detailed events matter less here than the political evolution as a whole. Political currents, like currents of social thought, do not have as much force and vitality as when they come from a short distance in time. Moreover, it is very difficult for us to appreciate the influence that contemporary, if not witnessed, events exert on opinion, and the degree of their resonance, until we read the details in an accepted history. Nothing is more disconcerting than to ascertain that some fact we have hardly noticed, some gesture or word or formula we barely remember, may arouse energetic and passionate reactions in masses of people as far away as the most distant provinces, and likewise the converse. Therefore, in what follows we have no thought of establishing relationships of cause and effect between details of political events that we shall recall and monthly variations in suicides. We grant that we took an interest in noting cases where rather clear decreases in the number of suicides

*Zola's letter, 'J'Accuse,' to the President of the Republic, was published in Clemenceau's *L'Aurore* on 13 January. The first Dreyfus court-martial had taken place in December 1894. The Court of Cassation would order his rehabilitation in July 1906 – Tr.

accompanied the vicissitudes which, in our view, were the most dramatic of the crisis concerning us. If the facts do not appear sufficiently convincing we shall very willingly admit that we have sometimes gone astray because of having wanted to establish too much.

To make these comparisons, we calculated the number of suicides for each month of the years 1899–1904 relative to the average of each of the months in the six preceding years, 1893–8, set equal to 100. Thus, a number falls below 100 when the number of suicides that month is below the average for such months during the six years preceding the crisis.

It may be pointed out that the date assigned to the beginning of the crisis is set too late, that the year of the Dreyfus Affair, 1898, should have been included in our period. We set that year aside deliberately, however, because, total figures only considered, it does not appear to exercise any direct influence whatever on suicides. The proportion of suicides (244) is higher in 1898 than in the six preceding years, noticeably higher than in 1896 and 1897, and much higher than in 1899. The Zola trial runs from 7 to 20 February: there are more suicides that month than on each February of the three preceding years. In May and June, to be sure, fewer killed themselves than in the same months of each of the six previous years. However, there had been elections in May. The discovery of the Henry forgery* brings about its author's suicide, but it is not accompanied by a diminution of voluntary deaths. Their number clearly falls below the monthly average for October. On the 25th of this month, General Chanoine, Minister of War, tenders his resignation and determines the fall of the Brisson ministry. Perhaps it is a simple coincidence. One's first impression is, as Seignobos has said, that 'the Dreyfus Affair, complicated by incidents, embroiled in maneuvers, obscured by fictional accounts, did not interest the mass of the public which never understood it.'[12]

Table 11.7   *Suicide rates in France, 1899–1900*

	Jan.	Feb.	Mar.	Apr.	May	June	July	Aug.	Sept.	Oct.	Nov.	Dec.
1899	99	91	94	94	99	92	90	102	96	96	95	85
1900	103	92	92	92	99	93	93	97	92	93	92	95

Table 11.7 shows the suicide rates in France in the first two years of our period, in relative numbers (100 equals the monthly suicide

* A document purporting to be decisive proof of the guilt of Dreyfus, forged by Lt-Col. Henry, Chief of the Intelligence Bureau of the General Staff – Tr.

rate in 1893–8). During these two years, the proportion of suicides remains at 230, instead of 244 as in 1898, a decrease from 100 to 94. A strong decline is produced in February of 1899. This is a rather agitated month: the death of Félix Faure on the 16th, the election of Loubet on the 18th, the funeral of Félix Faure on the 18th (Déroulède* endeavours to involve a regiment, etc.). An almost equal decline is enumerated in June: the annulment of the judgment against Dreyfus by the Court of Cassation is made public on the 4th of this month: the President is insulted at the Auteuil races on the 4th, acclaimed by the Republicans at the Longchamps Grand Prix on the 11th; the Dupuy ministry falls on the 12th; the Republican Ministry of Defense (Waldeck-Rousseau) is constituted on the 26th. A still stronger decline is produced the following month. The minimum is reached in December. This is the greatest monthly decline during the whole of the 1899–1900 period. We do not see any additional sensational event to which to call attention that month.

In 1900 there is a strong decline in February, March, and April, which resumes in June and July, then in September, October, and November. The battle against the congregations was enjoined by Waldeck-Rousseau from the last months of 1899 onward: the filing of a draft bill on congregations† in August; the draft of a bill on school probation at the end of November. On 11 April 1900 he denounces 'the League friars and the business friars,' and on 20 November, in his address at Toulouse, he speaks of the 'thousand congregations' and of the 'two youths.' This entire year is a period of tension (congregationist agitation, clerical demonstrations, etc.).

Table 11.8   *Suicide rates in France, 1901–2*

	Jan.	Feb.	Mar.	Apr.	May	June	July	Aug.	Sept.	Oct.	Nov.	Dec.
1901	93	78	83	94	102	99	92	92	95	101	92	96
1902	100	87	90	94	89	91	95	89	92	94	93	90

A very strong decrease of suicides during the months of February and March 1901 resumes, less markedly, in July and August and in the last two months of the year (Table 11.8). What is happening at this time? The discussion of the draft bill on the associations (directed against the congregations) begins in the

*Anti-Dreyfusard chief of the League of Patriots who endeavors to involve a regiment in an abortive *coup d'état* – Tr.

†A bill to laicize primary education, which very often was given by members of religious congregations, monks, or nuns – Tr.

Chamber on 15 January and ends at the beginning of April. The Senate examines it in May and accepts it by a strong majority. The law is promulgated on 2 July.

Thus [says Seignobos] the conflict with the clergy led the Republican party, after twenty years of waiting, to complete totally the program of political liberty which dated back to the Empire, and at the same time gave the Republicans a weapon to subdue or destroy the congregations.

The suicide rate becomes minimal in 1902: 224, instead of the 244 it had been in 1898, a decrease from 100 to 92. This minimum is exceeded in February, March, May, and August. The elections which bring the radical party to power take place in May (27 April, 11 May). The campaign began following the end of January (the pastoral letter of the Archbishop of Paris on 19 January). Waldeck-Rousseau tenders his resignation on 28 May. On 1 June Bourgeois is elected President of the Chamber, defeating Deschanel. On 11 June the Combes ministry is presented to the Chamber. On 12 July the closing of congregation schools, which had been open before this law, is decided upon. During August and September there were demonstrations in the churches of Paris and of the departments. The faithful install themselves on the premises and to dislodge them requires the police and even the troops. At the end of December, armed with a new law punishing infractions of the law of 1901 with fines and imprisonment, the government closed all unauthorized schools except where a secular school did not exist.

Table 11.9   *Suicide rates in France, 1903–4*

	Jan.	Feb.	Mar.	Apr.	May	June	July	Aug.	Sept.	Oct.	Nov.	Dec.
1903	104	95	99	91	98	87	88	90	92	99	97	92
1904	99	94	94	93	99	88	93	90	89	97	97	97

In 1903 and 1904 suicide rates remain almost at the level of 1902: 225 and 226 instead of 224 (Table 11.9). The Combes ministry remains in power from June 1902 to January 1905. In 1903 suicides decrease during the months of February and April, more strongly from June to September, and during December. In February 1903 the commission of the Chamber proposes to collect in a single bill all the demands coming from the congregations and to reject all of them without discussing particular items. From 12 to 18 March, after three very lively discussions, the Chamber rejects all the demands by a vote of 304 to 246. The measure adversely affects 3,040 preachers, 15,964 religious teachers, and the Carthusians. During the following months 'there was some resistance, barricaded convents, etc.' On 25 and 26 June the Chamber rejects collectively by a vote of 285 to 269 the demands of 81 congregations of women for the authorization of 517 institutions. The antagonism between the parties is at its height. The government, relying on the Council of States introduces an expeditious and revolutionary procedure. It extends the jurisdiction of its majority to the utmost. Enforcement measures implemented in all parts of the country set defenders and adversaries of the congregations against one another. On 18 December Combes introduces a bill forbidding instruction of any kind by any religious order or any member of a religious congregation. This bill will be voted on in March 1904.

The proportion of suicides remains low in 1904 until October (except for May), especially from June to September. The struggle continues on the ground of the concordat. Following the publication of a Vatican note to Catholic sovereigns protesting the visit of President Loubet to the King of Italy in March, the government recalls the French ambassador attached to the Pope (end of May). The decisive rupture occurs at the end of July. However, the end of the Combes ministry is approaching. The publication of the memoranda occurs in October. The ministry no longer has a majority. Combes will fall in January 1905.

The suicide rate for the whole of France jumps very plainly in 1905 from 226 to 239. It is interesting to note that the monthly rate which, in relative terms, exceeded 100 only once since 1898, acquires the following values during 1905: 100 in April, 101 in May, 106 in June, 114 in July, 107 in August, falling again afterwards and not exceeding 100 again until June 1906. In April 1905 Wilhelm II landed at Tangier. In June Delcassé tendered his resignation and France accepted the German proposal of an international conference on Morocco.

So after more than six years of decline, at a time when a grave conflict of foreign politics temporarily suspends the struggle between parties, suicides climb again to their old level and exceed it.

To repeat: the objective of this recollection of known facts is above all to illuminate clearly the intensity of the political passions which are given free reign during this period. These events are external indications of states of thought and sentiment that we cannot grasp directly in their collective form. Which of these multiple coincidences result from chance and which are worth remembering? To discover this, other investigations of tests of the same order are necessary, allowing still more precision.

To complete this study, we will reexamine the trend of suicides during these years within a few regions of France. There is no evidence that different parts of the population all reacted to contemporary political events with the same intensity. We will limit ourselves to comparisons made from this point of view among a few groups of departments.[13] (See Table 11.10.) The absolute number of suicides in each group in 1898 is set equal to 100.[14]

Table 11.10 *Number of suicides in France by region (relative to 1898)*

	1897	1898	1899	1900	1901	1902	1903	1904	1905
Paris	110	100	86	79	86	84	86	70.5	
Seine	104	100	91	88	91.5	90	90	87	90
Ile-de-France, Champagne, etc.	101.5	100	93.5	92	90	91.5	90.5	90	93
Anjou, etc.	94	100	102	104	99	94	89	95	100
Poitou, etc.	97	100	94	97	100	87	106	99	102
Brittany	112	100	104	105	100	102	95	103	118
West	100	100	100	102	99.5	94.5	95	98	106
Burgundy, etc.	96.5	100	87	90	85	90	99	94	104
Lyonnais, etc.	96.5	100	94	107	98	90	91	104	103
Burgundy-Lyonnais	96.5	100	91	102	94	90	93.5	102	103
Midi (South-east)	96	100	91	87	92	91	96.5	96.5	92.5
Midi (South-west)	85.5	100	90	89	89	95.5	90	97	104
Midi	92	100	91.5	87	91	92	93	96	98
France	99	100	95	94.5	93	92	93.5	94	98.5

If we confined ourselves to total results for the four great regions studied, we would assume that the decline of the suicide curve was clearest in this period in Ile-de-France, etc., and above all in the Midi. In both regions the numbers representing voluntary deaths stand, for five consecutive years, below what they were in 1898 by 8 to 10 per cent. The decrease in the Midi in 1900 is as much as 13 per cent. In Burgundy, Franche-Comté, and

Lyonnais the decline is both less continuous and smaller. The influence of the economic crisis, bringing an increase of suicides in its train, is felt clearly in 1900. From 1904 onward the political crisis no longer appears to exert any influence. However, except for a sag of only 5 per cent in the west during 1902 and 1903, the suicide rate remains at the same level from the beginning to the end of the period. There is a very marked recovery in 1905. Seignobos says, apropos of the legislative elections of 1898:

> The regional distribution of representatives remains the same: the conservatives came from the west, some from the southwest. The radicals dominated in the formerly democratic regions of the southeast, Languedoc, the center, the industrial countries, and the big cities. The moderates came, above all, from Lorraine, the northern countries, and the region of the southwest, recently devoted to the Republic.

Did the west react so feebly to the politics of the Combes ministry because the conservatives were dominant there? How, on the other hand, explain the indifference, or at least the halfheartedness of Burgundy and Lyonnais, in lively contrast to the much greater political sensibility of the Midi and the departments surrounding Paris?

Now let us examine the smaller groups of which these regions are composed. Our impressions will be confirmed at certain points, while much modified at others. In the two groups of the Midi, in Seine, and above all in Paris, the downward fluctuations are always very strong, especially in 1900, the Waldeck-Rousseau period. In Paris, despite the crisis and the exposition this year, the decline is more than 20 per cent.[15] However, while the Midi seems to weary more quickly, the southwest Midi to react but little in 1902 (the start of the Combes ministry), and suicides there to rise to their normal rate from 1904 on, the decline in Seine and in Paris, accentuated in 1904, continues even after 1904. In Burgundy (in contrast to Lyonnais) the average decline is even stronger than in Seine until 1901 inclusive (the Waldeck-Rousseau ministry), still strong in 1902. In Lyonnais, on the contrary, suicides hardly decrease at all until 1901 inclusive. They increase very plainly in 1900, the year of the crisis. There is a rather perceptible decline during the first two years of the Combes ministry which, however, ends abruptly: after 1904 people again kill themselves with great frequency.

Brittany, analyzed separately, must hold our attention now. Confining ourselves to the period 1898–1904, we may say that of all the regions, Brittany is where the number of voluntary deaths appears least related to the march of political events. The only decrease in suicides enumerated during these seven years is a small one in 1903. In other years suicides are even a little more numerous, on the average, than in 1898. Here, however, is a very interesting fact. We have said that suicides increase in France in 1898, the year of the Dreyfus Affair. This is true of all the regions studied except two: Paris and, precisely, Brittany.[16] In fact in both places suicides decrease from 1897 to 1898 in nearly the same proportion. At the end of the period, however, they mount to a very high level in Brittany, clearly higher than in 1897. It is as if a rising movement of suicides developed in this region before 1898 which was abruptly interrupted in that year, and which did not recover until the day after the resignation of the Combes ministry in 1905. Is this correct? To verify, we calculate the relative number of suicides which were produced here before 1898 and after 1905, always setting the corresponding number in 1898 equal to 100 (Table 11.11). The rise is very clear and almost continuous.[17]

Table 11.11   *Suicides in Brittany (I)*

1893	1894	1895	1896	1897	1898	1905	1906	1907	1908	1910	1911	1913
98	111	104	110	112	100	118	118	134	120	142	138	143

We must therefore admit that the increase in suicides was abruptly interrupted the very year of the Dreyfus Affair. The result of this, however, is that all during the Waldeck-Rousseau and Combes ministries suicides diminished strongly relative to what their level should have been. To measure this decrease, let us calculate the relative number of suicides, in Brittany, setting equal to 100 the absolute number of suicides not in 1898, but in 1897. We then find the figures shown in Table 11.12.

Table 11.12   *Suicides in Brittany (II)*

1897	1898	1899	1900	1901	1902	1903	1904	1905
100	89	93.5	73.5	89	90	85	92	104.5

The average decline is almost as large as in Seine and larger than in the Midi. The minimum is lower than in every other region except Paris and, as in Anjou, occurs in 1903, or later than the minima of other groups of departments. However, a first minimum occurs the year of the Dreyfus Affair which is not found in any of the regions we have distinguished except in Seine and, especially, in Paris. (It is less accentuated here.)

Finally, we can compare suicides in the rural and urban population during this period for all of France (Table 11.13). Here are two parallel series of relative numbers. The first two lines represent, respectively, the absolute numbers of rural and of urban suicides relative to the number for 1897 set equal to 100; the last line, the absolute number of urban suicides relative to the absolute number of rural suicides of each year set equal to 100.[18]

Table 11.13   *Suicides in the urban and rural population of France*

	1897	1898	1899	1902	1905	1906	1907	1908	1910	1911
Rural (relative to 1897)	100	105	101	97.5	106.5	106	110	106	114	111
Urban (relative to 1897)	100	94	89	89	92	90	102	95	97	94
Urban (relative to rural)	102	92	91	94	88.5	86	95.5	92	87	87

The first two lines of Table 11.13 bring two important facts to light: first, that urban suicides very clearly decreased in 1898, the year of the Dreyfus Affair, contrary to apparent findings of rates for France as a whole in 1897 and 1898 (242 and 244), as well as findings from the preceding Table 11.7. Second, the urban suicide rates do indeed decrease more clearly in 1898 and 1899 than the totality of urban and rural suicides. (For all of France, the numbers relative to 1897 are 96 and 93.) Another, smaller decrease is found in 1905 and 1906. Finally, there is a third fact. Rural suicides do not appear to diminish except for a sag in 1902. We recall, however, from Table 7.1,* that the suicide curve in the countryside from 1866 to 1911 is clearly ascendant. From the very figures above, we found that suicides increased between 1897 and 1910–11 from 100 to 111–14. Now this movement was interrupted in 1899–1902. The sag of 1902 is therefore really deeper than it appears. Were we to calculate for the countryside the relative numbers corresponding to the same rate of increase from 100 in 1897 to 114† in 1910 (giving 106.15 for 1905, which is almost the same as in the Table), we would find for 1902, 103.85.[19] The difference between this number and 97.5 therefore measures the real decrease of suicides in the countryside in 1902, from 100 to 94

*Chapter 7, p. 110 – Tr.
† In the original, 110, a typographical error – Tr.

or about 6 per cent. This decrease is very much smaller than that in the cities: from 100 to 89, almost half.

Finally, let us add that, as in preceding years, the relation of female to male suicides hardly varied during the entire period: from 30 to 30.15 women per hundred men. If the political situation explains the decline in suicide during this period, we must assume that the two sexes experienced its influence to the same extent.[20]

Although the proportion of voluntary deaths rises in 1905 almost to the level of 1896, it drops again in 1906: from 352* to 239*. Moreover, we notice in Table 11.7 that, in Seine and the southeast Midi, that is, in regions where the decrease in suicides was most perceptible at the height of the preceding political crisis, this proportion remains as low in 1905 as in 1901–2. Actually, the political crisis is not ended. Upon briefly recalling the most important events of 1905 and 1906, we see that their relevance is not obviously less that the preceding ones and that we have still not come to the sea's low-ebb and the announcement of the return of the tide.

1905. Principal vote on the separation of church and state, 10 February; deposit of a bill by the Commission, 4 March. Vote on the two-year law by the Senate, February–March. Vote on the law of separation in the Chamber, 3 July, and in the Senate, 6 December. The foreign crisis (visit of Wilhelm II to Tangier and resignation of Delcassé) deflects the feeling of political struggle against the church a little. However, if one discards these five months, the suicide rate during the other seven, for all of France, is equal to 225, that is, as low as in 1902 and 1903. Thus, the decline continues at the same time as the crisis.

> By the law of 2 December 1905 France broke with the European tradition of concordats by which the State recognized religion officially; she passed to the American system which allows cults organized by private initiative. This was a revolution in the ecclesiastical regime of France. [Seignobos, *op. cit.*, p. 245.]

1906. Election of Fallières to the presidency of the Republic against Doumer: 'success of the Bloc against the coalition of adversaries of the Combes ministry.' The inventories of the churches (protests by the bishops, demonstrations, resistances, etc.), February. Ministry of Sarrien–Clemenceau–Briant, March. Elections (triumph of the Bloc, which gains 60 seats), April. Election of Brisson to the presidency of the Chamber. Clemenceau ministry, October. Conflict with the Vatican. The Pope forbids

*The original reverses these figures, a typographical error – Tr.

church associations, August. Briand expels Montagnini, the Pope's chargé d'affaires, and seizes his papers, December.

Thus, the political crisis begun in 1898 continues until 1907. We can say that, during this period, except for four or five months in 1905 when the Tangier affair gave rise to a war crisis, public attention is totally preoccupied with the struggle against the congregations and the Vatican. Since the suicide rise during the four or five months in 1905 seems indeed to be related to preoccupation with the war, we can also say that the suicide rate declines all during the period when preoccupation with internal politics is the salient concern, and that not even at the end of the period does it again climb to the level attained previously.

We have dwelt on this example. We believe that one well-chosen experience studied sufficiently closely can suffice to establish a causal relationship. However, France has been through similar circumstances on other occasions since the registration of voluntary deaths. Without going into as much detail, it will suffice to show that coincidences we can enumerate between trends in suicides then and political events do not appear accidental.

From 1872 to 1892, the proportion of suicides increases rapidly and continuously. We calculated that this increase had to be 4.7 per year on the average and thus obtained a series of (calculated) numbers to relate to the observed numbers. In Table 11.14 we show the difference between the calculated and the observed numbers. For a number of years located at the beginning, first third, middle third, and end of the series (1872, 1874, 1878, 1882, 1885, 1887, 1888, 1891, and 1892) these differences are too small for us to be certain that the theoretic curve (the calculated numbers) does indeed represent the overall trend of the phenomenon. The negative differences represent more or less prolonged interruptions of the ascending trend. What are the causes of these interruptions?

The first, from 1875 to 1877, occurs in an extremely agitated period when France, escaping the government of the monarchical parties, votes the Constitution of 1875 that establishes the Republic, and when the Republican Chamber holds its own against the President and the Senate conservatives (*coup d'état* of 16 May 1877, republican elections in October).

A new massive decrease in voluntary deaths in 1879–81. 'The year 1878,' says Seignobos, 'was a year of calm and of political inaction.'[21] At the beginning of 1879, MacMahon tenders his resignation. The republican party prevails. Gambetta is President of the Chamber. The struggle against the congregations begins. In March 1879 Ferry drafts a bill which excludes the bishops from the Superior Council of Public Instruction (voted by a small majority

Table 11.14   *Number of suicides in France per million inhabitants*

Years	Calculated numbers	Observed numbers	Differences
1872	144.8	146	+ 1.2
1873	149.5	153	+ 3.5
1874	154.2	155	+ 0.8
1875	158.9	150	− 8.9
1876	163.6	158	− 5.6
1877	168.3	160	− 8.3
1878	173	173	0
1879	177.7	174	− 3.7
1880	182.4	178	− 4.4
1881	187.1	179	− 8.1
1882	191.8	192	+ 0.2
1883	196.5	192	− 4.5
1884	201.2	199	− 2.2
1885	205.9	207	+ 1.1
1886	210.6	214	− 3.4
1887	215.3	215	− 0.3
1888	220	220	0
1889	224.7	214	− 10.7
1890	229.4	220	− 9.4
1891	234.1	232	− 2.1
1892	238.8	241	+ 1.2

in February 1880), and another which prohibits unauthorized teaching by the members of congregations: Article VII, directed against the Jesuits, is voted by the Chamber in July 1879, but rejected by the Senate in March 1880. 'The decrees,' March 1880, are followed by the expulsion of the Jesuits. This is the rupture between the Republic and the clergy. The law establishing free education is voted in June 1881. In the elections of August 1881 the Republican party is reinforced. Gambetta forms his great ministry in November 1881.

In 1882 suicides increase; they decrease again in 1883–4, increase in 1885, and finally decrease in 1886. We say 'finally' because the political situation is quite different when, after two years of decline, suicides again increase. The reform of primary education is achieved in 1886 by the law of 30 October establishing the secularization of the schools. We might assume that from a political point of view the entire period 1877–86 forms a whole. We are also tempted to link the entire series of years during which the differences between the calculated and observed numbers of suicides remain negative, that is, until 1886. (When one refers to the table this linkage seems natural.) However, how shall we explain the interruption of this trend by intermittent rises on two occasions, in 1882 and 1885?

In 1882 there was an exceptional financial crisis in France, resulting from the profound economic depression felt by all the civilized countries after 1881, and from speculation (the crash of the Union générale). In the next chapter we shall study the influence that economic crises appear to exert on the suicide trend, and shall see that suicides tend to increase in periods of depression and to diminish in periods of prosperity. Let us say at once that this influence seems thwarted and obscured in France from 1881 to 1913, undoubtedly because political circumstances intervene. To be sure, we could relate the decline in suicides that we examined in the first place from 1875 to 1882 (exclusive) to the wave of prosperity that begins in 1875 and continues until 1881 (also exclusive). However, how then shall we explain that during the period of depression from 1881 to 1888 suicides diminish five years out of seven? At present our attention is engaged by political events. Nevertheless we must assume that the influence of economic circumstances, possibly weaker in France during this period, is more obvious when they become exceptionally critical. This is indeed what seems to have taken place in 1882.[22]

Durkheim noticed that suicides diminished in August and September 1889, that is, during the elections, by 12 per cent relative to the corresponding months of 1888, and increased anew from October on, that is, following the cessation of the struggle. According to the figures in our table, this decline was actually a matter not of two months but of two years. According to his own data, it is 16 per cent in December 1889 relative to December 1888, 14 per cent in May 1889 relative to May 1888, etc. But the most remarkable characteristic of this decline is that it does not begin until 1889, when the Boulanger movement proper is coming to an end. General Boulanger's popularity is very great from the middle of 1887 on (departure for Clermont, review of July), reaching its zenith in 1888: triple election in Nord, Somme, and Charente-Inférieure in August and in Seine in January 1889. However, from February 1889 on, the Republican party recovered and reestablished the constituency poll. Prosecuted before the High Court, Boulanger fled to Brussels on 1 April, and very quickly disappeared from the political scene. Once again conservatives and Republicans come to grips with each other. At issue are the laws voted from 1879 on. The Republicans prevail on 22 September. Now, the proportion of suicides had risen in 1887 and 1888. It drops very rapidly in 1889 and 1890. It is not Boulangism but the struggle against Boulangism, or rather against the conservatives who have joined forces with him, which seems to have recreated a more exciting political atmosphere.

Albert Bayet, in the book that we have cited, writes:[23]

Suicides do not seem to have been particularly numerous during the heroic period of the Revolution. According to a legend circulated by Falret, there should have been thirteen hundred suicides in Versailles in 1793. But Des Étangs, enumerating all ascertained deaths in 1793 at the Town Hall of Versailles, arrives at a total of only 1,144; 'and suicide,' he adds, 'accounts for only a few.' I have not found any figure whatever for Paris, anywhere. The journals which publish the number of deaths do not indicate those of the suicides. However, some statements provide grounds for thinking that suicides are more numerous in 1790 and after 1794 than at the height of the heroic period .... After 1795 registers and official police reports agree in indicating an increase in the number of suicides .... Now, although complaints are made about the great number of suicides before and after the heroic period of the Revolution, I have searched in vain for an analogous complaint during this period itself .... The only precise figure, indicating sixty suicides in 1797 (in Paris) for a five-month period, does not show an average higher than the annual average of 147 shown by Mercier for the years before the Revolution. Now, this number for 1797 relates to a period when, according to several testimonies, the number of suicides is in full growth. It will indeed have to be admitted, therefore, that at the height of the Revolution, at the time of the Terror, the average annual number of suicides in Paris is lower than during the course of the last years of the old regime.

All of this seems to justify Durkheim, and Rousseau who said: 'Outbreaks and civil wars give rulers rude shocks, but they are not the real ills of people .... A little disturbance gives the soul elasticity; what makes the race truly prosperous is not so much peace as liberty.'* (*Social Contract*, Book III, Chapter IX.)

*(Translation from the American edition of Everyman's Library, New York, E.P. Dutton & Co., Inc., 1950, p. 84 – Tr.)

However, let us avoid a hasty conclusion. We have shown that while suicides diminish during war, the structure of society is transformed at the same time. Life is simplified and standardized. Under these conditions it is rather natural that people behave differently from in time of peace. The decrease in voluntary deaths may only be due to the exaltation of national sentiment to a limited extent, and may result more often from the group's having passed from the industrial to the military type. Is the same thing true in a period of revolution or of political crisis or agitation?

We are entitled to be doubtful, for in such periods society is not externally modified. Functions are fulfilled by the same organs. Men are not separated from their families and continue to practice their professions. Economic life is pursued. Nothing is changed if it is only some members of the group who are more preoccupied with political activity and who devote to it a larger part of their time and attention. Here the explanation that Durkheim proposed remains therefore wholly valid. It is because people are caught up in a vast collective current that life interests them more. Dominated by a sentiment of being indistinguishable from others, they become less sensible of motives of despair and discouragement that impose on the conscience of the isolated individual.

We do not always know whether political crises may not have other effects than to intensify thus an entire special order of collective sentiments. Revolution, like war, simultaneously excites the passions and more or less relaxes and paralyzes all of society's functions. A revolution and a political crisis differ only in degree. The same indirect effects may be produced in both cases. While it is not possible for us to verify this hypothesis at this time, we must consider it.

The main point is the outcome of the tests we have analyzed: suicides diminish in times of political crisis as well as during wars. This fact must be held on to whatever explanation one might give for it.

Chapter 12

The effect of economic crises: fluctuations in Prussian and German suicides

To show that economic crises affect suicide, Morselli recalled that when a financial crisis erupted in Austria in 1873–4, suicides there increased immediately by at least 40 per cent, in Vienna by almost 70 per cent. At the beginning of the chapter devoted to 'anomic suicide' Durkheim lays stress on the same fact: 'The increase,' he says, 'is 70 per cent. This financial catastrophe is the sole cause of the increase.' Now let us quote an observation by Father Krose:

> Until 1872, the number of suicides in Austria only increases slowly. This same year publication begins of the medical enumerations prescribed by the Higher Council on Hygiene permitting completion of the data of the registries kept by the priests. Now, the number of suicides increases from 1,677 in 1872 to 2,463 the following year, or nearly 50 per cent.* No doubt the financial crash in Vienna in 1873 accounts for a small part of this increase. However, it results principally from the greater accuracy of enumerations, since it continues the following year.

This example only proves that certain precautions must be taken in the study of suicide statistics. Economic facts are rather complex, however. What is a crisis? Economists understand by this an abrupt passage from a perod of high prices to a period of low. However, the wholesale and retail prices of stocks and bonds negotiated on the Bourse do not decline at the same time. A financial crisis must not be confused with a crisis in prices: the former often precedes the latter, so much so that the latter can occur in a different year. Many authors speak of a crisis of inflation, Durkheim even speaks of crises of prosperity. The decline in prices will be a catastrophe or a benefit depending on

* Exactly 46.9 per cent – Tr.

the economic status of a country, on its being principally agricultural or industrial. Finally, there are nations, and periods in the life of nations, where commerce and industry are the principal interests of the people. In other countries, and at other times in the same countries, politics are salient.

In this study of the relation between economic crises and suicides, we shall confine ourselves to one great industrial country, Germany, and to the period following 1870, because during the forty years preceding the world war, political life there was slack while productive and commercial activity absorbed all the nation's forces. For the same reasons, we shall take as indices of prosperity and depression in Germany only the trends in wholesale prices.

We shall first compare suicide statistics in Prussia (or in Germany) and in France for all periods following 1827, because between 1880 and 1890 is when the industrial rise of Germany began and its foreign commerce surpassed that of France. If we were to ascertain that, after this, the increase in suicides slackened in Germany, but not in France, at least not to the same extent, that would already allow us to infer that a relationship exists between industrial activity and suicide, and that the latter declines when the former increases.

Table 12.1   *Proportion of suicides in Prussia, Germany, and France, 1827–1924 (per million inhabitants)*

	Prussia	Germany	France
1827–36	93.5		60.8
1837–46	103.9		82.4
1847–56	115.3		101.7
1857–66[2]	118 (138)		119.1
1867–76	129.5 (155.5)		141.6
1877–86[3]	191.2 (213)	210[1]	186.8
1887–96	199.7	206.3	231.3
1897–1906	198.1	206.9	232.2
1907–13	210	220	250
1914–18	161.5	175.6	174.6
1919–24	202.7	212	224

We must not forget that before 1883 (the date when suicide statistics in Prussia were improved) the enumerations in this country allowed an important number of suicides to escape attention, probably a sixth (as in the year 1883, for which the results of the two methods could be compared). We do not absolutely know to what extent a first reform in this statistic, in 1867, increased the number of registered suicides. However, for 1867–86 we can increase the numbers corresponding to the years 1857–82[4] by a sixth, compensating for the probable error of underenumeration as we have just indicated. We obtain, thus, the higher average proportions shown in the table between parentheses. If these new figures are almost accurate, it would follow that between 1827 and 1877–86 inclusive (for the numbers prior to 1877 are certainly flawed), that is, during over fifty years, the suicide rate should have been higher in Prussia than in France.[5]

After 1886 this was no longer so. In fact, from 1887 until 1913 for Prussia, and until 1924 for Germany, the proportion of suicides was lower every year (except in 1915 and 1918) than in France. During the twenty years from 1887 to 1906 it was 16 per cent higher in France than in Prussia (12 per cent higher in France than in Germany), and from 1907 to 1913, the brink of the war, by 19 and by 14 per cent, respectively. During the war, and this is rather remarkable, it was equal in Germany and in France. During the six years following the war, from 1919 to 1924, it was again higher in France than in Germany, but only by 6 per cent. From 1886 to 1887 is very clearly when the ratio changed direction and the suicide rate, hitherto favorable to France, became favorable to Prussia and to Germany.[6]

To have a more accurate idea of the suicide trend in the two countries during the entire period beginning with 1867, let us show the proportionate increase in the suicide rate for each decade (increasing the German figures prior to 1883 by a fifth) (Table 12.2).

The French rate exceeds the German after 1887 because it had

Table 12.2 *Increase or decrease of the suicide rate in France and Prussia*

	France (percentage)	Prussia (percentage)
1867 to 1876	+ 20	0
1877 to 1886	+ 27	+ 10
1887 to 1896	+ 12	− 2
1897 to 1906	+ 2	+ 2
1907 to 1913	+ 2	+ 11

become considerably higher during the previous twenty years. This was not the case in Germany because the suicides, which had greatly declined during the war of 1870–1, mounted only slowly in its aftermath to the level attained in 1867.[7]

Not only was a politically new era heralded by the military victory but, even more, by the foundation of the Reich. Probably not since the beginning of the nineteenth century has the German people been aroused and carried away by so irresistible a current of national enthusiasm. This explains the prolonged halt in the ascending trend in the proportion of suicides in Germany. No other example is found before this period. In order better to show to what extent this is exceptional, as well as the fluctuation which occurs ten years later, we have calculated for Prussia, as we previously did for France, the average suicide rate for three consecutive years since the beginning of Prussian statistics (Table 12.3). (Excepted is the triennial period 1882–4, where we increased the number corresponding to the year 1882 by a fifth, for reasons indicated above.)

The increase occurring from 1848 to 1882–4 was visibly

Table 12.3   *Average suicide rate in Prussia, per million inhabitants*

Years	Suicides	Years	Suicides
1816–18	71.1	1864–6	121.3
1819–21	77.1	1867–9	144.3
1822–4	84.3	1870–2	117
1825–7	83.7	1873–5	120.3
1828–30	91	1876–8	163.3
1831–3	92.3	1879–81	175
1834–6	99.8	1882–4	218
1837–9	101	1885–7	211
1840–2	102.7	1888–90	192
1843–5	107	1891–3	205.3
1846–8	108.3	1894–6	200.7
1849–51	102	1897–9	192.7
1852–4	120.3	1900–2	196.7
1855–7	127.3	1903–5	204.3
1858–60	116	1906–8	202
1861–3	118	1909–11	209

interrupted. There was a sudden and profound drop during the war years of 1870–71 and immediately following, and a depression lasting over six years.[8] The decline in the suicide rate, enumerated above, during the third period, which really begins in 1887, was equally deep in 1888 and 1889. We note that after this epoch and during all of the following periods the suicide rate tends to approach this minimum, in no case ever becoming much higher.

None of the national political events are sufficient to account for this second decrease in voluntary deaths (after 1887). The death of the old Emperor and the accession of Wilhelm II in 1888 constitute expected and secondary events; they were not of a type to arouse and incite the German masses in a prolonged manner. We must look elsewhere, directing our attention principally to the economic evolution being achieved at this time beyond the Rhine. Precisely between 1880 and 1890 is when the industrial and commercial rise of Germany begins. Although productive wealth and power undoubtedly developed there in greater proportions during the two following decades, until 1913, never was the change more profound or felt more profoundly than around 1887.[9] The hypothesis is that with the political transformation accomplished during and after the war of 1870–1, the beginning of the industrial revolution in Germany lowers the suicide rate there. This hypothesis will gain in credibility if we can establish that a relationship exists between alternating periods of economic prosperity and depression, and variations in the number of voluntary deaths.

This is what we shall prove for Germany after 1880. First, however, let us examine the Prussian figures for the period before this date, laying stress on the years of crisis. We reproduce in Table 12.4 the price index at Hamburg of 28 imported articles.[10]

Prices rise from 1849 to 1873 and decline from 1873 to 1896: both of these long-term trends must be taken into account to appreciate the significance of the amplitude of the short-term cyclic trends. As Aftalion remarks about this, 'the long-term trend prolongs the cyclic trend that takes effect in the opposite direction.' Accordingly, we must assume that downward trends are attenuated until 1873, that is, are more important than they appear to be.

We shall not dwell on the years following 1848. The revolution made its influence felt in Germany later than in France. Suicides diminish in Prussia after 1848, especially in 1849. On the other hand, we know that 1848, 1849, and 1850 were very good harvest years. Of course, we must distinguish between principally industrial and commercial countries, which profit from rises in prices and are severely disturbed by their decline, and principally agricultural countries, which may gain less from the rise in prices of agricultural products than they lose (because the rise is due to bad harvests), and which are not affected by the general rise in prices. We must not forget that at this period Germany is not yet very developed industrially and commercially. When Durkheim says that suicides increase 13 per cent in 1850, at a time when the wheat trade is declining in Prussia to the lowest point attained during the whole period 1848–81, he is not taking into account the delayed influence of the revolution of 1848, which lowered the suicide rate by precisely 10 per cent from 1848 to 1849. The suicide rate was actually lower in 1850 than it had been on the average in the whole period of 1842–8.

In 1857 there is a severe international crisis. However, since 1854, and especially since 1855 and 1856, suicides have increased in Prussia. Wholesale prices in Germany were exceptionally high in 1854 and 1855. They dropped a little in 1856. However, the prices of essential foods were raised in 1854–6. We may assume that in the countries which were not yet very industrialized, it was less the crisis of prices (going from high to low) than the cost of living which created a state of malaise and trouble in the mass of people. In fact, in 1858, when wholesale prices had just dropped 20 points, the suicide rate remained clearly below the level it had attained in 1855–6.

The extremely abrupt increase in the suicide rate in Prussia from 1866 to 1867 held the attention of Durkheim, who concluded from this that crises of prosperity as well as crises of poverty have an unfavorable effect in this respect.

> In 1866 [he says] the kingdom (Prussia) received a first enlargement. It annexed several important provinces, while becoming the head of the Confederation of the North. Immediately this growth in glory and power was accompanied by a sudden rise in the number of suicides.*

Unfortunately, the data we possess on suicides during these years, so important in the history of Prussia, are not quite reliable. We have said that it was very possible, even probable, that the new methods of enumeration, officially introduced in 1868, had already been employed a year earlier, at least on a trial basis. Now, there is no evidence that figures of previous years have not been inaccurate. (We recall that suicides will increase in 1883 at the time of a subsequent reform by more than a sixth.) We have every reason to cease searching any longer for meaning in a fluctuation which may be entirely imaginary.

---

* *Suicide*, p. 244 – Tr.

Table 12.4   *Indices of wholesale prices in Germany from 1850 to 1887*

1850	120	1860	141	1870	135	1879	123
1851	112	1861	139	1871	140	1880	128
1852	118	1862	141	1872	155	1881	127
1853	134	1863	136	1873	160	1882	127
1854	153	1864	140	1874	147	1883	121
1855	161	1865	139	1875	138	1884	114
1856	147	1866	142	1876	134	1885	108
1857	150	1867	143	1877	132	1886	101
1958	130	1868	139	1878	124	1887	103
1859	136	1869	139				

We come now to the great crisis of 1874. According to Durkheim,

> A new transformation occurs in Prussia on the eve of the war of 1870. Germany is unified and placed entirely under the hegemony of Prussia. An enormous war indemnity enlarges the public fortune; commerce and industry expand. Never has the development of suicide been so rapid. From 1875 to 1886 it increases by 90 per cent, going from 3,278 cases to 6,212.

The rate of increase in suicide from 1875 to 1886, although unprecedented up to then, is not as high as Durkheim believes. Not taken into account is, first, that from 1882 to 1883 the reform introduced into the methods of enumeration increased the official number of suicides by one-sixth. Also, he calculates the increase in the absolute number of suicides rather than their proportion in relation to the increased population. According to our calculations, the growth of the suicide rate from 1875 to 1886 (increasing the 1875 figures by one-sixth) would have been only 47 per cent, not 90 per cent.

> This increase is no less marked. On the morrow of the war of 1870 [wrote Durkheim] a new accession of good fortune took place. Germany was unified and placed entirely under Prussian hegemony. An enormous war indemnity added to the public wealth; commerce and industry made great strides. The development of suicide was never so rapid. [*Op. cit.*, p. 244 – Tr.]

Durkheim wished to establish that it is not the cost of living or the slackening of economic activity but rather crisis, as such, which brings with it an increase in voluntary deaths. Now there are, he thinks, crises of prosperity as well as crises of depression. Must one believe that the increase in suicides from 1875 to 1886 is the result of a surge of prosperity, of a crisis which, however fortunate it may be, remains no less a crisis?

Durkheim forgets that in 1869, 1870, and, especially, 1871, the Prussian suicide rate drops sharply and remains at a very low level until 1875 inclusive. Now, this decrease in suicides seems to be related to the national ebullience and political rise of Germany at this date. While in France the curve of suicides again mounts in 1871 and, after 1872, surpasses the level to which it rose in 1868–9, in Germany it troughs, and until 1876 remains below the figure attained at the outbreak of the war.

We can even say that the influence exerted on the suicide rate by this crisis of national growth, tending to lower it, is stronger than the economic crisis of 1874, which tends to make it rise again. However, the influence of the economic crisis soon becomes the stronger. In fact the period of depression, following the abrupt fall of prices, lasts at least ten years, though an agricultural crisis came along to prolong it in 1884–6.[11]

We have said that in 1883 a new reform in the statistics of voluntary deaths in Prussia increased their number by a sixth: if the numbers of suicides in the preceding years (1876–82) are increased in the same ratio, suicide rates are found as given below:

1876	175
1877	198
1878	210
1879	203
1880	210
1881	217
1882	223
1883	221
1884	210

Suicides undoubtedly increased independent of this correction, but that is explained by the continuous drop in prices between 1873 and 1886 from 160 to 101.

Here is the suicide rate in Saxony during the same years:

1876	352
1877	403
1878	408
1879	385
1880	396
1881	416

1882	371
1883	391
1884	357

Although the absolute numbers of suicides in Saxony are one-fifth as many as in Prussia during this period, the suicide rate, clearly higher in Saxony, varies in almost the same manner. Now, it clearly diminishes from 1881 to 1887. Hence, there are indeed grounds for correcting the Prussian figures before 1881. It is even advisable to increase them by a little more than a sixth.

After 1881 we command a more important collection of data for Germany as a whole than the preceding. From 1883 to the present, we no longer have to take account of statistical reforms, such as that in Prussia from 1867 to 1883, which would render comparisons from one period to another difficult and obscure.

In Table 12.5 below, we show the suicide rate, number of bankruptcies, and prices of goods in Germany for every year from 1881 to 1916.[12]

Table 12.5   *The suicide rate, bankruptcies, and prices in Germany*

Years	Suicides per million inhabitants	Bankruptcies (relative numbers)	Wholesale prices (relative numbers)
1881	198	66	105
1882	198	62	100
1883	223	60	99
1884	210	56	90
1885	215	59	85
1886	216	61	80
1887	210	62	80
1888	194	67	87
1889	198	67.5	96
1890	201	76	102
1891	212	93	109
1892	211	98	96
1893	212	86	89
1894	217	95	82
1895	202	91	80
1896	206	86	81
1897	206	89	88
1898	199	94	93

Table 12.5 continued *The suicide rate, bankruptcies, and prices in Germany*

Years	Suicides per million inhabitants	Bankruptcies (relative numbers)	Wholesale prices (relative numbers)
1899	195	99	94
1900	203	109	100
1901	208	134	93
1902	214	126	93
1903	217	123	92
1904	210	122	95
1905	213	120	99
1906	204	120	101
1907	206	126	113
1908	219	148	106
1909	223	140	106
1910	216	137	103
1911	217	140	109
1912	225	154	123
1913	232	162	113
1914	218	133	120
1915	166	82	161
1916	173	49	173
1917	164	—	203
1918	157	—	246
1919	184	—	471
1920	217	—	1,686
1921	207	—	2,169
1922	219	—	38,799
1923	214	—	—
1924	232	—	139
1925	245	—	148
1926	261	—	142
1927	—	—	157

We note, first of all, that the trend in wholesale prices during this period is cut by the year 1896 into two opposed and nearly symmetrical parts.[13] The trend from 1880 to 1896 drops from 110 to 80 in relative numbers. This ends the great downward trend which begins with the crisis of 1874 while prices are 160. The trend climbs again in an equal number of years between 1896 and 1912–13, from 80 to 110–20. However, this decline and recovery are not continuous. We count five crises in Germany during this period, in the years 1881, 1892, 1901, 1908, and 1912.

The first two crises are the strongest; downward currents are indeed more plentiful. In particular, prices fall lower between 1881 and 1886–7 than in France and England, as low as in 1896, while the drop in the latter two countries during this period is half as great. For Germany, we calculated the average suicide rates for each of the 9 periods alternating between low and high, with the results shown in Table 12.6.

Table 12.6   *Price movements and suicide rates, Germany*

Year	Price movement	Average suicide rate
1881–7	drop	210
1888–91	rise	201
1892–95	drop	210.5
1896–1900	rise	201.8
1901–3	drop	213
1904–7	rise	208.2
1908–10	drop	219.3
1911–12	rise	221
1913	drop	232

As we see, the average suicide rate is higher in periods of low prices, lower in periods of high prices. The only exception occurs in 1911–12. Prices drop the following year, however, and the suicide rate climbs again very plainly. Also, the crisis of 1913 undoubtedly began as early as 1912, the year in which the number of bankruptcies increases noticeably. Finally, we must take account especially of the fact that the secular suicide trend traversing these lows and highs rises: the series of figures corresponding to the low and high years, taken separately, are both increasing. We can say that the agreement, or rather the opposition, between the trend in prices and the trend in the suicide rate is quite remarkable. The relationship can also be expressed this way: the average rate of suicides in the years of low prices is 215.6, and in the years of high prices, 206.

Comparison of the number of bankruptcies and the suicide rate very plainly confirms this finding. The number of bankruptcies has increased continuously from the beginning of the period until the end, more than doubling. Above all has it increased after 1887, the very year that seems to mark the beginning of Germany's economic rise. Four pairs of years can be distinguished where the number of bankruptcies is maximum relative to the years which follow, as well as to the years which precede. The four maxima are in 1891–2, 1901–2, 1908–9, and 1912–13. Now, corresponding to all four pairs of years are very plain increases in the suicide rate. In the first two cases, the increases last one or two years after the maximum in bankruptcies but the suicide rate finally drops nonetheless. (In the first case, a secondary maximum in bankruptcies in 1884 corresponds to the delayed tabulation of the suicide rate; in the second case, one finds by calculating the average rate of suicides and the average number of bankruptcies for the years 1895–1900, 1901–3, 1904–7, respectively, 202, 213, 208; 95, 128, 122. There are indeed two maxima and two minima.) An increase in the suicide rate does not always coincide with the years in which the number of bankruptcies is maximal. There are also years when the suicide rate is maximal relative to subsequent or preceding years (until a new maximum before or after it).

The importance of such a finding depends, first, on the validity of the German suicide statistics. They cover one of the largest European populations (15,564 suicides in 1913, compared with 10,339 in France). Second, the test that yielded such results was done during a period when, on the whole, the suicide rate was not increasing much and was tending to stabilize. In fact, from 1881 to 1913 it increased not quite 12 per cent in Germany, while in France the increase during the same period was 32 per cent. Finally, there was nothing in Germany resembling a revolution or a profound political crisis during the last twenty years of the nineteenth century and the first twelve or thirteen of the twentieth, nor had this country engaged in war, not even a colonial war. Its entire attention appears to have been concentrated on commercial and industrial activity. That is why we see the rhythm of economic life so plainly reflected in the rhythm of suicides.[14]

The findings are much less clear in France. Since the increase in the suicide rate there is much more rapid than in Germany, and political crises indeed exert a stronger influence on the trend of voluntary deaths, it is difficult to discover a relationship in France of like direction between fluctuations in wholesale prices and in the suicide rate. However, let us calculate the same numbers for 9 periods.

Table 12.7 *Price movements and suicide rates, France*

Years	Price movement	Average suicide rate
1881–7	drop	200
1888–90	rise	218
1891–6	drop	240.7
1897–1900	rise	235.4
1901–4	drop	225.5
1905–7	rise	244
1908–9	drop	242
1910–12	rise	249.3
1913	drop	260

As in Germany, the same inverse relationship is again found between the two phenomena during the five periods 1888–90, 1891–6, 1897–1900, 1910–12, and 1913: when prices are rising, suicides diminish, when prices are declining, suicides increase. This is not the case in the other four periods. Of course, from 1881 to 1887 the suicide rate increases by 16 per cent and is found to be clearly higher than it was in the preceding years of high prices. However, even if the rising secular trend from 1881 to 1913 is eliminated, the suicide rate in 1881–7 remains lower than in 1888–90.[15] From 1900 to 1909, account must be taken of the drop in the suicide rate of 1899–1904, lasting until 1906, which seems to be explained by an important political crisis that is equivalent to a revolution. Taking these influences into account as well as the very rapid increase during this period, we can say that the law formulated for Germany is verified in France.[16]

Not the crisis as such (an abrupt passage from high prices to lower prices), but the period of depression following the crisis is what causes an increase in voluntary deaths. One might wonder about people killing themselves especially when prices drop. We have said above that the increase in suicides in Prussia in 1856 appears to be explained by the high prices, the period of exceptional inflation preceding the crisis of 1857. However, Germany before 1860 must be distinguished from after 1880. The German population increased from 1811 to 1861 by 13.1 per cent and from 1861 to 1911 (likewise fifty years) by 26.8 per cent. Germany before 1861 presents the image of a country in which economic life is relaxed. On the other hand, after 1880–5 especially, it is aroused, intensified, and accelerated. The psychological inclinations of the merchants and manufacturers, their hopes, fears, enthusiasms, and panics modify the moral atmosphere of the country altogether, like clouds or rifts in the clouds. The woes of unemployed workers, the bankruptcies, failures, and downfalls are not the immediate cause of many suicides. Rather, an obscure oppressive sentiment weighs on every soul because there is less general activity, because there is less participation by people in an economic life transcending them, and because their attention is no longer turned towards externals but dwells more, not merely on their distress or on their bare material competency, but on all the individual motives they may have for desiring death.

chapter 13

Suicide, mental illness, and alcoholism
The statistical data

There is no record whatever in history [says Montesquieu][1] of the Romans putting themselves to death without cause. The English, however, kill themselves without anyone being able to imagine any reason for it; they kill themselves even in the midst of good fortune. Amongst the Romans, suicide was the effect of education and resulted from their principles and customs. Amongst the English, it is the effect of a sickness, results from the machine's physical condition, and is independent of any other cause. Apparently, there is a deficiency in the filtration of fluids of the nervous system. [And he concludes,] It is clear that the civil laws of some countries have had reasons to stigmatize the self-murderer: but in England, one cannot inflict further punishment on him without punishing the effects of madness.

Let us speak, not of Englishmen and Romans, but of two groups of people. Instead of 'deficiency in the filtration of fluids of the nervous system,' let us speak of deficiency in secretions of the endocrine glands. Montesquieu's thesis could be advanced today in almost the same terms. It would correspond well to the most advanced stage of our medical attainments in this area. That is, there has been scarcely any progress.

Reading ancient works on suicide is interesting from more than one point of view. Even though most of the authors who have written on this subject in the first part of the nineteenth century were physicians specializing in the study of mental illness, their minds were not too systematic. They explained a large number of deaths as voluntary because they labeled hypochondria and lypemania as madness, melancholy, and delirium. Nevertheless, they thought that the passions, shame, anger, and remorse, could impel people of perfectly sound mind towards death.

There were exceptions, to be sure. Among the very authors of whom we are speaking, we find texts which could appeal today to partisans of purely physiological or psychiatric explanations of suicide. Thus, Esquirol had already written in 1838, 'Suicide offers all the characteristics of mental derangement, of which it is really only a symptom.' He cites an English author, Dr Burrows, who declared in 1820, 'Today it is generally recognized that suicide is a mental illness.' For his part, Falret says in 1822 that the condition of the soul which leads to suicide 'must be considered a delirium.'

Other passages by Esquirol, however, can be interpreted quite differently. For example, 'It is certain that he who lays violent hands on himself almost always at the moment of execution resembles a desperate man in delirium.' Or again, 'The general opinion regards suicide either as a neutral act [from the moral point of view] or as the effect of an illness.'[2] As for Falret, he enumerates as causes of suicide, love, jealousy, ambition, anger, domestic worries, reverses of fortune, etc.[3] As Bayet correctly observes, the idea that suicide is only an illness continued to gain ground throughout the first half of the century. In 1845 Dr Bourdin stated categorically, 'Suicide is always a sickness and always an act of an unhinged mind.'[4]

Today, the discipline of psychiatry does not ignore all that the statistics have taught us about this phenomenon and its relationship to social conditions and does not consider every subject who puts himself to death to be ill. The most frequent suicide, however, the prototype, remains nonetheless the act of a depressed or unstable person. Really voluntary deaths probably do exist. These, however, are not facts of the same order. It would be better not to force into the same category acts which sometimes result from a nervous malady or mental weakness and other times from reflection and will exerting themselves normally in a man sane of mind. This is the point of view of moderate defenders of the psychiatric thesis. Other, however, as we shall see, go much further and hold that almost all suicides are pathological, not merely the majority. They would find ludicrous Voltaire's expression of regret that 'not all who arrive at a decision to depart from life leave their reasons in writing, with a word about their philosophy,' since to do so 'would be useful to the living and to the history of the human spirit.' For them it is certainly the reflective and deliberate suicide which represents a sort of monstrosity and which would be better designated by another noun.

We would have to assume then that people were always mistaken in speaking of suicide, and that nothing was more absurd than to condemn, excuse, or approve an act which depended neither on society, nor on the individual. Bayet has done research in the law texts, in the codes, and in canon and civil law, but principally in literature on how suicide has, in fact, been appraised in our country during the course of the centuries which have elapsed since the Roman period. A short while ago suicide was condemned by the Church, the state, and public opinion. This indicates that society suffered from it as from an unquestionable illness without, however, believing it to be at all fatal to society. Society believed, on the contrary, that it had the power to eliminate suicide or to reduce it. Sometimes, principally under the influence of the cultivated classes, society showed greater indulgence for the voluntarily dead. Not that it considered suicide irresponsible. This is, on the contrary, the time and milieux when the sentiment of liberty and the rights of the individual were strongest. In any case, society even believed that upon it depended whether to tolerate or suppress suicide. The arguments which have been presented either against or for suicide may have been faulty. They may not have exerted the influence expected of them. As soon as society formulated them, however, or they were formulated in its name, society was convinced that suicide did not always result from mental illness or from delirium. It is improbable that such an illusion would have lasted so long if it had no basis.

The contrary opinion, defended by psychiatrists, is partly explained by the fact that, having seen many insane and neurasthenic suicides, they naturally are led to believe that all suicides are ascribable to mental pathology. This thesis is based, at the same time, on a popular prejudice. Suicide seems so abnormal an act that one is unwilling to assume that it could have been accomplished by anybody who was not ill. Would it, therefore, be possible to establish that a constant relationship exists between the increase in suicide and variations in the number of mental afflictions? Dr Burrows, of whom we have spoken, depended on the number of suicides in Paris and London for the conclusion that the number of insane must be greater in Paris than in London. There must then have been, in his view, a close relationship between insanity and suicide. However, this relationship is not obvious. Its existence is not certain until demonstrated.

Durkheim, who devoted the first chapter of his book to the study of suicide and psychopathic states,[5] could have found an indication of the physical and mental state of the suicides in the very numerous statistics on motives which most countries publish. However, he categorically refused to resort to such data.

What are called statistics of the motives of suicide [he writes] are actually statistics of the opinions concerning such motives of officials, often of lower officials, in charge of this information service.... We make it a rule not to employ in our studies such uncertain and uninstructive data [pp. 148, 151].

Since this type of statistic has multiplied since Durkheim wrote his book, and since most authors have taken account of it, we shall cite figures solely for the purpose of showing to what extent the proportion of suicides attributed to the mentally pathological condition of the subject varies according to country, and, since so many reasons explain why their number is increasing, how large a part of them, even given these arbitrary estimations, is linked to other motives.

In Prussia in 1906–8 nervous and mental maladies would be the cause of suicide in 25 cases per 100 for men, and in 42 to 47 per 100 for women. In Bavaria from 1881–90 to 1906 the proportion would have increased for the total population from 32.5 per cent to 40. In Saxony in 1905–8 it would have been 30.4 per cent for men and 50.7 for women (von Mayr). (See the figures given by Durkheim for Saxony in 1854–78 and 1880.) In France and Italy for the period 1878–87 the proportion would have been, in France, 30 per cent for men, 40 per cent for women;[6] in Italy, 25.3 per cent for men, 44.2 per cent for women. (See the figures given by Durkheim for the periods 1856–60 and 1874–8 in France.) In Serbia in 1902–6 only 11.6 per cent of the suicides are attributed to mental illnesses; there is, it is true, an extraordinarily large proportion of 'unknown motives.' In Japan, on the contrary, the proportion of pathological suicides is very large: 50.5 per cent of the suicides in 1897, and 48.5 per cent in 1906, would be explained by mental illnesses. Women exceed men by very little, only by 2 points (Schnapper-Arndt and von Mayr).

Contrary to what would be predicted, the proportion of suicides of this type is larger in the country than in the big cities: in Bavaria (1902–6) from 26.5 to 35.9 in the cities, from 41.5 to 49 in the rural districts. In Denmark (1896–1900), we are told, 23 per cent of male suicides and 39.3 per cent of female in the big cities, 30 per cent of males and 48.1 per cent of females in the countryside killed themselves on account of melancholy, delirium, etc. While in Prussia in 1908, 32.9 per cent of the males and 54.6 of the females who commit suicide are thought to be stricken by nervous or mental maladies, in Berlin these proportions fall to 21.2 and 33.3 per cent. It is curious to note that, according to the official records of the Prussian ministry, of 350 scholars who killed themselves from 1883 to 1905, the count of those who were stricken by a mental trouble or a malady was only 42. However, the motive that had decided them was not known for 277. Is it quite certain that the proportion of truly unknown causes had been much lower in the other tabulations?

The statistics on motives do not inspire confidence because they result from declarations accepted or inquiries carried out by a number of different physicians, physicians of the civil service or private physicians, unequally conscientious and unequally concerned about reaching the true cause of suicide. A large number of them undoubtedly fill out the official forms as one carries out an administrative task. A medico-sociological inquest recently conducted in Paris by Dr Suzanne Serin, physician of mental hospitals, for the clinic of mental therapy which Dr Toulouse directs, seems to us, on the other hand, more serious and instructive.[7]

This research which [from January 1925] until July 1926 dealt with 307 cases, 420 until October 1926, was conceived in the following way: where completed suicides are concerned, a social assistant, especially trained for this work, proceeded immediately to the home of the desperate person and at the setting gathered from neighbors and family all information able to throw light on his previous history, his attitude during the days preceding the suicide, and the motives he may have given for his act. For the others, we proceeded [still quoting the author] either to the survivor's home or to a hospital in order to initiate a psychiatric examination.

It is a question, as we see, of attempted as well as completed suicides, but we are not told the proportionate figures of these two categories.[8]

These cases have all been divided into five broad categories according to their causes: psychopathy, alcoholism, deep-seated anxieties, incurable maladies, and destitution. The table that can be drawn up from these is reproduced as Table 13.1.

Thus, a third of the suicides studied appear to be the acts of psychopaths. A little more than half of them

presented before the suicide well-defined mental troubles which must have aroused special notice. We have enumerated in order of frequency, melancholy, depression, mental troubles that accompany alcoholic intoxication, senile degeneration, *dementia praecox*, epilepsy, traumatic psychoses, suicidal depression, chronic deliria, organic dementias, general paralysis, puerperality, fevered delirias, and the after-effects of lethargic encephalitis.

The other half 'is constituted by the unbalanced, sometimes alcoholic, sometimes epileptic, whose suicide is not, however,

Table 13.1   *Psychiatric causes of suicide*

Causes	Suicides and attempts
Deep-seated anxiety (no sign of imbalance)	72
Destitution or reversal of fortune	50
Painful maladies	44
To escape punishments involving loss of civil rights	3
Total of non-psychopathic suicides	169
Well-defined mental troubles	78
Imbalances (neither delirious nor demented; the suicide's motives are, in general, plausible, but disproportionate to the act)	72
Total of psychopathic suicides	150
Suicides of drunkenness: in the course of a fit of drunkenness, excluding epileptic seizures, hallucinatory episodes, or delirious ideas, among subjects showing no sign whatever of imbalance	130
General total[9]	449

directly related to alcoholism or epilepsy.' They do not kill themselves under the influence of a delirious idea or in the course of a seizure; 'their gesture is neither unconscious nor demented.' However, though their acts have plausible motives, a quarrel, a reprimand, etc., these are inappropriate to the suicide which they appear to determine. The author includes in this category the suicides of very emotional subjects who allow themselves to be influenced by an example or news item reported in some journal, the imitative suicides. Another third of the enumerated suicides appears to be caused by alcoholism. We shall return to this a little later.

What first strikes us when we examine the results of this research is that suicides which are unquestionably psychopathic represent only one sixth of the total: 16 to 18 per cent. This time we are faced with a classification of mental troubles which is inspired by all we actually know of these conditions and their diverse forms. Regrettably, however, though observing that the majority of these psychopathic suicides, *stricto sensu*, are explained by melancholy depression, the author does not tell us their number or proportion. This is 'the period of depression of the periodic psychosis' by which Dr de Fleury desires to explain all or almost all suicides. This is the cause of the 'melancholy suicide' of which Durkheim speaks when he says,

> Very often the normal person who kills himself is also found in a state of despondency and depression, like the insane person [let us say like the recurrent- or manic-depressive]. There is always the essential difference between them, however, that among normal persons the condition and the act resulting from it are not without objective cause, while among psychopathic suicides they are unrelated to external circumstances.

This is a clinical entity on which the attention of psychiatrists is increasingly being concentrated.[10] The author of the research could not be mistaken in linking to this type of troubles a number of suicides not exceeding 10 to 15 per cent of all those she distributed into well-defined categories.

We note, secondly, that a very clear line of demarcation exists between suicides resulting from 'well-defined mental troubles' and those that are explained by instability or by the suggestibility of the subject, and which also represent a sixth of the total. The author in fact distinguishes these suicides from those we have just mentioned in that the former 'are more difficult to succor,' while 'an observation post or opportune internment' would be needed to prevent the latter.

> The prophylaxis of these suicides is a long and exacting labor, partly extra-medical, which would be all the more effective if begun in childhood. A judicious professional orientation, transplantation to a favorable environment – since the familial environment is almost always bad – appear to be the most certain means for this.

That is, these suicides, contrary to the others, remain more or less subject to the influence of social conditions.

Above all, however, in considering this second category of suicides, which probably can be called psychopathic only by attributing a rather large meaning to this word, we ask whether it is always possible and easy to distinguish them from those that could be called normal. We are in fact told that here the instability is recognized by the disproportion between the suicidal motive and the suicide itself. That notion, however, is indeed relative. Of course, when someone kills himself following failure in an examination or a reproach or vexation which appears mild to us, we think that he must be abnormal since no normal person should have acted in a like manner under the same conditions.

Had he not undergone this failure, however, not been reproached, would he have killed himself? There are extremely sensitive natures, as there are extremely insensitive ones. There are natures which are reserved, suggestible, impressionable. It is probable that almost all suicides are more impressionable than the average person since, under given conditions, only a small number of people kill themselves, while most people do not. Actually, we pass through a series of imperceptible transitions from abnormal cases to normal, from maladaptive impressionability to what is nothing but a very lively sensibility. The line of separation between the two is necessarily arbitrary. Nothing shows this better than how impossible it sometimes is to indicate which of several possible motives, each apparently disproportionate to the suicide, really explains it. That is because we ignore the condition of the subject's sensibility, the liveliness and direction of his thinking, the force of his imagination, and the relative importance that apparent circumstances assume in his eyes.

Lacking sufficient indication of the mental condition of the suicides, we looked to see whether there was any relation between the number of insane and the number of suicides in a given country.[11] This is why Durkheim drew up the two tables in his book (VI, p. 74) on relationships between suicide and insanity in different European countries. (Almost all the data are prior to 1871.)

The opposition between these two facts being measured by 4.5, their independence by 2.25, we find an average distance of 3.3. There is rather more opposition. It is still more marked in the second of these two tables: opposition = 6.5; independence = 3.25; average distance = 5.53. Durkheim therefore had the right to say, 'The countries where there are the fewest insane are those where there are the most suicides.'

Krose compiled an analogous table for a larger number of states (20 instead of 9 or 13) based on data which is a little more recent, though none goes beyond 1885. This time it is a question of comparing, not insanity, but mental illnesses and suicides. Calculating the same indices as above, we find: opposition = 10; independence = 5; average distance = 6.8. Here again, therefore, there would be opposition on the whole. Having been gathered in different countries, however, these figures are of unequal validity. If we take a given state, Prussia and its 12 provinces, we find from our calculations that the opposition being measured by 6, the independence by 3, the average actual distance is equal to 3 exactly. The two phenomena are totally independent. The finding for the 17 Austrian provinces is the same (opposition = 8.5; independence = 4.25; actual distance = 4.7). Moreover, the term mental illness confounds with insanity many troubles such as idiocy and cretinism which do not at all appear to predispose to suicide (see Durkheim, p. 75).

Durkheim wrote (p. 76), 'In short, as insanity is agreed to have increased regularly for a century and suicide likewise, one might be tempted to see proof of their interconnection in this fact.' He added, in a note, 'Completely conclusive proof of it, to be sure, has never been given. Whatever the increase has been, the coefficient of acceleration is not known.' Krose compared, for France, the ratio to the total population of patients confined in insane asylums, by five-year intervals from 1835 to 1893 (data published in *L'Annuaire statistique de la France*, volume XV, 1892–4), and the corresponding proportion of suicides. There is a certain parallelism between these two orders of facts, since they increased steadily in all periods, the one from 100 to 449.4 (inmates of asylums), the other (suicides) from 100 to 317.1. The rate of increase, however, is quite different. From 1835–9 to 1865–9, the increase is 180 per cent for insanity but only 77.6 per cent for suicide. From 1865–9 to 1891–3, it is 160 per cent for the number of insane and 179 per cent for the suicides. To be sure, the last two increases are very close. What requires even more consideration is that the number of *confined* patients, in relation to the totality of patients, appears to have increased notably from the beginning until 1876 (and perhaps beyond then).[12] However, it may be necessary to avoid a too hasty conclusion that alienation and suicide are related from the fact that both increased at the same rate over a period of twenty-five years. If suicide figures were compared with other series of numbers increasing continuously in the course of the century, for example the increase of railway traffic, or the number of tons of coal mined, we would certainly find many parallels of this type.[13] We can conclude nothing from this unless we previously compared suicide with all other facts which may be related to it without establishing even closer and more constant analogies between their evolution and that of suicide.

In his study on relationships between suicide and drunkenness, published in 1895, Prinzing tends to explain a certain number of details revealed by the statistics of suicide by more or less heavy overindulgence in alcoholic beverages.[14] For example, Jews have committed suicide infrequently during the past several decades because there are few alcoholic Jews. Women generally commit suicide less than do men because not many become intoxicated. The proportion of female suicides is a little higher in the northern countries because women become intoxicated more here than in the central or southern countries. (Of every 100 suicides in

England in 1872–6, and Norway, Sweden, and Denmark, the proportions by women were, respectively, 25.9, 23.6, 23.2, and 23.1 per cent, as compared with 21.3 per cent in France, 18.5 per cent in Prussia, and 15.4 per cent in Belgium.) People destroy themselves more often in the big cities than in the countryside partly because alcohol causes more havoc there.

Suicides that are explained by economic distress or by domestic troubles are often indirect effects of drunkenness, or drunkenness occurs at the same time as these other motives. For poverty or marital separation can be the effect or the cause of habitual overindulgence in alcoholic beverages. In short, Prinzing declares that if we confine ourselves to men from 30 to 60 years of age, drunkenness is the most frequent motive for suicide:[15] 'More than a quarter of masculine suicides, or, if we consider only fully adult people, a third, must be attributed to alcohol.'[16]

Dr Serin, the author of the Parisian research we spoke of above, arrives at the same conclusion.

A third of our suicides [she says] appear to be caused by alcoholism. We are not including in this category those which are due to mental troubles engendered by alcoholic saturation, suicides that have arisen in the course of panophobic seizures, hallucinatory episodes, or driven by a delirious idea of toxic origin. These have been classified as suicides of insane persons. We include here the acts of those who are 'in their cups,' who drown themselves or hang themselves without a perceptible motive in the course of excessive drinking and, if saved, thereafter are quite incapable of explaining why they wanted to die.

Though they are not truly capable of explaining why they wanted to die, it does not follow that their act had been unconscious. They may have been under the spell of an indefinable sadness, of a diffuse but intense sentiment of physical suffering, or thoughts may have been active in their minds which were only as stable as the affective states. Nothing is as quickly forgotten as such states. We regret, however, not being told more precisely on what occasions the drunks killed themselves, for it is necessary to distinguish drunkenness proper from the period of depression which follows drunkenness and which sometimes lasts until one again begins to drink. When he discusses the relationship between drunkenness and neurasthenia, Prinzing describes the diverse conditions under which a drinker kills himself in greater detail. The majority of suicides accomplished under the influence of drunkenness he links to this period of depression.

Durkheim compared suicides, misdemeanors due to

drunkenness, cases of alcoholic insanity, and alcohol consumption, using figures produced by Dr Lunier for the French departments in 1872–6. (See *Suicide*, p. 78 and Chart I, p. 393.) Confining ourselves to them, we will compare the consumption of spirits per person with the proportion of suicides in different countries, using tables drawn up by Prinzing, pp. 58 to 75. We calculated all the figures in Table 13.2 ourselves. A comparison is established here, with no indication to the contrary, between series of numbers referring to decennial or quinquennial periods or to successive years. As the figures on suicides in Russia, England, and Holland are uncertain, we have taken them into account only in the first two tests.

Table 13.2 *Comparison between the consumption of whiskey and the suicide rate*

		Opposition	Independence	Correspondence	Average actual distance
1	13 countries (1884–91)[17]	6.5	3.25	o	2.8
2	13 countries (1886–92)[18]	6.5	3.25	o	3
3	Norway (1831–90)	5	2.5	o	0.8
4	Sweden (1821–88)	4.5	2.25	o	4
5	Finland (1869–88)	2.5	1.25	o	2.4
6	Austria–Hungary (1873–7)[19]	7	3.5	o	1.6
7	Italy (1871–82)	4	2	o	1
8	Italy (1871–7)[20]	4.5	2.25	o	1.8
9	France (1830–85)	4	2	o	0.25
10	France (1872–6)[21]	7.5	3.75	o	4.7
11	France (1872–6)[22]	7.5	3.75	o	4.9
12	Germany (1881–90)[23]	11.5	5.75	o	6.8

We are not stressing the first two tests, which show that there is independence, that is, the lack of a relationship between these two comparative facts. The statistics of diverse countries differ in too many respects for us to be able to draw anything more from this comparison than a rather vague indication. On the other hand, there is a correspondence in tests 3 (Norway), 6 (Austria–Hungary), 7 and 8 (Italy), and 9 (France: here the comparison is between successive years separated by five-year intervals, for the first two figures by twenty-year intervals). In France, alcoholism and suicide increase simultaneously after 1830: the correspondence is very exact. The case of Norway is the most striking: there, alcoholism and suicide decrease in a parallel and continuous movement from the beginning of the period to the end. As Durkheim has already observed, however, and as is clear from our table, there is opposition between the two facts in Sweden, almost maximum opposition: alcoholism diminishes, suicide increases. And the same is true in Finland.

As we have already noted, for suicides and the consumption of alcohol per person to increase concomitantly does not suffice to demonstrate that the latter explains the former. If we were to compare suicides with other facts such as the aggregate population of a country, the rise of its exports, etc., we would find more than one concomitance of this type.

More important are the three last tests which compare diverse regions of a given country during the same period. Now, in France as well as in Germany, the actual average distance remains rather close to the coefficient of independence and indicates no correspondence. There are, to be sure, some departments in France which occupy nearly the same rank in the consumption of alcohol and in suicide: Eure, Orne, Pas-de-Calais, Finistère. On the other hand, the distance between alcoholism and suicide is very large in Seine, Seine-et-Oise, and Mayenne. While suicides may be more numerous among alcoholics in some places than elsewhere we must confine ourselves to the aggregate figures. By no means does it follow from them that the number of suicides is related to overindulgence in liquor. Durkheim had already observed that proportionately fewer suicides are found in the German province of Posen, which is in the forefront in consumption of alcohol, than in all the other regions of the Reich. Prinzing explains what he considers an exception by the fact that the population of Posen is Slav, and that Slavs are less inclined to suicide than Germans. Let us also discard Hohenzollern. Suicides are very few here but we are not told the consumption of alcohol per person (and assume it to be nonexistent). We find, then, that in Germany, without Posen or Hohenzollern, the opposition equals 10.5; the independence equals 5.5; the correspondence equals 0; and the actual average distance equals 4.7. The two facts compared are always independent. Undoubtedly, there are both many suicides and a large consumption of alcohol in the provinces of Saxony and Brandenburg (Berlin included). However, the reverse is the case in the kingdom of Saxony and in Schleswig-Holstein, which have the highest suicide rate in Germany, and a consumption of alcohol below average. Here, again, we must confine ourselves to general findings.

Thus, in Germany as in France, if one compares the number of suicides and the consumption of alcohol per person in the diverse states or provinces (in France, in the departments), these two facts appear independent.

The effect of laws which limit the manufacture and sale of alcohol rather strictly is to diminish alcoholism. Do we find a recession of suicides in countries where they are in force? Norway, one of the few European countries in which the proportion of suicides has very plainly diminished since the middle of the nineteenth century, has been an example of this. Now, from that time on they succeeded in reducing the importation and manufacture of alcohol considerably. There may be a relationship between these two facts. Durkheim has already observed, however, that in Sweden, where alcoholism has also diminished and in the same proportions, suicides have continued to increase. Let us, however, examine the figures reproduced by Prinzing, without going further back than 1850 (Table 13.3).

Table 13.3   *Norway: suicides and alcohol consumption*

Periods	Consumption of alcohol per person (in liters)	Proportion of suicides per million inhabitants
1850–4	3.2	107
1855–7	2.7	98
1860–4	2.2	86
1865–9	2.4	77
1871–5	2.8	75
1876–80	2.4	72
1881–5	1.7	67
1886–90	1.5	66

The consumption of alcohol diminished between 1850 and 1890 from 100 to 47 and the proportion of suicides from 100 to 62. However, the concomitance is not exact, for from 1860–4 to 1871–5 the consumption of alcohol increased while suicides continued to diminish. From 1871–5 to 1886–90, the consumption of alcohol diminished from 100 to 54 but suicides only from 100 to 88. These irregularities are not negligible, for if less alcohol is consumed, and if alcohol is the cause of suicide, voluntary deaths should diminish immediately. We know too little of Norway and its social evolution during this period to be in a position to say whether the diminution of alcohol on the one hand, and the diminution of suicides on the other, do not both result from a third factor, for example, from a general increase in welfare which could reduce motives for suicide and, at the same time, allow the inhabitants of this country enough leisure and freedom of spirit for organizing a war against habitual drunkenness. However, it is possible. Moreover, the number of suicides concerned is quite small: 144 per year in 1901–5, instead of more than 8,000 in France.

We cannot neglect an experiment which is being undertaken on a very large scale on the other side of the Atlantic. In the United States 27 states had already prohibited alcohol when the Congress (House and Senate) in 1918 voted an amendment to the Constitution, prohibiting the manufacture, sale, importation, and exportation of alcoholic beverages. In a study published in 1922 under the title *Prohibition in the United States, History and Social Impact*, Jean Appleton wrote, 'Arrests for public drunkenness have since diminished by 70 per cent. Criminality has dropped by 45 per cent.' Table 13.4 is a table of suicides in the United States that we have compiled from four sources: the figures in the first column are taken from John Rice Miner; those in the second, from the *Handwörterbuch der Staatswissenschaften*; they refer to the entire United States. The two other series of figures are reproduced from the *Statistical Abstract for the United States*, 1922 and 1924: the first refers to 100 large cities (94 after 1921), and the second to cities having 100,000 inhabitants or more in 1900 (from 24 to 28 million inhabitants for the first, from 20 to 24 for the second). We are displaying the wholesale price index numbers (Bureau of Labor Statistics).

We do not know why the numbers reproduced by the *Handwörterbuch* are a little higher than those of John Rice Miner. As might have been expected, suicides are more numerous in every year in large cities, above all in cities of more than 100,000 inhabitants, than in the total United States. Variations in all these numbers are the same from one year to the next, however: they diminish and increase concomitantly. If we had not taken account of the movement of prices, we would say that suicides diminish after 1916 as a consequence of the war. They continue to diminish after 1918. Is this the effect of the legislation against alcohol? They clearly go up again after 1921, however, though the dry regime continues anyway. Now let us consider the movement of prices. Prices drop slightly in 1914 while suicides increase (except for the contrary indication in the *Handwörterbuch*). Prices increase by a series of very marked upward movements the following years until a maximum in 1920; suicides drop very strongly until the same year, from 100 to 68, 59, or 64 (in the last three columns)

Table 13.4 *Proportion of suicides in the United States per million inhabitants, and wholesale prices*

	J. R. Miner	Handwörterbuch Selected cities	Cities of 100,000 inhabitants or more	Index of wholesale prices
1913	158	163	197	199	100
1914	166	161	209	215	98
1915	167	164	208	215	101
1916	142	149	180	185	127
1917	134	146	167	177	177
1918	122	133	146	152	194
1919	114	120	143	143	206
1920	—	111	123	127	226
1921	141	148	157	160	147
1922	—	—	—	153	149
1923	—	—	—	153	154
1924	—	—	—	157	150
1925	—	—	—	160	159
1926	—	—	—	168	151

relative to 1913. The influences of economic prosperity and war probably hold sway at the same time. Prices fall abruptly and profoundly in 1921, a year of economic depression following the crisis of 1920. Suicides increase (from 34.28 or 26 per cent). Prices go up again slightly after 1921 while suicides drop slightly. If the suppression of alcohol has exerted an influence, it is entirely masked. As we have discovered in Germany, suicides in the United States diminish in times of prosperity and increase in times of economic depression without exception during this whole period.

Finally, Table 13.5 is a table compiled by us from Polish data which permits comparison of suicides (including attempts) certified by police investigations and the number of persons arrested per month for drunkenness in public places. All of these numbers are our calculations.

The maximum opposition is equal to 6, the independence to 3, the dependence to 0. We find as average distance: 4. There is therefore no relationship between the two facts.

Thus, the result of the comparison between suicide and insanity

Table 13.5 *Poland: suicides and arrests for drunkenness in 1927, relative numbers (100 = numbers corresponding to the monthly average)*

	Suicides	Arrests for drunkenness	Serial numbers Suicides	Arrests for drunkenness
January	79	76	11	11
February	82	73	10	12
March	112	85	4	10
April	99	94	6	8
May	120	102	3	5
June	130	92	1	9
July	122	96	2	7
August	106	112	5	3
September	98	124	7	2
October	85	134	9	1
November	92	108	8	4
December	74	98	12	6

in several countries is that these manifestations are independent or opposed to one another. In France, however, from 1865 to 1893 the number of insane and the number of suicides increase concomitantly. The result of the comparison between suicide and the consumption of alcohol per head in several European countries (Norway, Austria–Hungary, Italy, and France) is that alcoholism and suicide increase or decrease concomitantly. The reverse is the case in Sweden and Finland. If we compare the Prussian provinces and the German states with the French departments we find there is no connection between the two facts.

The thesis that alcoholism is one of the principal causes of suicide finds support, therefore, in some (but only some) of these tests. Again, it is a question solely of countries where the consumption of alcohol and voluntary deaths increase concomitantly over a rather long period. As we observed above, however, we have no right immediately to conclude from the uniformly concomitant variation of the two facts that there is a relationship of causality between them. During the course of the nineteenth century the average consumption of alcohol increased greatly in most Western countries because an increasing portion of income, a higher proportion of wages, particularly in the working class, is devoted to the purchase of wine, beer, and whiskey. As the standard of living of workers in heavy industry, that is, their expenditure on food, clothing, etc., certainly did not diminish in other respects, wages must have increased for the wage-earner to be able to devote a larger portion to the purchase of spirits. If the increase of wages and the growth of suicides in the last fifty years were compared, we would discover many relationships between the two movements. Should we conclude from this that the more wages increase, the more people kill themselves?

In the same way, we might suppose that bankruptcies and failures of every nature are the principal factor in suicide because suicides increase in time of economic depression. Thus, suicides should increase concomitantly with the number of merchants and commercial transactions. Let us compare the absolute number of suicides in France at different periods with the rise (in value) of special commerce, that is, imports and exports combined. Let us set equal to 100 the two numbers corresponding to the year 1870 (Table 13.6). These numbers correspond rather well. However, suicides accomplished by merchants represent only a small proportion of the total of voluntary deaths. But the development of foreign commerce, and growth in the consumption of alcohol may be two distinct and independent consequences of a given industrial and urban civilization.

Table 13.6   *France: suicides and the rise of special commerce*

	Number of suicides	Special commerce
1870	100	100
1880	160	150
1900	215	176
1910	237	236

Neither the statistics of insanity nor the statistics of alcohol therefore prove that the majority, or even a very large number, of people who kill themselves are insane or drunks.

chapter 14

Examination of the psychiatric thesis
The pathological and social aspect of suicide

Not without some surprise does one read in a work published two or three years ago by Dr de Fleury[1] phrases of the type: suicides, *all* suicides, almost without exception, are explained by 'the fit of anguish produced during the period of depression in recurrent manic-depressive psychoses among subjects' who have an emotional temperament; 'Suicides accomplished calmly for completely discernible motives are extremely rare. One hardly encounters them.' Does not the author go too far? The number of individual cases of suicide he can have known represents but a quite small proportion of these facts dispersed over the whole territory. Undoubtedly, one test suffices to establish a law. It must, in addition, be decisive: one must know rather precisely what factors are put into play in order to be able to conclude with certainty that an effect will follow at such and such a moment. But what psychiatrist has ever predicted infallibly that a patient will kill himself, or at what moment? This reminds one of Molière's physician who could have said, 'Anguish produces the suicide, because there is a certain suicidogenic property in it. And that is why your daughter killed herself.'

Dr de Fleury's opinion, which is rather common among physicians, hardly seems reconcilable with what the statistics of suicide teach us. The statistics seem to be wrong. Or rather, this is how people claim to interpret them. It is true that more people kill themselves in France, Prussia, and Denmark than in Italy, Belgium, or England. That is because there are more psychopaths in the former countries than in the latter (but nothing justifies assuming this). It is true that, age held constant, the unmarried commit suicide one-and-a-half times as often as married people. One can assume that the unmarried man is predisposed to neurasthenia, or that neurasthenics do not marry voluntarily (but that also must be proven; we observe that the rule is presently applied to unmarried people of less than 25 years of age, the majority of whom will marry later; it applies also to the widowed, who kill themselves twice as often as do married people).[2] Do people kill themselves less often in time of war and political agitation than in normal times? That is because the number of psychopaths diminishes during such periods. (But why, on the contrary, does it not increase?) Do Protestants kill themselves two or three times as often as do Catholics? It may be because Protestants are proportionately more numerous in the cities than in the country and that mental illnesses are more frequent in the former than in the latter (but the second fact, at least, is not obvious). It is also because Catholics hide half or two-thirds of the suicides that concern them. (But, for the diverse reasons we have indicated, this is very unlikely.) All this, as we see, adds up to numerous assumptions.

They would be unnecessary if it could be established that two clearly distinct categories of suicides exist, the first of which is explained by social conditions while the second results from mental troubles. Let us state at once that we do not believe this can be established. This, however, is indeed the principle that has inspired the author of the Parisian inquiry we have just analyzed, when she classifies suicides as psychopaths and non-psychopaths. Georges Dumas also appears to concur in this thesis when he writes,[3]

> One cannot, in our judgment, conclude from the large role
> played by biological causes in the determination of suicides that
> social causes do not play any role, or even that they do not play
> as considerable a role as the biological causes. It is very likely,
> on the contrary, that Durkheim's social explanation retains full
> validity for the suicide who is exempt from psychopathic
> defects, that one must assign a role to the social explanation as
> well as to the biological for many psychopaths who go as far as
> suicide, and that, in certain cases which are rather difficult to
> diagnose, suicide arises only from a paroxysmal state of
> anguish so intense, and so befuddling to the conscience, that
> social restraints no longer function.

The moderate opinion of a psychologist who, in many cases, does not discard the sociological explanation, and undoubtedly reserves for himself a place among the majority. In fact, Durkheim placed himself at almost the same point of view: could it indeed have been shown that the majority of suicides were insane persons or psychopaths, there would, it appears, have been no grounds for searching elsewhere for the explanation of suicide. He has made that search because it seemed to him that the number of psychopathic suicides was so very small that they became lost in the totality, just as impurities disseminated throughout the mass of a homogeneous body do not at all alter its characteristics. He distinguished two fewer types of suicide among them. There would undoubtedly have been disagreement between Dumas and him only as to the proportions of the two.

Shall we assume then, like Dumas, that two categories of suicides exist, one normal, the other pathological? And shall we add only that some suicides of the first type do not at all escape social influences? They forget neither their family nor their religious persuasion and, because they are mindful of and concerned about them, can renounce killing themselves.

But Dumas allows us, at the same time, both too much and not enough.

He assumes in fact that only pathological suicides are explained by physical or physiological determinism. Social determinism explains the others. The majority of those who kill themselves are insane or unbalanced. But there are also some suicides which are caused by loss of money, a bereavement, etc. Here psychiatry has nothing to look at.

Is it true, however, that there are suicides that do not interest the psychiatrist or the psychophysiologist? We do not believe so.

We do not accept this separation of the totality of suicides into two species so different from one another that one cannot see how or why they are combined in the same genus. First, we do not believe that they would be given the same name or that society would react similarly to both, were they naturally and essentially different. We can pretend that society reacts differently when it is a question of the suicide of an insane person or the deliberate suicide of a normal person. But the difference is at bottom secondary. What comes to the fore is a quite definite sentiment which, in a given milieu, in a given period, is the same whatever be the suicide's motives. Side by side with the judgment passed upon the suicide, which can vary, is the sentiment one feels at the thought or the spectacle of every suicide. This does not vary within a given society. Similarly, one could distinguish deaths resulting from the violent introduction into the body of a knife, a dagger, etc. – all inorganic causes since the metal is a physical substance – from deaths produced by some sort of organic cause. Now, one undoubtedly reacts differently in the presence of a first-degree murder, and of the fatal termination of an illness. Death is always death, however, as suicide is always suicide. A particular impression is produced by death, as such, on each type of society. Thus, all suicides, like all deaths, are included in a unique genus whose unity is not at all artificial. If, however, all suicides are basically of the same nature, if they are so many species or varieties of the same genus, they must be explained by causes of the same order. In fact, we cannot assume that a given effect results from two types of different causes, depending on cases or circumstances. We apologize for insisting upon that principle. However, whenever a given phenomenon is explained, sometimes by one factor, sometimes by another, the only thing that is clear and could be considered established is that the cause of this phenomenon is yet to be found.

Now, as soon as we know that an important proportion of suicides, whether 20 per cent, 30 per cent, or even more, has psychopathic causes, we must assume that all the suicides result from analogous causes. We shall therefore go much further than Dumas in the direction of the psychophysiological thesis for we shall unhesitatingly assume that at the moment any individual commits suicide, and perhaps for some hours or even some days preceding, we would find some trouble of the nervous and cerebral functions, more or less deep-seated but always real. From this must result a psychic state similar to those found in the neurosis of anguish, depression, etc.[4] A great physical or moral suffering, whether it be a question of a sudden shock or disturbance or of a long succession of small, cumulative annoyances, a profound despair, a fit of anger against oneself or others, a fear of suffering born either of bodily illnesses, dishonor, or social declassment, all of these cause a state of nervous instability, either in the long run or abruptly. Common opinion is not mistaken here: someone will be said to be distraught because of passion, blinded by grief, drunk with fury, beyond himself, crazed by sorrow, etc. Violent and deep-seated affective states are accompanied by an organic perturbation which, except for its origins, and at least in its development, phases, expression, and effects, is scarcely distinguished from the agitation or nervous depression of a pathological nature.[5] Consequently, if we explain suicide by the organic condition in one case, why not invoke the same cause in every case?

There will be said to be always this difference between the normal and the psychopathic suicide: in the latter instability results from a cause within the body, an injury, intoxication, or functional trouble related to the state of the organs, a cause that carries its effect in its train independently of external circumstances.[6] Among normal suicides, on the contrary, organic trouble would not be prepared in the body only, as instability is in equilibrium. The cause that determines the normal suicide is external to the organism. Even when one kills himself to escape physical suffering, it is the idea of sufferings to come, that is, of something at the moment outside himself, which sets in motion his power to act. Between the normal and the psychopathic suicide there should therefore be all the distance separating a person who is perfectly sound of body from an ill person who has been carrying an organic defect in himself for a long time.

But the distinction between health and illness, stability and instability, is entirely relative. Is there certain to be a specific injury among so-called psychopathic suicides that could be discovered by autopsy and that would explain their nervous troubles? Possibly. But do we know whether injuries of this genus, perhaps less serious but no less real, would not be found among people who are sane in appearance but whose nervous systems are rather impressionable? Between an injury which is quite well defined, and the complete absence of injury, are all the intermediate steps. One is never entitled to assert that a well-marked difference exists between the organic constitution of a so-called psychopathic suicide and a so-called normal suicide. This may only be a difference of degree. Let us, however, continue to speak of injury since the subject is after all rather obscure. Let us consider only the mode of acting or of reacting of a person who is psychopathic and one who is not. Health is a condition of unstable equilibrium involving many fluctuations. What one observes in the psychopath is often only an exaggeration in intensity and in frequency of troubles to which the majority of organisms are also exposed despite their health. They differ, of course, in that the unhealthy person is badly adapted to the conditions of the normal milieu from which he suffers and that this suffering is strong enough in certain cases to push him to suicide. The normal person, on the other hand, is adapted to the normal milieu. Should the normal milieu change, however, for whatever reason, it would be an abnormal milieu to which the normal person would no longer be adapted. He would be in the very situation in which the psychopath has been and, undoubtedly, has remained. There will be said to be this difference, however: the cause to which there is no longer adaptation, but disequilibrium, is not and never has been within him. Where, then, will it be? When we say that a man who is adapted to marriage is no longer so to a state of widowerhood we appear to be abandoning the organic schema. We are speaking of a moral or psychic adaptation. Does there exist, however, a psychic state to which no organic state corresponds? The sorrow of a widow who cannot console herself is manifested by a state of depression, just as the depression of a manic-depressive is accompanied by a state of sorrow. An organ can be paralyzed either because of the effects of an injury internal to it or because the external milieu forces the organ toward a reactive effort of which it is incapable. It is no less paralyzed in the two cases. The psychiatrist will find that at a given moment a disequilibrium factor is manifesting its influence on the organism. The origin of this factor in no way modifies the nature of these troubles. There is, therefore, nothing to take into account here.

This is not, to be sure, a point of view at which one places himself naturally. Although common sense designates all suicides by the same name and greets them with the same reaction, there may be for common sense, as for the psychiatrists, two ways to explain suicide: either by a fit of madness or by a deliberate resolution. That is because common sense delights in clear distinctions and well-marked types. Now, these types probably exist. From antiquity, tradition has transmitted to us the memory of heroic suicides accomplished deliberately, without their author appearing to have been prey to a delirium, to some immoderate agitation, or even to experiencing the goad of an internal affliction. And on the other hand, examples are not lacking of suicides which, in their suddenness, their unforeseen character, and all the symptoms of aberration which precede them, resemble a fit of raving madness. In the first case, the person acts voluntarily under the influence of moral despair, while in the other, a profound organic disorder destroys all power of control in him. To the first, one links all the voluntary deaths which appear to be explained by a serious motive. A ruined, dishonored man whose life is devastated by sorrow or mourning decides to die with the same cold resolution with which in other circumstances he would agree to undergo a serious operation that barely offers him a chance to recover from it. He is as much master of himself when he abandons his body to the action of instruments he has chosen or of elements to which he has decided to expose himself as a patient who is stretched out on the operating table. On the other hand, to the category of suicides by the insane or mental patients are assigned all those for which one can find only insignificant motives, and which appear to belong to psychiatry more than to the moralist. It is not because there is an entire series of intermediary links between them that will and aberration join together thus in the suicide. It is, on the contrary, because extremes meet and because to meet death requires great resolution and very strong reasons, or indeed, facing it without seeing it.

Common sense is wrong, however, to consider as typical, forms of suicide which, in reality, are unusual if not altogether exceptional. These are extremes. The mass of cases, however, are found in between and do not lend themselves to so clear a distinction. Basically, it all comes down to saying that sometimes the person kills himself because he suffers morally, and other times because his organism burdens him and he feels a physical suffering which is all the more intolerable for being diffuse and imprecise. Moral suffering is caused by ideas and thought, that is, by changes in our relations to the world, while physical suffering is confined within the limits of our body. There is opposition between them, however, only when one considers extreme cases. Moral suffering is suffering only to the extent that it becomes settled in us and troubles the play of our bodily functions. Physical suffering is only irremediable when we picture the world as conspiring with our body to impose it on us.

> I see [says Rousseau][7] a healthy, cheerful, strong, and vigorous man; it does me good to see him; his eyes tell of content and well-being; he is the picture of happiness. A letter comes by post; the happy man glances at it, it is addressed to him, he opens it and reads it. In a moment he is changed, he turns pale and falls into a swoon. When he comes to himself he weeps, laments, and groans, he tears his hair, and his shrieks re-echo through the air. You would say he was in convulsions. Fool, what harm has this bit of paper done you? What limb has it torn away? What crime has it made you commit? What change has it wrought in you to reduce you to this state of misery? Had the letter miscarried, had some kindly hand thrown it into the fire, it strikes me that the fate of this mortal, at once happy and unhappy, would have offered us a strange problem. His misfortunes, you say, were real enough. Granted; but he did not feel them. What of that? His happiness was imaginary. I admit it; health, wealth, a contented spirit, are mere dreams.

We feel strongly that this reasoning is paradoxical. For the health, the well-being, the contentment of this man result precisely from the fact that he does not experience anxieties, that he enjoys a feeling of security, that his affairs go well, that no sight allows him to foresee a catastrophe. He sinks into despair because one representation of the world is suddenly replaced by another, calling forth on his part other reactions. The previous reactions, however, were also in keeping with the idea he had of the external world and of the place he occupied in it. The man is indeed required to adapt to the world, and the paradox is in wanting the world rather than himself to change; that is, his attitude toward the world also changes.

Here, now, is another man who has every reason to find himself happy. He is rich and respected. He succeeds in everything he undertakes. He finds only cause for satisfaction in domestic life. His friends envelop him in affection. He lacks nothing. He sees in the past only smiling images. No cloud obscures his future. One day, however, he is observed becoming self-preoccupied and gloomy. An organic trouble that has been developing for some time has just taken shape and he experiences a grave crisis of depression. This is not an illness which is exposing him to death nor even giving rise in him to definite, local sufferings. The void, the nothingness that he feels in himself in no way alters the world around him and is unrelated to the state of his fortune, his social situation, or the sentiments of those who surround him. Might one not say to him, 'Madness! Your illness exists only in your imagination. Turn your attention from this obscure foundation of your existence, from regions unreached by the normal conscience. Do not open this message which comes to you from obscure regions of the organic life. Confine your attention to what constitutes the solid web of your existence.' Said Rousseau, 'O man! Hoard your existence within yourself.' We could also say to the deprived person who is preoccupied with himself, 'O man! Extend your existence beyond yourself.' The person cannot follow either counsel, however. Inside and outside are too closely linked, like the obverse and reverse of a given object. The mental patient no longer sees things and men as they are. The representation of the world that he makes for himself becomes transformed. He projects his anxieties, suspicions, fears, and forebodings outside himself. Outside himself is where he seeks and in fact finds the reasons for his sufferings. Where, henceforth, are we to discover any difference between him and the man of sane spirit whom a real misfortune upsets and bewilders? It is the same state of maladaptation and disequilibrium, at once organic and mental.

If, however, every suicide is theoretically ascribable to psychopathology extended to its extreme limits, the converse is also true: there is scarcely even a psychopathic suicide which is not ascribable to sociology. It is going too far in the direction of psychopathology, much too far, and is not granting us enough, to assert that the majority of suicides of anguish, depression, or of alcoholic intoxication, accomplished in a state of drunkenness, etc., constitutes a well-marked category whose nature differs from all others.

Let us consider, in fact, some of the causes by which suicide is ordinarily explained and which do not call into play morbid mental factors, physical sufferings, pangs of love, jealousy, money worries, shame, fear of dishonor, fear of punishment, or sorrow caused by bereavement. Durkheim hesitated to see in these motives true causes of suicide envisioned as social fact: first, because they are very heterogeneous and because it cannot be understood how such different causes could account for the same effect; then, too, because the events or circumstances are too individual to determine a fact which is reproduced with such constancy and whose variations appear to be related to more general factors.[8] By themselves they do not suffice to explain the suicides. Can one assume from this, however, that they play no role in their production? Is it not possible to discover similar forces of nature underlying their diversity and, translating these individual facts into social terms, show them to be as many obstacles to the integration of the individual in society? Is it not possible to show, at the same time, that the other category of motives one distinguishes, namely, morbid mental factors, plays exactly the same role and tends to act in the same direction?

A culpable man who is responsible for some act which reflects on his honor feels diminished in the eyes of members of his own group, and isolated from it. Honor reposes on different considerations, of course, depending on the society. Frazer tells somewhere of a young savage who goes voluntarily to be buried alive because he is too skinny and sickly and is held up to ridicule by his tribe. Here, it is a point of professional honor; there, it is a point of aristocratic honor; elsewhere, the honor of the merchant is what intervenes. A man who has been insulted, an abandoned, unmarried mother, a gambler who cannot pay a gambling debt, all lose the esteem of those around them and the opinion which they prize most: they are violently expelled from social milieux far apart from which they cannot live. This, however, is also true of the merchant who is ruined, the wealthy man who loses his fortune, and the family head whose means are abruptly reduced.[9] All see their social level lowered. They are, to a certain extent, declassed. Now, what does being declassed mean? It is passing from a group where one is known and respected into another of which one is ignorant and whose appreciation one has no reason to expect. One then feels a void enveloping him. Those who formerly surrounded you, with whom you had so many ideas and so many prejudices in common, to whom you were linked by so many affinities, because in them you encountered yourself as they in you, suddenly become distant. You disappear from their concern and their memory. Those in the milieu in which you find yourself do not understand your bewilderment, your nostalgia, or your regrets. Detached from one group by a sudden disturbance, you are incapable, or at least you believe yourself incapable, of ever finding any support in another, or anything to take the place of what you have lost. When one becomes lost to society thus, one most often loses his principal reason for living.

Let us turn now to those who killed themselves because they

have lost a being who was dear to them, or to those suicides of passion which follow the separation or threat of being separated from the loved object.[10] Such despair also results from a ruptured bond. But is this tie indeed a social one? The passionate affection or attachment which unites two persons is of the order of individual sentiment. Let one be taken from the other. Nothing has happened to isolate the man or woman from his group of fellows. On the contrary, the sentiment that engrossed them may have been an obstacle to their entrance into closer union with the others. Since they had their own language and conventions, they formed, after all, a small society, though, at the same time, a very exclusive and very limited society. Once this group is dissolved, there is nothing more to prevent each of the two individuals who compose it from being linked to other milieux that he had forgotten, rediscovering his kinsmen, his friends, and tightening ties to them which had become slackened. When, however, sentiments of this type are sufficiently intense they sometimes survive the disappearance of their object. To remember others he must forget this person. This occurs during the interval when one is in despair for what he has lost without his imagining that anything could take its place. Recounting the story of a young girl who was seduced and abandoned, Goethe says,[11]

> Numbed, distracted, she finds herself at the edge of a precipice. Naught but shadows surround her. No perspective, no consolation, no presentiment. For the only one who made her feel alive has left her. She does not see at all how vast is the world, or the many others in it who could replace what she has lost. She feels herself alone, abandoned by all. The future closes up again before her.

As a current carries a swimmer far from the shore, so passion has carried the individual far from all his groups. When the beloved being disappears, he searches for her where he can no longer reach her, and he no longer has the courage or the will to turn again towards society.[12] Thus is explained how love's despair abruptly reveals to the person his solitude.

All the assumed motives of the normal suicide, however different they may appear to us, have the same character. They are facts or circumstances, sentiments or thoughts, which isolate man from society. To be sure one could maintain, to the contrary, that the person kills himself in many cases because he is unsufficiently detached from family and milieu and attributes too much importance to the prejudices, beliefs, and customs of his group. The fear of being dishonored, the desire not to fall at all, not to see one's own family at grips with life's difficulties, ambition deceived, and even the sorrow which certain mournings cause, these are sentiments which all presuppose social life and a certain degree of culture. They would be unknown to a person who took no interest in others. It is very evident, however, that the more narrowly certain social ties enclose him the more sorrowfully a person feels the rupture. The man who is born egoistical, or becomes so, yields to these motives of despair less than do others because his principal interest is himself. The most personal concerns occupy the void left in him by the absence of altruistic sentiments. He does not feel his isolation as long as he succeeds in deceiving himself thus, making himself the sole object of his affections by an adroit dissociation. However, when Silas Marner finds his hiding-place empty, had a human being not come crawling past his feet immediately, there would have been nothing left for him to do but hang himself. Grant, if you will, that it is not loneliness but the sentiment one suddenly has of being alone which impels one toward suicide in all of these cases.

The egoism of pleasure may not be accompanied by a painful sentiment of solitude because the egoist is really thinking of others even when he believes he is thinking only of himself. In the course of his pleasure he tells himself that he is getting the better of them, that he is envied, that many wish to imitate him. This sentiment, too, is rooted in society. There is, however, an egoism of sorrow, in which, on the contrary, the person finds himself firmly riveted to himself and walled in far from his fellows. Physical suffering is very often bearable only on condition that one is able, if not to share it, at least to express it, to communicate it, and to feel that others understand it. A patient finds relief in the thought that sufferings of his type are not unique, that they fall within the common lot of humanity, and that people who are sympathetic towards him know their extent and intensity. As long as this is so, the patient has not lost his bearings at all. All during his sufferings, even when they overwhelm him, he remains a member of a society whose invisible presence sustains and encourages him. When the pain becomes continuous, however, or exceeds certain limits, above all when the patient has no further hope that it will yield, his thought withdraws from the world, turns away from others and becomes centered in himself. He then is and feels himself alone. That is why suffering and illness have caused more than one suicide.

Do not, however, the frenzied and the depressed kill themselves for an analogous reason? To be sure, psychopaths, unlike many patients, do not during periods of depression appeal to the comprehensive sympathy of others. Instead, they conceal their illness and their suffering as if being ashamed of them. They appear to feel themselves like despairing patients cut off at the onset from the rest of the world. They are indeed isolates. Even though they appear to have little relationship to the other causes examined up to now which lead people to suicide, psychopathic states would represent in this sense only a particular case of a general phenomenon. Psychopaths, too, would kill themselves because they are on the periphery of society and can no longer find a point of support anywhere but within themselves.

Having thoroughly observed for years several subjects who were cared for at Salpêtrière, Blondel did indeed throw light on the social maladjustment that enters into the mental states of certain categories of neurotics, hypochondriacs, and paranoiacs. 'The morbid mentality,' he says, 'is an aberrant mentality, an asocial mentality.'[13] We cannot review all the forms of insanity, neurasthenia, or mental deficiency. It is, however, hardly unlikely that all are characterized by at least a partial interruption and an often profound alteration of the relationships which existed or should have existed between the patient and his milieu.[14]

To be sure, the illness, whatever it may be, makes the patient who is stricken with it conspicuous. Especially when they are suffering greatly, patients are somewhat misunderstood. That is why, in sanatoria and spas, they seek one another out and form small unique societies on the basis of a mutual comprehension of their ills. Whether they suspect it or not, those who feel themselves more susceptible to suffering and illness constitute a part of a silent and secret community from which healthy people in the vast human society are excluded. However, when his sickness is localized and his malady defined and classified, the patient again falls within the norm. While it is he who suffers, he nevertheless assumes that the physician knows as well or better than he the cause and nature of the condition in which he finds himself. Left to himself, he would invent and would propose an explanation. As soon as his malady is known, however, he enters into a category; he takes his place in the system of society's ideas. Even if he must drag his suffering along with him for a long time, he will advance down frequented paths that have been illuminated for him in advance. He places himself, body and soul, in society's hands, because it is from society that he expects both succor and explanations.

It is entirely otherwise, in this respect, with the mentally ill or depressed person. With him, emotional states which are found in such close relationship with the nervous system are altered at once and directly. Sentiments of anguish, apprehension, and terror succeed one another in him, dull anguish, vague restlessness, blind terror, and that is precisely what his illness consists of. This illness does not have a definite seat, is not localized.[15] It manifests itself only by such internal states as those in which we find ourselves when a misfortune which has occurred makes us unhappy, or when a misfortune we anticipate makes us apprehensive. Only, here, the cause of the sadness and apprehension cannot be found outside him. At least the patient's physician and associates cannot find it there, and they do their utmost to demonstrate to him that he is apprehensive and saddened without cause. On his part, however, the patient knows well that he is tormented. No demonstration prevails against this fact. Moreover, so real is the fact, to such a degree does it pass to the forefront of his conscience, that it must indeed be explained. The illness itself designs the explanation. We have said that the external milieux remain the same but the patient's attitude toward the world can change to such an extent that there is disequilibrium between them. As the delirious person can no longer adapt himself to the world, however, the world must adapt itself to him. That is why he will project the presumed causes of his apprehension on to his milieux. That is, he will interpret signs and circumstances which are insignificant or which do not have this implication in the light of his preoccupations. He will imagine perceiving what does not exist, remember what has never taken place. If events offer a glaring contradiction to his anticipations, he will not be disconcerted and will very quickly imagine another system of explanation which may or may not accord, or which will accord with the preceding only in part.

How, under these conditions, could he arrive at agreement with others and make himself understood by them or understand them? What first happens, as a rule, is that he is suspicious of all of them, including his relatives and above all the physician. The misfortune threatening him is hidden because it is the result of a conspiracy. But who are and who are not taking part in it? The arguments put up against him collide in him with such a powerful and complete conviction that, in his eyes, the gainsayers can only be accomplices or dupes of those who have mounted such a formidable machination against him. Thus, there is no one in whom he could confide, or who could be in a position to understand him. That, of course, is the situation in which is found more than one artist, more than one inventor, and more than one reformer who believes himself misunderstood. They, however, can wait, if need be. Not at stake are their very lives. What is cruelly contradictory in the case of the anxious or depressed manic-depressive is that he should need to make a clean breast of his terrible secret to the others immediately, and that they evade him. No one can understand what to him is so clear and admit the reality of what is imposing such tortures on him. What does it matter that both he and they speak the same language, have so many ideas in common, and can, in consequence, come to agree on everything that is not the actual theme of his anguish? For nothing else counts for him. He responds with an annoyed air when the conversation is turned to another subject. Underlying his words one catches a glimpse only of dulled thought lacking in resonance, of thoughts which are torpid and sluggish because they receive no heat from the central source his visions nourish. When a man is not in accord with the others on what he takes most to heart, and when their representation of beings and things no longer coincides with his own on any point of interest to him, he is clearly isolated in their midst, not so much because he does not understand them at all as because they do not agree with him. He is isolated by virtue of what is conspicuous and unique in him. God also is alone because he is unique. At least he has never lived in a society of other gods, so that he does not feel his isolation. The neurasthenic, on the contrary, turns all the memories he has carried away from social life into as many weapons against himself, for each memory makes him feel how much distance there is now between him and all the others. So much does he suffer from no longer being attuned to them that he imagines they are all in agreement against him.

Thus, psychopathic states produce the same effect as other causes of suicide. There is nothing that a thought formed by society is less capable of standing up to than a social void. This state of anguish and terror is alone what matters. There is nowhere beyond it to go when one wishes to explain suicide. Undoubtedly, there are many differences to examine between the depressed neurasthenic and the man who is ruined, exposed to dishonor, seriously damaged in his self-respect, or deprived of a being he loves. A special type of trouble has taken hold of each of them. A trait is common to them all, however. None perceives more of society than its hostile aspects, its steepest slopes. The term 'motives' must be retained for these events: mental illness, loss of money, mourning, or love-pangs, since they are so many different particular forms hiding the same condition. The unique cause of suicide, however, is the condition itself, that is, a feeling of a solitude which is definitive and without remedy. It is too easy to say, this man killed himself because he was manic-depressive, the other because of heavy money losses, etc. That is a somewhat crude kind of narration which sticks only to the most apparent and the most uncommon facts. Such explanations would be meaningless unless what determined the suicide in the nervous disorder was precisely what characterizes the loss of money. That is, one must extract from the former the condition of anguish and depression in which the person exposed to destitution and downfall is likewise found. It is, however, abundantly evident that the nervous disorder would not lead to suicide if it were not at all accompanied by this condition. It is because the same condition appears in both cases that the suicide occurs.

This is a point of view to which Durkheim never subscribed at all. He does not appear to have suspected that deleterious states are accompanied by a maladaptation of the individual to his milieu. More than that, in his latest book,* in which he studies religious ceremonies and festivals in savage societies, he was struck by the fact that just when the group is most concentrated, just when its members are overcome by the same sentiments and are dominated by the same images, is when a psychic exaltation, close to delirium, is manifested. 'A very intense social life,' he says, 'always does to the organism, as to the individual conscience, a kind of violence which disrupts its normal functioning.' He developed the idea that

> religious life cannot attain a certain degree of intensity without implying a psychic exaltation not unrelated to delirium. It is for this reason that prophets, founders of religions, and great saints, in a word, people whose religious conscience is exceptionally impressionable, very often present signs of an excessive or, strictly speaking, even pathologic irritability: these physiological defects predestined them to great religious roles.

Thus, while mental disequilibrium would, according to Blondel, correspond to an incapacity or a deficiency, according to Durkheim it is an excessive intensity of social life which would open up paths to delirium.

That the two explanations complement each other is credible. There are, in fact, different kinds of mental troubles. Above all, there are neurasthenics who pass more or less periodically through alternating phases of hyperactivity and depression, joy and expansiveness, sorrow and turning inward upon self. Durkheim is right to relate delirium to collective exaltation in the sense that, in both cases, the person puts forth more activity, an activity more feverish and disorganized than in normal times: he becomes exalted as if he were able to escape the narrow limits of his body, or as if he felt within himself an abrupt spurt of inexhaustible power. May this, however, not be the source from which this and all other forms of delirium derive? Durkheim did

**The Elementary Forms of the Religious Life*, 1912, translated, 1915, by Joseph Ward Swain, George Allen & Unwin Ltd, London; The Macmillan Company, New York – Tr.

not raise this question. We, however, know that nothing of the kind is the case and that in other circumstances, in other phases, the delirious person is depressed and condemned to mental isolation. He would have to be compared instead with the inhabitants of those ancient cities who, ravaged by pestilence or some scourge, felt themselves abandoned by their gods, no longer dared to go out of their houses, and dragged themselves along the streets to implore in vain for some succor. It is only in these circumstances that delirium leads to suicide.[16]

There is, however, a big difference between these periods of exaltation and depression, through which every member of society passes, and the similar troubles which develop in one individual alone, in the midst of a normal society. To be sure, there are collective deliriums.

> If one calls delirium [says Durkheim] every state in which the mind adds sentient intuition to the proximate facts and projects one's sentiments and impressions unto things, there may not be any collective representation which would not be delirious in a sense. The entire social milieu, in fact, appears to us as if peopled by forces which only really exist in our minds.

Now, to rise to this type of representation, to participate in this delirium, to put us in tune with an agitated, hyperexcited milieu, we need a certain amount of supplementary power. Where shall we find it? In the milieu itself. Describe for me an assembly in which passions dictate actions and words. Considering the state of calm and indifference in which I find myself, I shall believe myself unable to hold my place there. I shall turn myself into a spectator there. As soon as I have passed through the door of the room, I shall feel lifted out of myself by the sight of the assembled people, by their movements and voices. I shall adopt their attitude. I shall play my role in the social scene as if prompted in what I must say by the other actors and spectators themselves. It is the same when one is obliged to make a public appearance. One's mind is elsewhere. It is a drudgery one would willingly dispense with. One will be annoyed, will not open his mouth. One will encounter only indifferent people there. When you are among the others, however, the animation of the party reaches you. You enter into a sort of round where the music sets your steps in rhythm: in the same way, the utterances of those who surround you, their questions and responses, the attentiveness fixed upon you, communicate to your mind a kind of verve which you needed in order to sparkle in this circle and which you receive from its very self. Such is the contrast between the relative isolation in which we pass part of our days and those social milieux in which one must expend himself on others that, were we to depend only on our individual powers of the moment, we would not seek out the latter, would not try at all to intermingle with others. We know from experience, however, that upon contact we will draw from others the strength necessary to think like them and to put us in tune with their collective life.

The result is that periods of activity and social exaltation are not necessarily succeeded by others in which the people who have participated in these reunions and ceremonies feel themselves exhausted and depressed. That is because the energies they expended have not been drawn from within themselves, from their substance. To be sure, Australian savages are physically exhausted after those solemnities and feasts during which they have engaged in all sorts of dances and contortions for several consecutive days and nights. A short repose and sleep, however, suffices for them to forget this type of fatigue.

With the mentally ill person it is entirely otherwise in this respect. Only in the course of crises does the latter adapt himself to his milieu. Then he either does not attain or he exceeds the degree of intensity to which the social life around him rises. If depressed, he isolates himself, burrows as if into a hiding-place, and turns in upon himself.[17] He explains his anguish and his physical sluggishness by the attitude of other people who detest and despise him. For as soon as he ceases to be aware of the benefits of life in society, he naturally attributes to it all the internal sufferings he endures. The members of a society which is passing through a collective crisis of depression are not entirely separated from one another. The community of suffering holds them related. 'Children,' says Oedipus, 'young progeny of the ancient Cadmus, why do you hasten through these stages? Why these supplicant branches that I see in your hands? The incense is smoking in the whole city which resounds with both plaintive hymns and groanings.' They intermingle their lamentations and prayers. The mentally depressed person, on the contrary, endures his illness alone. He is rather to be compared to some member of a religious community who is passing through a crisis of unfeelingness and doubt and who is no longer capable of adapting himself to the other faithful, of opening himself to impressions, or of receiving the visions which exalt them. 'I was ill at the infirmary,' wrote Luther,[18] speaking of the time when he was a monk.

> The most cruel temptations (the temptations of the spirit)
> exhausted and martyred my body so that I could hardly breathe
> or gasp. No one consoled me. Those to whom I complained all
> responded, 'I don't know.' Thereupon, I said to myself, 'Am I,

then, the only one who must be so sad in spirit?' Oh! What horrible visions and figures I saw!

Luther blamed the papacy and the Church as the depressed accuses society. Society preserves its powers intact. He, however, is no longer in communication with it. He can no longer draw from the common reservoir.

Can we say that when the neurasthenic is, instead, in the phase of exaltation and euphoria, he is in more contact with society than other people? Does he draw the energies he feels overflowing in him from society? Is it true that 'an intense social life offers, then, a sort of violence to his organism, as well as to his conscience, which disturbs its normal functioning?' Far from accommodating himself to solitude during this period, he does not, to be sure, wait for others to come to him. He goes looking for them. He pushes every half-opened door, seeks out gatherings of people, awakens friendships which are almost extinct, renews interrupted relationships, creates new ones daily, and shows the same appetite for social life as does someone who has been deprived of it for a very long time. Moreover, this activity which is turned towards others, which is feverish, agitated, superficial, and vain, often gives the impression of a motor running in neutral. The excited person deludes himself as to the meaning of the effervescence of ideas and apparent deployment of energy whose center and source he is. He likewise deludes himself about the attitude that others have toward him. He is deceiving himself now, just as he deceived himself when he was depressed, but in the opposite direction. Feeling in himself an almost limitless capacity to adapt to diverse groups which are close to him or within his horizon, he is no longer aware of any of the obstacles separating him from such a center of social life, nor does he perceive any of the discords continuing to exist between him and those around him. The others' objections, their reservations, suspicions, or antipathies, that is, the natural barriers which prevent people, upon entering into contact, from blending entirely with one another, no longer exist for him. As it costs him no effort to transport himself from one group to another, he forgets in the latter the deceptions he may have experienced in the former. Also, he loves others, loves them excessively, not only because, smitten by social life, he really takes an interest in them, but because he is aware only of kindly, generous, and comforting aspects of groups.

Nevertheless, this could be naught but the illusion of an intense collective life. Society may by appropriate means create within itself states of exaltation in which the greatest number of its members participate. There are many differences between this case and one where a single individual carries his excitement from group to group. Even though the excited person apparently opens himself thus, does he not remain just as enclosed within his morbid self as the depressed? However similar the crises of megalomania that one observes in a manic-depressive person during a period of excitation may sometimes appear to the delusion of grandeur, which is a form of insanity, the manic-depressive undoubtedly differs from the insane in remaining related to other people, who are able to affect him, though only, it may be, by modifying the ends that he pursues and presenting to him new objects of excitement. He affects them also, less than he thinks, but more perhaps than a normal or average person. They usually have not invented the theses they develop, made up the plans they design out of whole cloth, or spontaneously conceived the sympathies, hatred, or enthusiasms that develop in them. We cannot say, however, that their excitation is the result of circumstances, or that society has lit this flame that is consuming them. They would not have become less agitated even if all those around them were calm. They draw their imageries not from society but from themselves. They are just as maladapted to their milieu in time of excitation as in depression.

None of this, however, distinguishes the neurasthenics from other candidates for suicide. We could describe the manic-depressive entirely in terms of adaptation to the milieu. We could, however, almost in the same manner describe the phases through which any person passes who is led to voluntary death by love-sorrow or by ruin. The successive phases through which a mental illness would pass that began with euphoric delirium and ended with a grave crisis of depression could represent the course César Birotteau* traversed from the night his wife surprises him in the process of piling up vast speculations to the moment when his fortune crumbles, when he hears only a 'noise of funereal bells' and thinks of suicide. Birotteau, who is religious, a family head, and moreover, weak-minded, does not commit suicide. He will traverse this course again, will be rehabilitated, and will die of excessive joy. Except for this ending we could anticipate that a great number of desperate persons would rediscover reasons for living if they were able for a time to resist the temptation to kill themselves. This would be true of a large number of depressed persons. We are not claiming, it must be added, that this would be so in every case. It suffices for us to have shown that nervous troubles play a role which is no different here from that of such events as ruin, deep-seated anxieties, etc., to which one usually relates suicide.

*The hero of *The Rise and Fall of César Birotteau*, novel of a merchant's career, by Honoré de Balzac, 1837 – Tr.

The reasons studied thus far only partially explain the state of social maladjustment which seems to us to be the cause of suicide. Another disintegrating factor is the weakening of the tie binding people to one another within a religious, domestic, or national group. Now, there is no difference in nature between the states of social deficiency resulting from these two circumstances; they become superimposed and reinforce one another, like debility produced by illness and that produced by overexertion. Durkheim focused his attention on religion, marital status, etc., because it is possible to measure them statistically, while it is hardly possible in each society to count the number of dishonors, monetary losses, vexations of love, intolerable physical sufferings, mental or nervous illnesses, etc. Now, however, we must ask ourselves whether psychopathic suicides clearly differ from all others in being entirely inaccessible at the critical moment to the social influences which are exerted on the members of a religious persuasion, a family etc. Since an important part of suicides appears to be committed under the influence of drunkenness, the same question must be posed concerning them.

Psychiatrists reason pretty much as follows. They do not contest the facts resulting from statistics, namely, that members of certain religions, persons of certain marital statuses, etc., kill themselves proportionately less than do others. They merely believe that social factors have no effect at all on psychopaths, and that, if one discarded the psychopathic suicides, retaining only the normal suicides, the influence of social factors would appear much greater still. Let us note at once, however, that if, on the surface, psychopaths escape social influences entirely, very probably a number of subjects considered normal are likewise, on the surface, no more amenable to them. For physical suffering, great despair, and even ruin or dishonor must cause a state of stupor among many people. Their concentration of thought on the event which overtakes them is sufficiently intense for them entirely to forget everything but their preoccupation of the moment. After that will be left only a very small proportion of despairing people who remain susceptible to this type of influence. These will be too few to account for the very clear regularities revealed in this respect by the statistics concerning the totality of suicides.

On what basis, however, does one assert that a mental patient in a state of depression is no longer susceptible to any of the social influences which act on the normal person? Is it sufficient to declare that he was psychopathic or that he killed himself under the influence of drunkenness for everything to have been said? It is indeed regrettable that psychiatrists do not indicate precisely when he killed himself, whether it was at the beginning of the crisis, at the moment of its culmination, in a period of agitation or of apathy, etc.[19] We do not believe, in any case, that generally the suicide immediately follows the impulse without the patient having time to reflect, like the sudden fall of a man seized by vertigo. Undoubtedly there are cases of 'seizures' of this type where sight of water, or encountering a weapon, acts instantly on a subject who until then appeared to be in control of himself and in equilibrium.[20] Anxious people, however, melancholics, allow a certain time to elapse between the moment when they think of killing themselves and the moment when they do kill themselves. The act of suicide is not produced by a sort of automatic trigger action. It is neither a purely organic process nor a mechanical reaction. Rather, it supposes sentient activity, however confused this may be. Nothing permits us to assume that the patient does not know he is putting himself to death at the moment he kills himself.

Some may say that while he is in fact aware of the impulse to which he is yielding, that impulse is, in a sense, no less 'external to him.' That is, all thoughts and sentiments which ordinarily occupy his consciousness are withdrawn from it, and a unique sensation invades his mind, the sensation of an internal state which is abnormal and intolerable,[21] with ideas that have been able to graft onto it of persecution, peril, or catastrophe. He could only escape them by disappearing. The automatism here will be of another genus, psychological rather than organic. It would, nevertheless, allow no greater place to thoughts foreign to the subject's actual illness or to the unique solution presenting itself to him.

We must *assume* all this, for we cannot apprehend the psychopath's state of awareness except through the words he utters, his gestures, and his attitudes. Now, it must indeed be recognized, as Blondel has shown, that these patients' states of consciousness are too peculiar and uncommon for them to be expressed by means of a language not made for it. It would therefore be unscientific to take literally what they tell us and interpret their conduct as if it were that of a normal person. The psychopath may declare, for example, that he has no further interest in his family, or that he no longer feels any affection for them. He expresses no desire to see them nor asks for news about them. All these utterances and this condition which, in a normal person, would simply reveal a total state of indifference may not have the same meaning at all in mental patients. They may only want to say that no one can understand the type of illness from which they are suffering or help them in their distress and that they no longer have the strength to think of anything else.[22] They do, strangely, occasionally declare at the same time that the (unknown or illusory) fault for which they feel responsible reflects on their relatives, friends, and members of their religion, and is dragging them along to a similar catastrophe. They grieve over this and blame themselves for it. Fearing for their kinsmen as well as for themselves, they humble themselves and ask their pardon. They become aware, on the contrary, of the solidarity uniting them even at the moment when all ties between them and their group are believed to be broken. They even represent it to themselves as both closer and more extensive than it is.

Psychiatrists especially go too far, however, when, from their inability to tell which social influences do or do not influence their patients, they conclude that social influences have no effect at all. They are then asserting much more than they are entitled to do. These influences may in fact be very weak and barely perceptible. That, however, does not prevent them from playing a decisive role. After all, not all psychopaths kill themselves. Many probably find themselves, in certain moments, in a state of exact equilibrium between the impulse impelling them to die and internal forces of conservation which retain them in life. The least little additional weight suffices to tilt the scale to one side rather than the other. Let us assume the psychiatrist fails to count among these infinitesimal forces the distant influence exerted upon the patient, across the type of barrier now separating him from the world, of his family or any other group to which he belonged until now. Psychiatry could in no way uncover this influence, given its means of observation.[23] Statistics, however, enable us to discover what no observer who examines an individual subject would be capable of apprehending. A physician or a psychologist, in the presence of a psychopath who has not obeyed an impulse to suicide, does not know whether he resisted because he was not at the last stage of depression, or because 'social reins' have retained him. Extensive statistics of suicides by psychopaths, distinguished, for example, by religion, marital status, etc., would, however, permit us to measure the influence that social forces exert on the mentally unbalanced, or to ascertain that they exert no influence. These statistics do not, of course, exist. As a result, psychiatrists cannot establish that the depressed psychopath is entirely withdrawn from the influence of his relatives, his religious group, etc., for only the statistical method enables us to measure this influence. For one to have the right to say that statistical findings concerning all suicides prove nothing about mental illnesses, the latter would, in fact, have to constitute a separate category different from all others in escaping social influences. Merely to assert that, however, is not sufficient.

Upon examining certain statistics, one is rather surprised at the high number of suicides that are attributed to alcohol and drunkenness. Neurasthenia is a lasting morbid state, a profound organic disturbance. Drunkenness, however, seems to create a temporary and superficial state of excitation and mental trouble. There is as much disproportion between drunkenness and suicide as between the shame which a child who has been reproached experiences, or the fit of anger provoked by an insignificant cause, and the act of self-destruction. We are less surprised upon examining the conditions under which drunks commit suicide.

> Drunkenness [says Prinzing][24] leads to death by different routes. One may make an attempt on his life because, under the influence of drunkenness, he imagines himself to be more unfortunate than he is, and because a mind troubled by alcohol magnifies real objects unduly. Sometimes the drunk is tormented by hallucinations, or drunkenness renders him really melancholy. Some drunken people happen to attempt suicide (and sometimes succeed at it) without any awareness of what they are doing, so that, should they escape death, they do not understand that they were capable of bringing themselves to such an act.

However, these cases, which may concern persons who become drunk occasionally just as well as habitual drunks, are less frequent.

> In *delirium tremens* terrifying hallucinations can provoke suicide. Monstrous forms threaten the patient which excite him to such an extent that under the influence of anxiety he throws himself out of the window, or puts an end to his life in some other manner.

The same is true in alcoholic psychoses. 'The patient sees dreadful images, hears voices which insult him, believes he is being followed, that he is a criminal and he must be executed, etc.' However, '*there is another explanation for the majority of suicides caused by drunkenness*. The sullen disposition in which the drinker finds himself when sobered up, or when he has not drunk for a long time, often arouses an intense disgust with life,' either because he is lacking the periodic excitation to which he has become habituated or because he becomes remorseful when he sees that he cannot renounce his vice. It is then that he thinks of death.

We can conclude from this that there are close relationships between those who give themselves up to drinking and the psychopaths of whom we have spoken who alternate between phases of excitation and depression. We noted many observations in Prinzing's book which authorize such a linkage. Not only do drunkards often believe themselves persecuted, but 'they find no ease, no comfort, whenever they are not under the influence of the excitant and stimulant which has become necessary to them' (p. 9). 'During the hours when he is not drinking, the habitual drunkard is ill-tempered, discouraged, depressed and taciturn, incapable of concentrating, often filled with anguish so that ideas of death surge in his mind' (p. 10). Many workers drink to forget their disorganized home-life, their family troubles, and to recover courage. Above all, however, they delude themselves that 'alcohol gives strength.' In our societies, where the human organism is often compelled to excessive outflows of energy, where work is both monotonous and exhausting, they seek a stimulant in alcohol. We do not know to what extent neurasthenia is the privilege of the upper classes. Its equivalent, however, will undoubtedly be found in the lower class in the form of habitual drunkenness. Now everything we have said about psychopathic suicides would apply to habitual drinkers who kill themselves. They, too, in hours of depression, feel themselves maladjusted to their associates and out of joint in relation to the groups to which they belong. They cannot stay at home, at the factory, or at the office. They feel ill at ease in a milieu which does not understand them at all and in which they take no further interest. There are too many misunderstandings between them and those around them. Their social capacities are paralyzed and warped. These awaken when they are intoxicated, and, as with an excited psychopath, become exaggerated. At this time the drinker generally becomes reconciled to life and ceases to think about leaving it. But, on the other hand, there is no evidence that, even when he is dejected and in a somber mood, even in periods of depression, the family and religion no longer mean anything to him or he is totally incapable of relating to life, for concern for others is not completely dead in him. Alcoholics do not at all kill themselves merely through egoism, under the influence of an illness or a sadness they cannot explain. Rather, during periods of lucidity, their sentiment of social downfall, their kinsmen's reproaches, and their shame as regards their friends can become added to this obscure suffering. Basically, the latter is of the same origin since the cause of both sentiment and suffering is naught but the false and abnormal situation in which they find themselves in society. Why should the thought of their next of kin and of the ties connecting them to one another not persist, like a flickering light, to the moment when consciousness is close to giving way? The observer is no more able in the case of the alcoholic than in the case of the psychopath to distinguish and measure all the influences which can restrain him or precipitate

him down the slope of suicide. Here again, statistics are needed to
give one the right to separate alcoholic suicides from all others and
to assert that social motives have absolutely no hold over them.

It is not sufficient, however, to establish that mental illnesses, like
all other circumstances impelling toward suicide, detach the
person from society, that is, produce social effects. Are they
themselves explained by society, however? To be sure, a psychic
trouble does not remain enclosed within the consciousness in
which it developed. Whether the individual turns from a society
from which he no longer expects anything, or becomes angry at
it, he only pictures his internal illness by reporting its imaginary,
external cause. On the other hand, society is no longer exactly
what it was, due to the very fact that a member of the group has
been violently separated from it. Society is not merely diminished
by one. Rather, the trace left by the person who has disappeared
and the disturbance communicated to the collective thought by
his act continues for some time. Still, mental illness is not itself, by
nature or by organic causes, a social fact. It is not a circumstance
comparable to the other occasions from which voluntary death
ordinarily results. The latter are produced in the milieux in which
the individual is immersed; the former is situated within his body.
In other words, there are suicides who succumb to a sort of social
fatality; others, mental patients in particular, seem to be victims
of a physiological or physical fatality.

Let us assume that states of nervous depression result only from
organic causes and that mental patients represent so many death-
points in the group because wherever they are found the social
current is colliding with an obstacle that is somewhat gross and
inert. Is this not true, however, of other circumstances which
cause the same states of anguish and internal distress among
normal subjects? We must not allow ourselves to be affected by
the words 'organic' and 'physical' as if by them was understood a
new sort of positive influence, that of matter, which would be
introduced into society. Actually, remaining on the sociological
plane, matter can be spoken of wherever a social void is revealed,
an interval when collective life reabsorbs itself. Forces of organic
nature, however, such as those which release a nervous and
mental trouble, represent only a part of the domain not reached
by the influence of the group. Accidents which leave an individual
disabled and adrift are produced within the society itself because
the social mechanism no longer functions well, or no longer
functions at all. The objective of industry, commerce, and all
gainful occupations is to support and perhaps to enrich all who
engage in them. Some become ruined because society does not do

all that it wishes and because there are limits to its power of foresight and organization. Custom does not regulate marital and extra-marital relationships between men and women, up to a certain point, for the purpose of making them unhappy: the vexations of love are accidents whose prevention and suppression does not depend on society. In this sense, we can say that social life collides against material impossibilities. It is materially impossible for everyone to become rich and for the enrichment of some not to entail the ruin of others; for more than one competitor to obtain the same post; that those in love should die simultaneously, etc. It is also materially impossible, however, among so many people as different as they must be for there to be a sufficiently great diversity of aptitudes, that none be born who are maladapted to their milieu. All these accidents are material to the same extent.

If so, however, these accidents, taken all together, measure the powerlessness of society to foresee all and to prevent all. Their number, their distribution in space and time, as well as their intensity, result from the structure of groups. So too, moreover, does the fact that they concern mental illnesses as much as other circumstances which impel toward suicide. Durkheim has not asked from whence they came, what was their origin. He refused to study them because he saw in them only individual accidents. He seemed to consider these accidents like so many obstacles distributed almost at random on a plain where horses race. To clear them, the latter must possess enough vigor and dash. The association which presides over the races must have trained them sufficiently. Those who lack training will collide against obstacles and will be thrown. According to him, however, the nature of the obstacle and its location matter little. A badly-trained horse will necessarily fall, in one spot or another.

However, these obstacles are not distributed at random. We may suppose that the association made every effort to level the terrain, but that it may not have had enough time nor commanded enough workers to cope with all the irregularities in the ground, to fill all the fissures, and to pull up all the brushwood. As a consequence, the disposition, number, and difficulty of these obstacles is also attributable to the racing association. A horse may fall because it has not been sufficiently fed and doped, but it may also be that the association has not covered a ditch or adequately carted off a tree trunk with which the horse collided. The same is true of the events that Durkheim reduces to the role of simple motives, but which are really causes. Not at all are they produced by chance. They result at every place and at every period from well-defined social conditions.

Is there a difference between mental troubles and other circumstances in this respect? We do not, to be sure, perceive immediately any relationship between the structure of a society and the number of neurasthenics encountered in it. What hold will the group have over phenomena which are mysteriously accomplished within the organism and whose existence physicians themselves do not ascertain until trouble bursts forth? That is as much as to say that death is a social fact, explained by society. We could therefore assert that mental troubles are distinguished from other causes of suicide as much as natural death is from other causes, such as marriage, migration, etc., which separate a member from his group: in the first instance, where it is a question of death or of mental illness, it is the organic which would come to the fore, in the latter instance, the social factor.

However, it is not at all absurd to assert that death is explained by society, for death results from life which is what the milieu makes of it. The mortality rate varies from one nation to another, from one professional group to another, and rises or falls from one period to another because society changes. As to mental troubles, even if we suppose that they result not from the milieu where the patient lives, but from congenital properties or defects, it must not be forgotten that births come from marriages and that, following the rules fixed for matrimonial unions, the rejected could be more or less predisposed to cerebral impairments. Durkheim himself has recalled that it seems indeed to emerge from certain observations that inbreeding increases the tendency to nervous ailments. 'Thus,' he says, 'the incontestable tendency of Jews to all varieties of neurasthenia may be due partly to an excessive frequency of consanguineous marriages.'[25] This frequency, wherever it is found, results from the laws and customs proper to a people. Let laws and customs change: the frequency of consanguineous marriages and the frequency of nervous ailments will vary. Add that certain social milieux attract or repel people of complex or unstable nervous organization and impel them selectively, toward certain professions, or predispose them to certain styles of life which, henceforth, more or less favor marriages that perpetuate, multiply, or reinforce certain types of mental instability. Thus, even if we assume that the milieu does not exercise a direct influence on these patients, neither creating nor aggravating their illness, their frequency and distribution, in the last resort, are explained through it. It is in this sense that we can say that the abnormal suicides, like the others, result from social conditions.

Likewise, it is up to society to reduce the sum of disturbance that the abuse of alcoholic beverages introduces into relationships uniting its members. No less certain is it that the number of bankruptcies, failures, or reverses of fortune increases during periods of economic depression. The same effects result, even during periods of prosperity, from causes peculiar to certain industries or branches of commerce, or from the customary speculations which characterize certain milieux. The same is true, however, of what we call the vexations of love. Two beings who are in love, or are loved, and who suffer for one another, imagine that their passion or despair is due solely to themselves, as if the surrounding society did not exist. This is an illusion. Statisticians long ago showed the astonishing regularities presented from year to year within a given country, or within a given, somewhat extensive region, in the number of men of given age who marry women of a given age, or the number of adulteries, divorces, or crimes of passion. These numbers increase or decrease in large or average cities, or in rural agglomerations, at diverse periods of the year characterized by a greater or lesser intensity of social life, the feast days, the exposition years, or years of war or of revolution. We can say, therefore, without sociological bias, that precisely in this domain is where social factors make their influence felt. We may conclude from all this that these diverse causes or particular motives for suicide do not result at all from individual accidents and that their relative frequency, could it be measured, would reveal very exactly the variations within groups of social temperature.

Life is said to be a struggle against death. Social life, too, offers the spectacle of a perpetual effort carried on by human groups with a view to victory over the factors that threaten disintegration. The weapons of society in this struggle are the collective customs and beliefs. When they are weakened or disturbed, we can say that the group's vital elasticity has slackened. On the other hand, causes of disintegration, troubles in functioning are produced in every machine that is somewhat complex, in every organism that is somewhat delicate. These are explained by the structure of the organism or of the machine. Let these troubles multiply, or let society's effort weaken – and the two can occur simultaneously, above all when passing from an old and traditional style of life to a new and more complex type of civilization – and hiatuses will be seen forming in society. It is within these hiatuses that the suicides are to be sought.

The group-oriented social observer can ascertain that hiatuses appear, grow larger, multiply, or disappear, depending on whether the structure of the collective organism changes, and on whether its vitality diminishes or increases. Psychiatry itself concentrates attention on what is going on within the hiatus. As there is a sort of social void there, it is entirely natural for the psychiatrist to explain the suicide by the suicided person rather than by the milieux from which the latter is separated. He does not perceive that the true cause of the suicide is the void that has formed around the suicided person, and that, if there were no such hiatuses, there would be no suicides.

It is unnecessary to believe that there are two categories of suicide, each explained by a different determinism, or that, depending on the individual, the organic determinism is sometimes in play, and sometimes the social determinism. Actually the suicide, every suicide, can be envisioned from two points of view. Depending on whether one places himself at one or the other, he will see in the suicide the effect of a nervous trouble arising from organic causes, or of a rupture of the collective equilibrium resulting from social causes.

Earlier, August Comte denounced what he called scientific materialism, essentially no less metaphysical than spiritualism, which consists in 'the tendency of each science to absorb the next in the name of an older positivism.' He warned scholars against the sociological materialism which pretends 'to explain everything in sociology by the purely secondary influences of climate and race.' We can add: and by the organic and nervous constitution of individuals. Thus is explained the conflict which today pits sociologists and psychiatrists against one another and which, as we see, is occasioned by a particular problem that conspicuously exceeds the boundaries of each of these disciplines.

chapter 15

Conclusion

I. THE DEFINITION OF SUICIDE: SUICIDE AND SACRIFICE

Study of the statistics has led us to findings which retain their validity whatever one's concept of suicide. We have not, however, pursued our research without inquiring into the nature of this phenomenon. Before indicating the general tenor of our conclusions as to its causes, let us attempt to see what suicide itself means. Is this the only phenomenon of its type? Do we not find, in ancient societies and among people who differ from us, institutions and customs which resemble and help us to understand it?

We recall the definition Durkheim proposed: 'the term suicides is applied to all cases of death resulting directly or indirectly from a positive or negative act of the victim himself, which he knows will produce this result.' It is easier to criticize this definition than to substitute another. Put to the test, it appears rather noteworthy for including all acts closely or remotely resembling suicide. Is not the definition too inclusive, however?

Durkheim did not say, 'the act accomplished by the victim with the intention or prospect of putting himself to death.' Often it is impossible for us to scrutinize intentions. Also, many acts are excluded thus which, however, are suicides according to him. Now, we do not always know intentions, of course, but we can infer them and society is certain to infer them. This is why society attaches more importance than might be supposed to the form of the act and the choice of instrument, that is, to the mode of suicide. Durkheim distinguished the choice of instrument from the suicide proper because they seemed to him to result from different causes. It is equally true that what distinguishes a suicide, externally, from every other case of death is that it is accomplished with instruments or by means which allow us to assume that the subject intended to die. If we hesitate to classify as a suicide a drowned person who has been pulled from the water, that is because the submersion could result from an accident. Most of the means chosen by those who wish to kill themselves, however, are such that we cannot mistake the meaning of their act. Not only did they know they were going to die, but they wanted to die.

To Durkheim, however, it seemed rather unimportant whether death had been accepted only as a necessary condition to which one had to submit in order to attain a certain desire, or whether death had been desired and sought for its own sake. It would be suicide in either case. 'The soldier who courts certain death to save his regiment does not want to die. But is he not the author of his own death? ... One can say the same of the martyr who dies for his faith.' Here we approach an order of facts which resemble suicide. Opinion distinguishes between them, however. Consider a person who through gluttony or intemperance refuses to follow a moderate diet although he knows this is the only way for him to postpone the expected date of death. We might say that such a person is killing himself, but not that he is committing suicide. The soldier, fallen on the field of battle, who has been courting certain death is not a suicide. It is also improper to call suicide the Christian act of a martyr who, knowing he will be punished by death, undertakes to overthrow idols.[1] Do we experience the same impression of terror and revulsion in the presence of their remains as when we discover the corpse of a suicide?

> On the 22 Floréal in the year 10 (12 May 1802) [Bayet tells us],[2] the First Consul, having learned that one of his grenadiers 'committed suicide for love,' had an order of the day read to the assembled Guard ... stigmatizing the voluntary death. 'It is as courageous to suffer the afflictions of the soul firmly as to stand fast under the grapeshot of a battery. To abandon oneself without resistance to melancholy, to kill oneself to escape it, is to abandon the field of battle before having been conquered.'

On the other hand, 'the officer who gets buried beneath the ruins of a fort rather than surrender, and the soldier who accepts death in an explosion in order to take the enemy with him, arouse only praise and admiration.'[3] One judges similarly the ship's captain who, remaining the last on board, goes down with his ship. There is no contradiction here, for the two orders of fact appear to be quite distinct. In one case, death was the condition of a value more important than the individual who killed himself. In the other it was useless, an end in itself. The Christian suicide does truly exist, but it is distinguished from the death that is accepted and submitted to in order to avoid sin. Saint Augustine condemns

Christians who seek death in order to defy the pagans, or who kill themselves to escape ravishment, or from shame at having been ravished. Those truly are suicides. He says, however, that 'it is better to die of hunger than to eat food consecrated to idols.' While he admits that one must 'flee to another city' when persecution comes, since to remain would be to seek death, he adds that this rule does not apply to bishops, for 'the Good Shepherd gives his life for his flock.' The Council of Elvira, which also condemns Christian suicide, 'has not a word to say of those who deliver themselves to the tribunals *in time of persecution*, or of the Christians who prefer death to dishonor.' That is because Christians are like combatants on such an occasion and set examples that are useful to all.[4]

Here then are two orders of fact, resembling two different species in that society does not react to them in the same way.

But these two species may be part of the same genus. Durkheim designated all suicides that result from the individual's being submerged in society as altruistic suicides and set them apart from the others. The individual who is entirely subordinated to the group does not hesitate to sacrifice his life for it. The act by which the soldier or the martyr courts certain death, the one for his country, the other for his religious group, is actually a sacrifice. Durkheim does not hesitate to place alongside of these facts the sacrifice of widows on the death of their husbands or of servants on the death of their masters. Sacrifice itself represents a rather vast species. For example, it can be optional or obligatory, though the transition from the former to the latter is gradual. Let us therefore consider sacrifices in their totality and see what a comparison of the sacrifice with the suicide can teach us.[5]

At Delphi, a very old legend told that the people, pressed by famine, besieged the king's residence. The king distributes provisions to many prominent persons. A young orphan, Charila, begs of him. He refuses and throws his slipper in her face. The child, 'beaten and expelled, goes off to hang herself in a lonely valley. The famine worsens. In order that prosperity return, Charila must be hanged in effigy.' An annual festival instituted by Pythias was celebrated in her honor. It began with a distribution of grain. Then a likeness of Charila was made. It was beaten, hanged, and buried. The sense of the myth is easily recovered, says Bayet. 'There is famine. A young girl hangs herself. The hanging is evidently destined to end the famine. The slipper on her head may be a ritual gesture consecrating the victim to an agrarian divinity.[6] Being an orphan, let us add, may also have predisposed her to sacrifice herself. Does not the legend confuse sacrifice and suicide because close analogies indeed exist between them?

To be sure, there seems to be the following essential difference between human sacrifice and suicide: in the former, the victim's death results from a group decision, while suicide is a voluntary death. But first, to what extent does suicide result from an act of individual volition? We notice that when Durkheim defines suicide as an act which the victim knows must produce death, he does not say that this act is voluntary. He was probably concerned not to exclude those that result from an impulsive action influenced by aberration or madness since the statistics do not distinguish them from the others.[7] But when the suicide is deliberate, or is committed 'wittingly,' as the common law of the Middle Ages put it, the suicide's volition is the same with respect to every goal except the issue of his life or death. The suicide's volition does not differ from that of other people, nor from what his had been before he decided on suicide. The act of killing oneself is most often accompanied by a feeling of renunciation and of aloneness. Before quitting life a desperate person will first have withdrawn from society into a sort of antichamber where he dwells for a longer or shorter time between the living whom he has already left and death which he goes to meet. Even so, his nature remains social. He turns over in his mind thoughts which come to him from the group and his volition remains as it was. It is in society that he has learned desire. Even when he is morally cut off from society and believes he will no longer participate in its life, he still partially obeys its promptings. We can say that an individual who deliberates before acting is turning back for a moment towards the human milieu of which he is or has been a part until just then, and that he must indeed think with the others and make up his mind with them before consummating, in isolation, the act they have chosen for him. In our individualistic societies we too often forget how much collective content enters into reflective and deliberate activity. We would be much less impressed by suicide did we not in reality perceive behind it a thought formed, like our own, in human milieux.

On the other hand, consider sacrifices in which humans are the victims. It is not easy to say to what extent they result from tribal, religious, or national decrees imposed on the individual against his will by a purely external form of constraint, and to what extent resignation, acceptance, and even tacit consent enter into the internal attitude of the sacrificed person.

> I shall know if an obedient victim is needed
> To stretch forth an innocent head to Calchas's sword,

says the Iphigenia of Racine. Obedient victims do, in fact, exist. The efficacy of sacrifice appears to be total only on condition that the immolated human or animal does not resist, or resists as little as possible. Before slaughtering them ritually, caressing and flattering words are murmured into the animals' ears as if to appease their anger and persuade them that no harm at all is wished them.[8] Why so many anointments, purifications, crowns, and garlands of flowers? Would one be so lavish of them if one did not believe that the victim would be honored by them, would accept and rejoice in them? But, above all, under force of the vital instinct, the human could well resist those who are leading him to death. The beliefs, for the sake of which he is being sacrificed, are just as much his. He has always held them and has undertaken to conform to them. Had the lot fallen on others, he would have applauded their sacrifice. We are entitled to assume that he accepts as soon as he has been designated. Would we know whether the captives and the vanquished who were executed, the widows who were burned, or the slaves who were buried alive had felt they were suffering violence unjustly, against their volition, had they not been bound and chained beforehand?[9] The human sacrifice did not consist in its inevitability or in resulting from rules as necessary to those who participated in them as are the laws of nature in our own eyes. The victims, designated not by arbitrary choice but by some mysterious decree of sacred powers, might well have lamented their fate, accused the gods and cursed the hour when they were born. But how could they have imagined an outcome other than death? The gods had abandoned them, the heavens had spoken against them, the valor which resided in their race and in their city had shown itself too weak, exhausted, lapsed. The powers that regulate the world order were definitely hostile to them. Their captivity, their defeat put a fatal sign on them. Moreover, they are equally resigned to a destiny they cannot avert whether they leave it to their enemies to draw the implications or whether they sacrifice themselves rather than allow themselves to be captured or led away to death.

But the death of a master or spouse produces the same effects as defeat. Durkheim says that:[10]

> in 1817, 706 widows killed themselves in the one province of Bengal and in 1821 2,366 were found in all India. Moreover, when a prince or chief dies, his followers are forced not to survive him. Such was the case in Gaul. The funerals of chiefs were bloody hecatombs where their garments, weapons, horses, and favorite slaves were solemnly burned together with the personal followers who had not died in the chief's last battle. Such a follower was never to survive his chief. Among the Ashantis, on the king's death his officers must die. Observers have found the same custom in Hawaii.

Sacrifice or ritual suicide? Half-consenting sacrifices, or suicides partially through persuasion? As long as the husband, the master, lived, wives and slaves had little individuality other than his. It was his will that, upon his death, they accompany him in departure from life. Was it not also their own? It was at the same time the will of the group in which they no longer had a definite place. In still other cases, a crime, an unclean contact, or a defilement cut them off from the community. As objects of horror to themselves and to others, there was naught else for them to do but to disappear. On what could an individual will to resistance have based itself when the laws, the customs, the living and the dead all agreed not to allow him a way out? Let us assume that the victims went to the sacrifice halfheartedly. Though they had not desired the cause they were resigned to the effect.

Is a like attitude also found among those who commit suicide? Seemingly, they decide all alone. They consult no one. Those who know them best are quite surprised to learn that they embarked on such a project. What offends society most about suicide is that its perpetrator has held counsel only with himself, has given a deplorable example of individual initiative. The Middle Ages put suicide on the same footing as homicide and even invented the expression self-homicide.[11] The suicide had lured into ambush and killed a creature of God, surrounding his premeditation with the same secrecy as the murderer. But while one could punish the latter, repair his act to a certain extent by discussing his motives for it with the criminal after the deed and making its nature quite clear during the course of a trial, punishment of the corpse would only be a meaningless parody, a ridiculous manifestation of powerlessness. While the sacrifice carried a dazzling proof of society's omnipotence, the suicide was solely the affirmation of an independence over which it had no manner of influence. In the former we have society sufficiently strong and with enough authority to obtain from its members the gift of their lives; in the latter, a multitude of scattered and unrelated rebellions that are clearly individualistic.

These individual wills are, however, obedient to laws, for the number of suicides remains constant within the group from one year to the next. Everything occurs as if society itself decided in advance what portion of its members it would consent to sacrifice. Thus, the suicide only appears to decide or choose to die of his own will. The choice is made without his being consulted. He yields to forces stronger than himself and, though he appears to give them his allegiance, since he carries out their commandment, he is like the sacrificed person. He also becomes aware of finding himself in a situation for which there is no other outcome. Should he succumb to the ruin of his business, be frustrated in his ambitions and overwhelmed by domestic sorrows; should he feel keenly his humiliation, his abandonment, his isolation; should he discover in himself a void he is unable to fill; should he, moreover, be victimized by his imagination or by circumstance in the battle men wage to attain wealth, prestige, power, and happiness, he will suddenly realize that he is only a person who is vanquished. It is not given to everyone to acquire the advantages life offers. Since he pursued and failed to attain them, fate must have declared itself against him. He no longer finds in himself enough self-confidence and resilience to keep his head in adversity. Life's vanquished form a long cohort of captives that society drags behind its chariot.

The majority of desperate persons, however, are able to shift responsibility for their misfortune on to circumstances such as result from social life. They are victims of society, since they are unfortunate, but society does not require them to die. Nay, more, society insists that they live and, if it sometimes excuses those who have not been able to bear too overwhelming a distress or too great a despair, it does not condemn them any the less for the suicide. The reason for this is apparent enough. It is sometimes said that modern societies are distinguished from all those that have preceded them because they are more individualistic. The result of this must be more respect for all liberties and, in particular, acknowledgment of the person's right to dispose of himself. When, on the other hand, the individual is considered more valuable, it is entirely natural for every act to be censured whose effect is not only to destroy him but to lessen the worship rendered him. In sum, it is less a question of liberty than of happiness and of carrying out all the activities which are reason for human living. That is why happy people, even moderately happy people, no matter to what other category they belong, resent as offensive the act of anyone who shows that, in his view, life is not worth the trouble of being lived. To be sure, one could say on the contrary that, since he kills himself from despair over being deprived of these values, the suicide accentuates their worth. Life is nonetheless the essential value, since it is the condition for all the others. Life is sacred, and whoever rejects it, whoever is not ready to endure all suffering in order to preserve it, commits a veritable sacrilege. There is no worship without sacrifice. This is why society claims the right to impose on its most unfortunate members that form of sacrifice which consists of enduring life even when they have so many reasons for unburdening themselves of it. This is the true meaning of those frequently invoked arguments that it is cowardly to prefer death to suffering, that suicide is a desertion. Similarly, one was able to say to a victim tempted to escape the sacrifice by fleeing that patience is the essential virtue and that it is a sin against the divinity not to accept the role assigned to him. Thus, those who voluntarily put themselves to death are, in our societies, not the resigned but the rebellious.

Society, however, is neither simple nor unitary. We have said that it condemns suicide because it believes that life is a condition of good fortune and because it does not want put into question the worth of values to which mankind subscribes. This general disapproval of suicide is diffused throughout society. In many milieux and on many occasions, however, sentiments of an entirely different nature come into play alongside of it. Also, there are suicides and suicides. Particular circumstances differ from case to case. Also, voluntary deaths can be divided into several major categories according to the attitude and internal disposition associated with them. Let us consider them, in turn, not only asking how the total society reacts in their presence, but which milieux are most affected or best prepared to accept them.

There are, first of all, suicides which appear very close to expiatory sacrifices. Killing is known to occur before a self-killing and homicide is sometimes followed by a voluntary death. How explain the succession of two such different acts and the triggering, in some way, of one by the other? Durkheim saw in this the effect of one of those states of exasperation and of irritated lassitude which, depending on circumstances, can turn against the subject himself or against others. Sometimes, he said, the subject's rage is such that two victims are necessary to relieve it. But what course does this fit of rage pursue? There would seem to be only one possibility here, namely, that suicide can follow after homicide but not homicide after suicide. There is, however, indeed occasion to distinguish the two cases. Sometimes the thought of suicide provides the impetus. Often, before killing himself, a man kills his wife, children, or other persons more or less closely related to him, because he believes that the same menace weighs on them as on him, that life is equally burdensome to them, and that they have as many reasons as he for leaving it. He would, if he could, lead the entire world into oblivion with the same intention. Sometimes the homicide comes to the fore. However, the suicide which immediately follows a similar, prolonged outburst of rage does not necessarily result from it. The person who has killed is doing justice. This form of suicide recalls the expiatory aspect of the sacrifice. Murder, however, is not the only act which calls for punishment, and plenty of men who are guilty, or who believe themselves guilty, of crimes or of less serious offenses commit suicide to punish themselves. The statistics of motives attribute a large proportion of child suicides, nearly half of them in the elementary grades, to fear of punishment. Do they put themselves to death because they dread a painful sanction or, at least in part, because they feel they have committed a serious offense? An alcoholic who views himself as responsible for his family's distress and a depressed person who is tormented by morbid remorse kill themselves in expiation. This is also true, however, of those who commit suicide to escape dishonor. Now, those who decide to die for such reasons, far from rebelling against society, are obeying it.[12] The person who killed yielded to an individualistic impulse. When he avenged his crime by doing away with himself he became the instrument of social justice.[13] Society condemns suicide, in general. At the same time, however, it orders the guilty to atone for his crime. It suffices that the sentiment to which the latter commandment responds be more intense for it to be better obeyed or respected than the condemnation.

But these cases may be exceptional. Is not suicide accompanied quite often by sentiments of exasperation, fury, and rebellion? 'Sometimes,' says Durkheim, 'there are blasphemies, violent recriminations ... threats, and accusations against a particular person to whom the subject ascribes responsibility for his mishap.' Suicide takes the form of a sort of bravado, malediction, and vengeance. The desperate person seems to wish to provoke a scandal by the outrageous or unexpected nature of his act to terrify and torture his survivors, to crush them beneath the weight of remorse, to project on to them clearly the responsibility for his death, and to persuade them that they are guilty and that his suicide is their crime.

Here, then, are people who no longer are killing themselves to obey certain conventions and collective beliefs. They kill themselves 'in opposition to society' or in opposition to a particular person who, in their eyes, represents society. The cause of their distress is indeed within the group which has offended them, mistreated them, and treated them unjustly and cruelly. But the group has not desired their death. It even wanted them to live, as if it had not measured the full significance of the injury it had done them. It must be that the group had to be forewarned, by the consequences of the offense or unjust treatment, of all the unconscious wickedness into which it had entered. The group did not desire the consequence. The injured person desires it. The volition is indeed his own, since it runs counter to the group's intention. These exasperated madmen resemble resigned and passive victims very little, still less people who are atoning for a crime. Such suicides, however, remind us nonetheless of certain forms of sacrifice of imprecation and vengeance. Antiquity offers us more than one example of these.

'Two Erigones hang themselves in Attica, one because her father Icarius was killed, the other to avenge upon the Athenians the acquittal of Orestes.' If it is true that victims were hanged to obtain a successful harvest, these may, of course, be myths invented to account for ancient sacrifices which had this other object. The very invention of the myth, however, suffices to prove that imprecatory suicides, viewed as vengeful sacrifices, did exist and that the idea of them was familiar.

> The daughters of Scedasus, violated by Spartans, killed themselves while cursing the native land of the guilty. Their father, having been unable to obtain justice, invoked the Furies and followed them in death. From this, though not until long afterwards, came the fall of Sparta at Leuctra.

Similarly,

> Melisseus the Argive unavailingly demands reparations from Corinth for the murder of his son killed by a Bacchant. After imploring the aid of the gods, he hurls himself from the top of a rock and draws down upon the accomplice city calamities which only cease with the removal of the guilty one.

Before throwing himself on his sword, Ajax, a suicide from the heroic era, appealed to the Furies against the Atridae, whom he held responsible for his death, and against the entire army.

> Suicide, the vengeance of the weak [says Glotz],[14] thus became an attack upon the community, requiring the individual, the family, the tribe, the city, all who were menaced by the specter, to break down its threats. The mutilation of suicides had no other cause, originally. All primitive societies which believe that to lacerate a corpse is to vanquish a vampire, attempt by posthumous tortures to deprive the suicide of all power. He is sometimes nailed to the ground with a stake, sometimes decapitated, sometimes his limbs are amputated. During the fourth century the Athenians cut off his hand, which was buried separately.

Here, by a curious inversion, the victim becomes the demon who will return after death to torment the living. For that, however, he will need the support of the higher or lower gods whose horizons extend further than a single city. Hence, to avenge himself he offers them his death, demanding their aid as the price of his sacrifice.[15]

This form of imprecatory suicide which is inspired by a thought of vengeance is again met in our societies. Now, whoever wishes, by an act of desperation, to compel people to recognize the wrong they have done him, and does the irreparable to put them in a culpable position, calls them before a tribunal. But a tribunal presupposes a society. The latter can be different from or superior to the one that has done the wrong, but it can also be the same, edified, enlightened, and capable of self-condemnation.

After a reprimand, a punishment which he judges to be undeserved or excessive, a child decides to kill himself. He is touchy, distrustful, and irritable. He goes through a period of lassitude. Many frustrations and vexations have indisposed and, little by little, exasperated him. The last offense is more cruelly felt and the child now contemplates an act which will emphasize in the eyes of his parents or teachers the baseness of their injustice and his own sensitivity or resentment. He imagines their shock, their regrets, their remorse and their grief, which will be like a punishment. The child appears alone in deciding or planning his act. By it, however, he secretly appeals from his unjust to his more enlightened kinsmen.

Anna Karenina's sentiments are more complex: she both loves and hates Vronsky. She hates him because she believes he no longer loves her. At the same time she is disgusted with life: 'Why not put out the light when there's nothing more to look at, when it's sickening to look at it all?' But the intention to avenge herself is present from the start when her thinking of suicide is still only very vague. It is still present when she throws herself under the wheels of a train in motion. 'Death presented itself to her mind as an unique means of reviving his love for her, of punishing him .... To punish him, only one thing was needed.' And further on: ' "There," she said to herself, looking into the shadow of the carriage, at the sand and coal-dust which covered the sleepers, "there, in the very middle, and I will punish him and escape from everyone and from myself." ' She entrusted the burden of her vengeance to Vronsky himself, not as he was now, but as he used to be, when he and she formed a little group whose customs he no longer obeyed but which would be reborn invisibly by virtue of her sacrifice.

'Oh! damnable land! Land of scorn! be cursed forever!' cries Chatterton, just as he was about to poison himself. This time it is a society larger in space and time which is invoked, it is posterity, justice, a world where the man of genius will not be offered a hireling's lowly employment. Life and people could be and ought to be other than they are. There are just and good powers into whose hands the desperate person entrusts his cause. He is bowing down before them when he rises in revolt against the wicked society. A volition which locates its base of operations in a collective world, even an imaginary one, is not purely individualistic.

Let us consider now those who kill themselves, not to expiate or avenge themselves, but from lassitude, discouragement, or disillusionment. This is the large mass of desperate people who find themselves, as Durkheim says, 'in a state of melancholy languor which slackens the springs of action.' Their disposition is the passive spirit of people who give up and lose courage, who perceive that it is useless to struggle. Have these in no way consulted society? Should they be said to have separated themselves from society like the dried leaves of a tree whose branches did not even need to be shaken? However, if nothing external occurs to incite them, if no stimulation reaches them from their environment, why should they not remain where they are? Why not resign themselves to their fate?[16] Shall we assume that they have lost the will to live? But Schopenhauer quite properly remarked that the will to die, seeing that it is a desire, presupposes that one is still attached to life. An unconscious being would be incapable of taking this step. To feel his isolation he must remain capable of reflection, that is, of describing to himself his relationship to the rest of the world. The desperate person does indeed reflect. He silently interrogates the beings and things around him, receives negative and discouraging responses which are but the echo of his sadness, and interprets them as an encouragement to take leave of life. Only then does he kill himself. That is because society has its shadowy as well as its illuminated aspects and shows only the most somber images of itself to the desperate person. All of the collective sadness and melancholy becomes embodied in him and rises through him to a higher awareness of itself.

> All of us are born to suffer; we know it and we invent the
> means of deceiving ourselves .... All is falsehood, all is illusion,
> deception, all is evil. In the houses, always people upon people,
> without end, all hating one another.[17]

Not until one is no longer capable of seeing the other aspects of the world are the discouraging ones so plainly uncovered. It is in society, not in himself, that the suffering person best perceives the image of his own destiny.

True, the spectacle of imperfections, injustices, and miseries scattered throughout the world can instead lead an unfortunate person to feel less keenly his own distress. The misfortune one shares with others is easier to endure. Since people generally resign themselves to living even though they have so many reasons' to die, why not imitate them? But society, when interrogated, does not merely reply that life is evil and that clinging to it requires an illusion of great strength. Society also makes him understand that he is more unfortunate than the others and that the miserable condition in which fate has placed him has nothing in common with the sorrows of every type to which they are exposed. People do not always know how to recognize misfortune and suffering. It does not in fact suffice for a person to find himself in a situation ordinarily considered tragic or desperate, since he will be affected by it differently according to whether he is energetic. heedless, weak, irresolute, or impressionable. There are hidden stresses that one passes by without noticing. Let us place ourselves, however, at the point of view of one whom a misfortune, real or imaginary, has overwhelmed. Someone is looking for employment and despairs of finding any. He makes a last attempt. Should he fail again, this time it would be a sign that no one wants to bother with him. The person to whom he applies does not wish him harm. He would, if anything, encourage him to continue looking and would give him reason to hope. At the moment, however, he has no opening. To the applicant this negative response is society's last word which, by refusing him any means of a livelihood, indicates that it is rejecting him. When the train comes to a halt at the station where she will commit suicide Anna Karenina no longer knows what she is doing. In the compartment where she is seated, a woman addressing her husband says quite loudly and a little pedantically: 'That's what reason is given man for, to escape from what worries him.' The words seem an answer to Anna's thoughts. 'To escape from what worries him,' she repeats. 'Yes, that is worrying me, and reason is given us to free ourselves .... Therefore, one must free oneself.' Society has spoken. It did not intend to give advice but a suggestion of this type, an unintended assent, is sufficient for one who is thinking of death to persuade himself that he is being shown the way.

Why do they refuse to hire him? Why is he made to understand that he must disappear? It is because he is excessively unhappy. To be sure, unhappiness is a necessary element of social life. Sorrows serve to enhance the value of joys. It is a commonplace that happiness is enjoyed more, and even an indifferent condition is appreciated, when compared to certain miseries. Desperate people, however, are approached by others with a feeling of uneasiness, revulsion, and even fright. We have learned to respect suffering and, when it is not irremediable, we consider it a duty (whether or not we always acquit ourselves of it) to do what we can to lessen it. Confronted, however, with distress that it feels itself powerless to abate, what role can society assume other than to localize the evil, to turn from the view of a spectacle which would weaken its vital force, and to keep at a distance those who could only cause it unnecessary sorrow. Let us again place ourselves at the point of view of the desperate person. He knows, or believes he knows, better than anyone, that his difficulty is without remedy. How should he not feel the same sentiments as those who were consecrated to the sacrifice because in them were concentrated all the malevolent principles which society harbors? And how should he not imagine that those about him, both the near and the distant, will consider his death a deliverance, even though they do not at all admit it?

We can understand why what seems to us most mysterious and most contrary to nature in suicide is that a person finds in himself, and in himself alone, the strength to want to die. The volitions which seem the most individualistic, however, only appear to be so. As Blondel, with whom we again agree on this point, has written,[18]

> there is no volition unless a system of collective imperatives of
> every order is present in the conscience to which conduct that
> does not conform must at least justify itself . . . . Only the
> presence [and, we shall add, the presence alone] of collective
> representations suffices to make our activity voluntary . . . . If
> volition is intelligence, reason, attention, foresight, and
> anticipation, that is because the person, upon acting, perceives
> himself acting and foresees how he will act. But this spectator,
> this conscience that is within us to organize our action, to
> foresee and evaluate it, though within us, is not ourselves . . . .
> This spectator is the conscience of the group installed within us
> with the group's principles of knowledge and action. The
> course of our thoughts and our actions unfolds before the
> conscience as before a judge.

Let us apply this thought to the explanation of suicide.

The reasons one gives to himself and sometimes to others to explain why people kill themselves are very diverse. Some we understand and we feel their strength. Others appear more questionable. Some we find absurd. To begin with, however, they generally are nothing but so many incomplete expressions of thoughts which are unfit for analysis or description. The reasons for suicide are both within us and external to us. When a person commits suicide he has the feeling of being carried away in a current of thought in which he is no longer capable of distinguishing what comes from himself and what from elsewhere. That is because, as a social being formed and disciplined by society, at the very moment when he is leaving it he obeys society's advice, impulses, and suggestions. How shall he discern in this ensemble of influences those which play the principal role? When he says, 'I want to die because life is a burden to me,' he is translating into the clearest language for him, that is, into individualistic terms, a conviction which may have been dictated to him by his milieu and which would be better expressed thus: 'I am killing myself because others are of the opinion that there is nothing else for a man in my situation to do than to die.' Certain suicides appear absurd to us, moreover, because they are not explicable from the point of view we call reason, that is, from the point of view of people whose thinking we share. There is more than one such reason, however, for not only is society partitioned into a certain number of groups but, in addition, one finds juxtaposed within each of them different and even contradictory points of view and ways of thinking. Now, depending on his state of mind, a person will hear in this welter of contradictory opinions only what he is capable of understanding.

Must he atone, he asks? Yes, but there is atonement other than suicide and they also are commended who, having committed a crime or a serious mistake, live on to submit to the punishment that law or opinion imposes. Must I avenge myself? Yes and no. And, besides, you can avenge yourself without disappearing. Am I going to withdraw from the sight of people an unfortunate person whose presence is a vexation and an anxiety to them? Yes, but it is also sufficient that you be resigned and keep silent. However, other nearby voices reply, perhaps simultaneously, that there is but one way for him to avenge himself, to atone, or to efface himself and that is to kill himself. Society is like a sibyl whose responses can be interpreted in more than one sense and who, moreover, offers several responses at once.[19] But one who is inspired by the oracles of a god is no less obedient to them because of the manner in which he hears them. Having delivered his volition into the hands of a power greater than he, it no longer belongs to him. This reconciliation of sacrifice and suicide must not lead us to confuse them, however. As we have said, they are two species of the same genus. What distinguishes them? No more than the sacrifice does the suicide accept advice only from himself. The latter, like the former, carries out an act whose reasons are found in collective representations or imperatives. But while society presides over the sacrifice that it has publicly organized, and accepts responsibility for it, society desires that it be impossible to say it intervened in the suicide. Society has advised and suggested it. Far from claiming the accomplished act as a manifestation of its volition, a consequence of its suggestions, however, society fails to recognize it, repudiates it: 'Society has not desired this.' This difference follows at once from the fact that the sacrifice is generally encompassed within ritual formalities, that it is accomplished in the midst of a gathering of people, and that sacred personages regulate its progress according to rules fixed by tradition. Nothing similar is found in the suicide. There are, of course, types of voluntary death which, whether one considers their apparent causes or the instrument and means that have been chosen, have been consecrated by custom and fixed by tradition. There are models for suicide and there is a publicity of suicide. That the voluntary death must be a ritual act, however, does not follow. Ritual is the form taken by a collective volition when, to achieve its ends, it must show itself plainly, must become so visible and sensible as to create among assistants and participants a community of sentiment and a unanimous decision. This necessity is imposed on it in the sacrifice. Even when a soldier voluntarily gets himself killed for his country, or a Christian for his faith, unless the gestures, attitude, and surroundings present a ceremonial aspect, society must appropriate and consecrate the act if it is to produce what is required of it. Its commemoration must be surrounded with conventional formalities: prayers to the martyrs, a cult of their relics, exceptional military honors, etc. Suicide, however, has no need to manifest itself externally. The suicide hides to accomplish his act. If he could disappear without trace the suicide would obtain in most cases exactly what he wants, namely, to eliminate himself, to withdraw from a world in which there is no place for him. If he kills himself to atone, it suffices for those whom his act has injured, or who have known him, to be informed that he is dead. He need not atone publicly unless a criminal trial and instituted proceedings have extended the consequences of his crime to other milieux. By killing himself, however, he has removed all justification for this procedure. If he kills himself for revenge, it suffices for the memory of his death to remain as a living remorse in the souls of those who have hurt him, that is, of a small number of persons too close to him for them not to become informed of it. If rage turns him against society as a whole, the latter, represented by those people with whom he is in most direct contact – his rivals, competitors, those who employ or supervise him, his creditors – will be forced to learn that their injustice, their wickedness, or their hardheartedness have pushed him to the end. Thus, if a human sacrifice such as that of a widow on the husband's tomb lost its ritual form, it would cease to be a sacrifice and would become a suicide.

Society claims the sacrifice as its own, an act to which it

committed itself totally, because its desire for it was in fact unanimous. Whatever objective it has in view, oblation, purification, atonement, or communion, the sacrificial act can only be accomplished in the midst of a community all of whose forces converge towards a given focus. The act would unavoidably lose effectiveness if a part of the group opposed it and doubted its efficacy. The community can include groups differing in other respects: all its divergent tendencies are suppressed when they assemble around the sacrifice and there is no part of the community whose entire volition is not engaged by it. As we have seen, however, it is entirely otherwise with suicide, particularly in our societies which are so complex and where so many distinct milieux and currents of opinion subsist side by side, or even partially penetrate one another. To be sure, the thought of suicide, the decision to commit suicide, have also taken birth in these milieux. In researching the roots of the motivations we will find them firmly embedded in the world of public opinion, yet strangely intermingled. There are indeed religious groups which condemn suicide. There is a common morality which is hostile to it. Elsewhere, suicide is judged with greater indulgence: it is excused, accepted, found legitimate and even necessary in certain cases. Reactions will differ, depending on whether the suicide concerns a friend or a stranger, the head of a family, a bachelor, an elderly man, an ill one, or whether the misfortune is of some particular nature, such as ruination, dishonor, grief, etc. A person who is tormented, to whom life seems too heavy a burden, traverses a part of these milieux, at least mentally. Even should he not actually question them anew, it suffices for him to know what people in them think, for him to remember, and for the echo of many ancient conversations to reach him. He has proceeded, hearing one echo, another, and still another. He himself has reflected on these matters long before he ever thought he would examine the question on his own account: on occasions when certain suicides occurred not far from him which for some reason occupied his mind. It suffices for him to recall how he then judged suicides for him to know how people like himself would now judge the act he is contemplating. Society in general, however, that is, those who do not know him intimately, can only ascertain that he has killed himself. Society in general does not know who has given him advice or in what locale he may have found examples and reasons for making up his mind. That being the case, what is astonishing about society's considering suicide to be an act which in no way emanates from itself, in which it has had no part? It is a natural child having all the attributes of a bastard, since it is not known at what moment it has been conceived. None of those who could be its father is disposed to acknowledge it. It is natural that society treat it as an illegitimate product, an accidental product, born under conditions which are too obscure for the entire blame not to be cast on the one that gave it birth, that is, on the suicide. If society can assert that it was absent from thoughts and deliberations which, however, are inconceivable without it or away from it, that is because it is easy for society to invoke more than one alibi.

Let us return to the definition of suicide that Durkheim proposed and whose last part we have modified: 'All cases of death resulting from an act accomplished by the victim himself with the intention or with a view to killing himself.' After what has gone before, are there not grounds and means for making it more precise? May one not add, '*and which is not demanded or approved by society*'? We have seen, however, that there are suicides demanded by at least a part of the society (suicides of atonement). Collective approval, moreover, is not presumed. What would be an accurate statement in countries and periods where civil law forbade and punished all suicides is inaccurate when opinion respecting suicide is uncertain and varied from one milieu to another. Shall we substitute the phrase, '*and which does not have an altruistic aim*'? Imprecatory suicides, however, are egoistic. Moreover, when one kills himself to atone, he thinks of others as well as, and perhaps more than, of himself. We shall therefore exclude as suicides all those cases where one departs from life in order not to be a burden to his family, or because one feels that he is an obstacle to someone's or some people's welfare. It remains, then, to distinguish suicide from sacrifice explicitly by saying, 'We classify as suicide every case of death which results from an act accomplished by the victim himself with the intention or with a view to killing himself, *and which is not a sacrifice*.' This restriction is not unimportant for there are sacrifices which are in fact accomplished by the victim voluntarily. We are not thinking primarily of human sacrifices, which no longer exist in our societies, although it would be of interest to know of countries such as India, where a very large number of female suicides are enumerated, whether all are really suicides. Durkheim's definition, however, applies just as much to acts such as the death of a soldier who voluntarily gets himself killed for his country, or to a believer who dies for his faith, as to true suicides. They are, moreover, difficult to distinguish from the same acts accomplished by people who only expose themselves to a danger of death but who as a result die from the same causes. Now, not all of these acts are suicides. We believe that a sociological definition must principally take into account the attitude of the society and the different judgments it brings to bear on externally similar acts. Once society admits being the inspirer and author responsible for certain acts, others that it considers to be purely individual, even though they may have been suggested, advised, or approved by it, enter into a different category. That is why it is useful to show that there are grounds for not confusing sacrifice and suicide at all, whatever be the real affinities between them. It is also the best way to recognize clearly the nature of each.

II. THE CAUSES OF SUICIDE

Suicide is an element of the normal constitution of peoples [said Durkheim]. In every society there are particular milieux where collective states do not penetrate without becoming modified. Depending on circumstances, they are either reinforced or attenuated. To have a given intensity in the country as a whole, a current must therefore exceed the average at certain points or not attain it.

He noticed that the tendency to melancholy whose reason for being exists side by side with an optimistic current develops proportionately as one rises in the scale of social types. 'Thus, it is a fact, noteworthy at the very least, that the great religions of the most civilized peoples are more deeply impregnated with sadness than the simpler faiths of earlier societies.' There must be a group of individuals who particularly represent this disposition of the collective temper. This is where the most suicides will be.

But if it is normal to encounter voluntary deaths in every society, it is even more necessary that their number not increase too much or too rapidly. 'The collective tendency to sadness is unhealthy' and unjustified; it fulfills a useful role in the social organism 'only on condition of not being preponderant.' Now, Durkheim observed, suicide has increased enormously over the past century:

By 411 per cent in Prussia from 1826 to 1890; by 385 per cent in France from 1826 to 1888; by 318 per cent in German Austria from 1841–5 to 1877; by 238 per cent in Saxony from 1841 to 1875; by 212 per cent in Belgium from 1841 to 1889; and in Italy since 1870, that is, in less than twenty years, by 109 per cent.

Durkheim calculated the increase in the absolute number of suicides without taking population into account. This is not a very good method. Here for some of these countries for the same period are the figures we find by calculating the increase in suicides as a proportion of the total population: by 140 per cent in Prussia from 1826 to 1890; by 355 per cent in France from 1827 to 1888; by 92 per cent in Saxony from 1841 to 1875; and by 78 per cent in Italy from 1870 to 1888. In Prussia, furthermore, there had been two reforms in methods of enumeration during this period which must be taken into account. This would bring the actual increase to around 90 per cent. If for France we replace the comparison between the two years 1827 and 1888 with the mean proportions in 1827–36 and 1879–88, we find that the total number of suicides increased in fifty years by 230 per cent.

These increases are still rather large, though not as great as Durkheim supposed. Are they explained by civilization, by the constitution characteristic of superior societies? Durkheim discards this hypothesis. Though Roman culture succeeded in propagating itself throughout Europe, raising societies to a new high of civilization, 'suicide was only feebly developed until the eighteenth century.' There is no historical reason to assume that the wave of suicides rises higher and higher with civilization. They have not risen to this point due to progress as such, but rather due to conditions under which progress is accomplished in our times, which must be abnormal since such an aggravation could only result from pathological circumstances.

Has Durkheim established, however, that the increased frequency of suicides in European countries in our times is an abnormal phenomenon? We will not dwell on the historical examples and precedents that he invokes. We have no way of knowing how often people killed themselves in the eighteenth or previous centuries.[20] Durkheim relates the present state of Europe to the epoch when the Roman Empire attained its apogee. 'One saw produced then,' he says, 'a veritable hecatomb of voluntary deaths.' But that was only a crisis. For 'Roman culture produced its most brilliant fruits long after this epidemic of voluntary deaths was no more than a memory.' Let us quote Bayet now.[21]

> Neither in the history books nor in the rest of Latin literature have I found a single text declaring or implying that Romans killed themselves *en masse* under the Republic or the Empire. To say that, in general, Roman society must have been disposed to suicide because it had been won over to Stoic ideas, or because it was impatient of tyranny, or because it was flabby and eroded by troubles at the end of the Empire, is to state hypotheses which are not supported by any evidence.

To be sure, a large number of suicides of illustrious or eminent Romans can be enumerated. But when Dr Lisle declares that 'a veritable epidemic of suicides extended by degrees to the whole

Roman world, lasted several centuries, and yearly harvested millions of victims,' this is naught but the echo of a legend invented by historians. Let us therefore resign ourselves to our ignorance of the frequency of suicides before the nineteenth century.

The increase in suicides during the course of the nineteenth century has been exceptionally strong. But considering the rate or amplitude of this increase, after what year are we entitled to say it is abnormal? That suicides should have doubled or tripled in thirty or forty years is a fact which would be surprising had it come about in countries which have scarcely changed in other respects. Were we to fix our attention on the development of great cities, for example, or on the progress of industry, we would measure them by figures of the same magnitude. Why should there not be a cause and effect relationship between the two?

Durkheim himself said that the most certain sign by which one recognizes that a custom, an institution, or a mode of collective behavior is normal is that it is general, that is, exists in all societies of the same species. Now a relatively high frequency of suicides is to be observed in all groups which have attained a comparable level of civilization. We have been able to establish this, from different points of view, in Europe at the end of the nineteenth century and at the beginning of the twentieth.

Let us first consider the evolution of this phenomenon through time. We have shown that in the thirty-seven years from 1840 to 1877 the average rate of suicides in eleven countries increased by 64 per cent, and that in the thirty-five years from 1877 to 1912 the increase was only 14 per cent. The increase in population had been nearly the same in one period as in the other. This notable slackening in the increase of voluntary deaths may be the sign that the inclination to suicide tends to become stable. In any case, it becomes firm. When the same phenomenon is found, not only in a great number of societies but, moreover, within each of them over so prolonged a period, we can say that it is general both in space and in time. Are all European societies ill? Can a given society remain in a pathological state for three-quarters of a century?

It might be said that not the higher rate of suicide but the rapidity with which it has increased is what is abnormal. Since this rapidity diminished by three-quarters during the thirty years immediately preceding the war, it must then have lost its pathological character to a large extent. It must be demonstrated, moreover, that the accelerated velocity of the antecedent development was abnormal and did not result from society's passing from a structure allowing of few suicides to one allowing of many. Upon comparing the height of a five-year-old child and of a twenty-year-old adult, one could also become quite frightened because the height has doubled, tripled, or quadrupled. The adult is not condemned to become a giant, however. He has grown quickly because he has passed in a short time through a phase of his development which allowed of a medium height to another to which a higher stature usually corresponds.

Elsewhere we have observed that the suicide rate tends to become stable, particularly in several countries where it increased the most and earliest. In other words, far from increasing unceasingly, it scarcely departs from the level it reached some time ago. What is most striking, however, when one observes the diverse regions of a given country, is that the increase in rate of suicide of the entire country is mainly explained by the increase of voluntary deaths in regions where, until then, they had been the least numerous. Everything happens as in a group of children and young people among whom the smallest grow the most rapidly while the growth of the tallest slackens more and more.

As a matter of fact, our study has enabled us to establish by a comparison of regional rates of suicide at different successive periods that more and more they are converging and all are tending to rise to a given level. This was by far the best way, undoubtedly the only way, to show that the very strong increase in the number of voluntary deaths, which appeared abnormal to Durkheim, is a very general phenomenon since it is encountered wherever the same style of life, the same type of civilization, succeeds in taking root.

Durkheim believed that it was the too-abrupt passage from one state to another that explained the increase in the rates of suicide. They result, he affirmed,

> not from an orderly evolution but from a pathological
> disturbance which has been quite able to uproot the
> institutions of the past, though without putting anything in
> their place. For the work of centuries cannot be reconstructed
> in a few years.

The rapid passage from one state to another, however, is not necessarily a pathological phenomenon. There are crises of growth in the social body, as in the individual organism, which are not at all morbid. On the contrary, society must adapt abruptly to new circumstances when it passes from a state of peace to a state of war, or when an agricultural region suddenly becomes covered with industrial cities. Can we believe that so much time is needed for people to habituate themselves to unfamiliar conditions? Why do suicides diminish in the first instance and increase in the second? Is it because they have passed rapidly from one state to another? Is it not rather because the state of war, as such, is accompanied by fewer suicides than the state of peace, while the industrial state entails more of them than the agricultural state?

If, however, a pathological disturbance has in fact been due above all to the abruptness of change in social organization, the consequences will only make themselves felt over several years, at most during the span of a generation. Now, it has not been established at all, however, that the number of suicides decreases in the regions which were transformed first and earliest. The number no longer increases as quickly, but it does not diminish further. The populations which are involved, however, have all the time to adapt themselves to new conditions. Let us therefore attribute the greater frequency of suicide to these persistent conditions rather than to the change which has long since been forgotten.

If the proportion of suicides in France is calculated in relation to the number of deaths among inhabitants aged twenty or more, we find it to be about 2 per cent (exactly 18.6 per 1,000). This figure can rise to 3 or at most 4 per cent in the group of departments where people kill themselves the most. This is rather appalling. Do you realize that of thirty, forty, or fifty persons, depending on the place, one will not die either a natural death or by accident?[22] Nevertheless, however frequent suicides may be today, they only represent a quite small fraction of all deaths, even assuming that they are still increasing. Let us take into consideration that there is a large number among these desperate persons who, being ill or aged, have only advanced a little the date when they would have appeared in the table of the causes of death under another category. How many of them, moreover, were or would have been a burden to their family and to their group, not primarily materially, but by the contagion of their gloom or because their imbalance was reproduced around them?

At first sight, therefore, there is nothing pathological or abnormal in the fact that a very limited number of the members of a society more or less voluntarily cut their lives short, particularly those who find existence a burden, a torture, or a cause of sadness and a weakening vitality. That a group puts its elderly, its infirm, and its sickly children to death is not necessarily an indication of a more pathological social condition.

But this utilitarian conclusion is a little too simple to be credible. It is not enough to know how many people kill themselves or to ascertain that this is, after all, only a limited loss of a substance which may not be healthy. Suicide is also a symptom. What is the extent and the nature of the social trouble it reveals to us?

> If life were in itself a blessing to be prized [wrote Schopen-
> hauer],[23] and decidedly to be preferred to non-
> existence, the exit from it would not need to be guarded by
> such fearful sentinels as death and its terrors. But who would
> continue in life as it is if death were less terrible?

A man must have reached a rather high degree of suffering for him to decide to pass through these doors. How many others are exposed to nearly the same torments but remain on the threshold? Naturally it is impossible to determine their number. As there are scarcely any reasons for assuming that the terror that death inspires is either greater or less in one epoch than in another, or in one society than in another, we can assume that the number of suicides is a rather exact indicator of the amount of suffering, malaise, disequilibrium, and sadness which exists or is produced in a group. Its increase is the sign that the sum total of despair, anguish, regret, humiliation, and discontent of every order is multiplying. These more or less scattered voluntary deaths, then, do indeed make us aware of whether the general condition is, on the whole, fortunate or unfortunate. Not without reason are we disquieted when they exceed a certain rate. Now, we have ascertained that there is a very marked difference in this respect, from once as much again to twofold and often more, between regions where traditional styles of life are maintained and areas where a more recent civilization has taken root: the urban settlements. During the nineteenth century and on up to the present, evolution displaced people from the country to the town, from small towns to big cities. In some extensive countries it is being accomplished with extreme rapidity and nothing indicates that it must come to a halt. A society can, to be sure, live in trouble and in suffering. We may assume that it is still in a transitional period and that one day it too will base itself on tradition and settle down to a corps of well-regulated customs which it is still lacking. Despite all this, when we compare the total number of suicides in principal countries today with fifty or sixty years ago, and when we imagine, behind the desperate ones who kill themselves, the mass of others who surely do not suffer much less, we are rather disposed at first to believe with Durkheim that modern societies have not yet found their equilibrium.

In comparisons between today's style of life and former times, however, we must take joys and satisfactions into account as well as sufferings. When the people of ancient or half-primitive societies offered the gods sacrifices they were guided by a basically rather sound sentiment, even when these were in the form of human victims. They believed that benefits must be purchased at the price of afflictions and privations. This conviction may have rested on the experience of an inescapable equalization and alternation of periods of prosperity and scarcity, power and humiliation. What is called social progress is the increase in the means at our command for satisfying our needs as well as the multiplication and enlargement of needs that we can satisfy. It induces as its counterpart a more complex existence, more disappointments and individual sufferings. Morselli, Durkheim, and Father Krose called attention to the rapid increase in the number of suicides over the past century as being an unnoticed and surprising phenomenon. Surprise would have been more appropriate had they not increased. This, however, does not necessarily indicate that there are more sorrows and deprivations now, relative to joys and satisfactions, than previously. For the latter became both more intense and more numerous.

Durkheim, it is true, did not hold this point of view. In the last chapter of his book he attempts to demonstrate that people in modern societies more often yield to the temptation to part from life because the bonds attaching them to society are slackening. It is not a question of knowing whether, released from their traditional obligations and freed from constraints and limitations which the family and religion imposed on them, they feel or believe they feel happier. For the group as a whole, the weakening of ancient customs and beliefs represents a loss not compensated by any gain.

We will examine this thesis only to the extent that it is offered as an explanation for the increased frequency of suicides. Durkheim in fact proved that, age held constant, single people more often kill themselves than do married people, and that married people without* children more often kill themselves than do married people with children. We have shown that more recent statistics confirm these findings. It appears equally well established that the tendency of married people to suicide strongly decreases in proportion as the number of their children increases. There is no evidence, however, that the preservative influence of the family diminished over a half-century or more. Durkheim recognized this himself.

> While the married [he says] have less tendency to kill
> themselves, their tendency increases with the same regularity
> and in accordance with the same proportions as that of the

*The original reads incorrectly, 'que les époux avec enfants se tuent plus que les époux sans enfants', a typographical error – Tr.

unmarried. The increase in Frse in France from 1863–8 to 1887 was 57 per cent for the married. The suicide rate of the unmarried was not much greater during this period: 67 per cent. *The increase that was produced during the century is therefore independent of marital status* [Durkheim's emphasis].

Similarly, there is no evidence that this difference between unmarried and married people must be greater in the regions where few suicides are committed than in the others. This is possible, but nothing is known about it. It has therefore not been demonstrated that suicides are more frequent because the family's influence over its members is weaker.

Is it true, on the other hand, that the Catholic religion protects the faithful from suicide because it 'imposes a vast system of dogmas and practices on them, and penetrates all the details of even their temporal existence as well'? Do people in modern societies kill themselves more often because Catholicism is in retreat here? All writers, as well as Durkheim, have asserted that suicides are more frequent among Protestants than in Catholic groups. We, however, have seen that the statistics which permit study of the distribution of suicides by religious persuasion can be interpreted entirely differently. They are few in number, moreover. When comparing two regions, one with a Catholic majority, the other with a Protestant, we must not forget that they differ in respects other than the religious point of view. Catholics and Protestants are sometimes linked with different nationalities: in Germany's eastern provinces the Catholics are Poles while the Protestants are Prussians. Elsewhere, the Catholics are peasants while the Protestants live in cities or in very urbanized regions and engage in industrial and commercial professions. Religion does play a role but, undoubtedly, a rather limited one. In any case, it is impossible to study the influence of religion separately from other factors. That diverse religious persuasions, as such, produce more or fewer suicides is one of the most impressive of the conclusions in Durkheim's study, but it may also be the most questionable.

If that is the case, however, where shall we seek the explanation for the increase in voluntary deaths? Another fact has interested us even more, though the statisticians are scarcely concerned with it: how shall we understand the increasingly uniform distribution of suicides within a given country or a given extended region?

Statistics tell us how many suicides have occurred within a group. They do not tell us, however, to what order of facts, social, domestic, religious, political, or economic, each category among them is related. An aggregate of suicides is thus a very complex fact that can only be related to a complex aggregate of causes.

Nowadays, one tends to call this 'a macrosociological fact'* which cannot be explained at all by simply one factor, but rather by a system of influences. These aggregates of factors and circumstances can be regional, regions being defined, not from the geographical point of view, but as zones of civilization. They are distinguished from one another not only by the different styles of life one encounters there but also because a given type of civilization presents a more or less advanced degree of development. In fact, there are regions which are, on the whole, rural and traditional and where the ancient customs preserve all their vigor but where social life has both slackened and dispersed. There are others which are more urban, progressive, industrial, and commercial, where the population is more mobile, circulation more intense, and collective life is simultaneously more concentrated, more rapid, and more disorganized. Between them are all the intermediate stages. Now, on observing the suicides in these categories, we have found that they varied very plainly from one to another, but that they were distributed within each of them, or tended to be distributed, with great uniformity. This is how we must pursue the study of this phenomenon if we wish to relate it to the group of causes that best explains it.

In any event, envisioning the suicides in a region defined in this way, and recalling the total milieu where they appeared, assures us of not allowing any circumstances to escape which could explain them. Family and religion have their place among these causes, to be sure, but only to the same extent as other organizations and customs from which they cannot be separated and which, moreover, contribute to strengthening, weakening, or modifying them. When a rural or provincial community is disturbed and is tending to break up, the collective customs of life and thought all become transformed at the same time as do its domestic sentiments and religious beliefs or practices. A common life circulates in this network of customs and manners bound tightly together. We do not see along what lines it could be analyzed. It must therefore be envisioned as a totality whose family and religious practices represent, again, one aspect. On the other hand, a type of civilization or style of life does not consist solely of habitual ways of behaving, or rules, or of a social discipline. It also allows of accidents and irregularities, of all those special, unforeseeable circumstances in which Durkheim saw only motives or pretexts for suicide and which, for this reason, he neglected. Though manifested in the form of individual situations or circumstances, these result nonetheless from the structure of the social body. Society determines the obedience or disobedience

*'Un fait de sociologie totale' – Tr.

of the individual to such religious or familial rules as much as it does the extent of his exposure to ruin, declassment, or the sorrows and frustrations, undoubtedly equally numerous in the diverse milieux of collective life, which result from his contacts with people. It follows that there is as much ground and as much reason for considering all occasions for shocks, conflicts, and disappointments to be causes of suicide as the weakening of traditional customs. The former undoubtedly multiply in proportion as the complexity of social life increases. Considered separately, each of these accidents may seem individual and even unique. All of them, however, even those we call deep-seated sorrows, even morbid emotional troubles and the neurasthenic's crises of depression, appear with the frequency they do only because of the nature or constitution of the group within which they are observed. Considered collectively, therefore, they are social facts.

Now we are retaining these accidents and their degrees of frequency within the styles of life we distinguish; they are a part of them. A type of civilization is a determinate arrangement of social life, consisting, on the one hand, of essential, relatively simple general functions, laws, and manners, and on the other, of an entire ensemble of local reactions and accidents consonant with these functions and with the general structure of the collective organism. When one devotes attention only to the family or religion, he is confining himself to general functions which undoubtedly do explain the frequency of suicides in part, but only in part. One must also take account of particular reactions and accidents. These manifest the tendencies and state of the milieu in other ways but no less energetically or effectively. It is impossible to eliminate any of these aspects of collective reality successfully except by grasping a form of life in full complexity rather than isolating single factors.

Social life multiplies or reduces the number of particular reasons one may have for killing himself in proportion to its complexity. Relating the frequency of suicides to this social complexity would aid us to understand why political wars and revolutions, on the one hand, and crises of economic depression, on the other, are reflected so exactly in the curve of voluntary deaths. That suicides diminish in time of war or revolution can, to be sure, be explained by a collective exaltation. People think of themselves less often and become excited by interests which surpass them. Even while assigning a part, a large part, to this type of influence, however, we do need to observe as well that life becomes simplified in such circumstances. A large part of the national effort is expended in forms which cause but few individual conflicts. Less of the national effort is left to influence the type of daily activity which maintains economic life or is the occasion for people to confront their values and their positions. One portion of the group is separated from the others either materially or morally. A man's thought not only turns from himself but from other individuals with whom he ordinarily agrees through self-interest or sentiment. What is there to be surprised at if suicides diminish as occasions for individual vexations are reduced?

An opposite phenomenon is observed, however, when a time of economic prosperity passes into a period of depression. Of course we can say that an economic crisis causes a state of disorganization and of disequilibrium in society. Falling prices indicate that consumers are avoiding manufacturers and merchants. Unemployment leaves many workers idle and in want. People are less able to satisfy their needs. Everyone is more preoccupied with himself. True, but at the same time this sum of suddenly available activity becomes employed in another manner and in another domain than the production or consumption of wealth. In the economic sphere there is slack time, sluggishness, and stagnation. But individuals who until this moment were carried along on the current of economic life now reencounter one another face-to-face. All kinds of new relationships are engendered between them that had had no time to form and of which they did not dream when totally occupied with producing and spending. Occasions for boredom, humiliation, disappointment, and suffering on account of others are thus multiplied. It is therefore entirely natural for a larger number of people to seek death during these periods.

There is better proof, moreover, that the social state is not identical with the sum of relationships of individuals to individuals or, as Tarde said, of inter-individual relationships. For the diminution of collective activity has as its counterpart an increase of relationships or contacts between individuals and conversely. Everything happens as in a crowd that is marching towards some assembly place. It overflows with energy and enthusiasm. None of its members thinks of anything but the diversion that is awaiting them, the action they are going to engage in. If an obstacle bars their route or a mishap compels them to retrace their path, the common sentiment animating them vanishes. Henceforth, each sees only individuals who are different from himself and who jostle and obstruct him. Above all, he becomes aware of what separates and puts distance between him and them. Likewise, when people are no longer caught up in a collective current of thought and action they find themselves face-to-face with other egos. This is when they have the most opportunities for giving offense to one another and when the weakest or the most unfortunate succumb.

Society as it evolves and becomes complex assembles larger numbers of people more closely together in space and multiplies contacts among them. Here is a kind of substance to which form is added. That is, customs and beliefs tend to establish a community of collective life among these people. Let us suppose now that society withdraws from a part of this structure temporarily and that some of these people no longer obey the influence of social forces. They have less strength, as well, to resist the impulse to suicide. They remain related and in contact, however, and therefore exposed to many more risks, conflicts, and shocks than if they continued to live dispersed. Society deprives them of support but keeps them in a situation where the chances of injuries and wounds of all kinds are multiplied. They therefore have more occasions to think of suicide.

The complexity of urban society is not identical with what Durkheim called anomie. What did he mean by that? According to Durkheim, 'Society is not merely an object which, of necessity, attracts sentiments and activity of individuals toward itself unequally. It is also a power that rules them.' Now, this regulatory influence is no longer felt or, at any rate, is very limited now, particularly in the economic domain. Industrial and financial crises increase suicides, not because they impoverish, but because they are crises, that is, 'disturbances of the collective order.' On the other hand, 'for the past century economic progress has consisted of emancipating industrial relations from all regulation.' Religion, which consoled the workers and the poor and which constrained the masters and the rich, 'has lost most of its empire.' The secular or governmental power that kept economic functions in a relatively subordinate state and limited their free play has become their tool and servant. Finally, 'the guilds, in regulating salaries, the price of products, and production itself, indirectly fixed the average level of incomes on which needs are at least partly based.' Since this corporate regime has disappeared, however, 'industry, instead of being regarded as a means toward an end, which it formerly was, has become the supreme end of individuals and societies.' Preoccupation with gain has become more and more salient. The result is an extension of appetites and a liberation of desires that no discipline can direct and limit any longer.

For our part, we have more than one reservation about these pessimistic conclusions. It is not obvious that economic and social life in ancient societies developed without shocks, without passing through critical periods, or that individual passions did not produce relatively the same quantity of discouragement and sorrow in them. We say, 'relatively,' taking into consideration the sum of activity expended and the needs that could be satisfied there. The corporate rules appear to have been introduced just when monopoly in the trades was threatened. We know that many struggles were engaged in between the artisans of the humblest trades and the other artisans; between the artisans and the merchants; and between the journeymen and the masters. On the other hand, how could they all have avoided the counterblows of wars, epidemics, and famines which depopulated the countryside and deprived them of their clientele and economic base if, as Adam Smith said, 'the city lives off the surplus of the countryside'? Would such severe laws have been prescribed against suicide, would they have been enforced with such rigor if, in many cases, life had not been hard and painful to bear? Should not the rationale for laws and institutions which have kept each person in his class be sought in social inequality? The latter was not tolerated any the less because accepted under constraint and by force. Society in its totality was too poor, offering few occasions for the high profits that would stimulate desire for the benefits of wealth. This was by far a more serious problem than maintaining oneself at a given social level. The distresses caused by the simple struggle for existence were as painful as the disappointments of those who today want to achieve wealth. Everything is relative. Today, we label 'unregulated' the quest for luxury and the gratifications of vanity. Formerly, however, the same term could have designated the simple desire for a minimum of comfort and security in humble milieux and even in classes of the middle level, when these benefits were reserved for only a small number. Ancient societies were unfamiliar with the particular species of disorder and disequilibrium that result from our more evolved civilization. Because of this we wrongly imagine 'the good old times' were a placid and disciplined age in which everyone was satisfied with his lot. We forget that those social bodies also had their maladies and fevers, their periods of agitation and instability, and that, undoubtedly, desires of every nature, such as ambition, the spirit of rivalry, and the passion for lucre, were no less unfettered there and claimed as many victims as among us. Thus, the city-dweller sometimes fancies that the countryman is happier than he because he escapes the pressure of urban life, as if preoccupations, anxieties, and troubles which are just as painful are not borne in the country. For us not to perceive them, however, it suffices that they occur in unfamiliar forms, just as we expressly forget old emotions that are no longer in harmony with the actual course of our life.

There is no evidence, on the other hand, that economic and social life are entirely unregulated in modern societies. More than one moderate program for state socialism is only the formulation of rules existing in today's world in the form of customs or habitual practices that constrain people even now. It is odd that one should be able to criticize such programs for this (assuming that one does criticize rather than definitely praise them for it). The monetary economy in general use obliges all who exchange goods or services to evaluate their payments-in-kind, workmanship, and efforts according to an instrument of uniform measurement. The law of the marketplace regulates the conditions of buying and selling. In working-class agglomerations, wages are set by price rates. Uniform standards of living tend to become all the more imperative in diverse groups to the extent that the latter are densely populated and extensive. A regulatory role is not played only until there is a crisis. Merchants, industrialists, and the workers as well undoubtedly feel its painful effects. But these are perturbations only to the extent that a remedy is a cause of agitation because it shakes up the patient. They restore the troubled equilibrium. It is not at all abnormal that in a society organized with a view to production the desire for gain becomes intensified. Moreover, that desire collides rather quickly with the limits resulting from the nature of things. Far from being unregulated and anarchic, social life in our modern civilizations is therefore consistent with a kind of spontaneous discipline that singularly restrains the free play of individual activities. We are bound by the rhythm of modern social life and must yield to its conventional forms. No society more pitilessly eliminates innovations to which it is unaccommodating, or more tyrannically regulates gestures and modes of thought and feeling. Nor is there any which does more to blunt human passions and channel them into one mold. Modern social life is undoubtedly too fragmented and prone to too many fluctuations to give birth to those vast collective currents which envelop and sustain people. At such times, at least, it lacks that authority, that prestige, and also that soothing and consoling characteristic which belong only to tradition. At any rate, while the influence of modern social life does not extend to all details of life, or to all the situations which are encountered, this was certainly also the case with old types of regulation, and nothing permits us to assert that there is relatively more anomie now than formerly.

On the other hand, social life is more complicated now than it has ever been. We have said repeatedly that urban and rural milieux appear from this point of view to be as contrary as two styles of life or two types of civilization. What, however, is a style of life? Though resulting from obvious and familiar experiences, this notion is itself poorly defined. That is not because no one ever tried to make it precise. Vidal de la Blache understood by it, 'A totality of organized, systematic customs deepening their grooves more and more profoundly, imposing themselves by force acquired over successive generations and impressing their mark on the senses.'[24] Above all, he viewed them in relation to the soil, its structure, and its qualities and peculiarities, that is, from the geographic point of view. Let us apply the notion to people and groups, and let us define style of life or type of civilization as 'a totality of customs, beliefs, and conditions of existence which result from the customary occupations of people and their mode of existence.'

While this definition is very general, we shall adopt an even more general perspective. Two styles of life, or two types of civilization, however they may differ, are alike in admitting of a rather large number of occasions for people to enter into amicable, indifferent, or hostile relationships with one another. Let us note in passing that motives of suicide can be nurtured equally by each of these three types of relationship. Now contacts between human beings are, on average, more numerous in urban milieux than in rural communities because of their more complex style of life. There are, it seems to us, certain reasons for this.

The peasant style of life is distinguishable from urban life in that work is carried on within the framework of the family group. No rural distinction is as sharp as in the city between the hours devoted to work and the time one spends with family or friends. When farmers meet, exchanging thoughts, communicating news, diverse sentiments uniting or dividing them, the two preoccupations, even though there is no relationship whatever between them, become intertwined, for the village is, in a sense, an enlarged family. The result is that the ties binding them to one another are stronger, the controversies and conflicts scoop out deeper abysses between them, and they inflict sharper wounds. At the same time, however, occasions for conflict and *rapprochement* are less frequent than in the city, where they can originate on the two separate terrains of business or the profession and family or kinship. Peasant life is deeply committed and all-absorbing in nature. From this it derives a special flavor and harshness, more spontaneity, primitive force, and savagery. It becomes weighted, however, with all of earth's burdens and unfolds in accordance with the slackened rhythm of country labor. This is collective living, at once very powerful and very simple, or simplified.

Customs derive their influence simultaneously from sentiments of kinship and from common professional occupations and preoccupations. To this they also owe their stability and continuity. They reach only limited groups, however, and apply only to infrequent actions. The two great collective powers, the family and religion, are more intact here than elsewhere. Their simple prescriptions become adapted without difficulty to a few rather uniform actions. Peasant life turns upon itself and moves in a rather restricted circle of occupations and events.

Progressive dissociation of the two domains of vocational activity and family life or sociability that in the countryside are joined together has not happened without resistance. Before allowing themselves to be shut in within bureaux, offices, and factories, those who were to become employees in commerce or workers in industry remained as long as they could in their shops, stalls, and domestic workrooms where the family was felt to be close at hand and the relationship of master-craftsman to proprietor remained patriarchal. The customs of the crafts were not concerned only with the technical side of vocational life. They placed their imprint on all events enacted in the bosom of the family, reunions of neighbors and friends, marriages and mournings. They kept the worker within the zone of human relationships. By proposing to him that he limit his goals, they moderated his activity. Thus, society intervened between the diverse workrooms and shops, hampering direct contacts between them and acting as a barrier to the spirit of rivalry and competition.

Well into the beginning of the nineteenth century, industry and the cities had plunged more than half as much again into the rural hinterland surrounding them. The force of custom and the simplicity of life would have seemed great to us here, too, not only in the associations of journeymen, artisans, and shopkeepers, but in the middle class of notaries, lawyers, and financiers as well. At that time kinship, marriage, and connections qualified one for office. How should one who carried hereditary responsibility not have thought of his ancestry and of his children? How should technical preoccupations not be intermingled with sentiments, preconceptions, and conflicts of family and class? So close were the connections between the family and its ancestral inheritance or its responsibility for descendants, on the other hand, that the entire thought of the family group would sometimes be concentrated on a legal problem, the history of a lawsuit, or the value of a claim. Just as the activity of a judge or businessman slackens to the extent that the cares of family and kinship encumber him, so family thinking became simplified because none of the attention it devoted to itself could be employed otherwise. Let us add that innumerable barriers separated the groups. Provincial, urban, and class barriers were more numerous and more rigid than now. Communication was more difficult. People lived their lives in the locality, adapted to one another, knowing too much of each other to be frequently exposed to shocks like those that occur when one passes from one locality, situation, vocation, or world to another. Commerce, being more limited and facile, carried fewer risks. Ambitions were less active and humiliations more rare. People thought and felt in unison. Sorrows and vexations, instead of being concentrated and confined within the individual conscience, were dispersed and absorbed within the bosom of the group. The division of functions and of activities was not carried so far as to leave each person confronting his pleasure or his duty in isolation.

Modern urban societies appear entirely different to us. Work places are distinct and ordinarily distant from the dwellings which constitute the physical framework of family life. Also, the times devoted to these two modes of existence are sharply separated and do not encroach on one another. A person who has finished or is going to his day's work is aware of a change of group and milieu. Vocations have become disengaged from the current of general social life in which they were rooted, have drawn together and group themselves according to their traits, to constitute their own framework. The same influence has caused all sorts of nonvocational relationships to become organized independently.

In each of these two milieux people are now only responsive to one type of preoccupation and think either of their work or of their family or relatives. We might suppose that their lives would be eased and simplified by this. Such would have been the case had all conditions remained constant and contributed the same sum of activity to the total as before. The effect of such differentiation, however, is instead to increase the intensity of the two functions which were formerly blended but are now separated. Employments come together and combine according to rules determined solely by the requirements of the occupation or production. Since a larger number of workers are placed side by side or brought into contact, relationships multiply among them. Operations of the same nature regulate one another. They form a chain which develops more rapidly than if they had to adapt to activities which had neither the same character nor the same objective. The same is true, however, of the whole order of relationships which become established between people in the sphere of life not devoted at all to practicing an occupation. The family is now separated from the estate, the farm, the workroom, or the shop. It must indeed be situated elsewhere, that is, amongst the totality of the other families on which the same requirement is imposed. Being no longer confined within the boundaries of the community of villagers or artisans, family life tends to gain in breadth what it may lose in depth. It undoubtedly comes up against boundary lines: just as employments become grouped in different industries, administrations, and occupations, so, too, do families have opportunities for coming together and encountering one another, above all within the same class. It is no less true of these *rapprochements* and encounters that they are more numerous than in those rural milieux where communication between villages is rare. At the same time that they multiply they come closer together in time. Thus, a faster current carries people along not only within the domain of professional activity but also within the family and in relationships which become established between them. The transition from one style of life to another and the progress resulting from it consists above all in the larger number of actions and proceedings and the greater diversity of more or less enduring situations which become concentrated in a given period, as if the network of social life was denser because its strands intertwined at closer intervals.

It is natural, therefore, that occasions for suicides should be more frequent in a society where contacts between people become multiplied. This, however, does not prevent the different species of motives which impel people to kill themselves from being distributed in the same proportions in these two types of society. A given number of people can very well have two or three times as many reverses of fortune in the city as in the country, even though, in both places, these occasions for suicide are in the same proportion to all the others.

Durkheim was surprised, however, that comparing in France two such different occupations as agriculture and the liberal professions, the relative frequency of the diverse reasons given for suicides should be almost exactly the same for both. 'The life of an artist,' he said, 'a scholar, a lawyer, an officer, or a judge has no resemblance whatever to that of a farmer .... The forces impelling the farm laborer and the cultivated man of the city to suicide are widely different.'[25] He concluded from this that motives were only accidental circumstances and that it was necessary to search elsewhere for the true causes of voluntary deaths. To be sure, the statistics on motives for suicide do, indeed, require caution. It is not at all accidental, however, that their distribution remains so constant. Why should the diverse circumstances which expose one to suicide not be distributed similarly (at least for the majority of these types) in both the city and the country? The same proportion of voluntary deaths is attributed in both places to the loss of employment, to a reverse of fortune, to misery. In both places, however, one must earn a living, and everywhere there are people who are miserable, that is, unsuccessful in maintaining themselves at the social level of their class. Why should economic preoccupations not play the same role in both milieux? The same thing is true, however, of family sorrows. Does family life not occupy the same relative place in both urban and rural groups? Do people love members of their family more in the country than in the city, and are bereavements felt there more cruelly? Why should thwarted love or jealousy not occur among causes of despair with the same frequency everywhere? And in what respect does it seem unlikely that mental illnesses are equally the cause of a third of the suicides in the two environments? The rural and urban styles of life are in reality two systems in near equilibrium and underlying both of them are to be found two great functions which complement and balance one another, namely, the economic organization and the family organization. That there should be an identical ratio to the totality of the maladaptations which are produced in these two functions is not unlikely if both of them develop and become complex simultaneously.

The difference between the two styles of life is of another kind, however. Though within groups risen to the level of urban civilization, the diverse circumstances exposing one to suicide retain almost the same relative proportions, each is more frequent in proportion to the total urban population than in rural groups or in those which resemble them. This is so because urban societies provide opportunity during a given period for more frequent contacts between people.

We are not restricting our attention exclusively to the great collective forces which originate and develop within the religious group, the family, or the nation. Will our conception be faulted as being insufficiently sociological on the grounds that only their weakening can explain why the individual who has been liberated from himself more easily separates from life, and that we are attributing a causal role to individual circumstances which are only unimportant occasions or pretexts? Durkheim, in fact, sometimes proposed that when these great collective interests command less of our attention, everything happens as if powerful supernatural personalities, who until then had been predisposed toward people and had poured out their favors upon them from on high, turned away abruptly and abandoned them to their own devices. Depending on how distant are these beneficent forces, a suicidal tendency of a given intensity will then be produced in the group with effects calculable in advance. The tendency will always find individuals who are weak enough and in sufficiently sorrowful circumstances for it to materialize.

> The reasons ascribed for suicide, therefore, those to which the suicide himself ascribes his act, are usually only apparent causes. They may be said to indicate the individual's weak points, where the outside current bearing the impulse to self-destruction most easily finds introduction.[26]

Every society, according to Durkheim, produces, naturally, enough more or less exceptional circumstances to explain and justify, afterwards, a wave of suicides which really have another cause entirely. These circumstances, however, are produced by virtue of the laws of chance, and like the reign of contingency and unpredictability, are opposed to the reign of necessity, of laws, and of order.

Let us again reproduce the list of these circumstances, enumerating the 'causes of suicide' according to modern French statistics: 'loss of employment, reverse of fortune, misery, family problems, thwarted love and jealousy, intoxication and drunkenness, suicides of perpetrators of crimes or delinquencies, physical sufferings, mental illnesses, disgust with life, and diverse frustrations.' Among these motives we can at once identify and combine in the same group those which result or which seem to result from the individual's physical and mental constitution: physical sufferings, mental illnesses, and intoxication and drunkenness, perhaps; perhaps also, though only partially, disgust with life. By so doing, we shall be in the domain of organic tendencies, of blind, materialistic influences, that is, at the antipodes of social life. Bichat stated previously that everything connected with the emotions arises from organic life and is independent of society. Durkheim says, on his part:[27]

> As for the individual qualities, they can play a role only if they exist in all persons. For strictly personal ones or those of only small minorities are lost in the mass of the others; besides, from their differences from one another they neutralize one another and are mutually eradicated during the elaboration resulting in the collective phenomenon. Only general human characteristics, accordingly, can have any effect. Now these are practically immutable; at least, their change would require more centuries than the life of one nation can occupy. So the social conditions on which the number of suicides depends are the only ones in terms of which it can vary; for they are the only variable conditions.

Thus, a method of explaining suicide would be legitimated which takes no account of individual traits.

But this division is undoubtedly too sharp. Is it quite true that the distribution of diverse organic peculiarities among groups is independent of all conditions of social life? Durkheim himself did not stop there. Almost immediately after the passage we have just quoted, he adds:

> the causes determining the social currents affect individuals simultaneously and predispose them to receive the collective influence. Between these two sorts of factors there is a natural affinity, from the very fact that they are dependent on, and expressive of the same cause: this makes them combine and become mutually adapted. The hypercivilization [which by disturbing the family, religion, etc., breeds the suicidal tendency] also refines nervous systems, making them excessively delicate; through this very fact they are less capable of firm attachment to a definite object, more impatient of any sort of discipline, more accessible both to violent irritation and to exaggerated depression. *

Is this not tantamount to acknowledging that an entire category of motives or of decisive individual circumstances, mental disorders and all conditions resembling them, vary through the effect of social influences and societal change? How could it be otherwise, however? We have shown that mental illnesses have a double aspect. They are organic disorders which are ascribable to psychiatry. At the same time, however, anyone who is mentally ill is no longer adapted to his milieu. A mental illness is an element of social disequilibrium and, by virtue of this, is ascribable to the science of society. It is a social fact which must be explained by social causes. Even without assuming that society does violence to the organism, how avoid taking into account the fact that certain environments are more favorable than others to the conservation and exercise of qualities and aptitudes which are linked to the greater development and sensibility of the nervous system? It may be that of all the people who have reason to commit suicide, only those who are irritable, delicate, or lacking in self-control, do kill themselves. Not at all by chance, however, are they found in greater number in liberal, industrial, and commercial occupations and in urban groups than in the others.

Shall we consider the other motives: loss of employment, reverse of fortune, misery, family troubles, thwarted love, etc.? They do not differ as to precedents. They lead to suicide because

---

* The citation is from Durkheim, *Suicide*, p. 323, where it reads, 'The hypercivilization which breeds the anomic tendency and the egoistic tendency also refines nervous systems ...' – Tr.

each of these events has the effect of morally isolating and separating an individual from the group to which he is linked, so that the person no longer finds himself adapted to his habitual milieu. Combined, these motives measure, exactly, the amount of disequilibrium which each type of society allows. How should their number or their prevalence result from chance? The laws of chance only apply to events which are independent or which result from independent causes. Now, although suicides are usually dispersed in time and space and although only exceptions can be explained by imitation, individual motives for suicide are nonetheless related to general causes and form part of the same system. This may not be perceived if the major currents of collective life are arbitrarily separated from these particular accidents as if there were no connection whatever between them. However, family sentiments, religious practices, and economic activity are not entities. They become embodied in the beliefs and customs which connect and bind individual lives to one another. Replaced in the social milieu, circumstances are no more than an aspect of general evolution. We therefore would really be going further than Durkheim along the route he committed himself to since we would be explaining by social causes not only the major forces that are deterrents to suicide but also the particular events which are not its pretexts but its motives.

Such a point of view could appeal for authority to common sense, which links the act of suicide to the special circumstances in which one finds himself. But common sense considers only the visible aspects of facts and retains only what it sees. Social influences escape it. Common sense does not understand, moreover, that the individual form in which these facts present themselves is only an appearance and that their number and distribution result from the structure and style of life of the society. We appeal, instead, to the statistical test. We were able to arrive at the most important results of our study, within the regional framework, by neglecting neither major collective currents nor the particular circumstances, and regarding them as a complex and indivisible whole.

Notes

INTRODUCTION

1 E. Durkheim, *Le Suicide, étude de sociologie*, Paris, 1897.
   [All translations are from John A. Spaulding and George Simpson's translation, *Suicide*, Free Press, Chicago, 1951 – Tr.]
2 Albert Bayet, *Le Suicide et la morale*, Paris, 1922, pp. 275 and 278.

CHAPTER 1 METHODS OF ENUMERATING SUICIDES IN EUROPEAN COUNTRIES

1 See Georg von Mayr, *Moralstatistik mit Einschluss der Kriminalstatistik*, pp. 263f., and Krose, *Der Selbstmord im 19. Jahrhundert*, pp. 7f.
2 To this we should add Russia, where 6,303 suicides were enumerated in 1925, 6,388 in 1926, and 6,552 in 1927, or 44.5 per million inhabitants this last year. Morselli counts only 1,711 suicides in 1875 and Krose an average of 2,574 from 1881 to 1890, or 26 per million inhabitants; we have at present, however, only very fragmentary data on Russia.
3 Morselli noted earlier that in Prussia the official figures were smaller than the figures compiled by church functionaries:

	1869	1870	1871	1872
According to the Bureau of Statistics	3,186	2,962	2,723	2,950
According to the church functionaries	3,544	3,270	3,135	3,439

Morselli, German translation, p. 338.
4 Of which about 58 per cent are for Austria, 42 per cent for Hungary (including Croatia and Slovakia).
5 It must be observed that in 1866, as a consequence of the annexation of Hanover and of other provinces by Prussia, the absolute number of suicides increased in this country from 2,485 in 1866 to 3,625 in 1867. The proportionate number of suicides (per million inhabitants) varied as follows:

1862	112	1865	122	1868	152
1863	125	1866	128	1869	131
1864	114	1867	150	1870	122

The strong increase in the proportion of suicides in 1867 is inexplicable. Father Krose explains the decrease from 1869 by the reform (at the close of 1868) and the difficulty that would have been encountered at the outset in applying the new method. It would indeed be perplexing. It would be prudent not to depend at all on the data of these years (1867–8) which have been enumerated under rather obscure conditions.

6 We do not know under what conditions officials of the civil registry fill out these statistical charts or forms. Are they dependent on notifications made to them? Are these notifications controlled by physicians? Then again, do the police officials and those of the civil registry operate separately or in concert?

7 According to Kürten, suicide statistics in the kingdom of Saxony were reformed in 1876, and so one passes sharply from 723 to 745 in 1873–5, to 981 in 1876, and to 1,114 in 1877, a number above which there is scarcely any rise until 1892.

8 It had been proposed (year X) at the time of the drafting of the Code Napoléon that, in case of violent death, the official reports of the police officer and of the crimes registrar were to be sent to the registry office in place of the death certificate. But the Council of State section ruled against this procedure, 'which would sully the memory of the deceased to no purpose.' The records of the registry office do not mention the mode of death of the deceased. A. Bayet, *Le Suicide et la morale*, p. 785.

9 This is not without drawbacks. We were able to verify this quite recently. In the report on the administration of criminal justice for 1923, published in the *Journal officiel*, 12,079 was indicated as a provisional number of suicides for this year, or an increase of nearly 50 per cent in relation to 1922 and 1921. We proceeded to the Bureau of Statistics of the Ministry of Justice in Paris, which informed us of tables (as yet unpublished) belonging to this year. It appeared to us that this increase was chargeable exclusively to the elderly, over eighty, and to the suicides of unknown age. The chief of the Bureau of Statistics consented at our request to require a revision in the returns furnished by the public prosecutors. This permitted bringing the assessment of suicides in France in 1923 to the perfectly normal figure of 8,458 (8,512 in 1922, 8,892 in 1924).

10 The Board of Public Assistance and Hygiene of the Ministry of the Interior has lately been publishing a *Statistique sanitaire de la France* in which are to be found retroactive tables of suicide. We have consulted only the first volume (for the year 1912, published in 1915). In it communities of 5,000 inhabitants or more are distinguished from those of less than 5,000. But in each of the years from 1906 to 1912 these numbers are appreciably smaller (by more than a thousand) than those of Criminal Justice. They appear to depend on the relations of the physicians to the registry office.

11 We note, however, that in recent years *la Revue hongroise de statistique* has published interesting research on suicide in this country.

12 Since the peace, Czechoslovakia is publishing suicide statistics annually.

13 The two principal sources of information on suicides are: *The Registrar General's Statistical Review of England and Wales* and *The Annual Return of Criminal Statistics (relating to Criminal Proceedings, Police, Coroners, Prisoners and Criminal Lunatics)*.

14 Father Krose wrote in 1906: 'Despite some progress, suicide statistics in England today still do not bear comparison with the statistics of Western Europe.' This opinion has been expressed now and then. But we do not know on what it is based. We shall see that, on the contrary, there is no decisive reason to discard these English data.

15 In Belgium, the declaration of the cause of death must be by the attending or certifying physician. One must depend in many cases on the declaration of the family of the deceased. (Jacquart, *Essais de statistique morale. Le Suicide*, p. 13.)

16 *Handwörterbuch der Staatswissenschaft*, 4th edition, p. 438.

17 The figures for Spain from 1880 to 1900, reproduced by Father Krose, are drawn from *Estadística de la Administración de la Justicia en lo Criminal*. They are very low (in 1900, 21.5 per million inhabitants). We find in von Mayr (p. 266), on the other hand, a much higher number of suicides than in Krose for the period 1896–1900: 1,808 suicides per year or 92 per million inhabitants instead of 360 per year or 21 per million. But von Mayr must have made an error, for 1,808 is

almost the total (and not the average) of suicides for these five years: he has forgotten to divide this sum by five. One could, however, remain perplexed when considering the number of suicides in Spain as enumerated by Enrico Ferri. Until 1905, he tells us, these figures are from the criminal statistics; however, only six of these numbers for the period 1883–1900 agree with those of Krose. After 1905, Ferri shows the number of suicides in Spain according to the statistics of the causes of death. Now they are three to four times higher. They pass sharply from 367 to 1,250 (this last figure corresponds to 67.5 suicides per million inhabitants). Now, von Mayr indicates 1,200 suicides for the period 1901–5 (Krose stops in 1900). But we are not at the end of our difficulties. For 1911–13, Ferri shows three figures whose average is 1,194 (statistics of causes of death). Now, in the *Handwörterbuch der Staatswissenschaft*, 979 suicides are shown for 1911–13 in Spain (according to the statistics of causes of death) and 1,924 (according to the judiciary statistics, or 66 per million). Has the *Handwörterbuch* cited its sources inaccurately and is the second figure drawn, like Ferri's figure, from the statistics of the causes of death? Then, on the next page, a total of 89 suicides per million inhabitants is shown for 1913 according to the judiciary statistics (instead of 66 for 1911–13), but *attempted suicides are included in it*. One sees what inextricable confusion the Spanish data present and the extent to which it is essential to use them only with precaution.

18 American cities of more than 100,000 inhabitants have been publishing statistics on the number of suicides each year regularly for the past twenty years. See p. 258 below.

19 This gap was partly filled for Turkey by Max Bonnafous, who, relying on police reports, compiled an enumeration of suicides in Constantinople from 1916 to 1926. The number of suicides appears to have increased very quickly from 27 in 1916 to 122 in 1921 and to 176 in 1926. This corresponds to nearly the proportion for a million inhabitants (the population of Constantinople scarcely exceeded this number in 1926). There are two recessions, in 1922 and 1925. The largest increase (100 per cent) takes place from 1918 to 1919.

20 René Maunier, published in *Metron*, 1 December 1926, the interesting 'Notes statistiques sur le suicide en Égypte (1887–1918)'. The weekly death bulletins assembled and published in the *Journal officiel* have been giving the number of deaths by suicide (by city, sex, age, etc.) since 1886 (with an interruption from 1901 to 1916). The proportion of voluntary deaths per million inhabitants was 5 in 1917 for the native population. Of all the countries that publish suicide statistics, therefore, Egypt would be the one in which fewest kill themselves. However, from 1913 to 1917 a proportion of attempts is enumerated equal to 130 for Cairo, 112 for Alexandria, 9 for the provinces of the Delta, and 4 for those of Said.

21 Prussia is, to our knowledge, the only country whose statistics indicate the place where the suicide occurred. In 1869–72, of 100 suicides whose location was known, 53.6 were done outside the house (7.5 in public establishments or places, barracks, reformatories, prisons, inns, etc.), 46.3 in private homes. But 21 per cent of the suicides could not be located. In 1907, all were located (except 1 per cent). Equal numbers are found then outside the home and within a private home. If suicides by drowning were discarded, the proportion outside would be much higher for men than for women. Let us add that in 1873–8, of 100 suicides in private houses, 66.6* are counted which were consummated in occupied dwellings, 35.4* in unoccupied dwellings. (Numbers calculated by us according to tables reproduced by Morselli and Father Krose.)

22 When Werther asks Albert in a note, 'Please loan me your pistols for a journey I am considering,' one can see in this only the contrivance of a novelist. It is so that Werther might cry, '... and you, Lotte, hand me the weapon – you, from

Sic – Tr.

whom I wished to receive death and now receive it. Oh, how I questioned my boy! You trembled, he said, as you handed them to him.' Nothing could be less plausible.

[Translation of Goethe's *Werther* by Catherine Hutter, New American Library edition, New York, 1962, p. 124 – Tr.]

23 In Prussia from 1871 to 1875, of 100 suicides by what are called sidearms (thrusting and cutting weapons), 77 cut their throats (*Halsabschneiden*), 9.5 stabbed themselves, 13.5 opened their veins. The proportions are the same for both sexes. According to the annual numbers reproduced by Morselli.

CHAPTER 2   A MEANS OF APPRAISAL: THE STUDY OF THE MODES OF SUICIDE

1 'But she did not take her eyes from the wheels of the second carriage. And exactly at the moment when the space between the wheels came opposite her, she dropped the red bag, and drawing her head back into her shoulders, fell on her hands under the carriage, and lightly, as though she would rise again at once, dropped on to her knees. And at the same instant she was terror-stricken at what she was doing. "Where am I? What am I doing? What for?" She tried to get up, to drop backwards; but something huge and merciless struck her on the head and rolled her on her back.' *Anna Karenina*, end of Part 7.

[Translation by Constance Garnett, The Modern Library edition, New York, p. 894 –Tr.]

2 Here, for each year from 1871 to 1875 in Prussia, is the proportion of 100 male suicides who cut their throats: 3.6, 3, 3.1, 2.7, 2.8. And for women: 2.8, 3.6, 3.3, 2.7, 2.2. Since the numbers involved are very small, their approximate constancy is indeed remarkable. From Morselli.

3 According to Krose, *Der Selbstmord im 19. Jahrhundert*, p. 79.

4 The figures which follow are our calculations from tables of Morselli, Krose, and von Mayr, who reproduce simply the proportions of averages of suicides, per 100 suicides.

5 This reasoning assumes that the Catholics in a country have exactly as many reasons as other inhabitants of the same country for choosing particular modes of death. But they may not. In Germany, for example, Catholics are proportionately more numerous in rural environments than in urban centers. Now, peasants do not tend to utilize the same means of suicide as city-dwellers. Hence, for the systematic concealment of a large number of Catholic suicides not to alter the average, it would have to be practiced *to the same extent* every year. One could, therefore, only conclude from the constancy of the modes of suicide, such as emerges from the statistics, that Catholics do not conceal any more suicides in one year than in another.

6 We must always note that the proportion of women who kill themselves is higher in England than elsewhere, and that suicides by soldiers are more scarce there. Now, women rarely use firearms to commit suicide, while soldiers do very often. These two reasons partly explain why suicides of this type are infrequent there.

7 Goethe, *Aus meinem Leben. Dichtung und Wahrheit*, Book XIII. On the particular aversion which suicides by hanging (and also by drowning) inspired, see Bayet, *Le Suicide et la morale*, 1922, pp. 99 and 295. 'Suicide by hanging is an impure death because it was originally a sacred death.'

8 We measure these gains and losses in numbers of points, and not in percentages, because we wish to know how many equal fractions (in hundredths) of a hundred suicides have passed from one category to another and how losses in one are counterbalanced by gains in the others.

9 It is strange that neither von Mayr nor Krose had thought to relate these two

facts (though well acquainted with them): on the one hand, the greater frequency of rural suicides in England by hanging, and on the other, the continuous decrease there of this type of voluntary death.

10 Of all the European countries, Norway and Denmark are the only ones where there is a decrease at the same time in the proportion of suicides by drowning and in the total number of suicides. Must one conclude from this that they are concealing a larger number of voluntary drownings than at first? In Norway, however, where the first decrease is slight, the measures taken against alcoholism were able to determine the second. In Denmark, on the other hand, the first decrease is stronger than anywhere else: from 24 drownings per hundred suicides in 1835–9 to 13 per cent in 1896–1900. Krose believes that a large number of these suicides are still being concealed there now. In Sweden, however, where suicides have increased, the proportion of drownings is hardly higher (15.4 per cent) and has decreased almost as fast.

11 In London, the proportion of desperate persons who drown themselves went from 14.3 per cent in 1846–50 to 20.8 per cent in 1872–6, or an increase of 46 per cent (in twenty-five years). In Paris, on the contrary, from 1817–25 to 1834–43 it diminished from 36.7 per cent to 21.4 per cent, or a decrease of 44 per cent (in twenty years), equal to the increased enumeration in England (however, the dates are not the same). In Milan, from 1821–32 to 1877, the proportion of suicides of this type decreased, in nearly fifty years, by 48 or 49 per cent, hence, much more slowly than in Paris. In Paris and in Milan about 1820, drownings were enormous: these numbers exceeded by far those which have since been enumerated in all the big cities (according to a table reproduced by Morselli).

12 We recall that in England this type of voluntary death includes, in 1889–93, only 27.7 per cent of all the suicides, instead of 47, the average for 16 nations (including England).

13 Averages for the following years: Norway, 1888–9; Denmark, 1890–4; Prussia, Switzerland, Italy, Saxony, Belgium, 1889–93; France, 1887–91; Spain (including, here, attempted suicides), 1881–4.

14 Had we included in the same calculation the four European states we have eliminated: Sweden, Bavaria, Württemberg, England, one would find the same relative deviation for suicides by drowning.

15 For cutting or piercing, etc., 14 nations; for poison, 15 nations; for jumping, 10; for asphyxiation, 8; for being run over, 11 nations.

16 Here are the main figures for these five nations for the following periods: Bavaria, 1887–90; Württemberg, Sweden, and England: 1889–93; Japan: 1887 to 1889–92.

	Hanging	Drowning	Firearms	Sidearms	Poison
Sweden	49.5	15.4	14	5.6	14.2
Bavaria	53.6	20.3	20.8	—	—
Württemberg	5.8	5.2	16.7	2.7	2.7
England	27.7	22.7	9.3	18.2	12.7
Japan	58.8	30.9	0.9	5.4	1

In Bavaria, the statistics relate only to the first three modes of suicide.

17 Attributable principally to women, who asphyxiate themselves three times as often as do men.

CHAPTER 3   ATTEMPTED SUICIDES

1 Von Mayr reproduced a certain number of facts on attempted suicides: in Vienna from 1901 to 1908 (106 abortive attempts per 100 committed suicides); in Munich from 1903 to 1909 (86 abortive attempts per 100 committed suicides; 39 female suicides are counted per 100 male suicides, and 85 female attempts per 100 male attempts); for Budapest, Brussels, Florence, London, and Buenos Aires (see below).

2 Maunier was able to study attempts in Egypt from police reports. According to figures he reproduced for 1917, 13.3 committed suicide per 100 attempts (successful or not) were counted among the Egyptian population and 37 per cent among the European population. But the modes of execution are quite different from those in Europe or Japan, where mechanical means predominate. In Egypt, more than 40 per cent of the native suicides are brought about by poisonings, principally with carbolic acid. Foreigners appear to utilize firearms more often. René Maunier, 'Notes statistiques sur le suicide en Égypte (1887–1918),' *Metron*, 1 December 1926, p. 12.

3 These numbers are taken from John Rice Miner's book. For France, Miner gives 17.7 for 1891–5 and 20.4 for 1901–5. Referring to the figures which are shown annually in the *Rapport sur l'administration de la justice criminelle en France*, and calculating the quinquennial averages, we find: 27.7 and 30.4. For the years 1910, 1911, and 1913, we find: 31.5. (However, as we do not have the data for 1909 and 1910 before us, we are not modifying the number shown by Miner.) We calculated the ratio for 1919–20 ourselves.

4 The ratio is 53 in Volga and Kama (Kazan), and Ural; 57 in Riazan and Toula; 59 in Volga; 60 in Northern Caucasus; 42.5 in the Moscow region which alone includes a sixth of all Russian suicides. From *Suicides en U.R.S.S. 1922–1925*, published in 1927 in Moscow. Certain figures may be partially explained by the Revolution since, for 1881–5 and 1886–90, von Mayr gives the ratios 28.9 and 30.2 for Russia. But as far back as this period, the figure 39.5 is reached in the Caucasus (47.8 in the districts) and 34.9 in Siberia (48 in the cities). These regions are indeed Asiatic. Von Mayr, *Moralstatistik*, pp. 298 and 300.

5 According to a *Sanitary Report* cited by von Mayr, *Moralstatistik*, p. 300. (No fewer than 11,112 suicides are concerned.)

6 We calculated the following numbers from the annual figures reproduced by von Mayr for Bavaria and by Morselli for Italy and England.

7 Von Mayr has been in communication with a Hungarian protective and rescue society (Freiwillige Rettungsgesellschaft) on a table indicating the distribution of modes of death among an annual average of 550 attempts completed in Budapest from 1903 to 1908. A small number of these (about an eighth) were followed by death. The attempts by poisoning represent 44 per cent of all attempts. Now, we do not know whether the two sexes are represented equally but, assuming that they are, we should obtain, according to the Roman figures, 47.5 or 54. The difference is not large (given the two very different cities). Nevertheless, one finds 30.4 per cent in Budapest for attempts by firearms. On the same hypothesis as above, the Roman figures (1920–2) should indicate 20 per cent. After this comparison the figures Bachi reproduced appear more credible.

8 Durkheim, *Suicide*, pp. 217, 234, 239.

9 *Der Selbstmord im österreichischen Heere, Deutsche Worte*, XIII, pp. 449f. See von Mayr, *Moralstatistik*, p. 295. Durkheim, who devoted only four pages to the 'style of death chosen by the suicide,' remarks in this connection, 'Man takes the path of least resistance ... and tends to employ the means of destruction most readily at hand and with which daily practice has familiarized him.' Thus it is that in England, according to a recent work by John Rice Miner, although 8 per cent of people who kill themselves do so with poison, 86 per cent of the

pharmacists and 85 per cent of the photographers who commit suicide choose this mode of suicide. In Milan, cooks kill themselves with knives, workmen who build bridges drown themselves.

According to the table compiled by Lisle for France in 1836–52, butchers, above all pork butchers, then artists, followed by metal workers, leather workers, and shoemakers kill themselves more than do others with the aid of thrusting and cutting tools. The proportion of suicides by asphyxiation is more than four times as high among laundrywomen as the average.

CHAPTER 4   THE DISTRIBUTION OF SUICIDES IN EUROPE

1 These numbers are taken from: Durkheim for 1866–70; Krose for 1836 to 1865 and for 1866 to 1900; *Handwörterbuch der Staatswissenschaften* for 1901 to 1905 and 1911 to 1913; *Statistisches Jahrbuch für das deutsche Reich* (volumes published in 1925–8) and *la Revue hongroise de statistique* (July 1928) for 1905 to 1906 and for 1922 to 1925.

2 1923–6.

3 1922–4.

4 1921–4.

5 1922–6.

6 The first category extends to 16 years of age, the second from 16 to 21.

7 Percentage increases. The rates of decrease are calculated by setting the lowest term, that is, the second, equal to 100.

8 It does not follow that there are grounds for correspondingly increasing the rate of Denmark proper, for it is calculated from this period on without taking account of Schleswig-Holstein. See Krose, *Der Selbstmord*, p. 48, note 1.

9 If very proximate terms, that is, very small deviations are concerned it would be better to calculate the *mean quadratic deviation*, also called the *standard deviation*, that is, to take the sum of the squares of the deviations, divide it by their number, and extract the square root of the quotient. In this way the importance of the largest deviations is increased and their value enhanced. But here, it will be seen, the deviations are always large enough, so that there is no ground for increasing them further.

10 Here is how to proceed. First calculate the ratio of suicide to the totality of the eleven countries (total of suicides divided by the population total). Multiply the number obtained by the population of each country. One obtains thus eleven numbers which show what the total number of suicides in each country would be if the suicide rate were the same throughout. Calculate the deviations among the eleven numbers, and the real numbers of suicides, in each country. Compute the sum of these deviations and divide them by the sum of all the suicides. It is all as though one had compared, not country with country, but fractions of countries each consisting of a million inhabitants, or, again, thirty-nine rates of suicide equal to the suicide rate in France, which counts 39 million inhabitants, 7 rates equal to the suicide rate in Belgium, which counts 7 million inhabitants, etc.

11 To calculate the adjusted indices we used the population figures in the censuses for the given years. For the intermediary years, when official publications did not show the population, we calculated it by interpolation.

12 The data for Spain are rather uncertain, as we have seen. For the years 1891–1905 we have had to substitute the suicide rate of 1906–10 for numbers obviously too low (15 to 20 instead of about 60, the average for 1906–25). All the numbers for the last period (1921–5) were calculated from the data of the *Statistisches Jahrbuch für das deutsche Reich*.

13 We are told in a note that the suicide rates shown for Denmark refer to the urban population only, except in 1919–22. Very likely this is an error. For

neither Krose nor von Mayr, who show these same rates (Krose until 1900, von Mayr for 1901–7), makes the same remark. The rates for Denmark are shown in Krose (*Der Selbstmord*, p. 70) by districts which correspond to these numbers. Now, these figures indeed appear to be calculated in relation to the total population. The strong decrease in the suicide rates in Denmark from 1914 to 1919–22 (a decrease of 25 per cent) can be explained by the return to Denmark of a part of Schleswig-Holstein. On the other hand, while we are not told so, we know that the Austrian suicide rate after 1914 refers to Austria's actual boundaries. (This explains why it seems to increase during the war, although it strongly decreased.) Finally, the figures for Spain are very irregular and, in general, very much lower. See our remarks in this respect, pp. 332–3, note 17.

14   1919–21.
15   Instead of 145 and 140, numbers published in the *Handwörterbuch*.
16   The urban population only, except in 1919–22.
17   1919–20.
18   For a part of the nation only. In 1911–13 and 1914–18, 24 states. In 1920–2, 35 states.
19   1920–2.
20   After 1915, only the suicides of civilians.
21   1841–50.
22   1923. Northern Ireland and the Free State.

CHAPTER 5   THE DISTRIBUTION OF SUICIDES IN FRANCE

1   For France, from 1872–6 to 1911–13.
2   *Tableau géographique de la France*, in *L'Histoire de France*, by Lavisse.
3   Stendhal, *Vie de Henri Brulard*, Champion edition, 1913, vol. 1, p. 240.

CHAPTER 6   THE DISTRIBUTION OF SUICIDES IN GERMANY, ITALY, AND
            ENGLAND

1   In *Der Selbstmord*, map plate.
2   Refer also to the map of suicides in Germany drawn up by provinces and states for the period 1903–13, [*Sic.* – Tr.], reproduced below on page 174.
3· Durkheim drew a map of suicides in central Europe (p. 395 of his book) based on Morselli, but does not tell us to what period the numbers he reproduces refer. For the Prussian provinces he borrowed from a table corresponding to 1868–74. Though the suicide rate in Silesia appears on this map to be only average, it is actually very high in the districts of Liegnitz and Breslau (over 325 in 1891–1900) and very low in Oppeln (from 76 to 125). It is as though one were to join together Seine-et-Oise and Vendée in France.
4   We also note that suicide rates at Lübeck, Bremen, and Hamburg are very high in 1903–13: 332 suicides per million inhabitants in Lübeck, 370 in Bremen, and 357 in Hamburg. The last two are the highest of the whole series (in 1903–13: Berlin, 340; Brandenburg and the kingdom of Saxony, 320; Schleswig-Holstein, 311; the province of Saxony, 317, etc.).
5   See Krose, *Der Selbstmord*. Actually, we calculated the average of the rates of suicide and not, more correctly, the average suicide rate for the totality of these eleven years. We do not know what procedure Father Krose followed; but there appears to be no necessity for findings that are obtained by these two methods to be very different.
6   Must we take the large Slavic population of these German regions into account to explain this exception? Studying the influence of race on suicide, Father Krose arrived at the following results for the period 1881–90. He classified the

European population into four large ethnic groups. From these he subtracts regions in each nation 'peopled allogeneously,' such as Posen and Bromberg in Germany, and Corsica and Brittany in France. He links part of Austria, Holland, etc. to Germany and finds for 92 million Teutons a suicide rate of 158; for 87 million people in the romantic countries, 113; for 12 million Celts, 55; for 93 million Slavs, 30. However, comparing the most purely Polish part of Posnania with Münster, which is purely German but just as Catholic and just as agricultural, he found for the 816,103 Poles a suicide rate of 71 per million and for the 493,147 Germans a rate of 69 per million. Religious persuasion and style of life (urban or rural) exerted, therefore, a greater influence than race. Krose, *Die Ursachen*, pp. 52–4.

7 Mario Bonsegna, *Il suicidio in Italia dal 1864 al 1918. Studio statistico*, Ostuni, 1924, p. 13.

8 The counties included in each group are as follows: southeast: Surrey, Kent, Sussex, Hampshire, Berkshire; south central: Middlesex, Hertford, Buckingham, Oxford, Northampton, Huntingdon, Bedford, Cambridge; east: Essex, Suffolk, Norfolk; southwest: Wiltshire, Dorset, Devon, Cornwall, Somerset; west central: Gloucestershire, Hereford, Shropshire, Stafford, Worcester, Warwickshire; north central: Leicester, Rutland, Lincolnshire, Nottinghamshire, Derbyshire; northwest: Cheshire, Lancashire, Yorkshire: West Riding, East Riding, North Riding; north: Durham, Northumberland, Cumberland, Westmorland; Wales: Monmouthshire, South Wales, North Wales.

9 Included in these English figures, along with the committed suicides, are the attempts which have been the object of judicial proceedings (felo de se), but which represent only an insignificant proportion, 2 or 3 per cent, of the total number of suicides.

10 Albert Demangeon, *Iles Britanniques*, vol. 1 of the *Geographie Universelle* (Colin), 1927, p. 20. The citations which follow are taken from this work. See Map 5.

11 Actually, four-fifths of the workers in wool in Great Britain are concentrated in the West Riding.

12 These wolds are the continuation beyond the Wash of the chalk cliff which begins in Berkshire, continues to the north of the Thames under the name of the Chiltern Hills, and slopes downward in the counties of Cambridge and Norfolk. See Demangeon, *op. cit.*, p. 208.

13 'South of the Thames, the Berkshire Downs present, facing north, a continuous front of cliffs at times exceeding 300 meters in altitude and rising to more than 200 meters above the plains of the Upper Thames. Their steep slopes, which are covered by a short grass and strewn with juniper bushes, resist cultivation. On the surface of the plateau, the flinty clay yields a rocky soil where rabbit warrens and sandy moors persist, and which must sometimes be cleared of stones prior to cultivation' (*ibid.*, p. 208).

14 The suicide rate in Devon would be lower had there not been to the south of this county an urban concentration formed of three towns: Plymouth, Stonehouse, and Devonport, or 210,000 inhabitants out of 710,000 for the entire county.

15 We are eliminating Bedfordshire, one of the smallest counties. With Durham, it has the lowest suicide rate, 82, in England, excluding Wales. The reason, as we have seen, is that this region is largely hilly. The highest suicide rate in all England, 129, is in Northamptonshire, which is contiguous. Norfolk has almost the same rate, 128. Northampton is the center of a very industrial region – heavy industry. Important iron mines and blast furnaces are grouped around this city at Banbury, Wellingborough, etc.

16 See Demangeon, *op. cit.*, pp. 280–1.

17 Middlesex, Surrey, Warwickshire, Derbyshire, Northumberland, Cheshire, Kent, Nottinghamshire, Sussex, Lancashire, Leicestershire, and the West Riding of Yorkshire.

18 We eliminated five counties whose populations increased greatly but whose suicide rates are below average: Essex, Durham, South Wales, Hampshire, and Hertfordshire. If Essex and Hampshire, whose suicide rates barely diverge from the average, are joined to the counties which have been retained, we obtain 32 per cent as the average increase in the suicide rates.

CHAPTER 7   THE DISTRIBUTION OF SUICIDES IN CITIES AND COUNTRYSIDE

1 If a number of countries are arrayed in two series, for example, as here, by increasing density of population and increasing frequency of suicides, each country can occupy the same rank in each series. The average distance between the two ranks will then be zero, the coefficient of maximal correspondence. If they occupy ranks as different as possible in the two series the average distance will be half the number of these countries (or smaller by a tiny fraction): the coefficient of maximal opposition. When the average distance is half of this last coefficient, that is, equals a quarter of the number of countries, we will assume that there is no relationship between the two rankings: this is the coefficient of independence. It is easy to see to which of these three coefficients a particular average effective distance approximates. We employ this rapid and sufficiently accurate calculation frequently in what follows.

[The following table compiled by the translator from figures given on pp. 109–10 illustrates Halbwachs's reasoning – Tr.]

Variable related to suicide	Coefficient of opposition ($^1/_2$n = maximal)	Average effective distance (Mean distance between ranks)	Coefficient of independence ($^1/_4$m = maximal)	Degree of correspondence (o = maximal distance)
Density (Krose, Table XXI)	11	6.3	5.5	o
Germany	35.5	19.7	17.75	o
Urbanization	9.5	5.52	4.75	o
Cities of 50,000 or more	9.5	5.15	4.75	o

2 We are not told how cities and countryside are distinguished except in Germany (the first two numbers), where cities have more than 15,000 inhabitants.

3 The following relative numbers for cities were drawn from data for 1850 and subsequent years, reproduced by A. Wagner: Prussia, 184; Württemberg, 188; Hanover, 165. (The meaning of these numbers is the same as in our text.)

4 Morselli's figures are given for the first three periods. The period 1897–1902 does not include 1898 or 1901, and the period 1905–11 does not include 1909. The suicide rates for each year are based upon the urban and rural populations

of the most proximate quinquennial census. Each calculated rate is the average of the annual rates.

5 *Statistique sanitaire de la France, Année 1912*, published in 1915 by the Board of Public Assistance and Hygiene of the Ministry of the Interior, gives figures on death by suicide in France in cities of 5,000 inhabitants or more, and in cities of less than 5,000, for each year from 1906 to 1912 inclusive. These figures (undoubtedly obtained from the death certificates) are noticeably smaller, by 10 to 16 per cent, than the figures of the criminal court. We calculated the average rate of suicide during this period for the populations of the two categories of cities. Setting the average proportion of suicides in cities of less than 5,000 equal to 100, we find, for cities of more than 5,000 inhabitants, 116, instead of the 122 that results from comparing for the same period cities of more than 2,000 with agglomerations of less than 2,000. We assume from this that the distance diminishes as the dividing line between more populated and less populated cities rises.

6 From a table reproduced in *la Revue hongroise de statistique*, July 1928, p. 726.

7 We assume a suicide rate in the 'other municipalities' equal to 100.

8 The numbers in this table refer only to 1920. But we can make the same calculations for the average of the suicides in Czechoslovakia during the four years 1923–6 (data are lacking for 1921 and 1922). We obtain the ratios of the suicide rates in cities of 10,000 inhabitants to those in the other cities: Bohemia, 122; Moravia, 158; Silesia, 146; Slovakia, 259; Subcarpathian Russia, 286. These numbers are lower collectively and individually than the figures in column 5. Like them, however, they increase proportionately as one passes to less urban regions. Silesia is the sole exception but, like Subcarpathian Russia, its population is small (each has less than a twentieth of the Republic), and its absolute number of suicides is very small. The suicide rates for the whole Republic and for Bohemia alone have been as follows:

	Number of suicides per million inhabitants						Increase from 1919 to 1926 (per cent)
	1919	1920	1923	1924	1925	1926	
Czecho-slovakia	209	233	261	250	265	295	42
Bohemia	280	320	335	320	327	378	35

9 The proportion of suicides in the large and small cities of Russia during 1925 follow. For every million inhabitants:

	Men	Women
Leningrad	431.1	201.8
Moscow	311.6	145
Large cities	276	136.4
Small cities	55.8	25.7

Large and small cities are not defined. See *Suicides en U.R.S.S. en 1922–1925*, U.R.S.S. Statistique, vol. XXV, book 1, section on moral statistics, Moscow, 1927, 177, p. 14.

The proportions of rural and urban suicides in the United States from 1914 to 1917 follow (John Rice Miner, p. 29, Table XXIII):

Suicides per million inhabitants in the United States (Registration states)

	1914	1915	1916	1917
Cities	194	191	169	159
Rural localities	128	133	110	103

10 In 1920, the suicide rate in Prague was 410 but in Czechoslovakia it was 233, or in relative numbers, 176 and 100. It was 320 in the province of Bohemia and 270 in Prague and its suburbs, or in relative numbers, 100 and 85.

In 1923–5 there were 465 suicides per million inhabitants in Budapest, and 289 in Hungary, or in relative numbers, 161 and 100. If the 356 suicides in the region between the Danube, Tisza, and Tarna rivers (excluding Nograd County) are set equal proportionately to 100, the relative number for Budapest was 130.

11 Based on the work of John Rice Miner, we calculated the proportion of suicides in New York in 1906–14 (1909 not included). There were 6,300 suicides out of 4,686,000 inhabitants, giving a suicide rate of 135. The suicide rate in the United States (Registration area) in the same period was 160. Assuming the rate for the United States equal to 100, the New York rate was therefore 84.5. It would clearly be higher, though always below 100, if compared to the suicide rate for New York State. (We have data for 1915–19 only, or 148. However, suicides have diminished greatly in the United States since 1916.) In general, the southern states have low rates; the far-western states high rates (287 in California in 1915–19). Suicide rates are much higher among the foreign-born inhabitants of New York (who are 42 per cent) than for the Americans living in this city: 345 for the English, 497 for the French, and 678 for the Germans, against 109 for the Americans and only 106 for the Italians.

12 In comparing the suicide rates of large cities and surrounding regions, we must take into account the respective compositions of the two populations as regards sex, age, marital status, religion, economic situation, etc. These are by no means the same in both places. The suicide rate in Paris, Berlin, Vienna, Rome, and New York is even lower than in neighboring districts or territories because the proportion of adults and women is higher, and that of the elderly lower, in very big cities than in the smaller cities nearest to them. Nevertheless, social conditions in the region resulting from proximity to the big cities do contribute to the frequency of suicides.

13 Hungary in 1920 contains three cities with over 100,000 inhabitants. The suicide rates in 1923–5 are respectively: 289 in Hungary, 465 in Budapest, 486 in Szeged, 582 in Debrecen, or, in relative numbers, 100, 161, 169, and 202. The rates for Hódmezővásárhely and Pécs (613 and 640 per million, or, in relative numbers, 214 and 222) are undoubtedly the highest that can be found in suicide statistics up to the present.

14 All of the figures were calculated by me from Table IVa of Bonsegna's study, *Il suicidio in Italia dal 1864 al 1918*, showing the suicide rate for each of the largest Italian cities annually from 1901 to 1914, as well as for the five-year period 1896–1900.

15 Average suicide rate for the cities considered.

16 These numbers are calculated by setting equal to 100 the suicide rate in the province where each city is located and taking the average of the numbers obtained for these cities.

17 How far does the influence of big cities extend? It does not seem to extend to the smallest localities. A table reproduced by Bonsegna shows the number of suicides per 10,000 inhabitants: 1. in 206 towns, judicial seats of provinces, and districts where this proportion should have increased from 1.2 in 1898–1901 to 1.4 on the average in 1902–13, or an increase of 17 per cent (almost as much as for the whole of Italy); 2. in 8,000 other, less important towns. Here, only one decimal place is given for very small numbers (less than unity) so that we can only fix the probable upper and lower limits of increase: 0 per cent and 19 per cent, or a probable increase of 9.5 per cent. A table reproduced by Morselli shows the suicide rate in 1877 in cities and in the countryside (less than 2,000 inhabitants) by province. The distance is greatest by far in Latium (Rome), than in Lombardy and Piedmont where, since this period, the largest number of urban industrial centers are found.

18 The rural proportion of the population falls from 80 per cent in 1770 to 50 in 1850, 35 in 1871, 22 in 1911. While 215 inhabitants per 1,000 live by agricultural work in France, the United Kingdom retains no more than 56.

19 We have calculated the simple coefficient of dispersion. The corresponding relative numbers follow (100 = the suicide rate or coefficient of dispersion in 1870–6):

	Average suicide rate		Coefficient of dispersion	
	1870–6	1920–6	1870–6	1920–6
1st group	100	154	100	32.3
2nd group	100	136	100	33.3
3rd group	100	162	100	59.9
4th group	100	155	100	93

20 Population growth has the same effect in each group. We calculated the increase from 1870–6 to 1920–6:

	Population in thousands of inhabitants		
	1870–6	1920–6	Percentage increase
1st group (Liverpool, etc.)	8,330	14,115	69
2nd group (London, etc.)	5,720	9,757	70
3rd group (Oxford, etc.)	2,940	3,494	19
4th group (Norfolk, etc.)	1,770	2,148	21

Suicide rates are most similar in the first two groups, where the population increased the most. The first group is the largest. We calculated the convergence in rates of suicide of the five counties of this group whose population increases were greatest. (These counties are Warwickshire, Leicestershire, Nottinghamshire, Lancashire, and Cheshire: their population went from 4,660,000 to 8,470,000, an increase of 81 per cent.) The dispersion in the suicide rates in these five counties decreased from 9.8 to 3.1 or, in relative numbers, from 100 to 31.5. In the five counties of this same group whose population increased least, the dispersion in the rates of suicide decreased from 10.2 to 5.5 or, in relative numbers, from 100 to 54. Thus, the greater the population increase in a group of counties, the greater the tendency for suicide rates to converge toward a level common to all the counties.

CHAPTER 8   SUICIDE AND THE FAMILY

1 'That married people are more often exposed to suicide than the unmarried is an idea often found in ancient works on suicide.' Krose, *Die Ursachen*, p. 93.
2 This table was prepared from an original study of 25,000 records of suicides maintained in the Ministry of Justice. Mauss did this tabulation alone. See in Durkheim, Table XXI, p. 178, and the corresponding Table XX for Oldenburg, p. 177. These data are particularly valuable because they have not been collected since Durkheim was able to study them. Before 1892 the public prosecutors sent to the Ministry of Justice as many individual forms, on which age and marital status were shown, as there were suicides. Since then the Ministry only receives tables which do not relate age and marital status to one another.
3 Durkheim calculated what he calls the *coefficient of preservation* of the spouses, meaning, in relation to the unmarried, for example, 'the number showing how many fewer in one group kill themselves than in another.' When the decimal point is omitted these coefficients really represent the relative numbers obtained for the unmarried and the widowed by setting the suicide rate of the spouses equal to 100 and, for the unmarried, by setting the suicide rate of the widowed equal to 100.
4 Age: for the husbands and unmarried men aged 15 to 20, Durkheim found relative numbers of 100 and 22, which proved that precocious marriage strengthened the suicidal tendency among men. For wives and unmarried women the reverse is the case: 100 for the wives and 239 for the unmarried women. This seems rather natural.
5 Ogburn, in a recent statistical study of marriage in America, observes that the death rate is higher for the unmarried than for spouses, age held constant. However, it is much higher for men: twice as high for men from 30 to 50 years of age, and almost twice as high for those from 50 to 70 years of age. As a result, the difference is very low for women: a death rate of 6.3 for women and 7.4 for unmarried women from 30 to 40 years of age. These data are for New York State, excluding New York City, in 1910. Comparing the married and the unmarried, he makes the same observation about criminality and about insanity. The distance between the two sexes always favors the men, who are better protected by marriage, but is smaller for insanity than for death and criminality. On the whole, marriage protects men more than it does women. Groves and Ogburn, *American Marriage and Family Relationships*, New York, 1928, pp. 137f.
6 In France, widows seem to be even less protected against suicide than single girls (see the total). However, this is only true from 25 to 40 years of age and over 60. From 20 to 25 years of age and from 40 to 60, widows appear to cling to life more than the unmarried women do. It may be that when very young they have greater hopes of remarriage, and when elderly are accustomed to the condition.
7 Durkheim questioned the Swedish statistics. (See *Suicide*, p. 175, note 8.) He called attention to several findings in the new Swedish table published by Krose which 'left him skeptical.' (See *Année sociologique*, XI (1906–9), pp. 512–13.) These improbabilities are undoubtedly due to the fact that for so small a country the statistics covered too short a period: 1891–4. Von Mayr's table for 1891–1900

does not show these improbabilities. There was no reason to ignore the Swedish data when based on more than 7,200 suicides.

8 The Norwegian population of $2^{1}/_{2}$ million inhabitants produced on the average 131 suicides per year from 1881 to 1895. This statistic is therefore based on 2,602 suicides. The proportion of voluntary deaths there was then 67 per million, which is one of the lowest rates observed in Europe at this period. Denmark produced 250 per million inhabitants during the same years, and Sweden 150 in 1891–1900.

9 Note also in Kürten's book a statistic of suicides by age and marital status for Saxony in 1908–9. Here, however, the age groups are larger. Here too the unmarried and widows of both sexes kill themselves more than do the married, at every age. Contrary to Durkheim's table, however, after thirty years the coefficient of preservation of married women in relation to unmarried would be higher than for the men.

10 The numbers in the first four columns are from Krose (*Die Ursachen*, p. 100). The relative numbers in the other columns were calculated by us.

11 Here are the same results for 1891–1900:

	Married	Unmarried	Widows	Widows	Unmarried
Men	100	184	255	100	73
Women	100	144	176	100	68

The gaps between the married and unmarried of both sexes are a little narrower than in France. Otherwise, all the stated findings are confirmed by these new figures.

12 For Switzerland in 1891–1900 we find [*Sic.* As in the Table to note 11 – Tr.]:

	Married	Unmarried	Widows	Unmarried
Men	100	184	100	73
Women	100	144	100	68

These numbers confirm the propositions formulated.

13 In Switzerland for the period 1891–1900 the difference between married and unmarried women is indeed at maximum from 20 to 29 years of age. It then diminishes, though only by a third. From 40 to 49 it increases a little, as in the provinces of France. Then, however, as in 1881–91, it again diminishes and disappears. The essential fact is that it diminishes from 20 to 60 years of age in the proportion of 100 to 42, exactly as in 1881–91.

14 Let us make the same calculation for the Danish and Scandinavian countries. If the difference between the suicide rate of unmarried and married women is equal to 100, the differences between the unmarried and married men are:

Sweden   122
Norway   138
Denmark   109

15 These numbers were calculated from 19,283 suicides by married people and

6,226 by widows. The proportions in each category per 100 married and per 100 widowed suicides are as follows:

Men			
Married without children	32.4	Widowers without children	34.2
Married with children	67.6	Widowers with children	65.8
Total	100.0		100.0

Women			
Married without children	39	Widows without children	40.6
Married with children	61	Widows with children	59.4
Total	100		100.0

16 The difference is much less when widowers and widows are concerned, whether with or without children, though always to the advantage of the women. The relative numbers are 198 for widowers and 229 for widows, or a ratio equal to only 1.15. Let us add that the relative numbers calculated by Durkheim which were based on suicide rates for 1889–91 are rather close: for married men, 192; for married women, 280; or a ratio of 1.46; for widowers, 134; for widows, 174; or a ratio of 1.3.

17 *Revue hongroise de statistique*, July 1928, p. 734. We are reproducing this table in a form different from the one adopted and are eliminating the numbers which refer to divorces.

18 Von Mayr, *Statistik und Gesellschaftslehre*, 3rd edition, 1909, p. 72.

19 Bourdon, 'La Statistique des familles norvégiennes au recensement de 1920', *Journal de la Societé de statistique de Paris*, Nov. and Dec. 1925 and Jan.

20 It took us a while to understand the meaning of this table, found on p. 27 of Rodine's introductory study of suicides in the U.S.S.R. in 1922–5, because the decimal point had by mistake been displaced to the left in each of the numbers, which were obviously too small. We had taken this into account, though hesitating to note the fact until we had found data in absolute numbers which would permit establishing the error and recomputing all the calculations. These numbers appear to be for two of the three years 1922–4 (total suicides: 12,125; suicides in 1925 numbered 6,303).

21 'In France, married but childless women commit suicide half as often again as unmarried women of the same age' (Durkheim, *op. cit.*, p. 188). That is, for every 2 suicides of unmarried women there are 3 suicides of married women of the same age. The ratio hardly seems lower in Russia (see the totals of the preceding table).

22 We are obviously formulating a hypothesis by assuming that the coefficient of preservation of married men without children relative to the unmarried is the same in Russia as in France. However, it is unlikely to be much smaller, as would be the case were unmarried women to kill themselves noticeably less than do married women without children.

23 We recall that the ratio of suicides for women compared to men is 48.5 compared to 100.

24 Birthrate in Russia:

Old Russia (per 1,000 inhabitants)		Soviet Union (per 1,000 inhabitants)	
1891–1900	49.2	1923	45.5
1901–10	46.4	1924	43.4
		1925	45.5
		1926	44.1

The birthrates in 1891–1900 were 36.1 in Germany, 35 in Italy, 29.9 in England, and 22.2 in France. These are maxima which are far from having since been attained. The rates in 1913 for these four countries were, respectively, 27.4, 31.7, 24.1, and 18.8.

CHAPTER 9   SUICIDE AND RELIGION

1 We note, however, that in Hungary in 1901–8 the proportions of suicides committed per year per million inhabitants of each religious persuasion were as follows. (Austria has not indicated the religion of suicides since 1865.)

Reformed Protestants	363
Evangelical Protestants	259
Israelites	166
Roman Catholics	158
Greek Orthodox	91
General average	177

Suicides by Jews remain relatively few.

2 *Année sociologique*, XI, 1906–9, p. 513.

3 'In Amsterdam, the number of deaths due to suicide per 100,000 inhabitants in 1905–14 was 8.2 among the Protestants, 5.1 among the Catholics, and 9.7 among the Israelites.' H. Van Zanten, 'Quelques Données démographiques sur les Juifs d'Amsterdam,' *Metron*, V (1925), pp. 36–68.

4 The numbers in columns 7, 8, and 9 show the relative value of Protestant suicide rates assuming the suicide rate of Catholics is equal to 100.

5 The numbers in column 10 show the relative value of the numbers in column 8, assuming each of those in column 7 equal to 100; the numbers in column 11 show the relative value of the numbers in column 9, assuming each of those in column 8 equal to 100. They measure the increase or decrease in the ratio of suicide rates of Protestants compared to Catholics.

6 Assuming the Catholic rate is equal to 100.

7 Here is the proportion of suicides in Bavaria by religious persuasion at different periods (according to von Mayr):

Suicides in Bavaria per million inhabitants of each persuasion

	Catholics	Protestants	Jews	Ratio of Catholic suicide rate to Protestant
1844–56	49	135	106	276
1870–9	74	194	115	263
1880–9	95	222	186	234
1890–9	93	210	212	225
1900–8	102	221	253	217

It is rather odd that the ratio of Protestant suicides to Catholic, which diminished from 100 to 78 in Prussia, has also diminished in exactly the same proportion, 100 to 78.5, in Bavaria during the same interval, 1855 to 1900–8. The suicide rate increased in almost the same proportions in Prussia and Bavaria for Catholics, from 100 to 202 and 207 respectively, and for Protestants from 100 to 158 and 164 respectively.

8 Krose, *Konfessionsstatistik Deutschlands mit einem Rückblick auf die numerische Entwickelung der Konfessionen im 19. Jahrhundert*, 1904.

9 Protestant suicide rate, assuming the Catholic suicide rate equals 100.

10 Legoyt, *Le Suicide ancien et moderne*, p. 113.

11 Bayet, *Le Suicide et la morale*, pp. 788–91.

12 Durkheim, *Suicide*, p. 170.

13 'Contribution à une étude sur la représentation collective de la mort,' *Année sociologique*, X (1907), pp. 48ff. Reproduced in 'Mélanges d'histoire des religions et de folklore,' by the same author, *Travaux de l'année sociologique*, 1929.

14 *Ibid.*, p. 97.

15 Bayet, *op. cit.*, pp. 330ff.

16 *Loc. cit.*, p. 369.

17 According to Bayet, the horror of suicide among the common people at the beginning of the Christian era is explained by the fact that the Romans, though recognizing the right of free men to kill themselves, punished suicide among their slaves by depriving them of burial. The disgrace of punishment will become linked increasingly to the act itself. We do not believe, however, that so strong a collective sentiment as this was not spontaneous.

18 Febvre, *Luther: un destin*, Paris, 1928.

19 Max Weber, 'The Protestant Ethic and the Spirit of Capitalism,' in *Collected Essays on the Sociology of Religion*, vol. I, 1920 (published in the form of an article in 1904–5).

20 Albrecht Penck, 'Das deutsche Reich,' in *Unser Wissen von der Erde. Länderkunde von Europa*, 1st edition, Prague and Leipzig, 1886.

21 *Ibid.*, p. 130.

22 Von Mayr, *op. cit.*, p. 329.

23 Moreover, it includes a rather high proportion of Poles.

24 Munich in 1885 is a city of artists and craftsmen. (Our statistics of suicide in Bavaria are for 1870–99.) The population then did not exceed 260,000 inhabitants. Only 12 per cent of it lives off commerce. In comparison with other large cities, this is a low proportion. Less than 45 per cent of the population is engaged in industry. An eighth of the total population, including 20,000 in the suburbs, consists of Protestants who migrated here since the beginning of the century, *Op. cit.*, p. 196.

25 'Population density is greater in the Palatinate than in any of the other mountainous regions of southwest Germany: 100 inhabitants per kilometer almost everywhere. The local agriculture does not produce enough to feed them: from 35 to 40 per cent of the population is engaged in industry, especially in textiles.' *Op. cit.*, p. 248. (All of this relates to 1886.)

26 Krose, *Die Ursachen*, p. 154.

27 Austria classified suicides by religious persuasion in 1851–9 and in 1865. However, these data antedate the reform introduced into this type of enumeration in 1872. National, cultural, and similar differences are more profound in Austria than elsewhere. It is impossible not to take them into account and they obscure the entire problem. This time Father Krose recognized as much, undoubtedly because the distance between Catholics and Protestants in Austria appeared quite small: 52.4 suicides per million Catholics compared with 64.2 per million Protestants, a ratio of 100 to 122. In Vienna in 1869–78 the Catholic rate was found to be 232 and the Protestant rate, 303, a

ratio of 100 to 130. Here again, we must look to see if Protestants are proportionately more numerous in commerce and industry.

28 Reproduced by von Mayr on p. 344 and by Krose on p. 158. Durkheim did not have these data. He reproduced a summary (*op. cit.*, p. 154) of statistics of suicide in Switzerland by canton and religious persuasion. He does not classify the population as industrial, agricultural, or mixed. Nor does he indicate the date, which must be much earlier than for our table.

29 Relative distances represent the Protestant suicide rates, setting the Catholic suicide rate equal to 100.

30 On Christian suicide, see Bayet, *op. cit.*, pp. 227–32.

31 The following, which became available only after this chapter was printed, must be added to the data reproduced above on pp. 157ff.

In 1926, suicide rates in Prussia by religious persuasion were Catholic, 148; Protestant, 294; Jews, 505 (*Zeitschrift des Preuss. stat. Landesamt*, Parts 3 and 4, 1929). Thus the distance between Catholics and Protestants continues to diminish. The ratio of Catholic to Protestant suicide rates falls from 250 in 1901–7 to 190 (see p. 160). The suicide rate of the Jews, meanwhile, increased constantly, and very strongly.

CHAPTER 10 SUICIDE AND HOMICIDE

1 There are inaccuracies in these tables. For example, he shows 3,602 suicides in France for 1846, whereas there had been only 3,102; and 9,332 for 1906 instead of 9,232; for Germany, he shows 13,664 in 1921 instead of 12,764. These are errors of transcription. But his figures for Prussia for the period 1869–82 are noticeably higher than those of Father Krose, who drew his data from the *Preussische Statistik* and does not seem to have made an error. For the period 1874–9 Enrico Ferri reproduced Morselli's figures (which, according to his bibliography, seem taken largely from secondhand sources). We do not know his sources from 1875 to 1882: they are higher by a seventh on the average than the numbers of Krose, who were well situated for access to good sources.

2 Tarde earlier remarked that the decline of the homicide curve in Italy in 1868 coincided with a decline, and not a rise, in the suicide [the original text reads 'homicide' here, a typographical error – Tr.] curve. *La Criminalité comparée*, 1890, p. 166.

3 As for France, Tarde wrote in 1890 that the horizontal and barely irregular curve of homicide generally corresponds to, and never at all opposes, the more accentuated undulation of the strongly ascendant curve of suicides. *Loc. cit.*

4 For Spain, Morselli's figures are unclear and, for the reasons already indicated, we can hardly make anything of them. However, we reproduce the following data from Bernaldo de Quiros, *Alrededor de delito y de la pena*, Madrid, 1904, first essay: 'el homicidio en España,' p. 27.

Periods	Annual average number of suicides	of homicides
1885–9	514	824
1890–4	448	369
1895–9	400	726
1900	551	810

If these figures are correct, suicides and homicides vary in the same direction between the first and second periods, and in opposite directions between the second and third.

5 In the German statistics, crimes and misdemeanors against the person are distinguished from injuries. Below are their absolute numbers. We also show the number of thefts and embezzlements so that one can better evaluate, through comparison, the importance of other crimes and misdemeanors mentioned, and their progression.

	1882–91	1892–1901	1902–11
Crimes and misdemeanors against the person	1,305	1,518	1,867
Injuries	74,129	114,997	127,811
Thefts and embezzlements	108,405	115,740	132,762

However, according to the comprehensive work of the Office of Criminal Statistics of Germany, published in 1901, murders, major crimes against the person, and even against property, have lost ground: the increase concerns above all petty violence (injuries, blows) and stealthy offenses. Paul Frauenstaedt, *Zwanzig Jahre Kriminalstatistik. Zeitschrift für Sozialwissenschaften*, 1905.

6 This appears to be the result of the following numbers drawn from a table reproduced by von Mayr, *op. cit.*, p. 829. In Germany we find:

		Per hundred thousand	
		Protestants	Catholics
Severe injuries	1882–91	130.2	227.7
	1892–1901	185.5	314.1
Simple theft	1882–91	242.6	280.5
	1892–1901	218.6	254.1

That makes for a distance (on the average) of 100 to 172 in the first case, and of 100 to only 116 in the second.

7 We calculated the distance between the ranks occupied by states and provinces when arrayed in two series according to the decreasing proportion of suicides and severe injuries enumerated.

8 Departments within parentheses exceed the limits indicated by a little bit.

9 Durkheim, *Suicide*, pp. 355–8.

10 In Corsica, the decrease is almost continuous:

1895	62	1910	56
1896	54	1911	39
1897	43	1920	22
1898	45		

CHAPTER 11 THE EFFECT OF WARS AND POLITICAL CRISES: FLUCTUA-
TIONS IN FRENCH SUICIDES

1 Father Krose, ordinarily more objective, quoted a prediction formulated in 1882 by the moralistic Protestant statistician Oettingen: 'One has only to draw all the consequences of the principles of Paul Bert to ascertain in a few years

that a generation formed in France by the public secular school furnished an exceptional contingent of suicides.' He adds, 'The facts have verified this prophecy' (p. 143). Now, if we assume that the secular school, established in 1882–3, did not produce its initial effects until after 1885, the following is established: in the thirty-five years prior to 1885, that is, since 1850, the suicide rate increased by over 100 per cent. In the thirty-five or thirty-seven years following 1885, if we take, not the figures for the war years or immediately after the war, which are obviously too low, but the highest figures, we find that the suicide rate did not increase exceptionally but only by a quarter (by 25 per cent). Rather, it tends to stabilize. It would also be unscientific to pretend that the introduction of the secular school had the effect of slackening the growth of suicides. Let us add that in Germany, where there were no secular schools, the suicide count per million inhabitants was 220 in 1901–5 and 228 in 1923. These figures are rather close to those enumerated in France in the fifteen years preceding the war.

2 As it might be assumed that the diminution of suicides in France during the war only applies to servicemen, whose suicides during this period were harder to enumerate, we reproduce Table 11.3 (p. 209) from the work of John Rice Miner. This table shows that suicides in England diminished for both sexes in 1916 and 1917 and, for the men, even since 1915. They also diminished for all age-groups. We note that in England during the war only civilian suicides were enumerated.

3 Note that to compensate for the decrease from 100 to 66, an increase from 66 to 100 would be needed, that is, from 100 to 151, or 51 per cent.

4 Figures were calculated for the period following the war, excluding the departments of Haut-Rhin, Bas-Rhin, and Moselle, until after 1926. The suicide rate for France in 1927 was 226.7 or 227. Adjusting for the three provinces, the rates would be lower: 230 for 1926 and 224 for 1927, confirming our expectations. The statistics of 1928 were not yet fully completed at the end of January 1930.

5 In cities of 100,000 or more.

6 New Austria, except in 1913.

7 Old Hungary, except in 1919.

8 Of course, the *coup d'état* having taken place in December 1851, the suicides had to decline from 1852. Durkheim observes, however, that the decline took place in Paris from 1852 onward and was prolonged there into 1853. We may assume that the repercussion of this political event did not make itself felt in the provinces until a little later. In 1863 Seignobos points out, 'political life is resuming.... At the elections of 1863, there were 35 opposition deputies.... Paris elected only opposition deputies' (*Histoire politique de l'Europe contemporaine*, p. 163). We recall that, according to Durkheim, simple electoral crises can have the effect of visibly slackening the rising trend of suicide (as in 1877) and making it decline at least slightly: e.g., 'the 1889 elections which ended the Boulanger agitation' (p. 204).

9 As far back as 1840, Cazauvieilh, in connection with the decrease of suicides in 1830, asked whether 'the political events of this period cannot explain this decrease in terms of the distraction of feeling, its redirection towards another goal' (*op. cit.*, p. 243). Falret wrote in 1822, 'Political upheavals ... revolutions ... present the most favorable conditions for the outbreak of madness and suicide.' He observed that, 'we almost never observe voluntary death during stormy times, however,' and explained, thus: 'Every citizen's life being in danger, all the powers of our soul are directed at such times towards a unique end, that of conservation.... Suicide is more frequent when political changes are imminent or when the changes have occurred.' As we see, this

interpretation is the reverse of what Durkheim proposed. (Falret, *De l'Hypocondrie et du suicide*, p. 75.)

10 Let us add that one of the periodic maxima in the number of bankruptcies is enumerated in 1904. Now these maxima take place in years when suicides increase: 1854, 1865, 1873, 1886, and 1899.

11 Exactly as in 1889, the year of the world's fair. Durkheim has shown that suicides increase during the years, or more precisely, the months of an exhibition. There is a decline in suicides that year because the Boulanger crisis neutralized the effects of the exhibition. We notice that 1900 is also an exhibition year. Economic crisis and exhibition are a double reason for suicides to have increased. But they have decreased.

12 Seignobos, 'L'évolution de la Troisième République,' in *L'Histoire de la France contemporaine*, by Lavisse, p. 197. This is the work we are following in our exposition.

13 These groups are constituted as before (see p. 76) with these modifications: Ile-de-France–Champagne includes Ile-de-France, Aube, Marne, Aisne, and Oise; Burgundy and Franche-Comté: minus Yonne; Lyonnais: plus Saône-et-Loire; Southeast Midi includes Aude, Haute-Garonne, Pyrénées-Orientales, Tarn, Gard, Hérault, Bouches-du-Rhône, Var, and Vaucluse; Southwest Midi includes Gascony and Guyenne, minus Aveyron.

14 If we had worked from the proportion of suicides instead of absolute numbers, these relative numbers would be lower by about a unity after 1901 since the population has increased (moderately).

15 In Paris, suicides decline in 1898 from 110 to 100 for the two sexes combined, but from 119 to 100 for the men only (see note 20 to Chapter 11). For each of the twenty districts, we compared the suicide rate in 1896–7 and 1901–2. (For all of Paris, it declines from 100 to 75.) In eight districts it diminishes by over 30 per cent. These are the 2nd and the 5th (maximum declines from 100 to 64 and to 66), the 19th, the 18th, the 12th, the 7th, and the 11th (the decline is from 100 to 67–8.5 in all except the 11th). In four districts it diminishes only from 100 to 85–9. These are the 10th, 16th, 13th, and 9th. In two districts it does not diminish at all: the 8th and 20th; and in the 1st it increases. Note that these last two groups (in which the suicide rate diminishes little or not at all) include the two richest districts, the 8th and 16th, and the two undoubtedly poorest, the 13th and 20th, and among others the 9th and 1st, which are also among the richest.

16 Suicides diminish in Brittany from 1897 to 1898 only in three departments out of five. The decline is very small in Morbihan. It is very large, however, in Ille-et-Vilaine and Loire-Inférieure: in relative numbers, from 100 to 71, or 29 per cent.

17 Here, for the same years, are the relative numbers measuring variations in the absolute number of suicides in all of France (in relation to the number in 1898 set equal to 100).

1893	1894	1895	1896	1897	1898	1905
96	102	97.5	97.5	99	100	98.5

1906	1907	1908	1909	1910	1911	1913
97.5	106	99	102	104	102	109

As we see, there is no trace of a rise, at least not until 1909.

18 We only found in our notes the absolute numbers of urban and rural suicides for these years. Also we had only the number of male suicides for 1918: for this year we calculated the number for the two sexes assuming that there are 28 female suicides in the countryside and 32 in the cities per 100 male suicides: this is the average for the years 1891–2 and 1910–11. (Between the first and second periods this number went from 28.3 to 29.4 in the countryside, and from 27.9 to 36 in the cities: we had no data closer to the 1897–1904 period for this computation.)

19 This operation eliminates a fluctuation of long duration. One calculates the difference between the beginning and end terms and divides it by the number of annual intervals included in the period. The quotient is a little less than 0.77. This is the average annual increase.

20 However, we observe that the proportion of female suicides, which appears to be a little higher in Paris, increased from 33.5 per hundred men in 1897 to 44.5 in 1898, from 35.5 in 1901 to 38 in 1902, and from 33.1 in 1903 to 37.5 in 1904. That is, female suicides declined perceptibly less than did male during this period.

21 *Op. cit.*, p. 47.

22 Moreover, this economic and financial crisis also had a political aspect. The Union générale des Banques, of Bontoux, presented itself as a Catholic enterprise. 'The nobles, the bourgeois, and the French priests, encouraged by the conservative journals, bought stock in the Union.... Their example carried the small investor along, particularly in the region of Lyon.' On the other hand, 'that same year the financial world, troubled by Gambetta's plans for conversion to 3 per cents and the redemption by the great companies, lowered the government stocks: the interest rate dropped 6 francs.' Seignobos, *op. cit.*, pp. 88–9. Here, the economic reaction is only the reverse of a political reaction, at least in part.

23 Albert Bayet, *Le Suicide et la morale*, pp. 698–9.

CHAPTER 12 THE EFFECT OF ECONOMIC CRISES: FLUCTUATIONS IN PRUSSIAN AND GERMAN SUICIDES

1 For the period 1881–6.

2 The numbers in parentheses represent the official figures increased by a sixth. This is the increase that results from the reform introduced into the enumerations in 1883.

3 Instead of 191.2, we find 184.2, according to the figures and releases in the *Zeitschrift des Preuss. statist. Landesamt*, Parts 3 and 4, 1929, p. 441.

4 We note that the corrected figure we obtained for Prussia in 1877–86 is very close to the figure the official statistic gives for Germany for the period 1881–6.

5 For each of the four years from 1883 to 1886 the suicide rate is higher in Prussia and in Germany than in France.

6 After 1924 Germany again surpassed France. Here is the proportion of suicides in the two countries in recent years.

	Germany	France
1919	184	213
1920	217	217
1921	207	228
1922	219	229
1923	214	222
1924	232	231
1925	245	234
1926	261	232

7 The years 1867–8 were years of crisis but 1876 was also characterized by an economic depression following the crisis of 1874. Had we calculated the variation in the Prussian suicide rate from 1869 to 1873, we would have found a decrease of 15 per cent instead of a plateau.

8 The decline, much smaller than observed in 1858–63, must be explained, as we shall see, by the commercial crisis of 1857.

9 We show here only the rising total of the foreign commerce of the two countries, imports and exports combined, in millions of francs:

	France	Germany
1880	8,501	7,074
1890	8,190	9,229
1900	8,807	12,817
1910	13,407	20,266
1913	17,121	25,770

In 1880 French foreign commerce still exceeded German foreign commerce; in 1890 the reverse was true. Between 1880 and 1890 is when the suicide rate became favorable to Germany.

10 According to the *Annuaire statistique de la France*, which recalculated these indices to give them the same base as the index numbers of French prices. See general index numbers of prices in Aftalion, *Les Crises périodiques de surproduction*, Paris, 1913, vol. I, pp. 21–2.

11 According to a table compiled by George de Laveleyes, reproduced in the *Handwörterbuch der Staatswissenschaften*, during the period 1871–1901 the years when the European states most reduced the issuance of bonds (relative to the two or three years preceding and following), were as follows:

1875 and *1876*; 1880; 1883; *1885*; 1887; *1892*; 1895; 1897; 1901.

The lowest figures correspond to the italicized years.

12 We have reproduced the price indices calculated by the Statistical Office of the Reich from the prices of 38 commodities (average for 1901–10 equals 100). Published in *Wirtschaft und Statistik*.

13 For this reason there is scarcely anything to learn from a comparison of the two arrays for these years in decreasing order of wholesale prices and decreasing order of suicide rates. The opposition being equal to 16.5, the independence to 8.25, we have found an average real deviation equal to 7.63 (that is, the two phenomena are independent). However, the same prices and the same suicide rates can correspond, depending on the half of the curve where they are observed, to a downward or to an upward trend.

14 We have calculated above the decrease in the suicide rate during the war and shown that the minimum occurs in Germany in 1918, while it is lowest in France in 1917. We show the most recent figures published. We make only the following observations. First, the armistice was not signed in 1918 until October. This means that the direct influence of the war was felt during most of the year and the influence of the revolution during the last months. Second, since 1924 the suicide rate has again climbed to its level in 1913 and plainly surpassed it in the two years following. Third, from 1918 to 1926 the suicide rate does not again climb continuously. Rather, there are two declines, the first only in Germany in 1921, the year when 100 marks, quoted at 123 francs 50 centimes at par, and worth 24 francs 63 centimes in 1920, are again at 16 francs 32 centimes; the other decline in 1923 both in Germany and France: this is the year of the Ruhr. Fourth, the proportion of women who commit suicide in Germany is abnormally high from 1920 to 1924; instead of 31 women committing suicide per 100 men, which is the average figure for the years 1907–12, the count then is 46.1, that is, 54 in 1920, 47 in 1921, 46.5 in 1922, 48 in 1923, and 37.5 in 1924.

15 Moreover, in this period 1881–7 a crisis of internal politics tends to lower the suicide rate and interfere with the play of economic forces.
16 It is likewise verified in the United States. See below, pp. 258–9.

CHAPTER 13 SUICIDE, MENTAL ILLNESS, AND ALCOHOLISM

1 *Esprit des lois*, Book XIV, Chapter XII. Voltaire asks 'whether there is not some other reason than climate that makes these suicides so common.'
2 Esquirol, *Des Maladies mentales*, 1838, vol. 1. Bayet quotes the same text, thus: 'the opinion which makes one regard suicide as the effect of an illness or a critical delirium seems to have prevailed ....' Undoubtedly, this is from a first edition (1821) which we were not able to consult.
3 Falret, *De l'Hypocondrie et du suicide*, 1822.
4 Bourdin, *Du Suicide considéré comme maladie*, 1845, p. 9. He goes on to say, 'Obliged to write a history of voluntary self-murder, I naturally found myself led to treat a question which was an essential part of my subject, namely, the diagnostic difference between the suicide and the insane person. To my great surprise, I recognized then that no distinguishable difference existed between these two species of suicides' (p. 8).
5 Durkheim has been criticized for being party to a classification of suicides of the insane which is out of date and which, even at the time he was writing, no longer corresponded to findings arrived at by alienists and psychiatrists. He does not even speak of manic-depressive psychosis which, according to Dr de Fleury, would explain the majority of suicides. However, did psychiatric work which studied suicides in the light of fresh knowledge acquired in the domain of nervous disorders exist at the time when he was writing? Objection cannot be raised to the author of the *Division of Labor* for having confined himself to the only sources of written information that were at his disposal on the special subject he was studying, and for not having displaced the psychiatrists in a task which they alone were competent to fulfill.
6 According to two tables on suicides in the Department of Seine reproduced by Falret, the proportion of suicides attributed to the following motives: 'Maladies, weariness of life, weakness and alienation of mind, quarrels and domestic worries,' would have been 36.5 per cent in 1817 and 45.5 per cent in 1818 (of 351 and 330 in total). Falret, *op. cit.*, pp. 95–6.
7 *La Presse médicale*, Paris, 6 November 1926, pp. 1404ff.
8 As there were about 1,000 completed suicides in Paris during the period January 1925 to October 1926, we see that the cases related to the research represent an important fraction of the total of Parisian suicides and attempted suicides, perhaps a fifth. Although the absolute number of married suicides is ordinarily clearly higher than the number of unmarried suicides, the breakdown of these 420 suicides is as follows: 200 unmarried, 138 married, 41 widowers, 24 divorcees. Likewise, the proportion of women is 75 per 100 men, that is, clearly higher than when attention is confined to completed suicides. Account must be taken of these observations when motives are referred to, for it is possible that single women, and very likely wives, are more exposed to mental troubles, psychoses, etc., than husbands and bachelors. Let us note, however, that almost all the suicides or attempted suicide survivors in question are French.
9 A total larger than the number 420 is found. It is possible that some subjects have been counted in two categories. We notice that 19 suicides of insanity or imbalance have been collective. Only 32 subjects presented a psychopathic heredity. We have been able to establish a heredity of suicide in only 8 cases.
10 This form of psychosis was already known to Esquirol. Apropos of certain cases of depression which accompany suicidal impulses, 'I have seen this malady

persist for several months, for two years; I have seen it alternate with mania and with perfect health. Some ill persons were maniacs or in good health for six months and, during the six months, overwhelmed by a sentiment of their physical, intellectual, and moral powerlessness which made them desire death.' *Des Maladies mentales,* 1838, p. 556.

11 A few anatomists have examined the brains of suicides. We cite only the results at which Heller arrived from 300 brains: no lesion, 8 per cent; a moderate lesion which does not lessen responsibility, 21.8 per cent; strong lesions which do not directly influence responsibility, 9.6; moderate lesions which may influence, etc., 18 per cent; strong lesions which limit responsibility, 43 per cent. These observations depend on a quite small number of cases. In order to be in a position to assert that there is a constant relation between such lesions and suicide we would have had to be able, as von Mayr observes, to make the counter-test, that is, examine sufficiently the brains of persons who had not committed suicide. See also Brosch's book, *Die Selbstmörder,* which rests on 327 autopsies of military suicides. The brain appeared affected in 40.7 per cent of the cases whose autopsies revealed some organic defects.

12 According to Levasseur, *La Population française,* I, Paris, 1889, p. 347, in France at the census of 1861, 2,250 persons were affected by mental troubles per million inhabitants, of whom only 844 were in asylums, while in 1876 the two corresponding numbers were 2,420 and 1,218. Cited by Krose, pp. 46-7.

13 From a table reproduced by Nicefero (*Les Indices numériques de la civilisation et du progrès,* 1921, p. 90) we draw the following figures which prove that our supposition is not absurd:

Years	Coal consumption	Suicides
1873-7	100	100
1878-82	114	113
1883-7	122	131
1888-92	138	138
1893-7	153	150

There is evidently nothing to conclude from this.

14 Prinzing, *Trunksucht und Selbstmord,* Leipzig, 1895.

15 Falret, on the contrary, said, 'In the production of insanity and particularly of suicides, great influence has been attributed to overindulgence in alcoholic beverages. I myself long believed this from general tabulations.' However, he now thinks that too much importance has been accorded to this cause. 'Almost always, I have been able to trace the real source of these mental illnesses to a moral infection.' *De l'Hypocondrie et du suicide,* 1822, p. 60.

Cazauvieilh makes the same observation. 'There is a general conviction that overindulgence in alcoholic beverages has a strong influence on the production of insanity and suicide. I think, as do some other authors, that too large a role has been attributed to the influence of this cause.' *Du Suicide,* 1840, p. 78.

16 *Ibid.,* p. 79.

17 Denmark, Switzerland, France, Germany, Austria-Hungary, Belgium, Sweden, Great Britain, Norway, Holland, Italy, Finland, Russia.

18 Calculated by Krose for the same countries, for somewhat different periods (*Die Ursachen,* p. 127).

19 Comparison among 14 provinces.

20 Comparison among 9 provinces.

21 Comparison among the 15 departments where the most whiskey is consumed.

22 Comparison among the 15 departments where the least whiskey is consumed.

23 Comparison among 23 Prussian provinces and German states.

CHAPTER 14 EXAMINATION OF THE PSYCHIATRIC THESIS

1 Dr de Fleury, *L'Angoisse humaine*, 1926, pp. 100–58. See also the account given of this work by Georges Dumas, in the *Journal de psychologie*, 15 December 1926, p. 1059.

2 This objection, based on the fact that the immunity of married people to suicide could be due 'to what may be called matrimonial selection,' was foreseen and discussed by Durkheim (*Suicide*, p. 180).

3 Georges Dumas writes in the report cited above: 'I asked myself what my personal experience taught me on the question (of suicide). After having carefully eliminated all the suicides I have known professionally because I practice psychiatry ... I counted thirteen suicides that I have known directly or indirectly from personal experience in the past forty years and sufficiently close at hand to hold an opinion about the nervous or mental condition of the suicided person .... Of these I found four who, it could be said, appear to have been exempt from psychopathic troubles .... I count three who were hyperemotional and who committed suicide under the influence of a fit of anguish. The six others were all recurrent depressives who committed suicide in a period of anxious depression.'

4 'When the soul is strongly disturbed by a violent and unforeseen predilection, organic functions are upset, reason is troubled, and the person ... is in a real delirium.' As for the person who is 'secretly undermined by hatred and jealousy, by disappointed ambition and fortune': 'Although they act slowly, the passions do not weaken the organs any the less; several (desperate persons) assured us that they remembered nothing of what they had done; several had had peculiar hallucinations. That, however, is voluntary suicide .... Whoever attempts suicide is almost always certain, at the moment of execution, to resemble a person who is desperate and delirious.' Esquirol, *Des Maladies mentales*, pp. 532, 536–7.

5 'Melancholy is too often spoken of as if it were a malady which must last a certain time and keep a certain unity .... I do not see why the individuals of whom Durkheim speaks, who are exhausted by efforts and fears which give birth to troubles, by financial ruin and terrible responsibilities, would not fall into melancholy states of short duration, capable of bringing on suicides which are wrongly considered normal acts. Pathological troubles must not be separated from functions one rather arbitrarily considers normal.' Pierre Janet, *De L'Angoisse à l'extase*, vol. II, *Les Sentiments fondamentaux*, 1928, p. 369. Suicide, for Janet, is always 'a morbid form of reaction to frustration.'

6 The life of normal individuals is full of incidents similar to those that the associates of patients, and the patients themselves, allege to explain their state. In the immense majority of cases they fortunately provoke only normal emotions whose consequences unfold normally. If, therefore, the emotion they produce carries the appearance of mental troubles in its train, that is because the emotion owes its morbid characteristic not to the incident from which it results, but to the soil in which it germinated.' Dr Charles Blondel, *La Conscience morbide*, 1914, p. 335.

7 *Émile*, Book II. [Translation by Barbara Foxley, London, Everyman's Library, 1966 edition, p. 47 – Tr.]

8 'Motives thus attributed to the suicides, whether rightly or wrongly, are not their true causes .... The reasons ascribed for suicide, therefore, or those to which the suicide himself ascribes his act, are usually only apparent causes .... They may be said to indicate the individual's weak points.' Durkheim, *Suicide*, pp. 149 and 151. Durkheim refuses to see in them true causes of the phenomenon, above all because the proportion of motives scarcely varies when the number of suicides increases in a given country or when one passes from one profession to another.

9 'Destitution,' says Dr Serin, author of the inquiry analyzed above, 'is a great purveyor of voluntary deaths.' Of 169 cases of nonpsychopathic suicide, she finds 50 attributable to destitution or to reverses of fortune. 'Sometimes this destitution is the consequence of alcoholism and of psychopathology; many unemployed are unstable.' However, it is indeed on account of their distress that they kill themselves. 'It is sometimes also because of illness, more often because of age, infirm age, solitary or abandoned age. Much more rarely, death is the deed of a sudden ruin, or an unfortunate speculation, or of a failure which appeared inevitable.' If the inquiry had been undertaken in a year of economic crisis, this last category would probably have been more important. Besides, one can become declassed from a lower social level as well as from a higher level.

10 In Dr Suzanne Serin's inquiry into 169 nonpsychopathic suicides, 72 would be explained by 'deep-seated grief.' 'They are the suicides of widower or widow on the death of spouse, husband, or abandoned lover ... of parents who cannot survive the death of a child.' It seems that 'certain so-called passionate suicides are feigned with a sentimental song in view. [But then it is a question of attempts.] On the other hand, it is sometimes difficult to know whether these tragic griefs may not conceal a constitutional disequilibrium or a psychosis unrecognized from the beginning.'

11 *Die Leiden des jungen Werthers*, jubilee edition, p. 55.

12 Often he does not even declare it. In *La Nouvelle Héloïse*, Lord Edward refutes the arguments assembled by Saint Preux in favor of suicide. 'One says, "Life is evil, but sooner or later one will be consoled." "Precisely that, however," one goes on to say, "is what doubles my distress: thinking that the distress will end." ' Cited by Bayet, *Le Suicide et la morale*, p. 625.

13 Charles Blondel, 'Psychologie pathologique et sociologie,' *Journal de psychologie morale et pathologique*, 15 April 1925, XXII, 4, p. 345. 'The more the morbid mentality berates itself, the more it shows itself incapable of contributing to the organization of any collectivity whatever' (*ibid.*, p. 345). Previously, Esquirol wrote, 'Those who no longer feel the goodness of living [this concerns hypochondriacs] ... no longer have sensations or desires. They have drained the well-springs of life. They experience a frightful emptiness, are *completely isolated in the midst of the world*, which hurls them into a state they prefer to exchange for death.' *Loc. cit.*, p. 598.

14 Blondel has opposed his thesis to the interpretation by Janet, for whom neurasthenia results from a sentiment of 'unfulfillment.' 'For Janet, mental activity derives from its own bosom. Nothing essential and irreplaceable comes to us from outside, from our social milieu. To explain why our activity no longer has its normal yield ... he is obliged to invoke the existence of a psychic deficit.' For Blondel, on the contrary, there is no deficit, rather superabundance and excessive riches, with the result that 'the collective framework no longer applies to the states of the morbid conscience,' and so the purely individual elements in the latter, being no longer repressed or eliminated, come to the forefront. What is suppressed is what comes from outside, namely the habitual relationship with the social milieu. *Op. cit.*, p. 303.

15 'Suffering,' said Montesquieu, 'is a localized illness which inclines us to want to see this suffering end; the burden of life is an illness which has no particular place at all, and which makes us want to see this life ended.' *Esprit des lois*, Book XIV, Chapter XII.

16 The depressed person is also, undoubtedly, a restless soul, ordinarily. But 'restlessness must not be confused with excitation. Excitation consists essentially of a rapid rise in psychological tension above the level which had remained constant over a certain time .... Restlessness sometimes consists of a complete activation of certain very weak tendencies, sometimes of a very

incomplete activation of certain tendencies a little higher but still below those that the subject would have to use.' Pierre Janet, *Traité de psychologie* of Dr Dumas, vol. I, pp. 935 seq.

17 Charles Blondel: 'The material and moral isolation in which constitutional psychopaths live amongst one another is well known to alienists .... Each remains alone and, so to speak, enclosed in his delirium.' Article cited, p. 341.

18 *Mémoires de Luther*, translated and edited by Michelet, 1837, vol. I, p. 10.

19 We must again refer to Esquirol to find some indications of this. 'Maniacs also kill themselves at the beginning of the illness, pushed to despair by the *moral disease* which caused the delirium, or which coincided with its outburst, *the memory of this disease not being destroyed by the delirium which has not yet invaded the whole intelligence*. These patients also kill *themselves because they feel the illness which is beginning* and which plunges them into despair. Some kill themselves *during the convalescence from the mania*, despairing because of the excesses they have committed or ashamed of having been mad.' Our italics.

20 'Maniacs kill themselves without reflection having any role in this act; they are ordinarily hasty, which proves that they obey a blind impulse .... Maniacs live off illusions, misapprehend relationships .... They are the playthings of their sensations or of hallucinations .... One, believing he is opening the door of his apartment, opens the casement window and hurls himself out, having wanted to descend by the staircase. Another, miscalculating distances, believes himself on a level with the ground and throws himself out the window. One, wishing to do violence to a serving-woman, throws himself from the third flight of stairs, hoping he will arrive at the bottom before the woman who is fleeing from his pursuit .... Others, believing they have some foreign body in the skull, hope to make it leave *by opening the head*.' Esquirol, *loc. cit.*, p. 541. See also, p. 542, three examples of suicides caused by mystical hallucinations. One may ask whether the majority of these cases are not accidents rather than suicides.

21 'I questioned several hypochondriacs and a large number of lypemaniacs ['a form of insanity characterized by extreme mournfulness,' *O.E.D.* – Tr.] who had attempted suicide. All assured me that they were carried along toward death voluntarily .... But all added that nothing was more frightful than the physical or moral state they were in ... and that death presented itself as the only means of delivering themselves from it.' Esquirol, *loc. cit.*, p. 597.

22 That is an example of the 'affected paradox' that Blondel has so well clarified. 'The question is whether it is necessary to take literally this lack of affect (of which the mentally ill complain) .... It may be the negative formulas which complicate the problem, above all, by affecting the patients' (p. 160). And further on, 'The irreducibility to conceptualized and collective experience of morbid affective states carries with it the negation of physical and moral sensibility. When the patient makes an effort at thought and analysis, he no longer finds in his conscience anything plainly equivalent to our physical impressions, pleasures, or difficulties. These impressions, pleasures, and difficulties constitute, in his eyes, all the normally imaginable forms of sensibility such as he had earlier imagined them to be when he was with us. He concludes from this that what he is experiencing no longer has any connection with what he has experienced and that he is anaesthetized physically and morally.' *Op. cit.*, pp. 302–3.

23 It is not at all that suicides are too numerous for physicians to be able to subject each one to an individual examination. John Rice Miner says that suicides represent from 0.2 to 1.4 per cent of all deaths (depending on the country) and that they produced in the United States, in 1919, a few more deaths than typhoid fever, but less than appendicitis. One does not see, however, how this sort of influence could be measured or even perceived since, as we have seen, the subject himself is incapable of explaining to us, and undoubtedly of himself

understanding, which external influences are or are not exerted on him.
24 Prinzing, *Trunksucht und Selbstmord*, Leipzig, 1895.
25 'Mémoire sur l'inceste,' *Année sociologique*, I, p. 35.

CHAPTER 15   CONCLUSION

1 Bayet is of the same opinion on this point as Durkheim, whose definition he accepts. He is surprised that 'in the current conversation one has only to plead to the adversaries of voluntary death the example of the sailors of the *Vengeur*, or of martyrs defying the magistrates, for them to reply without hesitation, "those are not suicides." ' Bayet, *Le Suicide et la morale*, p. 92. Is this so only because 'the word suicide is taken amiss' or is there not a quite obvious difference between these two orders of fact independently of all moral evaluation?

2 Bayet, *op. cit.*, p. 754.

3 During the Revolution, Beaurepaire killed himself after the surrender of Verdun. Bayet was greatly struck by the fact that this heroic death 'was the object of reservation amounting to censure.' Only a few German officers wanted to treat him like an ordinary suicide, his corpse thrown on the garbage-heap. But the Beaurepaire platoon changed its name and in a report to the Convention expressed regret 'that this officer had not been killed in the breach or in the citadel by the enemy instead of putting himself to death.' The voluntary death of Beaurepaire would not have been a suicide had he blown up Verdun and himself at the same time. *Ibid.*, p. 158.

4 Bayet, *op. cit.*, pp. 336f.

5 In what follows we shall take the expression *human sacrifice* in its broadest sense to include the cremation of widows on their husbands' funeral piles, the putting of the slaves of the deceased to death, and the execution of captives and even of criminals. The theory of sacrifice distinguishes these facts and excludes a large number of them. They have two traits in common, however, namely that they result from and are accomplished according to ritual forms.

6 Bayet, *op. cit.*, p. 297, note 3. See also Hubert and Mauss, 'Essai sur la nature et la fonction du sacrifice,' *Année sociologique*, II, p. 122. 'Greek mythology knows "hung" goddesses such as Artemis, Hecate, and Helena.' Charila is of the same type.

7 Durkheim's definition does not even exclude a certain number of suicides of madmen who do not even know that their act will entail death, such as those who throw themselves from the top of a staircase to reach the bottom more quickly, These, however, are not, of course, actual suicides.

8 Hubert and Mauss, *loc. cit.*, p. 64. 'But above all it is a case of inducing (the victim) to allow himself to be sacrificed peaceably for the welfare of humans, and not to avenge himself, once dead.' See also Oldenberg, *La Religion du Véda*, p. 306. 'As among many other peoples, the fatal act is designated by euphemisms …. The victim is told that he is not dying at all: "You will not die, no harm is being done you, you are going from here to God by a beautiful route" ' (*Rig Veda*, I, 162, 21). The knock-down is called 'Obtaining the animal's consent.'

9 Oldenberg says (*op. cit.*, p. 311, note 2), 'The cremation of the widow which still shows up vaguely in the Veda is not a sacrifice. His wife is sent to the deceased in the other world by means of the funeral pyre for the same reason as all of his other possessions.' We indicated above (Chapter 15, note 5) the reason for taking the word 'sacrifice' in a more inclusive sense.

10 Durkheim, *Suicide*, p. 219.

11 According to Bayet, in the Middle Ages, 'not only is the suicide considered an assassin but certain traits make one think that suicide excites even more horror

than assassination.' Not only are they hung on a gibbet (women are burned) but their bodies are dragged along the ground 'as cruelly as possible' and 'the stones beneath the terminus of the pathways over which they must pass or exit from the house must be torn up.' *Op. cit.*, p. 441. On the other hand, the punishments inflicted on the attempted suicide are not severe: flogging; if the culprit is repentant, a spiritual penitence sometimes suffices. Thus, what society abhors in the suicide is not so much the intention as the accomplished fact that allows society no possibility of intervention. *Ibid.*, p. 445.

12 'Contemporary law is entirely indulgent to those who kill themselves through desire to save their honor,' says Bayet. 'There is no declaration of bankruptcy if a merchant strikes himself just as he sees himself compelled to suspend his payments. Similarly, there can be no verdict of guilt, or sentence of condemnation if an accused person kills himself .... Since the Renaissance, all French jurists have been familiar with the Roman principle that suicide does not extinguish the crime. In refusing to adopt it, the men of the Revolution undoubtedly knew what they were doing.' *Op. cit.*, p. 82.

13 This is not the case when a criminal kills himself to escape prosecution and, at least in part, the punishment he has incurred. 'Roman law under the Republic and at the start of the Empire establishes a real premium on suicide by granting that whoever kills himself under threat of prosecution or during the course of a lawsuit escapes all condemnation .... At the start of the Empire, the *mortis arbitrium* (right to commit suicide) is a favor which the prince grants easily, at least when the accused is of a certain rank. However, it was not maintained in classic law. A text of the *Digeste* reveals an entirely contrary doctrine. Those who kill themselves under threat of prosecution, or capture in the act, do not have heirs. There is never any confiscation if the suicide is due to remorse at having committed a crime, but not to fear of being prosecuted.' Bayet, *op. cit.*, pp. 276, 277, and 289. Let us also observe that 'during the seventeenth century the majority of jurists hold that there is no ground for suit (against suicide) except when the person who does away with himself is under threat of indictment.' *Ibid.*, p. 607.

14 Gustave Glotz, *La Solidarité de la famille dans le droit criminel en Grèce*, 1904, pp. 65–6.

15 Numerous suicides of this type in China's feudal period are mentioned by Granet (*La Civilisation chinoise. La vie publique et la vie privée*, 1929). 'Warriors consigned to death are sent *to start* the battle. Upon contact with the enemy they must cut their throats while uttering a great cry. A raging spirit emanates from this collective suicide. It clings to the enemy like an ill-omened fate' (p. 313). The banished vassal, 'for as long as he wears the vestments of mourning and practices abstinence, holds his lord under threat of a gesture of suicide. This threat has a horrible power and suffices, even addressed to a stranger, to restrain his whims' (p. 353). 'The threat of suicide, characteristic of the relations of vassal to lord, is always included, though latent, in the disavowal proceeding which is the remonstrance' (p. 403). To this very day, 'suicide is very often a manifestation of the offended ego, an indirect form of the vendetta. Even the suicides committed by beggars are acts of vengeance.' Matignon, 'Le suicide en Chine,' *Archives d'anthropologie criminelle*, XII, 70.

16 Roman law of the imperial epoch does not carry a penalty against suicide, and it expressly indicates seven cases in which suicide does not entail the confiscation of goods. That is when there is: disgust with life (*taedium vitae*), desire to avoid sickness, suffering, grief caused by the death of a son, shame at being unable to pay one's debts, etc. What is said of the *taedium vitae* is to be found in the *Digeste*. Bayet, *op. cit.*, p. 275.

17 Tolstoy, *Anna Karenina*. [Translation by Constance Garnett, in Modern Library edition, New York, pp. 892ff. – Tr.]

18 Chapter 5 ('Les Volitions') of the *Traité de psychologie* (Dumas), pp. 397–8.

19 Bayet contrasts thus another series of simultaneous and contradictory responses: 'Suicide is cowardice; it is a proof of courage; it is the solution of petty souls; it is the recourse of a great soul; it is a "jade's" undertaking; it is not the undertaking of a "dear little wife"; it is lamentably banal; it is beautiful and poetic; one must not kill oneself when one has children; one must kill oneself to save the honor of one's children.' *Op. cit.*, p. 118.

20 A number of writers in the eighteenth century repeat that more and more people are killing themselves in France. 'Mercier says in 1782 that there have been many suicides in Paris during the past twenty-five years.' According to Bayet, 'the writers of the second half of the century may be under the impression that the number of suicides has been increasing; this may partly be because those who keep the statistics are less hesitant to enter suicides on their registers since the court "settles" the affairs of the suicide.' *Op. cit.*, p. 681.

21 Bayet, *op. cit.*, p. 290.

22 This proportion would be distinctly higher if only men were considered. It also increases with age. We recall that the relation of male suicides to female is 3 to 1, and that people 40 to 50 years of age kill themselves almost twice as often as those from 20 to 30.

23 *Die Welt als Wille und Vorstellung*, Book 4, Chapter XLVI, 662. [Translation by R. B. Haldane and J. Kemp, *The World as Will and Idea*, London, Routledge & Kegan Paul, Ltd., 1964, vol. III, Supplement to Book 4, p. 389 – Tr.]
    This is somewhat the same thought previously expressed by Erasmus: 'MARCOLPHUS: But is death as horrible a thing as it's commonly asserted to be? PHAEDRUS: The road leading up to it is harder than death itself. If a man dismisses from his thought the horror and imagination of death, he will have rid himself of a great part of the evil.' This text was brought to our attention by M. Febvre. [Translation by Craig R. Thompson, 'The Funeral,' *The Colloquies of Erasmus*, Chicago, University of Chicago Press, 1965, p. 359 – Tr.]

24 In two articles from the *Annales de géographie*, XX, 15 May and 15 July 1911. See also Lucien Febvre, *La Terre et l'évolution humaine, introduction géographique à l'histoire*, Paris, 1922, p. 288.

25 Durkheim, *op. cit.*, pp. 149, 151.

26 *Ibid.*, p. 151.

27 *Ibid.*, pp. 321ff.

Bibliography

We list here only particular works which have appeared since 1897, that is, since the publication of Durkheim's book, and which have been used in this work. (Yearbooks and official statistical publications are excluded.) Several listings of the most important antecedent works will be found in Durkheim's book on pp. 52, 57, 82, 104, 123, 217, etc. More recent bibliographies will be found in the works of von Mayr and of John Rice Miner. See also the *Bibliographie des Selbstmords*, by Rost, mentioned below.

Angiolella, 'Sulle tendenze suicide negli alienati e sulla psicologia del suicidio,' *Rivista sperimentale di Frenatria*, 1900.

Bachi, Mario, 'La micidialità dei tentativi di suicidio,' *Giornale degli economisti e Rivista di statistica*, May, 1924.

Bayet, Albert, *Le Suicide et la morale*, Paris, 1922.

Blondel, Dr Charles, *La Conscience morbide*, Paris, 1914.

Bodio, L., *Confronti internazionali, Parte II, Statistica delle morti negli anni 1874–1894*, Rome, 1897.

Bonsegna, Mario, *Il suicidio in Italia dal 1864 al 1918, Studio statistico*, Ostuni, 1924.

Brosch, *Die Selbstmörder, mit besonderer Berücksichtigung der militärischen Selbstmörder*, Leipzig and Vienna, 1909.

Dumas, Georges, 'Compte rendu du livre du Dr. de Fleury,' *Journal de psychologie*, 15 December 1926.

Durkheim, E., 'Compte rendu du livre de Krose: *Die Ursachen*,' *Année sociologique*, XI (1906–9), pp. 512–13.

Ferri, Enrico, *Un secolo di omicidii e di suicidii in Europa*, Rome, 1925.

Fleury, Dr de, *L'Angoisse humaine*, Paris, 1926.

Froberger, *Moralstatistik und Konfession*, Halle, 1911.

Fullkrug, Gerhard, *Der Selbstmord in der Kriegs- und Nachkriegszeit, Eine moralstatistische Untersuchung*, Schwerin im Mecklenburg, 1927.

Heller, 'Zur Lehre vom Selbstmord nach 300 Sektionen,' *Münchner medic. Wochenschrift*, n. 48, 1900.

Ichok, Dr, 'Peut-on parler en France d'une épidémie de suicides?' *Journal de la société de statistique de Paris*, July–September 1926, pp. 278–91.

Jacquart, Camille, *Essais de statistique morale: I. Le Suicide*, Brussels, 1908.

Janet, Pierre, *De l'Angoisse à l'extase*, vol. II, *Les Sentiments fondamentaux*, Paris, 1928.

Krose, S.J., Fr, *Der Selbstmord im 19. Jahrhundert nach seiner Verteilung auf Staaten und Verwaltungsbezirke*, Freiburg-im-Breisgau, 1906.

Krose, S.J., Fr, *Die Ursachen der Selbstmordhäufigkeit*, ibid., 1906.

Krose, S.J., Fr, 'Die Selbstmorde 1893–1908,' *Vierteljahrhefte zur Statistik des deutschen Reichs*, I, p. 108, 1910.

Kürten, *Statistik des Selbstmordes im Königreich Sachsen*, Leipzig, 1913.

Leoncini, 'Considerazioni sopra alcuni dati statistici sul suicidio,' *Rivista sperimentale di Frenatria*, XLVIII 3–4, 1924.

Massarotti, Vito, *Il suicidio nella vita e nella società moderna*, Rome, 1913.

Miner, John Rice, 'Suicide and its Relation to Climatic and Other Factors,' *The American Journal of Hygiene*, Baltimore, 1922.

Rost, Hans, 'Der Selbstmord in den Städten,' *Allgemeine statistische Archiv*, VI, 2, 1904.

Rost, Hans, *Der Selbstmord als sozialstatistische Erscheinung*, Cologne, 1905.

Rost, Hans, *Bibliographie des Selbstmords, mit textlichen Einführungen zu jedem Kapitel*, Augsburg, 1927.

Schnapper-Arndt, *Sozialstatistik*, Leipzig, 1908.

Serin, Dr Suzanne, *Une enquête médicosociale sur le suicide à Paris*, Communication à la société médicopsychologique, *Annales médicopsychologiques*, Nov. 1926, pp. 356–63.

Suicides en U.R.S.S. 1922–1925, U.R.S.S. Statistique, vol. XXXV, Part I, Section de la statistique morale, Moscow, 1927.

Von Mayr, Georg, *Statistik und Gesellschaftslehre, Moralstatistik*, pp. 258–404 (*Selbstmordstatistik*), Tübingen, 1917.

Zahn, Friedrich, *Selbstmordstatistik, Handwörterbuch der Staatswissenschaften*, 4th edition, parts 69 and 70, 1926.

Index